Changing
Human Behavior
PRINCIPLES OF PLANNED
INTERVENTION

McGRAW-HILL SERIES IN PSYCHOLOGY
CONSULTING EDITORS
Norman Garmezy   Lyle V. Jones
Richard L. Solomon   Harold W. Stevenson

Adams Human Memory
Beach, Hebb, Morgan, Nissen The Neuropsychology of Lashley
Berkowitz Aggression: A Social Psychological Analysis
Berlyne Conflict, Arousal, and Curiosity
Blum Psychoanalytic Theories of Personality
Brown The Motivation of Behavior
Brown and Ghiselli Scientific Method in Psychology
Butcher MMPI: Research Developments and Clinical Applications
Campbell, Dunnette, Lawler, and Weick Managerial Behavior, Performance, and Effectiveness
Cofer Verbal Learning and Verbal Behavior
Crafts, Schneirla, Robinson, and Gilbert Recent Experiments in Psychology
Crites Vocational Psychology
D'Amato Experimental Psychology: Methodology, Psychophysics, and Learning
Deese and Hulse The Psychology of Learning
Dollard and Miller Personality and Psychotherapy
Edgington Statistical Inference: The Distribution-free Approach
Ellis Handbook of Mental Deficiency
Ferguson Statistical Analysis in Psychology and Education
Fodor, Bever, and Garrett The Psychology of Language: An Introduction to Psycholinguistics and Generative Grammer
Forgus Perception: The Basic Process in Cognitive Development
Franks Behavior Therapy: Appraisal and Status
Ghiselli Theory of Psychological Measurement
Ghiselli and Brown Personnel and Industrial Psychology
Gilmer Industrial and Organizational Psychology
Gray Psychology Applied to Human Affairs
Guilford Psychometric Methods
Guilford The Nature of Human Intelligence
Guilford and Fruchter Fundamental Statistics in Psychology and Education
Guilford and Hoepfner The Analysis of Intelligence
Guion Personnel Testing
Haire Psychology in Management
Hirsch Behavior-genetic Analysis
Hirsh The Measurement of Hearing
Horowitz Elements of Statistics for Psychology and Education
Hurlock Adolescent Development
Hurlock Child Development
Hurlock Developmental Psychology
Jackson and Messick Problems in Human Assessment
Krech, Crutchfield, and Ballachey Individual in Society

Changing
Human Behavior
PRINCIPLES OF PLANNED INTERVENTION

RALPH K. SCHWITZGEBEL

Department of Psychiatry
Harvard Medical School

DAVID A. KOLB

Sloan School of Management
Massachusetts Institute of Technology

McGraw-Hill Book Company

New York   St. Louis   San Francisco   Düsseldorf   Johannesburg
Kuala Lumpur   London   Mexico   Montreal   New Delhi
Panama   Rio de Janeiro   Singapore   Sydney   Toronto

**Changing
Human Behavior**
PRINCIPLES OF PLANNED INTERVENTION

234567890KPKP7987654

This book was set in Times Roman by Black Dot, Inc.
The editors were Robert P. Rainier and Phyllis T. Dulan;
the cover was designed by Edward A. Butler;
and the production supervisor was Thomas J. LoPinto.
The drawings were done by ANCO Technical Services.
The printer and binder was Kingsport Press, Inc.

Library of Congress Cataloging in Publication Data
Schwitzgebel, Ralph K date
    Changing human behavior.
    (McGraw-Hill series in psychology)
    Bibliography: p.
    1. Behavior modification. 2. Personality change.
I. Kolb, David A., date joint author. II. Title.
[DNLM: 1. Behavior therapy. WM400 S415c   1974]
BF637.B4S38   153.8   73-15702
ISBN 0-07-055739-X

Contents

Preface   ix
1   Introduction   1

ILLUSTRATIVE PROCEDURES
2   Reciprocal Inhibition   12
3   Operant Shaping   39
4   Reinforcement   58
5   Stimulus Control   88
6   Observational Learning   122
7   Achievement-Motivation Training   148

A SOCIAL-PSYCHOLOGICAL PERSPECTIVE ON BEHAVIOR CHANGE
8   Self-directed Behavior Change   160
9   Behavior Change in Transitional Roles   182
10   Problems in the Assessment of Behavior Change   206

RESEARCH ISSUES
11   Observation and Recording of Behavior   227
12   Toward an Ethic for Research on Human Behavior   253
References   273

Indexes   319
   Name Index
   Subject Index

Preface

Nearly ten years ago this book began as do all books as an idea. The idea was that planned intervention in human systems should be based on scientifically verified principles of behavior change. The behavior to be changed should be empirically defined, and characteristics of the behavior should be accurately measured over a period of time. Also, the procedures used to change behavior should be described in such a way that they are replicable by others. Principles such as these, rather than allegiance to any particular theory, should guide the growth of behavior change as a discipline. These principles are frequently mentioned and discussed throughout the book.

There is another central concern expressed in this book: Research and the practical application of behavior change techniques should be directed toward meaningful and personally significant human behaviors. There have been literally hundreds, perhaps even thousands, of "scientific" studies of shock-avoidance behavior in rats and the memory of nonsense syllables in humans. But we see little indication that these studies have generated (or will generate in the foreseeable future) methods for changing human behavior any more effectively than the flogging of lunatics in the eighteenth century, the moralistic sermons of the nineteenth century, or the elitist psychoanalytic interviews of the early twentieth century.

One of the difficulties with many current psychological studies is that they deal with trivial behaviors confined within a laboratory. However, we know that the most meaningful human behaviors or events occur outside the laboratory in natural settings where people "fall" in love, feel embarrassed, experience illness, confront or deny the inevitability of death, and share with others the intimacy of music or feelings too deep to take the shape of words.

During the past several years, we have watched the development of behavior change as a discipline, and, fortunately, we have seen an increased willingness for researchers and change agents to move into the "real world" of homes, schools, businesses, and barrooms. This reflects a growing awareness that the determinants of behavior are seldom exclusively psychological in origin. To understand and change human behavior, we must understand the ways in which behavior is determined by factors in natural social situations.

The chapters in this book are generally arranged according to the development of the behavior change discipline from its early days when it focused upon techniques in the laboratory, such as systematic desensitization, to the more current use of observational learning in daily life settings. The content is also arranged so that readers with very little or no prior knowledge of psychology can gradually acquire a general understanding of this rapidly emerging area of study. We have attempted to explain new technological concepts as they are introduced. In addition, we have attempted to provide enough detailed descriptions of procedures so that readers can decide whether certain methods might be utilized in particular professional or personal situations. If so, references are usually noted which give more detailed descriptions and evaluations of effectiveness. In short, we hope to provide a practical, conceptual tour for the reader.

This book began as an idea; it ends as a hope. Tomorrow there will be new procedures and probably new disciplines. Behavior change will itself be a matter of history. But we can only proceed using our current knowledge. Although we would like a large, continuing readership for this book, we would gladly accept, in fact welcome, obsolescence if the procedures we discuss here can be replaced by the use of new, more effective methods.

We extend our special appreciation to Dr. Alfred S. Alschuler for his contributions to our thinking about achievement-motivation training. Professor Kenneth Gergen has greatly extended and enriched our thinking about human experimentation. We are also deeply indebted to Professor Norman Garmezy for his very helpful review and encouragement of our writing in its early stages. This help and the support of friends have made this book possible.

RALPH K. SCHWITZGEBEL
DAVID A. KOLB

Changing
Human Behavior
PRINCIPLES OF PLANNED
INTERVENTION

Chapter 1

Introduction

The desire to change human behavior effectively has been an ancient as
well as a modern hope. People often feel that they are unable to control
their destinies because they cannot control their own behavior. The
lament of St. Paul is familiar: "I can will what is right, but I cannot do it.
For I do not do the good I want, but the evil I do not want is what I do"
(Holy Bible, RSV, Romans, 7:18–19).

From a social viewpoint, there is the vision of a more noble and
humane world if man could somehow learn to express his positive
potential in behavior. Antoine de Saint-Exupéry (1942, pp. 205–206) has
described something of this vision which occurred to him a few years
after World War I while he was riding on a train in France. He happened
to sit down opposite a displaced Polish family and noticed a young boy
who had hollowed out a place between his mother and father. The boy
had fallen asleep. In the dim lamplight of the railroad car, he studied this
child's face.

1

I bent over the smooth brow, over those mildly pouting lips, and said to myself: This is a musician's face. This is the child, Mozart. This is a life full of beautiful promise. Little princes in legends are not different from this. Protected, sheltered, cultivated, what could not this child become?

When by mutation a new rose is born in a garden, all the gardeners rejoice. They isolate the rose, tend it, foster it. But there is no gardener for men. This little Mozart will be shaped like the rest by the common stamping machine. This little Mozart will love shoddy music in the stench of night dives. This little Mozart is condemned.

I went back to my sleeping car. I said to myself: Their fate causes these people no suffering. It is not an impulse to charity that has upset me like this. I am not weeping over an eternally open wound. Those who carry the wound do not feel it. It is the human race and not the individual that is wounded here, is outraged here. I do not believe in pity. What torments me tonight is the gardeners' point of view. . . . It is the sight, a little bit in all these men, of Mozart murdered.

Surely, attempts to change the course of human behavior, both individually and collectively, are not new. It is, however, only within the past few years that certain procedures for changing human behavior have been made explicit enough for scientific study. These recent advances have resulted in a new area of scientific inquiry—behavior change. A major purpose of this book is to present some of the therapeutic and social potentials of this new discipline.

CHARACTERISTICS OF BEHAVIOR CHANGE

The concept of *behavior change* as used here refers to the measurable modification of behavior through the use of duplicable procedures. The limits of behavior change are not yet well known, but there are certain concepts that help to outline the area. First, the behavior to be changed must be definable and subject to empirical investigation. Second, the frequency, duration, or other characteristics of the behavior to be changed must be measurable. The ability to observe and reliably record behavior is an important aspect of behavior-change programs. Finally, the procedures used to change the behavior must be capable of replication by others. This replicability may be achieved through methods such as verbal description, demonstration, or intensive individual training. However, a procedure for changing behavior that relied primarily upon the unique, nontransferable characteristics of a change agent would lie outside of the domain of behavior change as defined here.

A book that strictly applied these three criteria to the selection of studies for discussion would be quite thin—perhaps even nonexistent—and much of the authors' own research would have to be eliminated. It should be recognized that behavior change is still largely the goal of an emerging discipline rather than an accomplished fact, but it is a goal that appears to be increasingly obtainable.

The development of a new discipline usually involves a small number of dedicated persons who persistently attempt to demonstrate the practical value of new concepts over the old ones. Freud, Breuer, Jung, and Adler carried out this function very well for psychoanalysis. In addition, the emerging discipline is often characterized by a few note-worthy publications, a professional organization or society, and the creation of new job categories. All these events tend to focus upon increasing the general application of the new concepts.

No precise date can be set for the emergence of behavior change as a discipline.[1] Some of the intellectual origins can be found in the work of Ivan P. Pavlov on classical conditioning in the early 1900s; in B. F. Skinner's study of operant conditioning in the early 1940s; and in Joseph Wolpe's development of techniques for the inhibition of phobias in the late 1950s. In 1963, a new journal was begun in London entitled *Behaviour Research and Therapy*. It was edited by Hans J. Eysenck, who was well known by this time for his studies indicating that psychoanalysis was ineffective in the treatment of common neuroses.

Programs that change behavior in accord with the three criteria mentioned earlier (definability, measurability, and replicability) have been variously labeled. The labels vary according to the particular emphasis placed upon these criteria and the theoretical interests of the investigators. The term *behavior therapy* first introduced in 1958 by Arnold Lazarus (1958, 1968), has a heavy orientation toward learning theory. The therapeutic emphasis has been primarily, but not exclusively, upon the treatment of clinical problems such as phobias, sexual disorders, alcoholism, and compulsions.

The term *behavior modification*, which has been credited primarily to the work of Leonard Ullmann and Leonard Krasner (Krasner & Ullmann, 1965; Ullmann & Krasner, 1965, 1969), has somewhat broader social connotations than behavior therapy. Behavior modification techniques may be used not only to eliminate behaviors that are socially deviant (Ullmann & Krasner, 1969, pp. 243–244), but also to develop and increase socially desirable behaviors. Behavior modification may also include the use of psychoanalytically oriented techniques. These psychoanalytic techniques, however, are interpreted from the viewpoint of learning theory rather than unconscious forces. Behavior modification

---

[1] A brief, useful history of the development of the area of behavior change can be found in Ullmann & Krasner (1969, pp. 171–181).

tends to focus upon the systematic alteration of the physical and social aspects of the environment which elicit or maintain the behaviors to be changed.

The term *behavior change* is equally broad but is meant to have no connotations of therapy or deviance. Thus, although behavior-change procedures can be used to change deviant behaviors, they can also be used to enhance already adequate prosocial behaviors. Alternatively, behavior-change procedures should be capable of producing deviant behaviors, but for obvious reasons this is seldom done. There is also an emphasis upon learning new behaviors in natural, social settings.

These distinctions between the terms behavior therapy, behavior modification and behavior change are more conceptual than real in daily practice. Because the discipline is still emerging, these terms do not yet have clear, commonly accepted behavioral referents, and the terms are often used interchangeably.

PSYCHOANALYTIC CONTRIBUTIONS

Although psychoanalysis is not an often used behavior-change procedure because of its reliance upon many unmeasurable or non-replicable procedures, it has made some valuable contributions, perhaps inadvertently, to the area of behavior change. However, during the early years of the development of new behavior-change procedures, the concept of behavior therapy was often seen as the antithesis of psychoanalysis.

Exchanges between the founders of behavior therapy and psychoanalysis were sometimes quite heated. One of the early, noteworthy books in the area of behavior therapy, *Conditioned Reflex Therapy* by Andrew Salter (1949), began with the statement: "It is high time that psychoanalysis, like the elephant of the fable, dragged itself off to some distant jungle graveyard and died. Psychoanalysis has outlived its usefulness. Its methods are vague, its treatment long drawn out, and more often than not, its results are insipid and unimpressive."[2] Some psychoanalysts responded in a like manner to the behavior therapists.[3]

There surely were, and still are, important differences in orientation. Psychoanalysis places much emphasis upon past events, mental images and thoughts, patient insight, and therapeutic intuition. Nevertheless, psychoanalysis as a discipline has established a general, intellectual

---

[2]Some support for these statements was provided, as indicated earlier, by the studies of Eysenck (1952, 1955, 1961).

[3]For an additional discussion of exchanges between psychoanalysts and behavior therapists see Chapter 2.

outlook upon behavior that has greatly facilitated the emergence of newer, more scientifically oriented procedures of behavior change. The spirit, if not always the method, of inquiry during the early days of psychoanalysis has set an enviable record of astute observation and social courage worthy of serious consideration.

Early Psychoanalytic Inquiry

The somewhat solitary and brooding figure of Sigmund Freud, a Viennese physician, still pervades much of psychoanalysis. Freud's interest in hypnosis is one of the major links in a complex series of events that eventually led to the discovery, or more accurately, the development of psychoanalytic techniques. While attending some demonstrations of hypnosis shortly after finishing medical school, Freud met a physician, Josef Breuer, who took a fatherly interest in young Freud's career. It was Breuer's presentation of the remarkable case of Miss P. which captured Freud's attention and led to the development of the psychoanalytic method. It is a well-known story which Van den Berg (1964, pp. 115–117) has vividly described:

> In the two years between 1880 and 1882, a Viennese doctor, Josef Breuer, had been trying to gain insight into a disease which had been known since antiquity, but whose symptoms were so capricious and so unstable, and whose physical basis, even after accurate physical examination, appeared so entirely lacking, that nobody knew the outlines of the disease nor the meaning of its symptoms. A young woman—she was twenty-one years old—whom Breuer had been visiting regularly was suffering from this disease. She had a paralysis of the right arm, a disturbance of her eyesight, an annoying cough, and many more symptoms; these symptoms, however, without exception, were characterized by the amazing and in those days entirely unaccountable fact that they were not caused by a defect of a physical nature. Her arm was neurologically sound, even in a state of complete paralysis; the ophthalmologist found no signs of disease in her—nonetheless faulty—eyes; and the throat specialist could not find anything wrong with her throat, in spite of the fact that her cough continued to suggest a physical defect. In addition, she exhibited a remarkable disturbance: she had a tendency to go into a sort of unconsciousness, now and then, for no apparent reason. . . .
>
> As a result of the talks Breuer had with his patient, he acquired an increasing understanding of the nature of the disturbances which (and this cannot be emphasized strongly enough) had never before been understood. His understanding remained fragmentary and vague, however, until, in the summer of 1882, the patient suddenly complained of an entirely new symptom and after a few weeks got rid of it just as suddenly.

This symptom was a sudden inability to drink. Even when she was tortured by a bad thirst, she could not succeed in taking one sip from the glass Breuer offered her. She did bring the glass to her lips; but at the moment they were about to touch the liquid, she fell into a condition very similar to spontaneous hypnosis; and then, apparently horrified, she would put the glass back on the table. Again there were no physical defects.

The explanation of this extraordinary behavior came a few weeks later. Breuer was talking to her while she was in a spontaneous hypnosis and she suddenly told him, showing evidence of an intense nausea, how she had seen a dog drinking from a glass of a lady, who, ignorant of what had happened, had afterward drunk what was left. She had barely finished her story when she wanted a drink—still in a state of spontaneous hypnosis. Breuer handed her a glass of water; she took it from him, brought it to her lips—and woke up drinking. From that moment the symptom disappeared, and never reoccurred.

This "cure," however, was not quite adequate. Some of the other old symptoms would rather frequently reappear and would have to be "purged" away by this method which Breuer called *catharsis*. The patient, Miss P., more literally called it "the talking cure." Extreme and obvious physical symptoms had been greatly reduced or eliminated merely by talking; the discovery was a remarkable and astonishing one.

This story, as it relates to the development of a new discipline, is not yet complete. Eleven years lapsed between the discovery of "the talking cure" and its publication by Freud and Breuer in 1893. During this time, it became apparent to them that the success of the treatment depended, at least in part, on a close, positive relationship between the doctor and patient. Breuer and Freud must have noted that this was something more than the usual simple rapport between a physician and his patient. Near the time of the cure of Miss P., Breuer had been visiting her socially nearly every day for over a year. Later, she started an unfounded rumor that she was pregnant by him.

We are now familiar with the fact that during psychoanalysis an intense, lovelike relationship (called transference) may develop between the therapist and the patient in which the patient views the therapist as an unrealistic combination of parent and lover. At that time, however, such a situation must have been a source of considerable embarrassment to Breuer and perhaps accounts for his later lack of interest in such treatment. Meanwhile, Freud began to formulate a theory that the neuroses were caused by sexual disturbances. This theory was generally met by public and professional indignation.

Freud initially used hypnosis extensively in treating patients but then changed to the use of a technique known as free association. The patient was instructed to say whatever came into his mind no matter how trivial, embarrassing, or unpleasant it might seem. Freud assumed that the sequence of ideas thus expressed would eventually lead back to the discovery of the traumatic childhood sexual incidents which were the source of neurotic symptoms. Later, however, when Freud (1927) discovered that some neurotic patients did not have actual sexual experiences during childhood, he concluded that the mere fantasy or wish for such experiences could produce neurotic symptoms.

The Social Strategy of Psychoanalysis

The contribution of psychoanalytic methods to behavior change can perhaps be better appreciated if one considers the unusual, and to some extent radical, statements of the early psychoanalysts as viewed by their contemporaries. Not only were Freud and Breuer involved in the disreputable area of hypnosis, they also made claims for cures that seemed too remarkable to be believed. Furthermore, no conventional theory could be offered to explain these cures. Finally, rather than constructing a new, socially acceptable theory to account for the results, Freud developed one that emphasized childhood sexuality, a topic then generally regarded as disgusting as well as incredible.

Prior to the use of psychoanalytic methods in the nineteenth century, disorders such as delusions, paralysis, and irrational behavior were usually treated as physical ailments. The lack of success with these disorders was attributed to failure to understand enough about their physical causes. When neither physical treatment nor reason could produce a cure, the patient would often be referred to a psychiatrist who would experiment with bed rest, light work, good food, and massage. At this time, a few "quacks" such as Freud were experimenting with treatment by talking (Walker, 1957).

For several years, Freud felt socially isolated and his work was largely criticized or ignored. In 1906, a few therapists began to show positive interest, and in 1908 arrangements were made for the publication of a periodical about psychoanalysis edited by Jung.[4] There was still, however, no general acceptance of psychoanalytic methods. "The result of the official anathema against psychoanalysis was that the analysts began to come closer together" (Freud, 1927, p. 276), and in 1910 the International Psycho-Analytical Association was founded by Freud and his associates.

In broad historical terms, Freud opened up the possibility of the treatment of so-called physical disorders by nonphysical means—a major

---

[4]*Jahrbuch für psychopathologische und psychoanalytische Forschungen.* Two additional journals devoted to psychoanalysis were begun a few years later, *Zentralblatt für Psychoanalyse* and *Imago.*

intellectual contribution that has greatly facilitated the nonmedical treatment of psychosomatic or behavioral problems. Freud also provided a model of persistent and wide-ranging inquiry. His studies were called "investigations" and the persons initially treated by him were not called patients but "subjects of analysis."

This spirit of inquiry, which later diminished as psychoanalysis became a widely accepted treatment technique, is an attitude toward behavioral problems which can be very useful in producing new knowledge and more effective behavior-change procedures. There was a willingness to observe behavior, express opinion, and formulate theories about matters, such as infantile sexuality and the death instinct, even though there was much public and private disapproval. This courage has considerably increased the willingness of the public to accept, or at least tolerate, direct and honest discussions about behaviors that are socially disapproved, and such discussion is essential to the development of behavior-change procedures.

These contributions are independent of the truth of the psychoanalytic theories proposed. Very few, if any, behavior therapists will presently agree that the animals young children fear are symbolic substitutes for the father which the child seeks to kill in order to acquire his mother as his wife (the Oedipus complex).[5] There is persuasive evidence that childhood phobias can be experimentally developed without any real or symbolic involvement of the father and then rapidly and permanently eliminated without any psychoanalytic intervention (see Chapter 2). The therapeutic results of psychoanalytic procedures, when they occur, can often be explained more parsimoniously by learning theory than by psychoanalytic theory. This does not require a derogation of the results of the early psychoanalysts—the results of the discovery of America by Columbus are impressive even though he initially thought he had discovered the Orient. What is required is a reformulation of theory to fit more closely with observed facts.

DEVELOPMENT OF BEHAVIOR-CHANGE PROCEDURES

Although "the talking cure" can certainly sometimes produce dramatic changes in behavior, it is equally clear that there can be a considerable amount of talk with little or no change in behavior. Much of the traditional psychotherapy seems to produce changes localized within the region of the lips without affecting the hands or feet.

---

[5]An early exposition of the Oedipus complex in childhood phobias can be found in Freud's essay, "Analysis of a Phobia in a Five-Year-Old Boy," first published in 1909 (Freud, 1956).

The next several chapters present a broad survey of current behavior-change procedures. These chapters are arranged to present to the reader a broad outline of the development of the area of behavior change as it has grown over the past twenty years. Hopefully, this presentation of behavior-change procedures in their historical as well as theoretical contexts will enable the reader to experience somewhat vicariously the rapid growth, conflict, and sudden social significance of this emerging discipline. The next chapter, for example, discusses the experimental production and elimination of phobias and the use of reciprocal-inhibition procedures. The demonstrated effectiveness of reciprocal inhibition in cases ineffectively treated by psychoanalytic methods has severely challenged the theory and status of psychoanalysis. Psychoanalytically oriented therapists who have been living on the good faith of their patients (and the general, spontaneous remission of symptoms), have been put on notice that their credit is running out. The objective measurement of changes in the behavior of patients has rapidly become a criterion of therapeutic effectiveness (McNamara, 1972).

This use of measurable change as a criterion of effectiveness is a two-edged sword, however. Some researchers have recently suggested that the effects of the behavior-change procedure of reciprocal inhibition might be equally well or better produced by cognitive changes in the patients or by the subtle encouragement of nonphobic behavior by the therapist. Interest has thus increased in the use of operant-conditioning methods to produce new behaviors in the patient that facilitate social adjustment (Chapter 3). But, once a new behavior has been developed, it must be maintained or there will be a relapse. This requires an analysis of the contingencies and schedules of reinforcement that can be used to maintain behavior in natural social environments (Chapter 4).

Behaviors are controlled, however, not only by the environmental events that follow them but also by events that precede them, as illustrated by the studies of classical conditioning by Pavlov. This requires a consideration of the use of discriminative and eliciting stimuli in behavior-change programs (Chapter 5). The stimuli that evoke or elicit behavior can be as simple as a tone signal or as complex as a person acting as a model. The learning of some new behaviors seems to occur most rapidly through observing another person perform them (Chapter 6). It may be that some internal states (emotions or experiences) of people can be reliably related to certain observable changes in behavior. Achievement-motivation training represents an attempt to develop a behavior-change procedure relying heavily upon changing internal states (Chapter 7). Finally, if a therapist or change agent can reliably produce changes in another person, it is reasonable to ask whether this person might not become his own therapist. Thus, the possibility of self-directed behavior change has recently become an important area of investigation (Chapter 8).

The person who is changing or is being changed, does not live in a social vacuum. Provisions must be made not only for the maintenance of new behaviors once they occur, but also for the difficulty that the person may encounter while attempting to change his behavior. Transitional roles such as patient, client, student, and subject can, if carefully designed, help the person make the necessary changes in his social environment to support the new behaviors (Chapter 9). The design of these special, transitional roles and the future direction of the entire area of behavior change as a social endeavor depend upon the ability to assess changes in behavior accurately and reliably (Chapter 10). This, in turn, depends upon the development of better techniques for the observation and measurement of behavior in typical social settings (Chapter 11).

These observational techniques, as well as experimentation in behavior-change procedures, raise some difficult ethical issues which are not adequately handled by traditional formulations. A social-interaction perspective offers the possibility of developing ethical guidelines that are pragmatic as well as supportive of individual dignity and responsibility (Chapter 12).

The view of behavior change presented here does not attempt to impose an artificial, theoretical unity upon the area of behavior change (London, 1972). Theory is not considered as though it were a living thing that must be rescued by ingenious interpretations and ad hoc assumptions from the threats of recalcitrant data. Techniques such as the repeated practice of an unwanted behavior (negative practice),[6] the intense and direct exposure of patients to phobic stimuli without escape or adverse physical consequences (implosive therapy),[7] or even sky diving ("para-therapy")[8] are open to investigation without prior exclusion for theoretical reasons. The three criteria suggested earlier (definability, measurability and replicability) delimit the subject matter of inquiry within which theory serves as a guide for the formulation of hypotheses to be confirmed or refuted.

It should be noted that the emphasis upon measurable behavior does not necessarily exclude interest and concern about human experience. Behavior-change procedures such as operant conditioning which involve the use of "rewards" and stimulus-control procedures employing electric shock do indeed create experiences within the patients or subjects. Also,

---

[6]See, e.g., Dunlap (1932), Yates (1958), and Clark (1966).
[7]See, e.g., Stampfl & Levis (1967, 1968) and Levis & Carrera (1967).
[8]This technique has been recommended and used by a southern California physician, S. Delos Champaign. He suggests (*Medical Tribune*, 1965, p. 21) that, "There is a psychic innervation about it" and that there are no neurotics among sky divers (at least none that survive).

as the behaviors of stuttering, delinquency or the phobic avoidance of traffic are eliminated, the patient's potential range of enjoyable experiences is considerably enhanced. How one chooses to deal with the inseparable unity of human behavior and experience is perhaps one of personal preference or cognitive style. It may be possible to behave one's self into new ways of experiencing or to experience one's self into new ways of behaving; for example, by insight therapy.

Behavior change is always individual in nature. Even when one considers organizational change, this change is produced only by changes in the behavior of individuals within that organization because only individuals can, in a genuine sense, behave. Nevertheless, behavior-change procedures have major social implications and much of the current interest in behavior change derives from social as well as clinical concerns. The effective change of the behavior of persons treated individually or in groups raises the hope of broad-scale improvement in human behavior.

This hope has been expressed many times by Aldous Huxley. Not long before his death, he commented (1962, p. 291):

> In the course of the last three thousand years how many sermons have been preached, how many homilies delivered and commands roared out, how many promises of heaven and threats of hell-fire solemnly pronounced, how many good-conduct prizes awarded and how many childish buttocks lacerated with whips and canes? And what has been the result of all this incalculable sum of moralistic works, and of the rewards and savage punishment by which the verbiage has been accompanied? The result has been history—the successive generations of human beings comporting themselves virtuously and rationally enough for the race to survive, but badly enough and madly enough for it to be unceasingly in trouble. Can we do better in the future than we are doing today, or than our fathers did in the past?

Hopefully, the presentation of these methods may indicate the increasing ability of man to shape his own behavior and may serve as a sound basis for considering the related social and philosophical issues. The time may some day arrive when people will be able to design their behavior as a matter of choice rather than being forced, as is now the situation, by the inadequacy of knowledge, to follow the paths of historical and environmental chance. Beyond the study, research, and inevitable error in the development of behavior-change procedures, lies a vision of society in which people may become, by their own choice, what they most wish to be. Perhaps then man shall be free enough to begin the development of a genuinely humane community which has for so long remained only a dream devoid of substance because it has also been devoid of the means of attainment.

Part One

Illustrative Procedures

Chapter 2

Reciprocal Inhibition

Nearly every parent soon comes to realize that young children can be frightened very easily and that their fears are quite difficult to eliminate. Although this has been the situation for many generations of children, it is only within the past fifty years or so that very much has been learned scientifically about the nature and treatment of childhood fears. The procedures of *reciprocal inhibition* described in this chapter were developed primarily out of experimental attempts to understand and eliminate excessive fears (phobias) in children and adults.

HISTORICAL BACKGROUND

In an early experimental study of fear, Watson and Rayner (1920) displayed a white rat to an eleven-month-old child. The child, Albert, showed no signs of fear. The experimenters then again presented the rat to Albert and just as the child's left hand began to touch the rat, they made a loud noise behind Albert's head. He jumped violently, fell forward, and buried his face in the mattress. The procedure was repeated and Albert again jumped violently, fell forward, and began to whimper.

One week later when the rat was presented to Albert, he would not touch it. After seven more presentations of the rat and the loud noise, Albert cried when he saw the rat and tried to crawl away. Five days later Albert was still frightened by the rat. He was also fearful of a rabbit, a dog, a fur coat, and a Santa Claus mask. The fear had generalized to furry objects.

The experimenters concluded that they had experimentally produced a fear that could be described as a *conditioned emotional reaction.* They suggested several possible therapeutic procedures based upon a theory of classical conditioning. One of them was feeding Albert candy at the same time that the rat was shown to him. Unfortunately, Albert was taken out of the hospital where the experiment was being conducted and so it is not known whether little Albert ever overcame his fear of rabbits and dogs or was able to enjoy Santa Claus. The experimenters believed that his fears would be likely to persist into adulthood.[1]

This same combination of a traumatic, frightening event and a subsequent, generalized fear has been reported in a more recent case study by Bentler (1962). An eleven-month-old child, Margaret, tried to stand up in the bathtub, fell, and began screaming. After this, she objected with violent screams to further bathing and was finally removed from the bathtub. Within the next few days, her parents discovered that she was afraid not only of the bathtub but also of the wading pool, faucets, and water at any place in the house.

Margaret was successfully treated with a reciprocal-inhibition procedure (to be discussed later in this chapter), but if Margaret's accident had occurred only five to ten years ago very little professional help could have been given to her. For although Watson and Rayner's study had pointed to the possibility that fears might be conditioned responses, very little therapy was based upon this idea. One notable exception was the work of Mary Cover Jones in 1924. She successfully eliminated a child's fear of furry objects by bringing furry objects gradually closer to the child while the child was relaxed and eating as Watson and Rayner had suggested. Generally, however, the systematic use of a behavior such

---

[1]There are obvious ethical issues here. As the behavior-change field has grown there has been increasing recognition of the need to resolve the many complex ethical and moral issues that have been created by behavior-change technology. In Chapter 12 we address some of these issues.

This study by Watson and Rayner does not mention what happened to the white rat in the experiment. Presumably, the rat was just as frightened by the noise as little Albert who jumped violently and fell forward toward the rat. The poor rat was apparently not harmed, but, because many principles of learning can be demonstrated with both humans and animals, the rat may have developed a persistent fear of little children.

as eating to prevent or eliminate a fear was overlooked by therapists

In 1958 Joseph Wolpe reintroduced the idea of eliminating fear and anxiety by opposing them with positive emotions. In a noteworthy book *Psychotherapy by Reciprocal Inhibition,* Wolpe summarized twelve years of experimental work and concluded that approximately 89 percent of 210 patients treated according to the principles of reciprocal inhibition had either recovered or were much improved.

The central concept of reciprocal inhibition as proposed by Wolpe is as follows: "If a response antagonistic to anxiety can be made to occur in the presence of anxiety-evoking stimuli so that it is accompanied by a complete or partial suppression of the anxiety response, the bond between these stimuli and the anxiety will be weakened" (1958, p. 71). Anxiety is thus reduced by developing in the patient a response that competes with the anxiety response. Wolpe suggested three general classes of responses to inhibit anxiety: (1) relaxation responses, (2) assertive responses, and (3) sexual responses.

Relaxation responses are used in a special manner known as *systematic desensitization* to eliminate anxiety and fear. Systematic desensitization is thus a subprocedure of reciprocal inhibition. Because some therapists, including Wolpe (1969), believe that anxiety underlies many common behavioral problems, systematic desensitization has been used not only for the treatment of phobias but also for the treatment of a wide variety of difficulties such as stuttering, neuroses, frigidity, homosexuality, and compulsions.

SYSTEMATIC DESENSITIZATION

The purpose of this technique is to desensitize the patient to the stimuli which produce his anxiety or fear. The technique, as it is generally used, consists of deeply relaxing the patient and then asking the patient to imagine the weakest or least threatening item in a list of anxiety-producing stimuli several times until no more anxiety is produced. The patient is then asked to imagine the next item on the list, and so on, until none of the stimuli produce anxiety. This technique involves three major phases: the relaxation of the patient, the construction of hierarchies of anxiety producing stimuli, and the pairing of relaxation responses with the imagined stimuli.

This step-by-step exposure of a person to anxiety-producing stimuli is not new. Parents have often gradually introduced a fearful child to swimming by showing him the water, then encouraging him to splash in some shallow water, and then only much later teaching him to put his head under the water to swim. What is new about systematic desensitization is the careful use of relaxation to inhibit even mild or brief anxiety

lthough relaxation might be produced by hypnosis or drugs, a modifica-
on of Jacobson's (1938) progressive-relaxation technique is generally
sed. The emphasis is upon developing deep, muscle relaxation. As
/olpe (1969, p. 102) describes the method to the patient:

> I am now going to show you the essential activity that is involved in
> obtaining deep relaxation. I shall again ask you to resist my pull at your
> wrist so as to tighten your biceps. [The therapist pulls the patient's arm
> upward at the wrist.] I want you to notice very carefully the sensations in
> that muscle. Then I shall ask you to let go gradually as I diminish the amount
> of force exerted against you. Notice, as your forearm descends, that there is
> decreasing sensation in the biceps muscle. Notice also that the letting go is
> an activity, but of a negative kind—it is an 'uncontracting' of the muscle.
> In due course, your forearm will come to rest on the arm of the chair, and
> you may then think that you have gone as far as possible—that relaxation is
> complete. But although the biceps will indeed be partly and perhaps largely
> relaxed, a certain number of its fibers will still, in fact, be contracted. I shall
> therefore say to you, "Go on letting go. Try to extend the activity that went
> on in the biceps while your forearm was coming down." It is the act of
> relaxing these additional fibers that will bring about the emotional effects we
> want. Let's try it and see what happens.

The patient is encouraged to practice relaxation for a major portion
f his initial meetings with the therapist and is asked to practice
rogressive relaxation at home until, ideally, he can relax his whole body
 one or two minutes. Sometimes patients who are very skilled in
elaxation will experience deep relaxation accompanied by effects such as
almness, sleepiness, or warmth.

The patients are asked to practice relaxation at home involving
ifferent muscle groups. During the early meetings, the therapist also
xtensively interviews the patient and attempts to determine the stimuli
at evoke anxiety. When these stimuli are determined, they are classified
to themes such as a fear of heights, a fear of snakes, or fear of losing
onsciousness before an operation. Each of these themes is then broken
own into a hierarchy of items ranging from the least to most anxiety-
roducing such as the sight of bandages, the smell of ether, dizziness, and
e feeling of being about to lose consciousness.

During the early meetings, the patient is taught how to use a
ubjective scale of anxiety measurement. The patient is asked to think of
e worst anxiety he has ever experienced. This is rated as one hundred.
Ie is then asked to imagine complete calmness. This is zero. He is then
sked to specify his present state of anxiety. When the patient reports a
ating of fifteen or fewer units of subjective disturbance, the third phase
f systematic desensitization may begin.

In this phase, the first scene presented is a control scene that is no likely to produce any anxiety in the patient. This might be a typical stree scene. This test provides information about the patient's general level o anxiety and his ability to imagine scenes. Fewer than ten percent of adu patients have difficulty imagining scenes with suitable clarity and dura tion. Young children have more difficulty.

When the patient is sufficiently relaxed, the therapist presents th least anxiety-producing scene in a hierarchy. The patient raises his inde finger when the scene is clearly imagined and the therapist allows him t continue imagining it for approximately five to seven seconds. The patien is then instructed to stop the scene and to report the amount o disturbance it produced. If the patient has felt disturbed, he is give suggestions for relaxation and the scene is presented again. The sam scene is presented until little or no anxiety is produced by it. Then th next scene in the hierarchy is presented and the same procedure i followed until all of the scenes in the hierarchy are presented. This ma take from ten to fifteen sessions for the treatment of typical fears withou complications. More complicated cases may take from thirty to fifty-fiv sessions. This is a very brief period of treatment compared to the tim usually required for the treatment of similar cases by psychoanalyticall oriented methods. Some cases, however, have taken over two hundre sessions.

Effectiveness

Wolpe (1969) has reported that in several studies of neurotic patient totaling 618 cases, approximately 87 percent either apparently recovere or were very much improved. Although this exceptionally high rate o therapeutic success may be accounted for in part by the careful selectio of patients who are likely to be successfully treated by this method, it i still very impressive. There is little doubt that in some cases systemati desensitization, or procedures closely related to it, are effective. This ha been demonstrated in the laboratory under well-controlled condition (e.g., Lang, Lazovik, & Reynolds, 1965; Davison, 1968). In addition to th successful treatment of various animal phobias, systematic desensitiza tion has been used in the treatment of stuttering (Walton, & Mather 1963); blushing (Gibbs, 1965); exhibitionism (Bond & Hutchison, 1960 Wickramasekera, 1968); frigidity (Lazarus, 1963; Kraft & Al-Issa, 1967) homosexuality (Kraft, 1967; Huff, 1970); social anxiety (Cohen, 1965) hyperactivity (Graziano & Kean, 1967); alcoholism (Kraft & Al-Issa 1967); and smoking (Morganstern & Ratliff, 1969).

Paul (1969b) conducted an extensive study of systematic desensi tization covering all major published and unpublished reports up to

January 1967. There were seventy-five such reports; multiple reports of the same data were excluded. Paul (pp. 158–159) summarizes the findings in these reports as follows:

> These reports covered the application of systematic desensitization therapy to nearly 1,000 different clients in the hands of over 90 different therapists. While 55 of these papers were uncontrolled case reports of group studies without sufficient methodological controls to establish independent cause-effect relationships, 20 of the reports were controlled experiments, and 10 of the controlled experiments included designs which could potentially rule out intra-class confounding of therapist characteristics and treatment techniques. The findings were overwhelmingly positive, and for the first time in the history of psychological treatments, a specific therapeutic package reliably produced measurable benefits for clients across a broad range of distressing problems in which anxiety was of fundamental importance. "Relapse" and "symptom substitution" were notably lacking, although the majority of authors were attuned to these problems.

Paul (1966) also compared the effectiveness of systematic desensitization with the effectiveness of traditional insight-oriented psychotherapy. This study controlled for the personality and skill of the therapists as well as attention-placebo effects. Although the subjects in both the psychotherapy and the desensitization groups showed significant improvement in a stressful public-speaking situation, the desensitization group was consistently superior to the psychotherapy group. In addition, the desensitization group was the only group that showed a significant reduction in stress as indicated by heart rate and palmar perspiration.

Temporary Palliative or a "Cure"?

Closely related to the question of effectiveness is the question of the likelihood of the occurrence of other related behavioral problems following treatment. Does the procedure of systematic desensitization eliminate the symptom (the phobic behavior), but leave the underlying "disease" untreated? This question has been the subject of much heated controversy.

In the early 1950s and 1960s Hans Eysenck shocked and outraged some psychotherapists with the suggestion that "psychoanalysis is no more successful than any other method, and that in fact all methods of psychotherapy fail to improve on the recovery rate obtained through ordinary life experiences and non-specific treatment" (1965, p. 137). His conclusion was particularly distressing because it was based upon an extensive survey of various studies of the effectiveness of psychotherapy in many countries. Eysenck noted, however, one major exception to this generally discouraging finding; this was the work of Wolpe who used reciprocal inhibition procedures for treatment rather than psychoanalysis. About this work Eysenck (1965, pp. 131–132) commented, "Of all the hundreds of papers and books the writer has found this [reciprocal inhibition] to be the only one to give positive evidence in favour of one specified type of psychotherapy."

Although some questions can be raised about Eysenck's analysis and interpretation of data (Bergin, 1970), the effectiveness of psychoanalysis was clearly called into question and could no longer be accepted as a matter of faith. The replies of the psychoanalysts tended to accuse Eysenck of ignoring the subjective mental life of patients and of encouraging treatment methods which give only temporary relief rather than eliminating the underlying cause of the problem which may be unconscious.

The English psychoanalyst Edward Glover (1965, p. 161) replied to Eysenck in the following manner:

> Indeed, there is something at the same time forlorn and appealing in Eysenck's determined attempts to kick against dynamic and unconscious psychology. I don't agree with the frequently expressed criticism of him that he has a behavioristic and physiological bee in his bonnet. To my mind he belongs to that romantic rear-guard of Victorian ideologists whose members, fighting in the last ditch of a rationalistic and materialistic conception of mind, have come to the conclusion that it is better to die in the last ditch than to have any truck with modern dynamic psychology.

The psychoanalyst Elizabeth Zetzel (1965, pp. 146, 148–49) suggested that some behavioral symptoms may disappear merely because the person avoids threatening or disturbing life situations:

> It is common knowledge that many neurotic conditions appear to improve without formal therapeutic intervention. For example, the rapid symptomatic improvement of neurotic soldiers removed from combat areas is too well known to merit comment. Do we, however, accept symptomatic improvement contingent on substantial retreat from the physical, emotional and intellectual challenges intrinsic to human growth and development as evidence for recovery from neurotic illness? The young girl who becomes anxious on receiving her first proposal may indeed master her conflict and go on to a successful marriage. Sometimes she develops severe neurotic symptoms which may or may not respond to psychotherapy. She may, however, also "recover spontaneously" by increased inhibition. Though her symptoms disappear, she avoids men. She never marries; she supports her aging mother, and goes to an occasional movie with similar "girls" in her office. Is this recovery, or an unnecessary, even tragic waste? . . .

Anyone familiar with Dr. Eysenck's orientation over the past twenty years will not share his alleged "surprise at the uniformly negative results issuing from all this work." His enthusiasm for behavior therapy was also to be anticipated. Dr. Eysenck has no interest in the possible validity of an approach to mental life which demands recognition of the unseen and the unknown.

To this criticism of Eysenck, Wolpe (1965, pp. 173–174) replied:

In comparing the efficacy of psychoanalytic therapy and behavior therapy what is even more significant than the evidently higher percentage of success obtained by the latter is its much greater economy of time and effort. While psychoanalysis has an average duration of 3–4 years during which most patients are seen 4 times a week, i.e., over 700 sessions, behavior therapy requires an average of about 30 sessions and is usually completed in less than 6 months. Thus, *even if*, under controlled conditions psychoanalysis could match or exceed behavior therapy's figure of almost 90% of patients either apparently recovered or much improved, behavior therapy would remain the treatment of first choice. . . . The truth is that behavior therapy depends on the experimentally based conception that neuroses are nothing but persistent unadaptive conditioned habits. When the habits are deconditioned, nothing remains of the neurosis; and, at the follow-up, relapses or new symptoms are rarely encountered.

The issue of *symptom substitution*—the replacement of one symptom with a new symptom or behavioral problem—is still far from settled (Montgomery & Crowder, 1972). Symptom substitution is assumed to occur when a symptom is removed or blocked without treating the underlying cause of the symptom. A medical analogy would be taking aspirin for an infection, which might temporarily reduce the symptoms, fever, and temperature but would not cure the infection which might lead to a severe illness. In an attempt to determine whether symptom substitution occurs in regard to psychosomatic illnesses, Seitz (1953) hypnotically blocked the symptom of torticollis (a spasmodic contraction of muscles in the neck) of a patient. In a short period of time, this patient developed gagging responses. The gagging was then hypnotically eliminated and the patient developed severe headaches.

The procedure used by Seitz may not be equivalent to the procedures used in systematic desensitization, however, because the symptom was merely blocked abruptly without the development of a constructive patient-therapist relationship (Bookbinder, 1962). Also, in systematic desensitization the goal is not to block the symptom, but to reduce the underlying anxiety which produces it.

Another difficulty in determining whether symptom substitution actually exists in the treatment of behavioral problems as distinct from the treatment of physiological (medical) problems lies in the definition of a "symptom." There is much disagreement among therapists regarding which behaviors should be considered as symptoms except in extreme cases. Probably a patient should not be considered successfully treated if instead of feeling fearful of heights he stays in his house all of the time or regularly beats up his wife.

In study of sixty-two patients with phobias, Gelder, Marks, and Wolff (1967) randomly assigned the patients to systematic desensitization or to standard psychotherapy treatment groups. A three-year follow-up study of these patients showed nearly equal improvement in both groups, but the systematic desensitization group had improved somewhat more rapidly. In an analysis of symptom substitution, Gelder (1968, pp. 41–42) concluded:

> The use of a wide net of ratings made it possible to look for symptom substitution, bearing in mind that "symptom" must be interpreted widely, and that patients sometimes lose their symptoms at the expense of limiting their lives. No evidence was found that this was a special hazard of desensitization, at least in phobic patients; a few instances occurred, but they were seen equally in the control group and may possibly reflect the fluctuating course of the neurosis rather than the effect of treatment.

Symptom substitution does not appear to occur very frequently in patients treated by systematic desensitization or other behavior-change procedures (Crisp, 1966; Rachman, 1968). When it does occur, it seems to be in those patients whose initial symptoms are most severe. Nor does symptom substitution appear to occur in these cases more frequently than in cases treated by brief forms of standard psychotherapy. Psychoanalytic treatment, however, might be more effective in reducing symptom substitutions in cases of severe psychosomatic disorders (cf., Gelder, 1968; Eysenck, 1969).

In regard to the treatment of relatively simple phobias by systematic desensitization, one could agree with a suggestion made by London (1964, p. 117): "The odds against harmful aftermaths of symptom removal are great enough, apparently, so that given the choice, most patients would be wise to take the risk of future trouble against the certainty of present ones."

Essential Elements of Systematic Desensitization

Interest in discovering the essential elements of systematic desensitization has been stimulated by some recent criticisms of systematic desensitization theory. In a wide-ranging criticism, Breger and McGaugh (1965) called attention to the fact that behavior therapists tend to use terms such as *stimulus* or *conditioning* in a very general, imprecise manner. Also, they noted that the theories discussed by behavior therapists often do not fit with what they actually do in practice. And finally, Breger and McGaugh suggested that the particular learning theories used by behavior therapists were inadequate to account for the therapeutic results. The criticism was harsh (p. 340): "Counterconditioning is no more objective, no more controlled, and no more scientific than classical psychoanalysis, hypnotherapy, or treatment with tranquilizers."

Other researchers have called attention to the fact that systematic desensitization theory does not place much emphasis upon the interpersonal relationship between the therapist and the patient. But a positive relationship between the therapist and patient often occurs and this might account for the therapeutic results (e.g., Brown, 1967). Finally, Hoenig and Reed (1966) have reported that although several patients verbally indicated reductions in fear by systematic desensitization, their galvanic skin responses (usually thought to be a valid measurement of fear) did not indicate a reduction of fear. They suggested that patients may report improvement merely out of gratitude to the therapist or to deceive themselves.

In response to these criticisms, many analog (prototype) experiments have been conducted in the laboratory to duplicate specific features of systematic desensitization as it is used in clinical practice. Potentially, there are many factors which may influence the outcome of systematic desensitization such as the amount of relaxation, the graded presentation of anxiety-producing stimuli, the behavioral responses of the patients, and the therapeutic encouragement given by the therapist. No one study has been conducted which controls for all of these factors and therefore tentative inferences must be made from the examination of a wide variety of studies.

The learning theorist, Guthrie (1935), suggested several methods for breaking habits. One of them involved repeatedly exposing an animal to a stimulus at full strength until the animal became "fatigued" and no longer responded. A typical example of this is bronco-busting on western ranches in which the rider stays on the horse (or tries to) until the horse no longer bucks. This procedure in which a stimulus is repeatedly presented until it no longer elicits a response has been called *extinction*.[2] It is different from the procedure in which a very weak form of a stimulus is presented to an animal so that no response is elicited and then this

---

[2]The term extinction has also been used in operant conditioning theory to refer to the situation in which a behavior is not followed by reinforcement. See Chapter 4, Positive Reinforcement.

stimulus is gradually increased in strength without eliciting the response. Using this procedure, a horse could be taught to accept a rider without bucking by first placing a small piece of cloth on the horse's back and then gradually increasing the weight up to a blanket, an empty saddle, and a light rider. Systematic desensitization often involves a combination of procedures because the patient is not permitted to escape the anxiety-producing stimuli and these stimuli are presented in gradually increasing intensity. In addition, relaxation is induced in the patients to help to inhibit anxiety.

Merely teaching patients how to relax in general is not as effective as pairing relaxation with a gradually exposed hierarchy of anxiety-producing stimuli (Davison, 1965a; Cooke, 1966a). Although some benefit might be obtained by presenting a hierarchy of stimuli without relaxation (Cooke, 1966a), presentation of the hierarchy with relaxation appears to be more effective (Davison, 1968; Lomont & Edwards, 1967; Wolpe & Flood, 1970). Schubot (1966) found relaxation helpful for the most fearful subjects but not for the least fearful subjects.

The issue still remains open whether the gradual exposure to phobic objects with relaxation (systematic desensitization) is more effective than directly exposing the patient to phobic objects at full intensity without allowing him to escape (an extinction procedure sometimes known as flooding or implosion). Although some therapists have successfully used a direct exposure extinction method (Wolpin & Raines, 1966; Hogan & Kirchner, 1967), others have not found the procedure as helpful as the gradual presentation of phobic stimuli with relaxation (Rachman, 1966).

Goldstein (1969) has reported a well designed animal study to test the separate effects of counterconditioning (eating), gradual exposure to a phobic object, and direct exposure to a phobic object (extinction). Each monkey in the first group was individually exposed to a phobic object and was fed sugar to inhibit the fear. Another group was exposed to the phobic object at progressively closer distances and fed sugar. A third group was exposed to the phobic object at progressively closer distances but was not fed sugar. These three groups were then compared with monkeys exposed to the object in their cages without sugar and with monkeys with no experimental treatment at all. In summary, Goldstein found that all of these methods of treatment were better than no treatment. Although there were no extreme differences among the various treatment groups, gradual exposure appeared to be somewhat more effective than direct exposure. However, direct exposure with counter-conditioning (eating) was more effective than gradual exposure with no counterconditioning. The most effective procedure was gradual exposure plus counterconditioning—a procedure similar to systematic desensitization. With human subjects, there is some evidence supporting the value of counterconditioning (relaxation or other nonfearful behaviors) in reducing fear, but the need for the gradual presentation of feared stimuli is not so clear (van Egeren, 1971; Boulougouris, Marks, & Marset, 1971).

Some of the lack of agreement among studies may result from a failure to control important therapeutic elements such as the responses made by the subjects while they are experiencing anxiety or fear. Neutral tasks such as doing arithmetic may be used in place of relaxation with some success (Nawas, Mealiea, & Fishman, 1971). Perhaps the procedure called relaxation actually serves the function of distracting the patient or of encouraging him to confront the feared stimuli (Davison, 1971). In a study using albino rats, it was found that rats which "froze" or attempted to avoid a feared stimulus (a previously electrified floor) did not overcome their fear nearly as rapidly as those rats which were mechanically forced to explore the feared stimulus (Lederhendler & Baum, 1970).[3] Nonfearful responses apparently greatly facilitated the extinction of fear. A gradual presentation of the feared stimulus may allow these nonfearful responses to occur rather than avoidance, freezing, or excessive fear.

Although animal studies of human problems may appear somewhat humorous, they help to control a serious problem in evaluation of the effectiveness of various desensitization procedures. This is the problem of bias. The experimenter may inadvertently or deliberately give biasing suggestions to the subjects. A therapist is likely to suggest directly or imply that his procedures are effective. Some studies indicate that subjects who are told that systematic desensitization is therapeutic show more fear reduction than those who are not told that systematic desensitization is therapeutic (Oliveau, Agras, Leitenberg, Moore, & Wright, 1969; Oliveau, 1971; McGlynn, Reynolds, & Linder, 1971).

A very direct method of eliminating bias or the subtle influences of a therapist is to eliminate the therapist. This is very simply done by replacing the therapist with a machine. Melamed and Lang (1967) randomly assigned thirty snake-phobic subjects to one of three groups: automated desensitization, live desensitization with a therapist, or a no-treatment control group. The automated desensitization procedure involved the use of a Device for Automated Desensitization, a DAD. As described by Melamed and Lang (p. 3):

---

[3]A cautionary note: This study should not be interpreted as suggesting that a nonswimmer should be thrown into the water to teach him to swim. His response is likely to be avoidance, panic, or freezing rather than a nonfearful response in a *safe* situation. If the swimmer survives the *unsafe* situation, he is likely to be more fearful; if he does not survive, the persons who threw him in should be fearful of a large legal suit for damages.

DAD is essentially a double-decked tape recorder which stores hierarchy items and relaxation instructions on magnetic tape and presents them according to the desensitization format previously employed. It automatically presents the items in the subject's prerecorded hierarchy in sequence, but allows subject to control the length of visualization and speed with which progress is made. By signaling anxiety (by pressing a switch at end of chair), a given trial is terminated and relaxation is reinstated before proceeding. If the *S* indicates increasing anxiety on the second presentation of the item, he would automatically be returned to an item lower on the hierarchy and must work his way back up the sequence. The apparatus is flexible and can be preset to deliver the item any given number of times. In the present study, the criterion for successful completion of an item was two successive visualizations with no signaling of anxiety.[4]

The group receiving the automated desensitization showed as much decrease in the fear of snakes as did the group receiving live desensitization. Both of these groups showed less fear of snakes than did the control group. Fear was measured not only by the subjects' verbal statements but also by their willingness to approach and touch a harmless snake.[5] Similar success in the use of tape-recorded desensitization procedures for snake phobias has been reported by Nawas (1969). Of course, the therapist has not been completely eliminated. He still meets the patient or subject briefly and describes the procedure, administers tests, and is available if needed. Even a brief encounter with the therapist may be sufficient to influence the results of tape-recorded desensitization (McGlynn, Reynolds, & Linder, 1971).

There is no clear evidence that a positive relationship with the therapist is harmful. It may be helpful but not absolutely essential. Kraft and Al-Issa (1967b) reported an unusual case in which a patient became so dependent upon the therapist that he had to be desensitized to him. This was done by constructing a hierarchy of graded stimuli involving increasing amounts of time away from the therapist.

In a study of the effects of suggestion on human subjects, Howlett and Nawas (1969) reported that graded exposure and relaxation were more effective than graded exposure alone. This could be expected. However, those subjects who were given the negative suggestion that they would probably not be able to touch the snake performed better than those subjects who were given a positive suggestion. Although a positive suggestion was more helpful than no suggestion at all, a negative suggestion seemed to motivate the subjects to "go as far as possible" in performing the tasks.

[4]Two inexpensive cassette tape recorders can also be used (Wark, 1971).
[5]Tape-recorded desensitization has also been used successfully with small groups of subjects for test anxiety (Donner & Guerney, 1969).

Cognitive Factors

The possibility that suggestion may influence the outcome of laboratory experiments in desensitization brings us back to the earlier criticisms by Breger and McGaugh (1965). Perhaps not enough attention has been given to the cognitive aspects of behavior-therapy procedures. Some indication of this is provided in a study which exposed subjects to a stress-producing film showing accidents at a wood-mill (Folkins, Lawson, Opton, & Lazarus, 1968). Prior to viewing the film, the subjects were assigned to one of four groups. One group listened to tape-recorded relaxation instructions. A second group imagined accident scenes similar to those in the film without relaxation instructions. This was called *cognitive rehearsal*. A third group, designated the desensitization group, imagined similar accident scenes and listened to relaxation instructions. Finally, a fourth group, the control group, listened to a tape recording on study habits.

Heart rate and skin conductance were recorded during the treatment and the presentation of the film. No clear differences were found among the groups in regard to heart rate. The cognitive rehearsal group showed somewhat less stress reaction during the film than the desensitization, relaxation, or control groups. The control group showed the greatest stress reaction.

It may be noted that the treatment in this experiment did not involve a gradual approach with intervening relaxation as is done in standard, systematic desensitization. Also, the stress from viewing accidents may not be directly comparable to an approach toward phobic objects. Nevertheless, cognitive rehearsal does seem to have had some beneficial effect in reducing stress reactions.

In an experimental study by Efran and Marcia (1967), subjects were told that phobic stimuli would be presented to them by tachistoscope too rapidly for them to perceive and that unconscious responses to these stimuli would be followed by shock. The subjects were in fact shown blank cards. The pairing of electric shock with real or fantasied phobic stimuli should theoretically increase avoidance responses. Nevertheless, a group of subjects who expected that this "treatment" would reduce their fear of snakes or spiders showed significant improvement in a performance test measuring their willingness to approach and touch the objects. This group also improved more than a similar group which went through the same procedure but was told that a "crucial part" of the treatment procedure was missing.

The results of this study paralleled those generally found in the study of *placebos* (usually capsules filled with sugar or a similar substance). Headaches, nausea, warts, allergies, and other ailments can be remarkably reduced or eliminated if the placebo is given in a situation that induces strong expectations of therapeutic effectiveness in the patient.

Machines can also be used to induce these placebo effects (Schwitzgebel & Traugott, 1968). In a broader perspective, Ullmann (1970) has called attention to the important consequences that may follow from the way in which a person labels social situations, including psychotherapy. After labeling a situation, the person may behave in such a manner that the label becomes a self-fulfilling prophecy.[6]

Analog studies of the fear of snakes in a laboratory setting may not be exactly equivalent to the treatment of patients in a clinic. One important difference may be the person's view of the situation. In the analog studies, the fear is usually temporarily induced and is, in a sense, situational. The subjects are aware of the time-limited exposure to the phobic object and for most of them their fear of snakes or beetles does not constitute a problem which handicaps them in daily life or makes them feel inadequate. In contrast, the patient who comes to the behavior therapist for treatment is likely to feel that his phobia is causing problems in his daily life and that he urgently needs help. These differences in orientation may produce different expectations and interpretations of even externally identical treatment procedures.

In a study of adult patients with chronic behavior problems, Lazarus (1968c) designed a placebo treatment group that involved the patients in gradually more difficult exercises such as recalling past experiences, discussing the fulfillment of one's inner potential, and the mental visualization of pleasant scenes. Unexpectedly, the placebo group improved nearly as much as a similar behavior-therapy group. Both the behavior-therapy group and the placebo group improved more than a similar psychotherapy group which focused upon the historical origins of current problems and the symbolic significance of symptoms. Lazarus (1968, p. 142) has commented on this surprising outcome: "In opposition to expectations, a clinical experiment has yielded tentative evidence that structure may be one of the most potent aspects of behavior therapy. The application of specific techniques lends structure in and of itself, but when patients are enabled to experience a sense of achievement at graduating from one therapeutic phase to another, constructive outcomes seem greatly facilitated. The deliberate addition of graded structure to the usual behavior-therapy framework may well advance the therapeutic potency of this approach."

Support for this suggestion is found in a study by Davison and Valins (1969) in which subjects who believed that they had increased their ability to tolerate a shock were in fact able to tolerate a subsequent shock

---

[6]The concept of the self-fulfilling prophecy can be traced back to an early American sociologist, W. I. Thomas, who proposed the theorem: "If men define situations as real, they are real in their consequences." In his famous essay, "The Self-fulfilling Prophecy" (1965), Robert Merton discussed the application of the Thomas theorem to the development of "runs" on banks, racial prejudice, and mental illness.

better than those subjects who attributed their increased tolerance to the ingestion of a drug. Similarly, it was found that subjects who assumed (incorrectly) that their heart rate did not increase when they were exposed to a feared snake were later better able to approach the snake than control subjects. It appears that the patient's belief that he has changed or is not internally frightened can be helpful in producing changes in external behavior. A series of graded tasks and approval by the therapist may encourage a cognitive reevaluation by the patient of his ability.

In a review of desensitization studies, Goldfried (1970, p. 5) concludes, "These several studies clearly indicate that the individual's cognitions, particularly as they relate to expectancy for improvement and control over his own internal state, may play a significant role in the effectiveness of systematic desensitization." Recognition of the potential importance of cognitive factors has encouraged what Lazarus (1966) has labeled "broad spectrum" behavior therapy. In addition to systematic desensitization in cases of phobia, this may involve the analysis of the patient's relationship with others, his feelings of self-esteem, and his personal values. Attention may also be given to the management of practical, daily affairs.

Encouragement

It is also likely that approval or encouragement by the therapist can markedly improve the performance of the subject independent of relaxation effects (Wagner & Cauthen, 1968). The well-motivated subject may perform fear-producing tasks in an experimental situation with more anxiety than he would usually tolerate. A gradual approach toward a phobic object with the encouragement of a therapist, even without relaxation, might produce some reduction of anxiety by extinction (Goldstein, 1969). The timing of this encouragement may be important (Oliveau et al., 1969). It should probably follow immediately the approach behavior being developed.

The desensitization of patients in natural settings often seems to involve some reward of approach behavior. This is illustrated in the case of Margaret briefly discussed earlier in this chapter. Margaret developed a fear of water after falling in the bathtub and was treated primarily by her mother under a therapist's direction. The basic rule was that Margaret was to be gradually exposed to bathing situations only under conditions that produced little anxiety. Bentler (1962, pp. 187–188) has described the treatment as conducted by Margaret's mother:

> Treatment consisted of four parts and lasted approximately a month. First, toys were placed in the empty bathtub and Margaret was given free access

to the bathroom and the toys. She would enter the bathroom and remove a toy from the tub occasionally, but she did not stay near the tub and refused to play with the toys while leaning over the tub. She continued to scream if any washing was attempted, but became less emotional toward the tub. Free access of this type was allowed throughout the duration of treatment. Second, Margaret was twice placed on the kitchen tables surrounding the sink while the sink was filled with water and toys were floating in it. At first Margaret screamed when near the water. All toys were then placed on the other side of the basin, and onto a ledge above it so that Margaret would have to walk through the basin in order to reach them. After several vacillations, Margaret entered the water reluctantly. Some minor crying resulted from wetting her buttocks, but the kitchen sink helped desensitize Margaret to water. The third step consisted of washing Margaret, at diaper-changing time, in the bathroom sink. She was generally given a favorite toy to play with, but the mirror hanging over the sink proved more interesting, and initial crying soon turned to happy squeals. Margaret also started playing with the water, and during this time she again learned to play with the sprinkler in the yard. The fourth and final step was washing Margaret at diaper-changing time in the tub with water running. To this she objected at first, with screams, but parental hugging and firmness caused her to stop crying after two days.

A follow-up study six months later found that Margaret would gladly play in the bathtub and rush to play in a wading pool. Bentler observes that the procedure might have been accelerated if food in addition to toys had been used.

Tasto (1969) has reported a case in which a four-year-old boy who was extremely frightened by loud noises was gradually exposed to sounds made by dropping a board or popping a balloon. The boy's father showed much ingenuity by placing a dime inside each balloon. The boy had to pop the balloon in order to get the dime. To make this task gradually more realistic, the balloons were initially only slightly inflated and at the conclusion of treatment were fully inflated.

Tasto notes that earlier attempts to desensitize the boy to loud noises by having him imagine them in a hierarchy were not successful. The treatment of patients in the presence of the phobic object in the clinic, laboratory, or in their life situations has become increasingly frequent.

In Vivo Procedures

Studies have shown conflicting results concerning the transfer of imagined performance to actual performance with the phobic object (e.g., Cooke, 1966b; Ritter, 1968; Gruber, 1971). O'Neil and Howell (1969) found no significant differences between groups desensitized to snakes using color slides or live snakes. But, as mentioned earlier, desensitization in analog experiments, such as this one, may not be directly comparable to desensitization procedures with patients having more pervasive, functional phobias.

Clinicians have rather frequently observed the failure of patients to transfer from imagined performance to actual performance. Wolpe (1969a) has discussed one such case. An eighteen-year-old boy developed an extensive fear of urine, especially of contaminating others with his own urine. This resulted in an elaborate forty-five-minute ritual of cleaning his genitalia after urinating which would then be followed by approximately two hours of hand washing. In the morning, he would take a shower which lasted approximately four hours. Not unrealistically, the boy decided that getting up was not worth all the trouble and so two months prior to treatment spent most of his time in bed. Wolpe (pp. 263–264) has described the treatment procedures:

> Treatment in the first place consisted of conventional desensitization. Since he was even disturbed at the idea of anybody else's independent contamination with urine, the first scene he was asked to imagine was the sight of an unknown man dipping his hand into a forty cubic foot trough of water into which one drop of urine had been deposited. Even this scene produced some disturbance in Mr. T. at first, but it waned and disappeared in the course of a few presentations. The concentration of urine was then "increased" until the man was imagined to be inserting his hand into pure urine. At each stage a particular scene was repeated until it no longer evoked any anxiety.
>
> During the course of these procedures, which occupied about five months of sessions taking place about five times a week and lasting, as a rule, about twenty minutes, there was considerable improvement in Mr. T's clinical condition. For example, his handwashing time went down to about 30 minutes and his shower time to just over an hour; and he no longer found it necessary to interpose the *New York Times* between himself and his chair during interviews. A new series of imaginary situations was now started in which Mr. T. himself was inserting his hand into increasingly concentrated solutions of urine. During this time it became evident that there was diminishing transfer between what Mr. T. could imagine himself doing and what he actually could do. Whereas he could unperturbedly imagine himself immersing his hand in pure urine, to do so in actuality was out of the question. It was, therefore, decided to resort to desensitization *in vivo*. Relaxation was to be opposed to increasingly strong *real* stimuli evoking anxiety. Accordingly, Mr. T. was, to begin with, exposed to the word "urine" printed in big block letters. This evoked a little anxiety which he was asked to relax away. The next step was to put him at one end of a long room and a closed bottle of urine at the other end. Again, he had to relax away the anxiety; and then step by step the bottle of urine was moved closer

until eventually he was handling it with only minimal anxiety which again he was able to relax away. When the bottle of urine was no longer capable of evoking anxiety, the next series of maneuvers was started. First of all, a dilute solution of urine (1 drop to a gallon) was applied to the back of his hand and he was made to relax until all anxiety disappeared; and then, from session to session the concentration was gradually increased. When he was able to endure pure urine, his own urine began to be used; and finally he was made to "contaminate" all kinds of objects with his uriniferous hands—magazines, doorknobs, and people's hands.

By the time of completion of these procedures, the boy's hand-washing time was down to seven minutes and his shower time was down to forty minutes. A few months later the boy went back to school and was seen by the therapist only occasionally during the next six months. But, because there was no further improvement, the frequency of treatment was increased to weekly meetings for three months. He was then able to reduce his hand-washing time to three minutes and his shower time was reduced to twenty minutes. Approximately two-and-one-half years later, he reported that his hand washing took about ten seconds and that he "wasn't even using soap." A little over five years following treatment his recovery was still maintained.[7]

In vivo desensitization presents some difficulties because it often requires leaving the clinic or laboratory and thus reduces the control of the therapist over important treatment variables. Also, there may be difficulty in presenting the feared object gradually and in producing sufficient relaxation in the presence of the feared object.

On the other hand in vivo desensitization in the natural environment may be necessary when the patient cannot imagine the feared stimuli with sufficient clarity. Sometimes patients are not even aware of the environmental stimuli which produce the anxiety or fear. In these cases, the therapist may need to observe and treat the patient in the disturbing environment.

Rosenthal (1967) discusses a case of acrophobia in which the patient was successfully desensitized in a laboratory setting to scenes such as entering a plane and flying. In a therapeutic test flight, however, the patient again experienced great fear and reported the source of his fear as the feelings inside himself when the plane started to bank. These visceral, interoceptive stimuli had not been previously desensitized or even recognized until the in vivo treatment was begun. In vivo desensitization has been found considerably more effective in these cases than the usual

---

[7]In 1972 the *New York Times* reported that a college student from Texas claimed a new world record for the longest shower. The shower lasted 169 hours—slightly over one week. Hopefully, it was not this patient (*New York Times,* 1972, p. 4).

methods involving rest, psychoanalysis, or tranquilizers (Goorney, 1970).

In vivo desensitization may have two additional therapeutic advantages. A patient's ability to perform an activity that was previously impaired within his daily life situation may be very motivating to him and thus helpful in producing cognitive reevaluations that may stabilize or facilitate further improvement. Finally, the therapist may also be able to observe some of the social and interpersonal relationships that support the unwanted behavior and to change these relationships.

ASSERTIVE RESPONSES

As mentioned earlier, the reciprocal-inhibition technique has generally used three classes of responses to inhibit anxiety: relaxation responses (described above), *assertive responses*, and sexual responses. The term *assertive*, as Wolpe (1969a) uses it, has a somewhat broader meaning than usual. It refers not only to aggressive responses but also to friendly and affectionate responses. However, in most treatment situations, assertive responses are generally of an aggressive (but not hostile) nature. Assertive responses are typically used in those cases where the patient experiences anxiety in interpersonal relationships.

The use of assertive training has not received much professional attention. One of the early discussions of the use of assertive responses was contained in a book, *Active Psychotherapy*, written by a German physician, Alexander Herzberg, in 1945. He observed (pp. 38–39), "Many nervous patients have the idea that because of their trouble they must take care of themselves and not do too much work, nor indulge in any sport or social activities or have intercourse at all frequently; this all tends to keep their symptoms alive. If we remove their fear of effort by making them realize that what they need is not care but activity, this may enable them to lead a more satisfactory life and thus get rid of their trouble."

Herzberg would take detailed case histories of each patient's problems and would then attempt to persuade the patient that his passive attitude was incorrect. The patients were not permitted to relax or recline on a couch as this would favor a passive attitude. Patients who suffered from phobias were quoted Emerson's comment, "He has not learnt the lesson of life who does not every day surmount a fear" (p. 143). Tasks would then be assigned to the patient to diminish neurotic behavior and achieve more satisfaction in life.

The tasks assigned to the patient were appropriate to the intellectual, physical, and ethical capabilities of the patient, but not to his habits. Thus, athletic tasks would be assigned to physically inept patients and shy patients would be given the task of meeting people. These tasks were not given as demands or prohibitions but as goals to be achieved by the patient in order to overcome his problem. To avoid failure and to build up the patient's confidence, the tasks were given in a graduated series from the least to the most difficult for the patient.[8]

A more widely recognized work emphasizing assertive responses is that by Andrew Salter, *Conditioned Reflex Therapy: the Direct Approach to the Reconstruction of Personality* (1961). Salter differentiates the inhibitory personality which is withdrawn, self-condemning, and emotionally unexpressive from the excitatory personality which is spontaneous, direct, and free of anxiety. He suggests that some patients may have been conditioned into inhibitory modes of response by prior social incidents.

Conditioned-reflex therapy has utilized both direct suggestion and hypnosis in order to produce relaxation or assertive responses. Instructions also can be given to the patient to perform specific tasks in daily life situations. Some of the feeling tone of this therapy may be seen in the following excerpt. Salter (1961, pp. 69–70) describes a case in which he teaches a patient to relax in order to sleep more readily and to feel comfortable in social situations.

> J. R. is the tall, handsome son of a millionaire. He is twenty-five years old, a postgraduate student in sociology, and talks vaguely of improving the welfare of humanity. He is convinced he is uninteresting. He is an alert, if too agreeable, young man, and acts somewhat mule-like when I disagree with him. Though he does not find his studies difficult, he cannot concentrate on them because his mind "wanders constantly." He tosses restlessly for hours before falling into a fitful sleep. He wants to learn how to hypnotize himself so that he may be rid of his insomnia. I test him for hypnosis, but his attention wanders as he compares my technique with what he has read about the subject, and with what he thinks I should do. Needless to say, nothing happens.
>
> I then become stern, and tell him that I am utterly uninterested in the clap-trap that clutters up his mind. I am the authority, and he has come to consult me. He will do exactly as I say, if he wants to learn autohypnosis. All that he has to provide is the broken leg. I will decide the splints that are indicated. This approach is necessary with the spoiled-child type of adult, because our only means of communication with him (and with everybody else) is through his conditioned emotions.
>
> He is interested in music and possesses absolute pitch. I decide to mold my technique accordingly, and tell him to listen intently.
>
> I snap my fingers. "Can you still hear that pitch in your head, now that I have stopped snapping my fingers?"
>
> "Yes."

[8]Herzberg (p. 145) provides the following illustrative list: "First task, renouncing medicines; second, not lying down in the daytime; third, settling marital conflicts; fourth, resuming sexual relations; fifth, resuming work; sixth, tackling professional tasks which were previously avoided."

I tap my desk with my pen. "Can you hear this sound in your head?"
"Yes."

"That's fine. I see the procedure necessary, and we'll take it from there when I see you next."

"Aren't you going to hypnotize me today?" he asks.

I smile blandly. "If you want me to help you, it will have to be in my way. I can't be bothered having you tell me what to do. . . ."

Our young man is annoyed when he leaves, but he is very curious about what I have up my sleeve, which is precisely my intention.

When I next see him, I tell him that he simply has to listen to me and obey. He has my permission to waste his own time, but I resent his wasting mine, and unless he is completely and absolutely cooperative he might as well leave right now.

"What have I done to deserve this tirade?" he asks.

"You are guilty of being you. That's all. The fact that you bought a ticket doesn't give you a license to tell the actors what to say."

He smiles.

"Very well," I say. I point to the glistening thermos jug on my desk. "I want you to look at the spot made by the reflection of the light. Do you see that spot?"

"Yes."

"Now, each time I snap my fingers, I want you to close your eyes in a docile, browbeaten way. For your sake, please, close them in a docile, browbeaten way. You will find this very interesting."

Many persons go through life in a constant flight from boredom, and their cooperation can be enlisted only by promising them relaxation and entertainment. Ringing these bells involves no hypocrisy. Our therapeutic duty to a human being in distress is all the validation we need.

He relaxes in the easy chair and stares at the jug. I snap my fingers. He closes his eyes. I wait about three seconds and then say quietly, "Open them." He opens his eyes, and continues looking at the spot. I snap my fingers again and he closes his eyes. I wait another three seconds, and then say, "Open them." He does so. "That's fine," I say. "From now on I want you to think thoughts of blankness, relaxation, and quietness in a vague day-dreaming way. At the same time, as I snap my fingers, close your eyes without thinking and keep them shut, until I tell you to open them. Think 'relax,' and try to feel blank in every part of your body. Do you understand?"

"Yes," he says. I see that I have his complete attention, and that now, at least, he has no negativism toward me.

I snap my fingers. His eyes close. I wait three seconds and say, "Open them," and I snap my fingers again. He closes his eyes. I permit them to remain closed for three seconds and say, "Open them," and I repeat this ritual once more. After about forty times I stop. "How are your thoughts now?"

He is somewhat surprised. "I feel relaxed."

"That's fine," I say. "Now I'll tell you what," and without ado I snap

my fingers, although he is not fixating the jug. He blinks. "What happened?"
I ask.

"I blinked when you snapped your fingers."

"That's fine," I say, for this means that now his lid closure has become somewhat conditioned.

After the patient was taught how to relax, he became much more spontaneous in social situations. Following this, he was then instructed to become more assertive. Within a few weeks he reported social successes and a new feeling that people liked him.

It should be noted that even while the therapist was teaching the patient how to relax he was also serving as a model of a person who was socially assertive and successful. Salter has suggested several techniques for increasing assertiveness. Verbally express spontaneously felt emotions, deliberately use the word "I," express agreement when praised, and improvise rather than plan far into the future.

Although most therapists have not used assertive responses as extensively or enthusiastically as suggested by Salter, their application may in some cases be helpful. Weiner (1967) has described a case of a shy, fifteen-year-old boy with compulsive rituals involving washing, dressing, reading, writing, and the careful placement of objects. The treatment plan required the boy to replace these rituals with similar, time-limited activities that would interfere with his normal daily activities in only a small way. For example, one of his rituals was a compulsive checking and rechecking of his school locker. The boy was asked to give a good reason for it (to prevent things from being stolen) and then asked to decide what action would be necessary to insure the desired result. The boy was instructed to lock the lock, check it once, take one step back, and with his hands in his pockets say to himself: "I have checked the lock; and I can now be certain it is locked and everything in the locker is safe and protected; there is absolutely no positive reason for me to check it again; I am now going to walk away from it and go to class" (p. 28). He was also told not to be concerned when he could not succeed in this task but to attempt to complete it the next time. The boy's behavior markedly improved under these conditions.

Weiner (p. 29) has offered some reasons why this treatment procedure may have been effective:

> Much benefit seemed to accrue from the technique's simultaneous utilization and circumvention of his obsessive-compulsive personality style. On the one hand, his involvement in the treatment was probably promoted by the fact that his characterological emphasis on cleanliness and neatness and his preference to conduct his life in an orderly, scheduled manner were

neither demeaned nor denied him; rather, the therapist endorsed positive aspects of these values and encouraged him to continue to perform rituals, albeit rituals far more in tune with realistic necessity than those that brought him for help.

On the other hand, the therapeutic approach circumvented certain features of his characterological style that might otherwise have impeded his progress. First, he was instructed to act, to do things rather than to think about them, which steered him away from the ruminations and dread that initially incapacitated him. Secondly, by frequently telling him that he would probably not always be able to succeed in his assigned tasks and that failure should not concern him or prevent him from trying further, the therapist provided him with a set of standards much less harsh than his own rigidly obsessive code of success and failure.

Many of the more conventional forms of psychotherapy involve, almost inadvertently, some assertive training. In systematic desensitization, for example, some confrontation with the anxiety-producing situation or phobic object is required for completely successful treatment. If the patient has difficulty in performing the assertive response, the patient and therapist may rehearse the behavior together in a form of role playing. The therapist may first demonstrate the proper response while the patient observes. The therapist thus becomes a model for the patient and may gently guide the patient if necessary. There is rather convincing evidence that this modeling with guided encouragement toward increasingly difficult tasks is more effective in changing some behaviors than systematic desensitization or assertive training alone.[9]

SEXUAL RESPONSES

As previously indicated, strong sexual responses as well as relaxation and assertive responses may reduce anxiety. Discussion of the use of sexual responses to reduce anxiety generally focuses upon the treatment of impotence or frigidity (e.g., Wolpe, 1969b). There appears to be a reciprocal relationship between relaxation and sexual responses. When anxiety or fear is intense, some relaxation must be obtained in order to achieve a satisfactory sexual response. This sexual response may then help to reduce subsequent anxiety.

The typical treatment procedure for impotence, therefore, places much emphasis upon relaxation and the avoidance of anxiety (Lazarus, 1971). With the cooperation of his wife, the man with a problem of impotence is often told merely to lie beside his wife without feeling any

---

[9]Details of assertive training and behavior rehearsals can be found in Wolpe and Lazarus (1966). Modeling is discussed in Chapter 4, Observational Learning.

need to make any sexual advances. His wife is not to expect or require any performance on his part. When he feels some sexual arousal (hormones or tranquilizers can also be used), he may make some very limited sexual advances but never to the point where he feels anxiety. Progress is to be very gradual. An attempt to achieve complete sexual intercourse too early may greatly impair progress.

In thirty-one cases of impotence reported by Wolpe and Lazarus (1966) using this or closely related procedures, 67.7 percent were able to achieve completely satisfactory sexual performance, 19.4 percent showed some moderate improvement, and 12.9 percent showed very little or no improvement. The time the patients spent in treatment ranged from one week to over one year, with a median time of approximately eight weeks. Patients who improved with this treatment technique tended to do so in approximately six weeks or less.

Because of the social taboo regarding the discussion and experimental study of human sexual responses, relatively little is known about them in comparison to their personal and social importance. Thus the causes of sexual difficulties are still largely matters of speculation. There is some tentative evidence that sexual difficulties might be related to the three following situations:

1   A person's general fear of close, personal contact may create anxiety which is not specifically related to sexual activity. Although there is sexual interest and response to the opposite sex, this response is inhibited during approach or contact. Systematic desensitization and assertive training may be useful in these cases.

2   Although there is no anxiety caused by close, personal contact with the opposite sex, anxiety is produced by sexual activity. Initially strong sexual responses may diminish as sexual activity becomes increasingly explicit because of anxiety produced by sexual stimuli. This may result from the early, severe punishment of sexual activity. Also, the fear of failing to perform in a sexually adequate manner (as in cases of impotence) may give rise to additional anxiety. As in stuttering, anxiety about adequate performance increases the likelihood of poor performance, and this in turn produces additional anxiety and poorer subsequent performance. The use of systematic desensitization and assertive training with graded exposure may be helpful. Typically, the patient is relaxed and then is gradually presented scenes of increasing sexual intimacy until no anxiety is experienced (Huff, 1970; LoPiccolo, 1971). The treatment is very similar to the desensitization procedures used in the treatment of phobias described earlier in this chapter.

3   In some cases, there may be no positive sexual response to a person of the opposite sex. Heterosexual reactions are weak or absent rather than suppressed by anxiety. Sexual responses to the same sex or

opposite sex persons may be conditioned responses. McConaghy (1970) has used a classical conditioning procedure to develop sexual responses. Both heterosexual and homosexual men were exposed to motion pictures of attractive women or men which were immediately followed by colored triangles or circles. After several presentations, the triangles and circles alone were able to produce sexual reactions.[10] The patterns of conditioning in childhood and adolescence may be important developmental factors in later sexual orientation. Treatment may involve conditioning sexual responses to heterosexual stimuli and training the person in appropriate social and sexual skills.

Some sexual difficulties may derive from a combination of the conditions described above. It is also likely that many patterns of sexual behavior are maintained by the positive reinforcement from pleasant sexual experiences. The treatment of these difficulties will be discussed in subsequent chapters, particularly Chapter 5, Stimulus Control. The purpose of the discussion here has been to indicate that there is a close, reciprocal relationship between sexual responses and relaxation.

SUMMARY

It is only within the past fifty years that enough has been known about human fears and phobias to produce them reliably in the experimental laboratory. Many fears now appear to be conditioned-emotional reactions in which the feared object has been paired with a frightening experience. In the famous case of little Albert, a loud noise made just before he touched a white rat greatly frightened Albert, and he later became very fearful of the rat and furry objects.

If fears can be learned, then some experimenters have concluded that they can be unlearned. One of the major experimental procedures for eliminating or reducing fears, anxiety, and phobias is reciprocal inhibition as developed by Joseph Wolpe. The basic procedure consists of deeply relaxing the patient and then asking the patient to imagine the least fear-producing item in a list of fear-producing stimuli until no more fear is experienced by the patient. The patient is then asked to imagine the next item on the list, and so on, until none of the items produce fear. This procedure thus pairs relaxation responses with the gradual presentation of fear-producing stimuli. These fear-producing stimuli may be imagined,

---

[10]McConaghy has also suggested that there may be an inhibitory process that prevents heterosexual men from having homosexual responses. Similarly homosexual men may be inhibited in regard to heterosexual responses. This would fit with Freud's theory that all heterosexual men are also latent homosexuals because all persons are bisexual in either manifest or latent form (Freud, 1956, p. 347). Thus, homosexuals are also latent heterosexuals.

but if it is possible or convenient, actual fear-producing objects may be brought into the laboratory or the patient may be gradually introduced to them under conditions of relaxation in the natural environment.

As a therapeutic procedure, systematic desensitization appears to be equally as effective or more effective than traditional, insight-oriented psychotherapies. Although there are relapses, they do not seem to be more frequent than with the use of traditional methods. When symptom substitution does occur, which is rare, it usually occurs in patients with severe psychosomatic disorders. For these patients, long-term psychoanalytic treatment might be preferable to reciprocal-inhibition procedures. At least care should be taken to understand the personal or social utility that a symptom may have before eliminating it.

In addition to the treatment of phobias, reciprocal inhibition has been used to treat difficulties such as stuttering, neuroses, frigidity, homosexuality, and compulsions. The primary goal has been to reduce the anxiety or fear which may underlie or produce these behaviors. Generally, relaxation responses are used to reduce anxiety but assertive or sexual responses may also be used.

A large amount of research has been conducted to determine the essential elements of reciprocal inhibition. Some studies show inconsistent or conflicting results. Tentatively, it appears that in addition to any conditioning effects which may result from the pairing of incompatible responses, such as fear and relaxation, there may also be important cognitive factors involved. The patient's expectation of effective treatment, for example, may greatly enhance therapeutic effects. Also, the encouragement or approval given by the therapist to the patient as he learns a new behavior may be very important in eliminating old, incompatible behaviors.

Chapter 3

Operant Shaping

Man is used to feeling superior to animals even when the animals perform complex tasks. B. F. Skinner (1938, pp. 339–340) once trained a rat to pull a string to obtain a marble from a rack, which it then carried with its forepaws across a cage and dropped in a tube in order to receive a pellet of food. Most people are likely to view this as a mere stunt or joke.

An experiment with more serious social implications has been conducted by William Cumming (1966). By using operant-shaping techniques, he trained pigeons to recognize small, defective electronic components (diodes) as they passed by on a mock assembly line. After passing inspection, the components were fed into a large machine that then assembled these components into commercial products.

Thus far, nothing seems too serious until one is told that the pigeons did this inspection job very well, in fact, better than the men in the factory on the assembly line. The birds inspected approximately one thousand parts per hour, and Bird 119 could inspect at this rate continuously for four hours. Longer sessions of inspections were not tried because the human operator checking this bird's work was unable to continue at this rate. The bird showed no fatigue; in fact, its performance tended to improve rapidly the longer it worked.

In addition to inspecting electronic components better than their human competitors, pigeons cost very little (not over five dollars for the best), eat very little, require very little sleep, if any, and have been known to work for days, even weeks and months, without stopping. Furthermore, as Cumming notes, they will work for "chicken feed." But, as the possibility of replacing men with pigeons on the regular assembly line appeared increasingly imminent, organized labor objected. After all, it is embarrassing enough to be replaced by a machine; to be replaced by a pigeon is unbearable. Thus, in this company,[1] men are still sent to do a pigeon's job.

TECHNIQUES OF SHAPING

Perhaps the solution to the problem of the use of pigeons in factories is not to leave pigeons unemployed, but to train men to reach higher levels of skill and accomplishment than pigeons. One effective procedure for developing new behaviors in both men and animals is *operant shaping.* Because operant shaping is a special form of *operant conditioning,* it is helpful to understand a few very general concepts commonly used in operant-conditioning theory.

During operant conditioning, a specific behavior is followed by a prearranged environmental event that reinforces (or in popular language, "rewards") the behavior. The reinforcer may be food, money, or verbal praise. The behavior is known as a *response.* A group of very similar responses, such as the responses required to operate identical levers, is known as an *operant.* The term operant emphasizes the fact that the responses "operate" upon the environment to produce reinforcing consequences.

The frequency of a response prior to conditioning is called the *operant level* of the response. An environmental event is a reinforcer if it follows a response and increases the frequency of that response over its earlier operant level. It is clear that a response cannot be reinforced if it is not emitted by the subject. Operant shaping is used to obtain responses that would otherwise never, or very rarely, occur.

Operant shaping involves reinforcing successively closer approximations to the desired response until that response is emitted. For example, let us assume that we want to shape a behavior in a student

---

[1]The name of the company is withheld by request. Management and public relations problems also occurred in a similar experiment using pigeons as quality-control inspectors to locate faulty capsules for a drug manufacturer (Verhave, 1966b).

involving the scratching of his right ear with his right hand. Though one might have to wait quite a long time for this behavior to occur naturally, with shaping techniques and, of course, a willing student, this response can usually be obtained at high rates of frequency in ten to fifteen minutes.

Staats and Staats (1964) have described the procedure used to shape an ear-touching response in a student. Essentially, the experimenter begins by waiting for any movement of the student. If the student becomes restless and moves in his chair, the experimenter reinforces this movement. Initially, the experimenter reinforces any movements that occur so that the general class of "movements" becomes reinforced and increases in frequency. During these general movements, the student will probably move his right shoulder. The experimenter then reinforces this shoulder movement as well as general movements of the upper body and right side. Then as the shoulder movements become more frequent, the experimenter reduces the reinforcement of general movements (differential reinforcement) until all movements that are clearly not tending toward the desired, final response are no longer reinforced.

As movements of the right shoulder become more frequent, movements of the right arm are likely to occur. These movements are then strengthened, leading to more movements of the right hand, some of which may be toward the head. These are then reinforced until the ear is touched.

Sidman (1962, pp. 173–174) has suggested some useful principles in the shaping process.

1 Reinforce the behavior immediately. If the reinforcement is delayed, even by a fraction of a second, it is likely to be preceded by some behavior other than that which the experimenter intended to reinforce.

2 Do not give too many reinforcements for an approximation of the desired final response. Behavior that is initially reinforced must ultimately be extinguished as we move closer to the end point. If we reinforce intermediate forms of behavior too much, these once-reinforced but now-to-be-discarded responses will continue to intrude and will unduly prolong the shaping process. . . .

3 Do not give too few reinforcements for an approximation of the desired final response. This is the most common difficulty in shaping behavior; the experimenter moves too fast. He abandons a response before he has reinforced it enough and, as a consequence, both the response and the variations which stem from it extinguish before he can mold the next closer approximation to the final behavior. The subject may then return to his original behavior, as if he had never gone through a shaping process at all. . . .

4 Carefully specify the response to be reinforced in each successive

step. Before abandoning one response and reinforcing the next approximation to the final behavior, the experimenter must watch the subject closely
to determine what behavior is available for reinforcement.

Thus far, even with these principles, the ability to shape behavior is
still very much an art rather than a clearly specified routine.[2] Basically the
same procedures that are used to shape a rat to carry marbles or a pigeon
to inspect electronic components can be used to train people to drive a car
or ski. The reinforcers used in these shaping procedures are usually those
that have indirect or secondary reinforcing potential.

Use of Secondary Reinforcers

There are two general categories of reinforcers: *primary reinforcers* and
secondary reinforcers. A primary reinforcer is a stimulus that does not
depend upon a prior history of conditioning. Water and food are typical
examples of primary reinforcers. A secondary reinforcer is a neutral
stimulus which has been closely and consistently associated with a
primary reinforcer so that it acquires reinforcing potential. This is
accomplished by presenting the neutral stimulus immediately prior to the
primary stimulus.

If a green light is turned on immediately preceding the presentation
of a primary reinforcer, such as food, to a hungry rat, the light will acquire
reinforcing potential. Later, even though all food is withheld, the rat will
press a bar to turn on the light.[3]

A secondary reinforcer, however, tends to lose its reinforcing
potential for an animal rather quickly if it is not eventually followed by a
primary reinforcer. The process during which reinforcement is no longer
given is referred to as *extinction*. The rate at which a response declines in
frequency during extinction depends to a large extent upon the previous
type and rate of reinforcement. Responses previously reinforced by
secondary reinforcers usually decline in frequency more rapidly than
those responses previously reinforced by primary reinforcers.

Secondary reinforcers that are paired with more than one primary
reinforcer are called *generalized reinforcers*. Money, social approval, and

[2]For example, the amount of reinforcement a response requires before shifting the reinforcement
to a new response may depend upon the operant level of that response. Based upon this assumption, some
statistical formulae are being developed, known as shaping indexes, to guide the shaping of human vocal
responses (cf. Lane, Kopp, Sheppard, Anderson, & Carlson, 1967). However, very little work has been
done in the area of human operant behavior discussed here.
[3]Secondary reinforcers are also sometimes known as *conditioned reinforcers*. This implies that a
neutral stimulus acquires its reinforcing potential through a conditioning process. This assumption needs
more experimental investigation before it can be completely accepted (cf. Hill, 1968). Secondary
reinforcers may also become reinforcing because of the "information" which they provide about the
likelihood of subsequent reinforcement (Hendry, 1969).

affection are sometimes considered generalized reinforcers for humans because they have been closely associated with several primary reinforcers.

The importance of secondary reinforcement in operantly shaping behavior may be seen in a simple example offered by Holland and Skinner (1961). The objective of the shaping process was to get a dog to touch a doorknob with his nose. The dog was first taught to respond to a secondary reinforcer, the sound of a dime store noisemaker cricket. This was done by clicking the noisemaker and immediately tossing a bit of food into the dog's dish. When this sound became a secondary reinforcer, the process of shaping was begun.

Successive approximations to the terminal response, touching the doorknob, were immediately reinforced by clicking the noisemaker. Initially, any movement of the dog was reinforced by a click, then gradually only those movements toward the door and doorknob were reinforced. Finally, when the dog's nose touched the doorknob he was given a piece of food.

The use of the click as a secondary reinforcer was important because the dog needed to be reinforced immediately, but tossing the dog a piece of meat would have made the dog move his head toward the floor. Thus, movement of his head toward the floor rather than movement toward the doorknob would have been reinforced, and the terminal response of touching the doorknob would not have been obtained as soon, if at all. In shaping, the reinforcer should not interfere with the behavior being shaped. The click served as an easily administered and noninterfering secondary reinforcer.

Chaining

Shaping can be used to produce not only one response but also a series or chain of responses. Several secondary reinforcers can be used so that an animal will press a lever to obtain a green light, then press another lever to obtain a white light, then press a third lever to obtain food. *Chaining* is accomplished by following a response with a stimulus that acts as a secondary reinforcer and as a signal that "sets the occasion" for the next response.[4] Under these conditions, an animal will work to receive a series of secondary reinforcers if they are eventually followed by a primary reinforcer.

Most behavior is actually a chain of smoothly performed responses.

[4]Chapter 5 discusses the use of these discriminative stimuli that set the occasion for a subsequent response. There is some controversy regarding whether these linked stimuli act as secondary reinforcers, discriminative stimuli, or both.

The pressing of a lever by an animal to obtain food is a series of responses involving at least the animal's rising, pressing, and lowering which is followed by seizing the food and eating it. If a secondary reinforcer which is usually present in this chain is eliminated, the entire chain of responses may be disrupted (Keller & Shoenfeld, 1950).

The shaping of chains of responses is often done, even inadvertently, in the daily life situations of humans. Little Jonathan, for example, decides that he wants a jelly sandwich. He follows his mother around the house whining, "I want a sandwich," which his mother attempts to ignore. Occasionally she says, "No, you can't have a sandwich," or some similar statement, but the whining continues. He begins to tug and hang on her skirt. In desperation to avoid further annoyance, she gives little Jonathan his sandwich. His mother has successfully shaped a chain of responses made up of whining, tugging, and eating. If little Jonathan merely says, "I want a sandwich," he does not get one. If he only whines or tugs at her skirt, he does not get one. But, if he does all these annoying things in proper sequence, he does get a sandwich. That mothers can successfully shape this, as well as other chains of annoying responses, is evidenced by the fact that the world is filled with whining cookie collectors.

Response chains may be weakened by at least three procedures. One procedure is to eliminate a stimulus that usually precedes one of the responses in the chain (e.g., hide the jar of jelly that initiates the request for the jelly sandwich). Another procedure is to withhold reinforcement of the terminal response (e.g., do not give Jonathan the sandwich). These two procedures involve primarily extinction. A third procedure is to shape responses that compete with the response chain to be eliminated (e.g., teach Jonathan to make his own sandwich).

Although shaping procedures have been fairly clearly demonstrated in the experimental laboratory, their application to humans in daily life situations requires considerable extrapolation. Only by allowing some imprecision and many unverified assumptions can one say that operant-conditioning procedures are applicable to humans in their natural milieu. To a large extent, the reasoning is by analogy rather than by deduction. Nevertheless, these analogies have permitted the development of techniques for changing human behavior which have produced rather striking results.

A CASE STUDY: SHAPING THE ATTENDANCE OF DELINQUENTS IN TREATMENT PROGRAMS

Earlier in this chapter, it was suggested that a student's behavior might be shaped so that he would scratch his right ear with his right hand. This could be accomplished within ten to fifteen minutes. While watching such demonstrations, a student of the slightly rebellious type might well ask the professor, "Why not just tell the student to scratch his ear and save all the time and effort?" The question would be a good one. If a person can perform the terminal behavior (if the behavior is in his *behavioral repertoire*), it is usually more efficient just to ask him to behave in a certain way. If the behavior is not in the person's behavioral repertoire, or if he is not cooperative, shaping may be necessary.

Delinquents are ideal subjects upon which to test the power of shaping procedures because they will not cooperate with a professor merely to be polite or to earn a better mark in a psychology class. (A colleague of ours once remarked that it was very understandable why psychology did not work with real people—psychologists usually test their theories on unusual organisms such as white rats and college undergraduates.) To test shaping procedures, a project was set up to obtain the attendance and cooperation of delinquents in therapy-like situations such as talking into a tape recorder and taking psychological tests (Schwitzgebel, 1964). Most of the boys had extensive court records and had spent time in reform school or prison. They were also generally known as serious "troublemakers" in the community.

In general, the shaping procedure was as follows. Delinquents who did not know the experimenter were met on the street corner, or in the typical meeting places of delinquents, and offered a part-time job of talking into a tape recorder as an experimental subject. The job paid from one dollar up to two dollars an hour for, on the average, two or three hours a week. The subject was invited to bring a friend or two along, look over the laboratory situation, then make up his mind as to whether he wanted to participate. During this initial conversation, he would be casually offered a cigarette, free games on a pinball machine, or food as a reinforcer of his attention. The experimenter, the subject, and his friends would then ride the subway back to the laboratory where they were immediately offered a Coke and more to eat. The delinquents were generally willing to come along with the experimenter because they were bored and apparently had nothing more interesting to do.

At the laboratory, the subject and his friends would usually play with the tape recorder, ask numerous questions about the electronic equipment and the secretaries, and play with a white rat used in experiments. They would then participate in an informal, tape-recorded interview. At the conclusion of the interview, the subject would be given an unexpected "bonus" of one dollar.

If the subject seemed willing and able to keep appointments, he was scheduled to meet the experimenter at the laboratory at his convenience the following day. If the subject missed this meeting or if the experimenter decided that the boy could not keep appointments, the experimenter went out to meet him the following day at the original meeting place. One subject, for example, who was initially met in a poolroom failed to arrive at the laboratory for his second interview. The experimenter then went back to the poolroom and spent considerable time there for the next several days and found the subject. The boy appeared glad to see the experimenter and both of them rode the subway back to the laboratory. The third meeting was arranged for the next day at the same time outside the subway entrance nearest the poolroom. When the subject arrived at this location, he was immediately reinforced by being offered a cigarette and was complimented by the experimenter. The experimenter paid the subway fares. The fourth meeting was arranged inside the subway station after the toll gate. (Part of the previous day's wage was paid to the subject in the form of subway tokens which he could not easily spend elsewhere.) The next meeting was arranged just outside the subway exit nearest this laboratory. Finally, the subject was met at the laboratory.

This arrangement of meetings at locations increasingly close to the laboratory did, of course, appear strange to the subject. He was honestly told at the second meeting that delinquents often have trouble arranging their schedules and getting to appointments on time. This shaping procedure was being used as part of an experiment to see if it could make his attendance less difficult and more reliable.

The attitude of the experimenters toward the attendance problem is also very important. The problem of delinquent nonattendance was considered to be very different from the problem of nonattendance at therapy sessions by middle-class neurotic patients. If a middle-class person pays for therapy and then fails to attend, it may be a sign of the severity of his problem. He has had much experience with keeping appointments and recognizes their importance to himself and to the therapist. If a delinquent fails to attend a meeting, he may just have been doing something more interesting at the time and not have realized the importance of the meeting to the experimenter.

If a subject failed to attend, this was interpreted to mean that the shaping procedure was inadequate, that the boy had forgotten about the meeting, or that the laboratory situation was not attractive enough for him. The solution to this was to improve the shaping procedure and the incentive, set a time for another meeting, and let each boy know that no matter how many meetings he missed he was still welcome.

Unless a boy was in jail or had a severe physical or mental disability, his failure to attend was not seen as his fault but the fault of inadequate techniques. In one extreme case of nonattendance, the experimenter and a project assistant, a very attractive girl with long blond hair, drove to the boy's home located in a low-rent housing project in a new, white convertible, the kind most highly prized by the delinquent subculture. The boy, who was standing on the corner with his friends, was immediately impressed (or, more accurately, stunned) and eagerly came along to the laboratory for the ride. Afterward, the boy commented to the experimenter, "It was just like out of the movies when you drove up."

Of twenty-five delinquent subjects in this project, only two failed to develop reliable attendance patterns within fifteen or fewer meetings. One of these boys was arrested and went to reform school. The other boy took a job that occupied most of his available hours.

It could be argued, and should be, that at least some of the delinquents in this experiment would have attended the meetings at the laboratory without the use of shaping procedure. To test the usefulness of the shaping procedure more carefully, a second experiment was conducted. Fifteen boys between the ages of fifteen and nineteen were met in a poolroom and were told about an "opportunity" to participate in some research. The poolroom was a well-known meeting place for delinquents. The proposed research involved getting some very brief questionnaires filled out by local businessmen. (This task was selected in order to encourage delinquents to contact businessmen, of whom they are usually frightened, and to ask them for jobs.) The boys would be paid fifty cents for each questionnaire completed.

The boys were asked to come to a church office about twelve blocks away the next day if they were interested. Most of the boys were clearly not interested and were hesitant to talk with the research assistant, a college senior.[5] Two of the boys said that they might stop by the office the following day, but they did not show up. None of the boys were willing to offer their names or telephone numbers.

The boys who were contacted and showed no interest in the project were designated as the subjects in the experiment. (The two boys who said they might show up were eliminated as they were considered too cooperative to be included in this study.) The goal was to shape the attendance of the remaining thirteen boys. The research assistant returned to the pool hall the next day with mimeographed questionnaires and a pocket full of change. He met many boys he had seen the previous day and offered each of them fifty cents for getting the manager of the pool hall to fill out a questionnaire and sign it. The manager had previously indicated his willingness to participate. The boys vacillated between perceiving the entire situation as a "gag" and questioning the

---

[5]We wish to thank Richard J. Solomon for his excellent help and pioneering spirit.

assistant as to whether the questionnaire would get the manager into trouble. In the assistant's own words (Solomon, 1966):

> After some intensive verbal prodding, I finally got three boys to ask [the manager] for his signature; though each boy took his own sheet, they approached [the manager] together as if there were some security in numbers. By this time many more boys had gathered around to see what all the commotion was about. The boys returned with the signature and following Sidman's advice,[6] I immediately gave them fifty cents each. This seemed to change the entire complexion of the crowd. Formerly reluctant members of the [experimental] group who were not even interested enough to question me about the project became the first to ask for a chance to "get a signature." Luckily for my pocketbook, I had only a few more mimeographed sheets with me which I gave to those who asked first.

A time was set up for meeting the boys at the church office the next day. None of the boys showed up. The behavior had not yet been adequately shaped and all of the thirteen subjects had thus twice failed to attend. The research assistant then returned three more times to the pool hall with more questionnaires and money. He gave special attention to those subjects who seemed to be least interested. At the fifth scheduled meeting, six subjects showed up at the poolroom and three arrived at the church office near the scheduled time. On one occasion, a boy, thinking that he was supposed to meet the research assistant at the church, arrived at the church early, waited for a while, then realizing his error hurried back to the poolroom in time to keep the original meeting.

After three more meetings, the following pattern emerged: nine of the thirteen delinquents who had previously failed to attend now arrived regularly at the church office, three attended occasionally, and one did not attend at all. Thus, this small experiment tends to confirm the possibility that delinquent attendance and cooperation can be shaped even in activities that delinquents initially reject.

Although delinquent subjects may arrive dependably at a laboratory or church office, their arrival may not be prompt. It may be as many as several hours early or late. The next step in the project was to shape prompt arrival.[7] This was achieved primarily through the use of cash "bonuses" as reinforcers. For example, a subject might arrive an hour late for the tenth meeting. The experimenter would welcome him, mention that this was much better than the previous day when he was an

---

[6]See Sidman as quoted earlier in this chapter.

[7]It should be noted that shaping attendance involves both spatial and temporal dimensions. In most laboratory experiments the temporal dimension is ignored; the animal is merely placed in the cage or the subject, usually a cooperative undergraduate, arrives on time.

hour and a half late. For the "good effort" the boy was given a twenty-five cent cash bonus. The next day the boy might arrive within fifteen minutes of the appointed time—hoping perhaps for a dollar bonus. The experimenter might mention nothing about his arrival, but the boy would be likely to call attention to the fact and ask about his bonus. It would then be explained that the employee can always expect to receive the basic wage but that bonuses depend entirely on the amount of money the experimenter happens to possess and on his feelings at the time. The boy might be disappointed until, later in the hour, he receives a fifty-cent bonus for, say, showing curiosity about the meaning of a recurring dream. He might then realize that he could never be sure what he might receive a bonus for or what the bonus would be, but in general the whole thing seemed to be an interesting game. At the following meeting, the experimenter might take the subject to a restaurant for a sandwich if he arrived still more promptly.

Using the procedures we have outlined, it was possible to shape arrival to within a few minutes of the scheduled time for most subjects. Figure 3-1 shows the arrival times for a typical subject, S_2, for the first twenty-two meetings.

In a subsequent study of youthful offenders ranging in age from twelve to twenty-one years, the subjects showed a group mean of thirty-eight minutes late during the first four meetings (Schwitzgebel, 1969). One group of these subjects then received reinforcers (bonuses)

Figure 3-1 Arrival times of experimental subject S_2 for initial twenty-two meetings. R. Schwitzgebel and D. A. Kolb. Inducing behavior change in adolescent delinquents. *Behavior Research and Therapy,* 1964, **1**, 297–304.

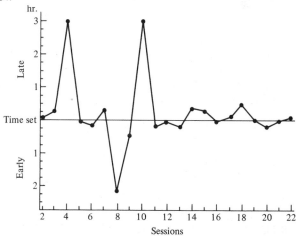

contingent on prompt attendance while a matched group of subjects received none. They received bonuses for other socially desirable behaviors (e.g., putting Coke bottles away at the end of an interview). Both groups improved in the promptness and dependability of their attendance over the first twenty meetings. The contingent-reinforcement group, however, had a significantly lower mean discrepancy between appointment time and arrival time (11.2 minutes) than the group without contingent reinforcement (15.6 minutes).

It should be noted that bonuses were not offered immediately following each more prompt arrival by the subjects in this study as is customarily done in shaping new responses. This might have been a more effective procedure. On the other hand, a certain amount of intrigue and adventure throughout the period of shaping might have served as a reinforcer. Also, it is possible that the experimenters inadvertently greeted a subject more enthusiastically or treated him more considerately than usual when he arrived close to the scheduled time. This may have served as an implicit but consistent reinforcer.

Although the shaping procedures discussed here may sound somewhat rigid, they were not carried out in a harsh or mechanistic manner. Rather, the subjects were genuinely liked by the research staffs, and the experiments were carried out in a spirit of enthusiasm. This attitude may have significantly contributed to the positive results.

An interesting experiment by Rosenthal (1966, pp. 165–176) points to the importance of the experimenter's attitude in shaping behavior. Laboratory rats were randomly assigned to two groups of experimenters. One group of experimenters received rats that were arbitrarily labeled "bright"; the other group of experimenters received rats that were arbitrarily labeled "dull." There was, in fact, no difference in the learning ability of the rats because they all came from the same carefully controlled animal colony. Experimenters who thought their rats were "bright" and expected positive performance shaped the behavior of their rats to press a bar considerably better than those experimenters who thought their rats were "dull." The experimenters had "biased" the results.

Evidence from Rosenthal's experiment also suggested that those experimenters who worked with the supposedly "bright" rats felt more relaxed and were more friendly and enthusiastic. They handled the animals more and observed the animals' behavior more closely than those experimenters who thought they were working with the "dull" rats. This closer observation by the experimenters working with the "bright" rats could allow more accurate and rapid reinforcement of those behaviors approximating the terminal response, bar pressing. In the same manner experimenters who expect positive performance from delinquents and are friendly and enthusiastic may be more successful in shaping behavior than experimenters who expect failure. In a broader sense, that which is called experimenter bias in the laboratory may be called therapeutic skill in the clinic.

DEVELOPMENT OF COOPERATIVE AND FRIENDLY BEHAVIOR

Shaping procedures have been used to modify a wide range of behaviors. Children have been trained to eat (White, 1959), use the toilet (Marshall, 1966), follow orders (Davison, 1964), read (Staats, 1968), speak (Risley & Wolf, 1966), wear glasses (Wolf, Risley, & Mees, 1964), and use experimental equipment (Ferster & DeMyer, 1961). Of broader social significance, however, is the use of shaping procedures to develop cooperation. However, work in this area is still at a very exploratory level.

Some researchers have been moderately successful in developing cooperative responses in the higher apes (cf. Crawford, 1935). Under carefully designed conditions, even rats have been trained to cooperate so that they will both avoid shock and obtain adequate food—though this involves using intense electric shock and a severe deprivation of food (Daniel, 1942). It is encouraging to note that Wolfe and Wolfe (1939) found that cooperative responses were somewhat more frequent in children than in apes when both were tested in similar experimental situations.

In the study by Wolfe and Wolfe, some cooperative responses were probably in the behavioral repertoires of the children prior to the experiment. In a study of four mute schizophrenic children by Hingtgen and Trost (1966), cooperative behavior had to be carefully developed by making reinforcement contingent on behaviors that successively approximated cooperation. The reinforcers were coins that could be put into a vending machine to obtain candy. The subjects were seen in pairs and the shaping procedure was divided into four phases.

During the first phase, reinforcement was given when one subject approached, then accidentally touched, then deliberately touched the other subject with his hand. In the second phase, reinforcement was given only when there was physical contact by hand also accompanied by a simple vocalization. Reinforcement during the third phase required vocalization plus contact with both hands. During the fourth phase, reinforcement was contingent upon both subjects making vocal responses and touching each other with both hands.

A high frequency of cooperative responses was shaped in approximately forty-six sessions. Only one coin was given for each cooperative response and this resulted in frequent competitive behavior such as pushing, tugging, pinching, and hugging to prevent the other from getting the coin. In short, they began to act like typical children—laughing and smiling when cooperative behavior was developing well and expressing anger when cooperation was not developing well. These new responses generalized from the laboratory to the ward and home.

Although competition may not be the exact behavioral opposite of cooperation (cf. Lindsley, 1966), competitive behavior may need to be reduced in order to construct the social situation necessary for the reinforcement of cooperative responses. For example, Dennis, a seven-year-old boy at a state training school, was so aggressive that he was not allowed to associate with the other children in the institution (Bostow & Bailey, 1969). He was given tranquilizing drugs and was sometimes tied to a door in a hallway where he was able to strike only an occasional passerby. During the treatment program, each time he bit, kicked, scratched, or butted his head against another person he was placed in a small "timeout" booth for two minutes. Alternatively, each time two minutes elapsed without such aggressive behavior, Dennis was given a small amount of milk, carbonated beverage, or a bite of cookie. Within this situation of alternative contingencies, the frequency of aggressive behaviors rapidly declined and within a week he was allowed to associate with the other children for increasing periods of time. Occasionally during the periods of reinforcement, he would approach other children to hug and embrace them. It is likely that some of the effectiveness of this procedure resulted from the combined use of both punishment and reinforcement contingencies.

One of the early attempts to develop cooperation in pairs of children was by Azrin and Lindsley in 1956. Their experiment followed closely an earlier experiment by Skinner (1953, p. 306) in which cooperative responses had been developed in a pair of pigeons. Essentially, Azrin and Lindsley placed two children at opposite ends of a table. At each end of the table, there were three holes and a stylus in front of each child as shown in Figure 3-2. The children were told that they could play the game any way they wanted to and were shown how to put the styli into the holes. They were also shown some jelly beans that would fall into a cup on the table.

If the styli were placed in directly opposite holes, a red light flashed on the table and a jelly bean fell into the cup. Although the children were not told about this requirement, all ten teams of children (two children in each team) learned to cooperate within the first ten minutes. Leader-follower relationships generally lasted throughout the experiment. When

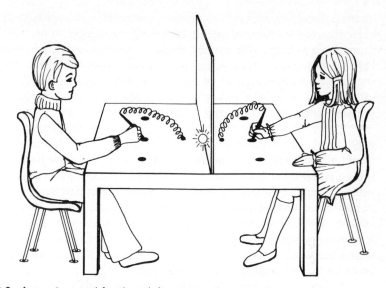

Figure 3-2 Apparatus used for the reinforcement of cooperation between children. N. H. Azrin & O. R. Lindsley. The reinforcement of cooperation between children. *Journal of Abnormal and Social Psychology,* 1956, **52**, 100–102.

reinforcement was temporarily terminated, cooperative behavior clearly declined in frequency. When reinforcement was again initiated following this period of extinction, the earlier rate of cooperation was almost immediately restored.

Using more elaborate equipment and experimental controls, Lindsley (1966) induced cooperation and competition in teams of adult subjects by changing only the contingencies of reinforcement. In teams with a history of cooperation, complex patterns of cooperation were developed, usually involving alternating leadership so that each gave the other equal opportunity for individual reinforcement. Lindsley also noted that "altruistic gifts are not accepted as debts unless the donor provided the gifts by sacrificing reinforcement to himself. In other words, an unavoidable 'gift,' one with no other alternative, is not responded to as a gift" (p. 495).

ADVANTAGES AND LIMITATIONS OF SHAPING

There is no doubt that shaping procedures can be used to develop new behaviors that were not previously in a person's repertoire. Whether shaping is the most efficient procedure to use depends on a number of factors. Surely, shaping is inefficient, comparatively speaking, if a new behavior can be obtained merely by asking the subject to perform it. For example, a subject will usually display more assertive or cooperative behaviors in a social situation if he is asked to do so and is assured that such behaviors are appropriate and acceptable. The fact that it is difficult to discuss the desired behavior with a rat or pigeon surely does not preclude such discussion with a human.

There is fairly consistent evidence that a person's awareness of the conditions of reinforcement can greatly improve his performance if he wants his performance to improve (e.g., Spielberger & DeNike, 1966). In fact, a person's belief about the conditions under which reinforcements will be given may influence rates of behavior more than the contingencies of reinforcement actually in effect (e.g., Kaufman, Baron, & Kopp, 1966; Dulany, 1968). This should not be too surprising because we often see people behaving in ways that will not produce the results they expect—which is usually another way of saying that they do not accurately perceive the contingencies of reinforcement.

When shaping procedures are not successfully used, it is often not clear, especially in the case of children, whether the subject did not know what the contingencies of reinforcement were for the appropriate behavior, knew the contingencies but chose not to participate, or wished to participate, but lacked the required behavior.

Behavior-change methods that emphasize shaping procedures to obtain a desired behavior often assume a behavioral deficit. Although this may be true, it should not be assumed without clear evidence that the subject was aware of the reinforcement contingencies. Shaping may change consequences for a person. In natural settings as the subject displays the desired behavior, other people may observe and interact with him more frequently, thus increasing the frequency of reinforcers associated with the desired behavior. Attention and praise may be effective reinforcers easily overlooked in the natural environment, especially when the researcher is used to observing more tangible reinforcers such as food or coins.

A study of the social development of a child by Buell, Stoddard, Harris, and Baer (1968) illustrates this possibility nicely. Polly, a three-year-old girl, showed no cooperative play with other children, rarely used the outdoor play equipment, and would hang onto the teachers. The behavior-change technique focused exclusively on getting Polly to play on the outdoor equipment by placing her on it each day and holding her there at least thirty seconds (a procedure called *priming*). She was reinforced for staying on the equipment by the teacher's interest and approval. Equipment use by Polly as well as behaviors such as touching

other children, using children's names, and cooperative play were carefully observed before, during, and after this technique was used. Not only
did Polly's use of the outdoor equipment markedly increase, but so did the
child-oriented behaviors of touching, cooperative play, and use of names
although these behaviors were not deliberately shaped or reinforced.

One can agree with the researchers in this study that the collateral
development of these social behaviors resulted from Polly's increased
contact with peers and availability of peer-group reinforcement. Thus,
changing the reinforcement contingencies for one behavior produced
changes in that behavior which in turn changed the contingencies for
collateral behaviors. If these collateral behaviors were also being shaped,
an investigator could be easily misled to believe that shaping produced the
behavior change rather than the changed contingencies of peer-group
reinforcement.

Another factor to be considered in the analysis of the effectiveness
of shaping procedures is the availability of alternative procedures that
may be used to produce new behaviors. Modeling is a particularly likely
alternative. If a subject already has available the basic components of a
new behavior, he may be able to imitate a new behavior quite readily.
Shaping the new behavior is likely to take longer, require more effort, and
involve more exposure to physical or social risk. In this regard, Bandura
(1969, pp. 143–144) appropriately notes:

> In laboratory investigations of learning processes experimenters usually
> arrange comparatively benign environments in which errors will not pro-
> duce fatal consequences for the organism. In contrast, natural settings are
> loaded with potentially lethal consequences that unmercifully befall anyone
> who makes hazardous errors. For this reason, it would be exceedingly
> injudicious to rely primarily upon trial-and-error and successive approxima-
> tion methods in teaching children to swim, adolescents to drive automo-
> biles, or adults to master complex occupational and social tasks. If rodents,
> pigeons, or primates toiling in contrived situations could likewise get
> electrocuted, dismembered, or bruised for errors that inevitably occur
> during early phases of learning, few of these venturesome subjects would
> ever survive the shaping process.

On the other hand, if the new behavior requires the learning of many new,
internal, physiological cues, as in water skiing, modeling procedures may
be much reduced in their effectiveness. It is, of course, sometimes
possible to combine procedures, such as shaping and modeling, to
increase the rate of behavior change. Modeling and imitation are discussed in more detail in Chapter 6 on observational learning.

Another combination of behavior-change procedures that is often useful is shaping and extinction. The nonreinforcement of one behavior may facilitate the shaping of an incompatible or competing behavior. This was illustrated in the earlier case of Dennis who was placed in a "timeout" room following aggressive behavior and positively reinforced when his behavior was nonaggressive or friendly (Bostow & Bailey, 1969). Because friendly responses are generally incompatible with aggressive responses, the shaping of friendly responses may reduce aggressive responses—in somewhat the same manner as whistling can be reduced by reinforcing the eating of crackers, an incompatible behavior.

Not many carefully designed treatment programs have incorporated the extinction of one behavior and the systematic reinforcement of an incompatible behavior. An exception is a study by Wahler (1969) in which parents were taught to isolate their children in a bedroom for five minutes immediately following "oppositional" (destructive and stubborn) behavior and reinforce cooperative behavior by parental approval and play. The changes in behavior were marked and stable, the spontaneous approaches of the children to their parents increased, and the social reinforcement value of the parents was enhanced.

An increasing number of studies are using parents or paraprofessional personnel to shape and reinforce behavior (e.g., Marshall, 1966; Patterson, 1965a; Tahmisian & McReynolds, 1971; Wagner, 1968; Wolf et al., 1964). If verbal instructions to the parents are not adequate, a gradual, step-by-step training procedure, including videotape feedback, can be used to shape the parents' behavior which will in turn modify the child's behavior (Bernal, Young, & Shannon, 1970). Thus, it may eventually become possible to change behavior on a much broader scale than is now possible with only the use of highly trained professionals.

SUMMARY

During operant conditioning, a specific behavior is followed by a prearranged environmental event that reinforces that behavior. A reinforcer, such as food, money, or verbal praise, increases the frequency (probability) of the behavior. The behavior is called a response and a group of similar responses is known as an operant.

Operant shaping is a special form of operant conditioning. It is a procedure used to develop new behaviors which are not in the subject's behavioral repertoire. During operant shaping, successively closer approximations to the new, desired behavior are reinforced until the new behavior is finally emitted.

A primary reinforcer is a stimulus that does not require the subject to have a prior history of conditioning or learning in order for the stimulus to act as a reinforcer. Food and water are typical examples of primary reinforcers. A secondary reinforcer is a neutral stimulus which has been closely associated with a primary reinforcer often enough so that it acquires reinforcing potential. Secondary reinforcers which are associated with more than one primary reinforcer over a period of time are known as generalized reinforcers. Typical generalized reinforcers for humans are money, social approval, and affection. They are frequently used in the shaping of human behavior and the maintenance of high levels of behavioral activity.

Shaping procedures have been used to develop a wide range of behaviors such as eating, speaking, reading, and cooperating with others. In one demonstration project, juvenile delinquents were met on street corners and in poolrooms and their participation in therapy programs was shaped through the use of generalized reinforcers. The shaping of human behavior does not need to be done in a harsh and mechanistic manner. In fact, shaping appears to be most successful when it is done with enthusiasm by the experimenter and with a positive attitude toward the subjects.

Shaping generally seems most effective if the subject is aware of the shaping procedure and its objective. If, however, the subject has available the basic components of a new behavior but has never integrated them, demonstrating and modeling the behavior to the subject and then asking him to imitate may be more effective than shaping. Sometimes shaping and modeling procedures can be combined. Shaping procedures can often be taught readily enough so that parents or paraprofessional personnel can assist the therapist in changing a patient's behavior in natural settings outside of the clinic or laboratory.

Chapter 4

Reinforcement

Thus far in this book there has been considerable discussion of technical terms and laboratory experiments. This may seem to be a somewhat harsh and insensitive approach to the life and spirit of man. In this period of rapidly expanding technology, noise, and speed, it is tempting to think that man would be far better off if he would live without supersonic planes, audio amplifiers, and neon signs. Surely, so it seems, we do not need "secondary reinforcers" and "extinction curves," but rather a return to that time when man was more "natural."

But even if such a return were possible, we could not escape the contingencies of reinforcement that shape and maintain our behavior. We could only be more ignorant, less effective, and less human. The story that follows brought an end to Rousseau's myth of "natural man" living nobly and freely in the wilderness. This myth met its sudden and shocking demise late in September of 1799 near the Caune Woods in France.

THE WILD BOY OF AVEYRON

For several years, there had been rumors in the city of Aveyron that a naked child, a stranger to humanity, was living in the nearby woods. In September, a young boy of twelve or thirteen who had lived alone in the woods at least seven years was captured, but he soon escaped and wandered through the woods during the extremely cold winter months draped only with a tattered shirt. Then, perhaps forced by hunger or cold, he entered an inhabited house and was recaptured.

This time the boy did not escape. He was shipped to Paris and was, for a brief time, one of the most popular public spectacles. The people who crowded the streets did not see Rousseau's natural man. Instead, they saw "a degraded being, human only in shape; a dirty, scared, inarticulate creature who trotted and grunted like the beasts of the fields, ate with apparent pleasure the most filthy refuse, was apparently incapable of attention or even of elementary perceptions such as heat or cold, and spent his time apathetically rocking himself backwards and forwards like the animals at the zoo" (Humphrey, 1962).

> When watched inside his own room he was seen swaying with a tiresome monotony, turning his eyes constantly towards the window, looking sadly over the airy plains outside. If at such a time a stormy wind chanced to blow, if the sun behind the clouds showed itself suddenly illuminating the atmosphere more brightly, there were loud bursts of laughter, an almost convulsive joy, during which all his movements backwards and forwards very much resembled a kind of leap he would like to take, in order to break through the window and dash into the garden. Sometimes instead of these joyous movements there was a kind of frantic rage, he writhed his arms, pressed his closed fists upon his eyes, gnashed his teeth audibly and became dangerous to those who were near him.
>
> One morning when there had been a heavy fall of snow while he was in bed, on awakening he uttered a cry of joy, left the bed, ran to the window, then to the door, going and coming with impatience from one to the other and finally escaped half dressed and gained the garden. There, giving vent to his delight by the most piercing cries, he ran, rolled himself in the snow and gathered it by handfuls, feasting on it with incredible eagerness.

Fortunately, the boy came into the care of a young physician, Jean-Marc-Gaspard Itard, who spent five years giving daily care to the child whom he named Victor. Itard's methods were extraordinarily advanced for his time. In historical perspective, it now appears that many of his successes resulted from the application of operant-conditioning procedures which were not known or formalized until well over a hundred years later. Surely no one can accuse Itard of biasing his account to give undue credit to operant conditioning.

To make Victor's surroundings tolerable and to increase his sensibilities, Itard provided much pleasant, gentle stimulation. In Itard's own words:

> I let no occasion pass of procuring happiness for him: and certainly this was neither difficult nor costly. A ray of sun reflected upon a mirror in his room and turning about on the ceiling, a glass of water let fall drop by drop from a certain height upon his finger tips while he was in the bath, and a wooden porringer containing a little milk placed at the end of his bath, which the oscillations of the water drifted, little by little, amid cries of delight, into his grasp, such simple means were nearly all that was necessary to divert and delight this child of nature almost to the point of ecstasy (p. 18).

Thus, Itard gradually helped Victor develop sensitivity to touch and taste and, in this way, not only reinforced the boy's attendance and cooperation but also developed a wider range of reinforcers for subsequent use.

One of the early games Itard played with Victor reinforced the boy's attention by using food as a reinforcer. In the early stages of this game, Itard placed a nut under several small cups and then after showing the boy the empty cups allowed him to select the one remaining cup concealing the nut. In this way, the success and interest of the boy was assured. Gradually, the game was made more complicated until nuts were hidden under two or three cups which were then rearranged among the other empty cups.

Through the use of matching games, Victor learned to recognize letters. Then by pairing the letters LAIT with milk, the boy began to learn the meaning and use of words. It was in the area of speech, however, that Itard had his most disappointing failures. Victor greatly enjoyed one of the lessons in which he was blindfolded to prevent distraction and then instructed to raise a finger when Itard made a sound. Between these lessons Victor would sometimes come to Itard with the blindfold in his hand, apply it to his eyes, and stamp with joy when Itard would finally tie it firmly on his head to begin the lesson.

As the difficulty of these lessons increased—Victor was required to raise a particular finger corresponding to a particular vowel—Victor's joy also increased. His displays of delight became so lively that he would become distracted, confuse the sounds, and raise his fingers indiscriminately with impatient bursts of laughter. Although Itard removed the blindfold and looked somewhat menacingly at him to discourage gaity, this only increased the boy's laughter and produced more distraction.

I again put the bandage on his eyes and the bursts of laughter were repeated. I then tried to intimidate him by my behavior since I could no longer hold him by my expression. I took one of the drum sticks which we had used in an experiment and struck him lightly upon the fingers when he made mistakes. He treated this as a joke and in his glee became even livelier. In order to undeceive him I thought it necessary to make the punishment a little severer. He understood me, and it was with a mixture of pleasure and pain that I saw in the lad's clouded expression how the pain of the blow was lost in the feeling of insult. Tears rolled down from under his bandage. I hastened to raise it but whether from perplexity or fear from a profound preoccupation of the inner senses, he persisted in keeping his eyes closed although freed of the bandage. I cannot describe how unhappy he looked with his eyes thus closed and with tears escaping from them every now and then. Oh! how ready I was on this occasion, as on many others, to give up my self-imposed task and regard as wasted the time that I had already given to it! How many times did I regret ever having known this child, and freely condemn the sterile and inhuman curiosity of the men who first tore him from his innocent and happy life! (p. 59).

Victor never learned to talk. A feeling of fear had now replaced that merriment and the lessons were even more disrupted than before. After speaking a vowel, Itard would wait as long as a quarter of an hour for Victor to hesitantly raise his finger. Then, even though the reply was correct, if a slight noise or movement would be made in the room, Victor would suddenly withdraw his finger and in fearful slowness raise another. The lessons remained blocked over the following years of training.[1]

During the first years after his capture, it was difficult to tell whether his displays of affection toward his governess, Madame Guérin, were genuine or merely attempts to gain more satisfaction for himself. Five years after his capture, however, external reinforcers of his affection were no longer necessary. The following incident illustrates this:

The last time when his memories and his passion for the freedom of the fields, led our savage to escape from the house, he turned in the direction of Senlis and gained the forest. He soon came out, however, doubtless driven by hunger and the impossibility of providing for himself any longer. Drawing near to the neighboring fields, he fell into the hands of the police who arrested him as a vagabond and kept him as such for a fortnight. Recognized at the end of this time and again brought to Paris, he was taken to the Temple, where Madame Guérin, his guardian, came to claim him. A

[1]This may have been a form of traumatic-avoidance learning as seen in Chapter 2 with little Albert and the white rat. One wonders whether systematic-desensitization procedures using relaxation, food, or drugs known at the time, might have been helpful in reducing Victor's fear.

number of inquisitive people had assembled to witness this interview, which was truly affecting. Scarcely had Victor caught sight of his governess, when he turned pale and lost consciousness for a moment but, as he felt himself embraced and fondled by Madame Guérin, he suddenly revived and showed his delight by sharp cries, convulsive clenching of his hands and a radiant expression. In the eyes of all the assistants he appeared less like a fugitive obliged to return to the supervision of his keeper, than like an affectionate son who, of his own free will, comes and throws himself in the arms of the one who has given him life (pp. 89–90).

Thus, by small steps of progress reinforced by tangible expressions of love and affection, this boy's entry into the human condition was shaped. Yet, there was always a sense of sadness about him, for when in the course of lessons he struggled in vain to understand a word, he would suddenly moisten with tears those unintelligible characters that he could never fully comprehend. The years passed, Madame Guérin aged with the loss of her husband, and Itard's interest waned and turned to disappointment.

Little is known about Victor's later life. It is clear, however, that the early patterns of reinforcement that had initially encouraged Victor's growth and participation in social life were not maintained. In 1828, Victor died a mute farmhand in an obscure part of France, having precipitously declined in social and human stature from that time when, as a teenager, he dined in town with his companion, the young physician, Itard.

The purpose of this extended story is to suggest that because Itard labored without the advantages and successes of modern behavior-change techniques, the full potential of Victor's life was not realized. The richness of human life need not be diminished by technical understanding and complicated procedures any more than understanding a map and driving skillfully to a friend's home diminishes the enjoyment of meeting him. Rather, it makes the event possible.

SCHEDULES OF REINFORCEMENT

Patterns of reinforcement, particularly those involving the secondary or generalized reinforcers of attention and approval, make the "humanization" of a child possible. Only in a social context, through the transmission of cultural perspectives by learning, can the child become human. In fact, so powerful are the forces of cultural learning that if, by some fantastic miracle, we were able to transport a bright, young, prehistoric child of the Upper Paleolithic Age across fifteen thousand years to our present age and raise him in a modern city, he would probably grow up as a typical teenager racing his motorcycle Sunday afternoon to Malibu Beach. The difference between the late prehistoric man and the modern urbanite is not so much the result of a different biological endowment as it is the result of a different physical and social environment.

Operant-learning theory is one scheme, among many, for analyzing the effects of the environment. This theory suggests that one of the pervasive characteristics of all social environments is the scheduling of reinforcers that maintain consistent patterns of behavior without which there could be no social order. The rules used in determining when a response is to be reinforced are called *schedules of reinforcement.*

If the rule specifies that the response is never to be reinforced, the schedule is one of *extinction.* If the response is reinforced every time it occurs, the schedule is one of *continuous reinforcement.* If the response is occasionally reinforced, the schedule is one of *intermittent reinforcement.* Many, if not most, human behaviors are intermittently reinforced. The letters we look for in the mail box are there only occasionally, but we may go to the mail box many times before they arrive.

An interesting effect of many intermittent-reinforcement schedules is that after all reinforcement has stopped (extinction), subjects will continue to respond more frequently than if they had previously been on a continuous-reinforcement schedule. In other words, extinction of a response is slower following an intermittent schedule than a continuous schedule. The different effects of these schedules can be very great. For example, if a pigeon has been on a schedule of continuous reinforcement for pecking at a light and all reinforcement is discontinued, the pigeon may emit roughly one to three hundred more responses before ignoring the light. But, if the pigeon has been on a certain type of intermittent schedule before extinction, it may emit over sixty-thousand responses before the frequency of the response significantly decreases (Ferster, 1963).

This does not mean that intermittent reinforcement is better for obtaining high frequencies of a behavior in all circumstances. A behavior's durability is greater following intermittent reinforcement than continuous reinforcement, but continuous reinforcement will often produce higher frequencies as long as the reinforcement is being given. A child will tend to reach for pieces of candy more often if they are given to him each time he reaches (continuous schedule) than if one piece is given to him only after he reaches ten times (intermittent schedule). However, when no candy is left, he will continue to reach more often after the intermittent schedule than after the continuous schedule.

Which type of schedule is better depends in part upon whether the experimenter, or mother, wants high frequency or durability of behavior. There are also some other considerations. Continuous reinforcement may more rapidly produce satiation and fatigue than intermittent reinforcement. Because a child can eat only a certain amount without getting full or sick, the experimenter should consider whether he wants temporary high frequency or a longer period of response at a lower frequency. Also, eating may interfere with a response such as singing. Thus, behavior maintained on intermittent schedules tends to be more easily weakened by physiological changes in the subject, punishment, or emotional factors, than continuously reinforced behavior.

A variety of different rules determine when reinforcement is due on intermittent schedules. The *fixed-ratio* schedule allows the subject to be reinforced only after he has emitted a number of responses. If the subject was reinforced only for every tenth response, he would be on a fixed-ratio schedule identified as an FR 10. There is also a *variable-ratio schedule.* The same procedure is used, but reinforcement is contingent upon a mean (average) number of responses. On this schedule, the number of responses emitted to obtain reinforcement may vary widely from one reinforcement to the next. For example, if the mean number of responses per reinforcement is twenty (a VR 20 schedule), the number of responses needed to obtain a reinforcement might randomly vary from five to thirty responses. The mean and the range of the required responses are programmed prior to the experiment.

Fixed-ratio and variable-ratio schedules tend to produce different patterns of behavior.[2] Subjects tend to respond in bursts on fixed-ratio schedules. Responses are usually rapid just prior to reinforcement and slow immediately following reinforcement. If a person does not respond well on a fixed-ratio schedule, he may not get reinforced for long periods of time. He may then respond even less frequently, and finally, the schedule may become completely ineffective in maintaining his behavior. Generally, a person responds either quite well or quite poorly on fixed-ratio schedules. Slot machines, horse races, and dice cages usually pay off on a variable-ratio schedule that seems very effective in maintaining steady rates of response in subjects for a long period of time.

Although the discussion of intermittent reinforcement has thus far centered around fixed-ratio and variable-ratio schedules, intermittent reinforcement can also be based upon the amount of time that has elapsed since a prior event such as previous reinforcement. This is known as an *interval schedule.* Ferster (1963, p. 243) has provided some helpful examples of the difference between ratio and interval schedules:

[2]In 1957, Ferster & Skinner published a noteworthy book, *Schedules of Reinforcement*, that details many types of schedules and their effects.

Climbing stairs is reinforced on a fixed-ratio schedule. A fixed amount of behavior is required to get to the top, similarly, with digging a hole, turning a piece of metal in a lathe, writing a letter, shaving, telling a story, or persuading someone. In each of these cases, the final consequence maintaining the behavior does not become more probable with passage of time but only with the emission of the necessary amount of behavior. Interval schedules occur somewhat less frequently in human affairs, but nonetheless are of great theoretical importance. Under interval schedules of reinforcement, a response (the first response after the interval elapses) produces a reinforcement periodically. Here, the number of responses per reinforcement is not specified, and only passage of time makes possible the reinforcement. Looking into a pot of water is reinforced on a fixed-interval schedule by seeing it boil; looking down the street while watching for the bus is reinforced on an interval schedule by the sight of the bus; dialing a telephone number after a busy signal is reinforced on an interval schedule by the telephone being answered. The appearance of the bus is not hastened by the number of times one looks down the street, and it is proverbial that watching the pot does not make it boil. Nevertheless, the relevant response is reinforced after sufficient time has elapsed.

On a *fixed-interval schedule*, a response is reinforced only after a preset interval of time has elapsed since the last reinforcement (or other specified event). For example, the first response following a forty-second interval since the preceding reinforcement would be reinforced on a fixed-interval schedule (FI 40). On a *variable-interval schedule*, a mean interval is used to determine when reinforcement is due instead of a fixed interval between reinforcements. For example, in a variable-interval schedule of three minutes (VI 3), reinforcement might randomly occur following intervals ranging from five seconds to ten minutes, but the mean interval would be three minutes.

The different effects of fixed-interval and variable-interval schedules may be illustrated by assuming that a musical program on the radio is arranged so that the top two or three hit songs are played only at the end of the program each day (a fixed-interval schedule). The listener will tend to tune in only toward the end of the program (fixed-interval). On the other hand, if the top songs are scattered throughout the program (a variable-interval schedule), the listener is likely to tune in to more of the program. On a fixed-interval schedule, the frequency of responses tends to increase near the time of reinforcement (Holland, 1958). On a variable-interval schedule, the response frequency is relatively constant over time (Sidman, 1960).

On some of these schedules, the responses of normal adults have become predictable and stable enough so that operant-response patterns can be used as a measure of mental disturbance. Using nickles as reinforcers, normal adults tend to pull a lever evenly at moderately high rates, 800 or more responses per hour, on a one-minute variable-interval schedule. When chronic, psychotic patients are placed on a similar schedule, only approximately 20 percent respond at the normal rate. There are usually long pauses during which they display their psychotic symptoms. As their psychotic symptoms decrease on the hospital ward, their response rates tend to become higher and more stable. This can provide an objective measure of their improvement (Lindsley, 1960).

It is possible to combine ratio and interval schedules so that reinforcement is determined by both the number of responses emitted and the interval of time since the last reinforced response. These schedules are known as *combined schedules*. A subject can be reinforced only when his rate of responding is high (or low) within a specified period of time, e.g., twenty responses per minute. Because these schedules can be efficient in producing a high number of responses with a low number of reinforcements, Skinner (1953, pp. 105–106) has suggested that

> Gambling devices could be 'improved'—from the point of view of the proprietor—by introducing devices which would pay off on a variable-interval basis, but only when the rate of play is exceptionally high. The device would need to be more complex than the slot machine or roulette wheel, but would undoubtedly be more effective in inducing play. Schedules of pay in industry, salesmanship, and the professions, and the use of bonuses, incentive wages, and so on, could also be improved from the point of view of generating maximal productivity.

POSITIVE REINFORCEMENT, NEGATIVE REINFORCEMENT, AND PUNISHMENT

There are two major types of reinforcing events: (1) the introduction of stimuli, e.g., the presentation of food, water, or sexual contact; (2) the removal of stimuli, e.g., the elimination of electric shock, loud noise, or extreme heat. The first type of event involves *positive reinforcement* whereas the second type of event involves *negative reinforcement*. Reinforcement, whether positive or negative, increases the probability of a specified response. If the introduction or removal of stimuli reduces the probability of a specific response, then a process other than reinforcement is operative such as punishment, extinction, or interference.[3]

Negative reinforcement by the removal of an aversive stimulus is

---

[3]There seems to be some consensus that punishment implies at least some contingency between a response and a noxious stimulus. Punishment can be avoided by responding in a specific manner (active avoidance) or by not responding (passive avoidance). The term *negative reinforcement* usually refers to the termination of a noxious stimulus as used in escape or avoidance experiments (Campbell & Church, 1969, p. 518).

likely to have more immediate effects than positive reinforcement. *Punishment*, the presentation of an aversive stimulus or the removal of a positively reinforcing stimulus, is also likely to have more immediate effects on behavior than positive reinforcement.

Punishment is usually effective in suppressing behavior for at least a brief time. If, however, a schedule of reinforcement continues to support the previously punished behavior, that behavior may reoccur at rates near the former frequency. Thus, although delinquents may be severely punished for stealing cars by being put in prison, the excitement and adventure of stealing is not diminished when they return to the community. The likelihood of stealing cars again is high.

Suppression of a response by punishment appears to be more effective when the punishment is of a fixed duration than when the subject can escape from it. Suppression may also be more effective when there is an alternative, unpunished response which the subject can use to obtain the same reinforcement he was obtaining by the punished behavior (cf. Fowler, 1971). For example, stealing cars can probably be more effectively suppressed by punishment if the delinquent is allowed to borrow a car from a friend or rent one than if his only source of a car is a stolen one.

A special effect may occur if a neutral stimulus is presented just before a person receives intense, aversive punishment. Suppression by punishment under this condition may be very prolonged. For example, if a dog barks at and then bites a woman as she walks home from the store, she may take a different, longer route home from the store the next time, particularly if she hears a dog barking. Having gotten home safely using the different route, she is negatively reinforced by avoiding the dog that would have bitten her (so she thinks) and is positively reinforced by getting home. Thus, she continues to use the longer route even though the dog that bit her is not present and the barking is by a very friendly dog securely tied in a yard. This combination of initial punishment, the negative reinforcement of avoidance responses, and the positive reinforcement of an alternative behavior maintains the alternative behavior that may look quite unreasonable to an observer. If the woman was gradually exposed or systematically desensitized to the dog, walking the original, shorter route could then be positively reinforced and the old pattern of behavior could be reestablished.

Punishment appears to be most effective if the noxious or aversive stimulus is applied early in a chain of behaviors rather than after the final behavior. Swatting a dog with a newspaper just before he takes his first mouthful of food is more effective, (i.e., suppression is more enduring) than if the dog is swatted after he has eaten several mouthfuls of food or has finished it. If punishment for a behavior occurs repeatedly in one particular situation, the suppression of that behavior may become limited to that situation and not others. Driving above the speed limit may be effectively suppressed in the presence of a patrol car, but not in its absence.

Behavior can also sometimes be suppressed by the reinforcement of *competing responses*. The driver who reduces his speeding in the presence of a patrol car may also reduce his speed if he drives through a wooded area in which a sign has been posted saying "Nudist Colony." In this case there is interference between two schedules of positive reinforcement. When the reinforcement of the competing response is discontinued, however, the original response may reoccur, e.g., the driver speeds up after he leaves the wooded area. This "recovery" of the original response might be prevented if the competing response is reinforced for a long period of time or if the reinforcement of the competing response is slowly discontinued (Leitenberg, Rawson, & Bath, 1970).

The competition between two responses sometimes occurs very inadvertently. For example, a student in a course on behavior change decided to use operant conditioning to improve his studying, especially his reading of textbooks. To do this, he placed reinforcers back of every few pages in his textbook. One of these reinforcers was a note written to himself which said, "Mother says good, good." Another reinforcer was a picture of his girl friend. The student began reading and soon reached the note in which his mother congratulated him. His attention wandered momentarily as he thought about home, but he continued reading. In a few minutes he came to the picture of his girl friend. He thought about her, their last date, meeting her parents, the dinner together at the dorm, and their discussion about his roommate. He wondered if he really knew her very well, if he could predict her reaction if he would call her late at night just to say "hi." When he called her, she was glad to hear from him. The rest of the book went unread. The hoped-for schedule of reinforcement actually reduced the amount of reading he ordinarily would have done because it initiated competing patterns of behavior.

Use of Combined Techniques: Elimination of "Brat" Behaviors

Frequently the techniques of positive or negative reinforcement and punishment or extinction can be effectively combined. Bernal (1969) has provided an illustration in the treatment of "brat" behaviors.[4] Dennis, a

[4]We all know what a "brat" is when we meet one. But for those who prefer additional linguistic security, "a brat will be defined as a child who often engages in tantrums, assaultiveness, threats, etc., which are highly aversive and serve to render others helpless in controlling him" (Bernal, Duryee, Pruett, & Burns, 1968, p. 447).

five-year-old, was verbally and physically abusive toward both his younger brother and his mother. When there was abusive behavior, the mother was instructed to: "(a) Specify the desirable behavior, show anger, tell him you are angry with him, then ignore him; (b) Give him time to shape up. If he doesn't, repeat your command, express anger, and punish him by spanking; (c) Do not attend again until he does as you have asked. Repeat step b if necessary. (d) Once you specify a desirable behavior, if he doesn't do as requested, *always* follow with the spanking, i.e., be consistent" (pp. 381–382).

Emphasis was also placed upon the use of positive reinforcers such as smiling, praise, and physical affection to establish and maintain acceptable behavior. The mother, as well as researchers in the home, observed the parent-child interactions before, during, and after treatment. To assist in formulating the treatment plan and in training Dennis' mother, videotapes were made of Dennis and his mother in interaction. These videotapes were then played to his mother to help illustrate behavior-change techniques. The following graph, Figure 4-1, illustrates the marked reduction of brat behavior over a period of twenty-five weeks.

General abuse in the graph refers to behavior such as refusal to obey instructions, whining, threats, and profanity. Physical abuse refers to behaviors such as hitting, biting, throwing things, and tantrums. The improvement in Dennis' behavior was also reported by the boy's teachers at school. Unfortunately, his younger brother showed some increase in unacceptable behavior during this period but this declined in subsequent months and Dennis' behavior remained improved.

The success of such a procedure depends upon the cooperation and ability of the parents to maintain several schedules of extinction, reinforcement, and punishment simultaneously. This ability is gradually shaped in the parents by detailed instruction, comment, and praise by the therapist. Seven different categories of instruction, called interventions, were used by the therapist. These emphasized punishment, extinction, or reinforcement procedures, depending upon the progress of the case (see Figure 4-1). A subsequent report by Bernal, Young, and Shannon (1970) points out the need to shape accurate and reliable behavior in the mother if treatment is going to be successful.

In a study by Wetzel (1966), the compulsive stealing of a ten-year-old boy was successfully eliminated by removing a positive reinforcer whenever the boy stole. The reinforcer in this case was rather unusual—it was a person, a Mexican-American cook at the home where the boy lived. The boy looked forward to visiting the kitchen and home of the kind woman, but on those days when he stole, these visits

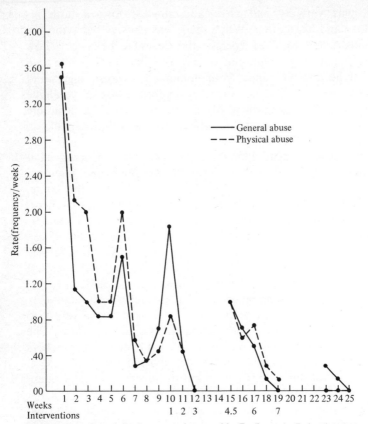

Figure 4-1 Dennis' abuse at home. M. E. Bernal. Behavioral feedback in the modification of brat behaviors. *Journal of Nervous and Mental Disease,* 1969, **148**, 375–385.

would be eliminated. As the boy stole less, his relationships with his peers improved and a more normal social adjustment became possible.

PERCEPTION OF THE REINFORCING EVENT

To talk about a response to a stimulus is deceptively simple. If a stimulus-response situation exists, it is clear that there must be an observer present to do the responding. Although it is desirable to define stimulus and response in terms of physics to communicate the information about experiments accurately, it is also necessary to consider some of the less tangible characteristics of the observer.

History of the Observer

Candy is one of the most frequently used reinforcers in operant-conditioning experiments with children. If, however, the child is allergic to candy or has just eaten two sundaes and three candy bars prior to participating in the experiment, candy will not be an effective reinforcer. With pigeons, the problem of satiation is handled more precisely by withholding food from the pigeons until they are at some specified percentage (often about 80 percent) of their usual body weight. This controls the subject's immediate prior history of eating.

An important aspect of the observer's history is his previous operant behavior. If the behavior to be reinforced is not in the subject's repertoire, it will have to be shaped before the subject is exposed to the schedule.

One method of controlling a subject's immediate history is the construction of a carefully monitored, total environment in which the subject lives. This has been done in space flights with an emphasis upon physiological monitoring. In the area of operant conditioning, one of the most thoroughly programmed environments for a single person has been described by Findley (1966). Eating, sleeping, exercise, use of toilet facilities, several kinds of work, reading, listening to music, smoking, and so on were programmed in the sense that an activity was allowed to occur only under specific conditions and once it was started it had to be completed before a new activity could be initiated. Completion of one activity illuminated a button indicating the next activity that could be selected. The selected activity was initiated by the subject's pushing an illuminated button. For example, if the subject was offered the possibility of sleep, he could push the illuminated button. The bunk was then automatically unlocked from the wall, the room temperature dropped, the lights were extinguished, and an outlet for a heating blanket was activated. The living arrangements allowed no radio, television, or visitors. The living chamber consisted of a main room eleven by eleven feet, an adjoining toilet room five by five feet, and a workroom five by five feet. Contact with outside persons could only be made verbally through an intercom.

A healthy, thirty-four-year-old male subject volunteered to spend three days in the chamber, and then later, after having become familiar with the situation, agreed to spend an indefinite period of time in the chamber until he wished to leave. A button was available by which the subject could indicate his desire to lengthen or shorten the duration of the experiment. He was also free to terminate the experiment at any time he wished. Throughout the 152 days of the experiment, the response frequencies of the various behaviors were automatically recorded. The situation was tolerable; but after approximately ninety days, the subject began to show behavioral strain or stress. This was indicated in part by the deterioration of his performance on specific tasks and a general "milling about," although he remained healthy throughout the experiment. Many behaviors for which there were no programmed consequences rapidly declined in frequency.

> On day 121 of the experiment the subject was informed that the experimenters were instigating a "vacation" during which the subject would be allowed full use of the bypass switches on the control panel. These switches made it possible for the subject to follow any one activity in the program by itself or any other activity. Once selecting an activity, however, the requirements had to be completed before selecting another. In this way the program was made maximally flexible and the subject was allowed ready access to the more rewarding activities without completing the less desired ones. During this "vacation" which lasted only 24 hours, the subject spent all of his time at first in the final part of the program consuming food, smoking, listening to music, and earning delayed reinforcements . . . . Although the "vacation" resulted in increasing activity and a general state of euphoria in the subject, very few effects could be detected lasting more than one or two days (Findley, 1966, pp. 839–840).

The overall environment was probably not highly aversive, but the building up of stress and decreased performance probably resulted from programming inadequacies and social isolation. Subsequent environments could provide for programmed interaction with other people.

Some schedules are effective only when there has been a history of prior conditioning. If an experimenter wants a pigeon to respond on a fixed-ratio schedule of one hundred, he cannot merely put the pigeon in a box with the reinforcement apparatus and set it to reinforce every one-hundredth response. Instead, the ratio of responses to reinforcements must be gradually increased from perhaps one reinforcement for every two responses, to one reinforcement for every five responses, to one for every ten responses, and so on up to one for one hundred responses. Once this learning is in the animal's history, he will respond to ratio schedules without this training procedure. Some schedules are more sensitive to this specific history than others. Interval schedules, for example, will tend to maintain a behavior in the animal's repertoire without this special training.

When schedules are used in natural social settings, the determination of those aspects of history that may be relevant is tremendously more complex. Stimuli may be variously perceived and responded to depending upon the interpersonal, social, and material contexts of the stimuli. A woman may like the smell of both French perfume and strong-smelling cheese, but only in the appropriate context. If we gave her perfume that smelled like cheese and cheese that smelled like perfume, she would probably be quite disgusted. Several schemes have been developed for observing and coding stimuli in natural settings (cf. review by Sells, 1963), but much research needs to be done to make these schemes broadly useful. At present, most research focuses upon the most salient stimulus in the total situation as perceived by the experimenter.

Adaptation Level of the Subject

An important and often overlooked aspect of the history of the subject is his immediately prior experience with the reinforcing stimuli. In an early study by Bevan and Adamson (1960), three groups of subjects were given high, medium, and low intensities of shock prior to performing a learning task. This was the adaptation period and determined the subjects' *adaptation levels.* During the learning task, a medium intensity of shock was used for all three groups of subjects as a negative reinforcer, i.e., the subjects could avoid the shock by making proper responses.

Although the intensity of shock was the same for all of the subjects during the learning task, those subjects who received the weak shock during the adaptation period and the medium shock during the learning task did better than those subjects who received medium shock during both the adaptation period and the learning task. As might be expected, the group of subjects who received the strong shock during the adaptation period and the medium shock during the learning task performed the poorest. It appears that the reinforcing potential of a stimulus depends more upon its intensity relative to the subject's previous exposures to it than upon its absolute physical intensity.

In another experiment in which the subjects were to detect a missing tone signal (Bevan & Turner, 1966), subjects received either the display of the word "right" in green for correct responses or the word "wrong" in red for errors. They performed at a 65 percent-correct response level during this task. Then, midway in the experiment, the group initially receiving "right" for correct responses was shifted to "wrong" for errors, and the group initially receiving "wrong" for errors was shifted to "right" for correct responses. The performance of these two groups jumped to a 75 percent correct response level indicating that a mixed reinforcement schedule was superior to a standard, single reinforcement schedule.

The reinforcement potential of a stimulus may also be affected by a preceding class of stimuli quite different from it. Two groups of rats were trained to respond at a stable, operant level to receive reinforcement by intracranial stimulation—a stimulation assumed to be quite pleasant (Pfaffman, 1962). The groups of experimental rats then received an intense electric shock to their feet just prior to operant testing on ten randomly selected days out of a total of twenty days. The control group received no electric shock on the test days. The results show that the experimental group responded at clearly higher rates on those days when they received pretest shock than when they did not receive shock and also responded at generally higher levels throughout the test period than the control group. The results were interpreted as being due to the increased pleasantness of the intracranial stimulation resulting from its contrast with the unpleasant foot shock.

Bevan (1968) has suggested that the adaptation-level model of reinforcement might help to explain phenomena such as adaptation with the repeated presentation of the reinforcer, the relative effectiveness of intermittent as compared to continuous reinforcement, and certain characteristics of extinction curves. "If our current optimism about its value is warranted, this conceptual approach will have accomplished yet one more thing: it will have provided the beginnings of a rapprochement between psychologists, on the one hand, and learning and motivational theory, on the other" (p. 710). Adaptation-level effects might also give us some understanding of the curious but common observation that compliments (reinforcement) from a stranger can be more effective than similar compliments from a person well known and liked.

A suggestion by Bevan (p. 711) is worthy of serious consideration: "What we must learn is to look beyond the literal view of the physical nature of stimuli and responses and their correlation and ask what they represent and reflect of function within a perceptual system." Physical stimuli that are carefully observed and recorded can also be classified and interpreted in terms of the behavior of the perceiving subject.

CONTINGENCY MANAGEMENT

The concept of *contingency management* is derived from operant-conditioning theory. In its most general form, it involves specifying a reinforcing event such as receiving compliments, eating, or playing baseball and then arranging the environment so that the occurrence of this reinforcing event is contingent upon the completion of the behavior one wishes to reinforce. The reinforcing event generally involves a behavior with a higher probability of occurrence, if it is freely permitted, than the behavior to be reinforced. Homme and Tosti (1965, pp. 14–15) offer the following example:

Suppose a student is scribbling, and looking-at-the-blackboard is the response desired. Notice that here is a very clear-cut case of two behaviors: one of high probability (scribbling) and one of low probability (looking-at-the-blackboard). If a plan can be devised to make the scribbling depend upon having looked at the blackboard, then the problem is solved. With most children, a verbal instruction like this will do: "Look at the blackboard while I write a word; then scribble some more."

The rule for this example can be summarized in this way: Notice what behavior is at a high probability at the moment, then instruct S (the student) that he can execute more of it if he will do a small amount of lower probability behavior first.

In contingency management, the term *reinforcing event* is used more often than the term *reinforcing stimulus* because the emphasis tends to be on responses rather than on stimuli. If a rat presses a lever to receive a pellet of food, discussion is likely to focus on the rat's eating of the food (response) rather than on the presentation of the food (stimulus). The concept of a reinforcing event is broad enough to cover both stimulus and response definitions of reinforcers. Sometimes the reinforcement can be best categorized in terms of its stimulus characteristics, for example, verbal praise. On the other hand, a reinforcer such as playing baseball might be more conveniently categorized in terms of its response characteristics. Of course, this does not preclude the precise specification of a reinforcing event as either a stimulus or a response, depending upon the investigator's particular conceptual model.

The Premack Principle

Contingency management relies heavily upon several propositions outlined by David Premack (1959, 1962, 1965). The underlying concept is that reinforcement refers to a relationship, usually between two responses, which specifies the probability of each of the responses rather than presupposing that some reward, benefit, or drive-reducing quality is inherent in the response or the reinforcing stimuli. From this, Premack has formulated several important propositions:

"Any response A will reinforce any other response B, if and only if the independent rate of A is greater than that of B" (Premack, 1959). "For any pair of responses, the more probable one will reinforce the less probable one" (Premack, 1965). "Reinforcement is a relative property. The most probable response of a set of responses will reinforce all members of the set; the least probable will reinforce no member of the set" (Premack, 1965).

The probability of a response is usually, but not always, determined by the rate of occurrence of the response in a "free" situation that allows a choice of several responses. The use of the principles cited above to change behavior was illustrated in an early study by Premack in 1959. During the first phase of the study, thirty-three first grade children were allowed either to play a pinball machine or to eat chocolate bits delivered one at a time on a conveyer belt. Sixty-one percent of the children made more pinball-machine responses than candy-eating responses. These children were called the "manipulators." The remaining children who ate candy more frequently than they played the pinball machine were called "eaters." Eating was considered the more probable response of the eaters and playing the pinball machine was considered the more probable response for the manipulators.

During the second phase of the study, one-half of the manipulator group could play the pinball machine only after they ate some chocolate. The other one-half of the manipulator group served as control subjects. One-half of the eater group could eat only after they played the pinball machine. The other one-half of this group served as control subjects. The control conditions were the same as those during the first phase of the study when the children could freely choose either activity.

When playing the pinball machine (high-probability behavior) was made contingent upon eating (low-probability behavior) for the manipulators, the frequency of eating significantly increased. For the control group the frequency of eating did not significantly increase. When eating (high-probability behavior) was made contingent upon playing the pinball machine (low-probability behavior) for the eaters, the frequency of playing the pinball machine significantly increased. For the control group, the frequency of playing the pinball machine did not significantly increase.

It is possible to view the results of this study as indicating that candy can reinforce the manipulation activity of the eaters, or that manipulation can reinforce the eating activity of the manipulators. This is consistent with the proposition that reinforcement is a relationship. Either eating or manipulation can become reinforcing by making that activity into a high-probability behavior. This might be done by depriving manipulators of food. Some additional evidence for this reversibility of the reinforcement relationship between two responses has been found in animal experiments that have made drinking contingent upon running and running contingent upon drinking (Premack, 1962). Under certain conditions, running can be used to reinforce drinking.

Whether Premack's very useful propositions will hold under all conditions is open to further study. If aversive stimulation such as electric shock is used to increase the probability of one of the responses, particular caution may be needed in generalizing from the results.[5] Most of the studies reported by Premack and those found in the contingency-management literature involve responses associated with neutral or nonaversive stimuli.

In order to use contingency-management principles, it is necessary to determine rather accurately the probabilities of the behaviors under consideration. High-probability behaviors can be identified as those behaviors in which the subject wants to engage at the time behavior-change procedures are conducted. Telling a student that he can do some spelling if he does some arithmetic is not likely to increase the amount of arithmetic he does. However, if the student is told that he may take a break following a few minutes of arithmetic, the amount of arithmetic completed is likely to be increased. One of the most frequent mistakes made by persons initially using contingency-management procedures is to require too much low-probability behavior before the high-probability behavior is permitted. As in shaping behavior, the principle of small steps and very gradually increased levels of performance should be followed (Homme, Csanyi, Gonzales, & Rechs, 1969).

In an early study of contingency management (Homme, de Baca, Devine, Steinhorst, & Rickert, 1963), it was observed that if four-year-old nursery school children were left without supervision they would seldom sit quietly in front of the blackboard. Instead, high-probability behavior in this circumstance was running around the room and yelling. A situation was then constructed in which running and yelling were made contingent upon sitting quietly. The children were instructed to sit quietly for a brief period of time; then they were told they could "run and scream" until a bell rang. After two days, sitting quietly was very readily obtained without the use of demands or threats. During a later stage of the experiment, the children were given tokens for engaging in socially desirable behaviors of low probability. These tokens were then used to "buy" the opportunity to engage in high-probability behaviors.

Following the work of Homme et al. (1963), Wasik (1968) has used contingency management with culturally deprived children in a second-grade classroom. The objective was to increase behaviors such as following directions, working independently, and sharing and helping

---

[5]Premack (1965) has, however, suggested that the probability relationship will hold for both positive and negative reinforcers. For example, in order to establish running in a continually rotating wheel (a high-probability behavior), a rat will lick a tube a specified number of times (low-probability behavior) to stop the motor from turning the wheel. Miller (1966) has raised the question, however, whether this running could be used to turn on the switch that starts the wheel. The problem here may be in the different definitions of the onset and offset of the high- and low-probability behaviors in the test situation.

others. Inappropriate behaviors to be reduced included pushing, hitting resisting instructions, and noise making to get attention. Two days befor contingency conditions were introduced, the nineteen children in th study were carefully observed to establish a base line of responses fo each child and for the class as a whole. During the first contingency perio lasting fifty days, the children were allowed to play with toys they ha previously selected only if they behaved appropriately. Thirty-six ob servations were made on each child on the 12th, 13th, 41st, and 42nd days

In the first contingency period, desirable behaviors increased on th average (mean) 20 percent above those of the base-line period. But whe the contingency conditions were removed and the toys were taken out o the room for one week, desirable behaviors markedly decreased, some o them below that of the base-line period. Finally, the contingency condi tions and toys were reintroduced. During this second contingency perioc the desirable behaviors increased, on the average, to rates as high as o slightly higher than during the first contingency period. Inappropriat behaviors decreased during those periods of contingency management a desirable behaviors increased.

After a high-probability behavior such as playing, eating, or swim ming has occurred, it may no longer have high probability because o satiation or adaptation-level effects until some time has passed. Also, th relative likelihood of generally high-probability behaviors may chang from hour to hour or day to day. Addison and Homme (1966) hav proposed a worthwhile solution. Following the completion of a specifie amount of the low-probability behavior, the person may select a reinforc ing event from a previously prepared list of generally high-probabilit behaviors. This list, called a "Reinforcing Event Menu," has severɑ advantages. An experimenter can develop a list of ten or twenty reinforc ing events uniquely suited to each subject. This list may help to remin the subject of things he would like to do and may, therefore, serve as prompting device for subjects not well motivated. In addition, differen amounts of low-probability behavior may be specified for the variou items on the list. Relatively large amounts of low-probability behavior ca be required for very special and difficult-to-provide reinforcing events.

A wide variety of stimuli and responses have been used as reinforc ing events for changing behavior. Some reinforcers reported have bee obvious ones such as food, money, or social approval. Others such as sal (Marshall, 1966), rides in a fancy car (Schwitzgebel, 1964), imagine situations (Cautela, 1970a), music (Barrett, 1962; Findley, 1966), tactil vibration (Schwitzgebel, 1968), running water (Sapon, 1967), sexuɑ intercourse (Stuart, 1969), religious services (Ayllon & Azrin, 1968), an pictures s of nudes and feeding a kitten (Lindsley, 1956) have not been s obvious. A list of available reinforcers developed jointly by the exper menter and the subject can permit the use of very individualized reinforcers while still applying contingency-management principles.

TOKEN ECONOMIES

It is clear that some reinforcing events, such as riding in a fancy car, cannot be offered to a person every few minutes without severely disrupting the behavior to be reinforced. This problem is solved by setting up a program of secondary reinforcers that eventually leads to the presentation of the primary reinforcer. This is often done by establishing a *token economy* in which "tokens" (poker chips, pieces of paper, coins, marks on a card, marbles) are dispensed according to a schedule of reinforcement. These tokens can then be exchanged at a later time for a different reinforcer. Merchandise stamps, coins given at gas stations, chances earned in mail-order contests, and poker games are some common token economies.

In an early study of token economics in 1959, Staats (1969) reinforced reading responses in young children by giving them plastic disks which they could later exchange for toys or other items.[6] Since that time, token economics have been frequently established and studied (Krasner & Atthowe, 1970). A noteworthy example of a token economy was set up at the National Training School for Boys, Washington, D.C. (Cohen, Goldiamond, Filipczak, & Pooley, 1968). This project was directed toward increasing the educational and social abilities of the delinquent inmates at the reform school.

The student-inmates earned points for activities such as completing programs on teaching machines, taking tests, assisting with clerical work, and working in the kitchen. To help control all sources of reinforcement, a special twenty-four-hour-a-day living environment was designed.

> Rather than designing a special cottage for the project, an effort was made to convert existing facilities, at minimal cost. Sleeping quarters were established in the ground floor of the building. This constituted a series of individual rooms, which insured a modicum of privacy for each student. These rooms were rented weekly by the students. If they wished, they had the option of not paying rent and sleeping in the open in double bunk beds, as is prevalent in the rest of the institution. There was an option of free open showers or private showers available on a rental basis. A special lounge containing pool tables, pinball machines, TV, and other leisure activities was available on the first floor. An admission fee was charged for use of the lounge, as well as activity fees for the use of equipment. A dining room was

---

[6]Wolfe in 1936 and Cowles in 1937 used tokens to modify the behavior of chimpanzees but it was long time after this until token economies were widely established to change human behavior therapeutically.

also located on this floor, and all meals were served here. Initially, the student could choose between Class A food (which included a variety of choices) or Class B food (fewer choices), for either of which he had to pay. He also had the option of having served to him the regular institutional food which was free. A small store on this floor sold magazines, candy, holiday greeting cards, soft drinks, and other consumable items, such as clothing, were made available through mail order catalogues (Cohne, et al., 1968, p. F1-3).

In addition to the purchase of activities and services indicated above, the students could purchase items such as radios, cameras, clothing, and cigarettes. They could also purchase more education (which some did) or convert the points to cash. By making these reinforcers contingent upon studying or other specified activities, the educational level of the students rapidly improved. Very often those students who had previously been very reluctant to study chose this activity over others even when extrinsic reward was small or nonexistent. In a sense, it could be said that studying had acquired intrinsic value and, in popular language, had become its "own reward."

Social behavior also greatly improved. This was achieved by allowing much freedom of activity which, even if initially excessive, came under control of the long-term contingencies of the environment. For example:

> The normal prison system devised for students this age severely penalizes possession of pictures of female nudes to the extent of exorcizing photographs of barebreasted native women in publications such as *National Geographic*. As Washington newspapers commented, this restriction occurs despite the fact that some of the students are fathers many times over. In CASE II, *Playboy* was available in the store, along with other magazines generally available on newstands. Again, in this respect the project was closer to the normal environment than is the artificial prison system. Many of the students cut out pictures from *Playboy* to use as pinups on their walls. These pinups often occurred side by side with reproductions of works by the great masters, as well as religious icons, pictures of home and family, pictures of cars, and abstract symbols. Whereas, in the initial flurry of the freedom, quite a few *Playboys* were purchased, their purchase plummeted to almost nothing; presumably, there was only so much space on the wall (Cohen, *et al.*, 1968, p. F1-7).

By being given a wide range of choices within this enriched, contingency-managed environment, the students came to look and act more like students in a typical high school than prisoners at a reform school. To help bridge the gap between institutional and community life, some researchers have allowed delinquents to purchase trips outside of the reform school (e.g., Burchard & Tyler, 1965).

Graubard (1968) arranged a contingency situation for institutionalized delinquents in which a contract was made with each delinquent for the amount of behavior that he would perform for a particular reinforcer. The reinforcers included money, listening to records, playing games, and dancing. In addition, a contract was made with the entire group which promised a prize of money to all members of the group if each member fulfilled his part of the contract. Conversely, each member had to fulfill his part of the contract before any member could get reinforced for his individual performance. This contract effectively used the group as a reinforcing agent to modify individual behavior.

Within the community, contingency management using money, food, dancing, weekend dates, outings with parents, parties, and car insurance payments has successfully changed delinquent behavior (Jeffrey, 1965; Thorne, Tharp, & Wetzel, 1967, Vannette & Heymen, 1967). Generally, these contracts are honored, but when a delinquent fails to complete his portion of a contract, this is considered not so much the fault of the delinquent as it is of the director who permitted the delinquent to offer to do more than he reasonably could. The failure is a result of the inadequacy of the program, not the delinquent. These efforts at contingency management in the community are encouraging because they indicate a willingness to apply methods successfully demonstrated in the laboratory to problems in the broader context of daily life.

One of the more imaginative and well-constructed studies of the use of token economics in natural settings is that designed by Stewart (1969) for the treatment of marital discord. Stewart's operant-interpersonal treatment method is derived from two basic premises. (1) The impressions which each spouse forms of the other is based on the behavior of the other. Thus, when one changes his behavior, there are corresponding changes in the impression the other has of him. (2) In order to change the patterns of social interaction in the marriage, each spouse must take the initiative in changing his own behavior before expecting changes in his spouse.

Each spouse is asked by the therapist to list three behaviors which he would like to see increase in frequency in the other. (Reduction of negative behaviors is avoided because so much of the couple's prior behavior has been unsuccessfully directed toward reducing or eliminating unwanted behaviors.) A behavior checklist is then used by each spouse to record the frequency of these three behaviors by the other. Finally, these desired behaviors are reinforced either by a mutual exchange of desired behaviors or through the use of a token-economy system.

In marriages which have not dissolved reciprocity into coercion or withdrawal, a simple exchange of behaviors is effective. Couples are asked to accelerate desired behaviors on an equal basis. For example, one husband complained that his wife failed to greet him at the door, that she did not straighten the family room in anticipation for his return home from work, and that meals were rarely ready on time. His wife complained that he failed to spend sufficient time with the children (it was agreed that 30 minutes before bed was sufficient), failed to take her out for an occasional movie, and failed to pay attention to meals when they were well prepared. Accordingly, each of these behaviors was restated as a positive (e.g., greet husband at door) and was listed on the Behavior Monitoring Form. Each person recorded the frequency with which the other completed the desired behavior. When these behaviors were accelerated at a sufficient rate, other goals were added (Stewart, 1969, p. 678).

If the marriage does not involve sufficient reciprocity, tokens may be used. In four cases, the wife desired that her husband not "close me out of his life when he is at home." A system was set up in which the husband would receive one token if during an hour their conversation reached a suitable level. His wife determined the suitable level which was negotiable with her husband and which varied from intense conversations to her feeling free to interrupt him with a question.

Husbands typically wanted to exchange the tokens they earned for various degrees of physical affection. Under a schedule in which husbands were charged three tokens for kissing and light petting, five tokens for heavy petting, and fifteen tokens for intercourse, the rates of conversation and sexual activity rapidly increased and were maintained through a forty-eight-week follow-up period. The couples also reported much greater satisfaction with their marriages.

Although the use of a token system may appear somewhat foolish or trivial, it has several important advantages over the use of primary reinforcers. Ayllon and Azrin (1968, p. 77) have summarized well some of these advantages:

Tokens have several valuable features as conditioned reinforcers: (1) The number of tokens can bear a simple quantitative relation to the amount of reinforcement; (2) the tokens are portable and can be in the subject's possession even when he is in a situation far removed from that in which the tokens were earned; (3) no maximum exists in the number of tokens a subject may possess, whereas dimensions such as intensity, as with volume of music, have practical maximum reinforcing value; (4) tokens can be used directly to operate devices for the automatic delivery of reinforcers; (5) tokens are durable and can be continuously present during the delay, in contrast, say, with a brief flash of light or sound; (6) the physical characteristics of the tokens can be easily standardized; (7) the tokens can be made fairly indestructible so they will not deteriorate during the delay; (8) the tokens can be made unique and nonduplicable so that the experimenter can be assured that they are received only in the authorized manner.

In addition, tokens permit the selection of a variety of primary reinforcers by the subjects, thus avoiding satiation or adaptation effects.

On the other hand, tokens do present some problems such as hoarding, stealing, and misuse in gambling. Also, very little attention has been given in most economies to the reinforcement schedules on which the tokens are dispensed. The most common procedure involves stretching the ratio from fairly frequent or continuous reinforcement to less frequent reinforcement, but consideration should also be given to interval and combined schedules. Laboratory studies have shown that schedules are often more important in maintaining behavior than is the nature of the reinforcer.

GENERALIZATION OF BEHAVIOR CHANGE

Although new patterns of behavior can be maintained by positive reinforcement in the laboratory or clinic, a reasonable and socially important question would be "Will these new patterns of behavior last when the patient enters the community?" The disappointing answer to this question is that behavior change is likely to be temporary unless new social arrangements can be made. *Response generalization*, the transfer of a set of responses from one environment to another, depends at least in part upon the actual or perceived similarity of the environments.[7] The contingencies of reinforcement in laboratories and clinics are likely to be considerably different from those found in community environments.[8]

Even when natural environments appear to be fairly similar, generalization may not occur. This was illustrated in an informal study of tie-wearing behavior conducted by the authors. Until recently, boys in private Eastern preparatory schools and in Harvard College were required to wear ties to dinner in the dining halls. The purpose of this was apparently to encourage them to become gentlemen as they grew up and to wear ties on appropriate occasions.

One hundred graduate students at the Harvard Law School and at the Harvard Business School were randomly selected for study as they

---

[7]Generalization is also sometimes used to refer to the broadened inclusion of stimuli or responses within a class of stimuli or responses, or to the durability of a response over time within the same environment.

[8]A helpful, intermediate step may be the use of specially programmed half-way houses in the community (Henderson, 1971).

entered the dining halls for dinner. (Wearing a tie is not required.) These students were briefly asked about their past experiences with tie-wearing requirements. It was found that those students who were required to wear ties to dinner in the past did not now wear ties to dinner more often than those students not required to wear ties in the past. In fact, there was a negative relationship—those students who had been required to wear ties in the past now wore them less often than those students who had not been required to wear ties.

Although the question of whether graduate students wear ties to dinner can hardly be considered a matter of great social significance, it does point to the need to examine carefully the generalization of behavioral responses. Generalization cannot be assumed.

Traditionally, it has been the view that the generalization of a response will depend upon the availability of reinforcers for that response in the new environment. If the reinforcers, such as food or money, are withheld or are not available, then the response rate will decline. The decline in this response rate will follow an extinction curve determined by the prior schedule of reinforcement. As mentioned earlier, extinction will usually occur more rapidly following a schedule of continuous reinforcement than a schedule of intermittent reinforcement. Also, extinction will tend to be more rapid following variable-ratio schedules with small mean ratios of reinforcement than variable-ratio schedules with large means. Sometimes animals put on extinction schedules will initially show a rapid burst of responses and then irrelevant, "emotional" behavior such as biting or striking the apparatus before the response rate declines. Similarly, when some patients are moved to a new environment without available reinforcers, their behaviors may briefly become even more troublesome than they were before treatment.

There is another way of viewing response generalization that utilizes the Premack principle rather than extinction theory. After the experimental contingency period, the subject can be placed in a situation in which both the reinforcing event (the previous, high-probability behavior) and the instrumental response (the previous, low-probability behavior) are freely available with no contingency relationship. Schaeffer (1962) has reasoned that if there are any residual effects of reinforcement, the rate of the less-probable behavior should be higher after the contingency period than before the contingency period.

With rats as subjects, Schaeffer found no systematic difference between the response rates of less-probable behaviors in the precontingency periods and the postcontingency periods. The results suggested that reinforcement effects were limited completely to the contingency condition. This was confirmed in a similar study by Wasik (1968) involving human subjects and bar-pressing responses. The conclusion was that "when the contingency between two responses is removed and reinforcement is freely available, no residual postcontingency effects of reinforcement are obtained" (Wasik, 1968, p. 88).

The practical significance of this finding can be seen in the frequent failure of responses developed in institutional token-economy programs to generalize to other community environments. Staats (1969) reports the case of a young girl whose temper tantrums and inappropriate social behavior were so greatly reduced in a special-contingency environment that she appeared ready to return to school. Contrary to the therapist's advice, however, she was placed in a traditional school situation with the usual patterns of reinforcement. Her former behavior patterns soon emerged. Staats (pp. 22–23) comments:

> Rather than challenging the learning approach, however, this case validates the approach in the strongest way. That is, the child had severe problems in her usual life circumstances. In a period of behavioral treatment, she improved and made normal progress. When she was returned to traditional circumstances, her behavior deteriorated and her progress was disrupted. . . . That is why working with a child for a semester or a year will not be enough. We have to create opportunities for continued application of desirable reinforcement conditions and other learning conditions through-out the child's educational years.

Treatment environments can be considered in a sense as "prosthetic environments" for people with behavioral deficiencies just as prosthetic environments with ramps are used for people in wheelchairs and traffic lights with bells are used for persons with physical deficiencies (Shah, 1968). Transition from these prosthetic environments to standard environments may have to take place slowly in some cases. Also, special techniques and social situations may need to be developed to assist in transferring behavior developed in one environment to a different environment.

Increasing emphasis is being placed upon associating token reinforcement, or other tangible forms of reinforcement, with verbal praise and compliments which are much more common reinforcers in most social environments. Another approach involves teaching the subject or patient how to apply behavior-change principles to his own behavior. This self-directed change may take place individually with a therapist or within a group of people similarly seeking to change their behavior. Finally, transitional roles may be used to support a person as he changes his behavior from that typical of a patient or inmate to that of a community participant. These several approaches to generalizing and maintaining new behaviors in the community are discussed in much further detail in subsequent sections dealing with self-directed behavior change and transitional roles.

SUMMARY

One of the characteristics of all social environments is the scheduling of reinforcers that maintain consistent patterns of behavior. The rules which determine when behaviors will be reinforced are called schedules of reinforcement. If the schedule specifies that a behavior (a response) is never to be reinforced, the schedule is one of extinction. If the response is reinforced every time it is emitted, the schedule is one of continuous reinforcement. If the response is occasionally reinforced, the schedule is one of intermittent reinforcement. Most human behaviors are intermittently reinforced.

There are many possible types of schedules of intermittent reinforcement. A fixed-ratio schedule reinforces the subject only after he has emitted a specific number of responses. A variable-ratio schedule reinforces the subject after he has emitted a mean (average) number of responses. The number of responses required for reinforcement on this variable-ratio schedule may vary widely from one reinforcement to the next. Reinforcement can also be based upon the amount of time that has elapsed since a prior event such as previous reinforcement. On a fixed-interval schedule, a response is reinforced only after a pre-set interval of time has elapsed since the last reinforcement (or other specified event). On a variable-interval schedule, a mean interval is used to determine when reinforcement is due.

It is possible to combine ratio and interval schedules so that reinforcement is determined by both the number of responses emitted and the amount of time elapsed. These schedules are called combined schedules. It is important to determine the type of schedule that reinforces a behavior because different schedules can produce markedly different frequencies and patterns of behavior.

Closely related to the concept of reinforcing stimuli is the concept of reinforcing responses. The Premack principle suggests that for any pair of responses, the more-probable response will reinforce the less-probable response. The probability of a response can be determined by observing what responses the subject prefers in a free choice situation, e.g., reading a book or eating chocolate candy. In contingency-management programs, highly probable responses, e.g., eating chocolate candy, are made contingent on performing a lower-probability response, e.g., reading a book.

Contingency management has been used to modify a wide range of behaviors in mental patients, delinquents, and marriage partners.

When defining reinforcing stimuli or events, it is important to consider the subject's prior history in regard to the reinforcer and his perception of it. Some schedules of reinforcement are effective only when there has been a history of prior conditioning on a similar or related conditioning schedule. Alternatively, over a period of time, subjects may adapt to reinforcers in such a way as to make them less effective. An integration of schedules of reinforcement and perceptual theory may lead to more effective procedures for changing behavior than those procedures traditionally developed exclusively from learning theories or motivational theories.

Chapter 5

Stimulus Control

Much emphasis in the previous discussion has been placed upon the environmental consequences of a subject's behavior, but it is also clear that the stimuli which precede a behavior may also be highly correlated with the occurrence of that behavior. The sight of food is highly correlated with thinking about food, salivation, and eating. Even reading about food—particularly large, bitter lemons—may produce salivation. A major question is how these important, preceding stimuli shall be most usefully analyzed to facilitate the design of behavior-change techniques. It appears that neither operant (instrumental) conditioning theory nor classical (respondant) conditioning theory can easily account for the full range of effects produced by these stimuli. It may be helpful, nevertheless, to consider briefly the approach and therapeutic implications of both these theories.

DISCRIMINATIVE STIMULI

In operant-learning theory, the concept of a *discriminative stimulus* is of central importance in explaining the high correlations between a behavior and the stimuli that precede it. A discriminative stimulus is a stimulus in the presence of which a response is reinforced and in the absence of which the response goes unreinforced. If, in the presence of a stimulus such as a green light, a response is always reinforced, but in the absence of the green light the response is never reinforced, the probability of the occurrence of the response will become greatly increased by the presence of the green light.[1] If the green light is on, the subject may respond at a high rate; if the green light is off, the subject may respond at a low rate or not at all. If a red light is also used when no reinforcement is given (extinction), then the red light will further reduce the probability of response and would be known as a *time-out* stimulus.[2]

For most people, a green traffic light is a discriminative stimulus and a red traffic light is a time-out stimulus. Under some circumstances, however, even the red light can become a discriminative stimulus (Cohen, 1968). If a pedestrian crosses the street successfully with the red light, he has saved time and has been reinforced. This increases the probability that he will cross the street again using the red light as a discriminative stimulus. Of course, if he is struck by a car or arrested, the probability of crossing again with the red light will be considerably reduced.

In operant-conditioning theory, the discriminative stimulus does not elicit a response but rather "sets the occasion" or indicates that reinforcement is likely to follow the conditioned response (Skinner, 1938; Terrace, 1966). On some occasions, the occurrence of a response may be highly correlated with a stimulus similar to, but not the same as, the original discriminative stimulus. Thus, the original bright light and a moderately bright light might be correlated with a response, but a dim light might not be. The intensity of light, then, would be a stimulus continuum that would determine the probability of the response.

In laboratory experiments, stimulus control through improved discrimination has been facilitated by either of two procedures. The traditional discrimination procedure involves the presentation of two stimuli, one which is correlated with reinforcement ($S+$) and one which is not correlated with reinforcement ($S-$).[3] In some training procedures the $S-$

---

[1]Discriminative stimuli may also be developed on schedules other than continuous reinforcement, but usually not as rapidly (e.g., Morse & Skinner, 1958). Some researchers have suggested that the establishment of a discriminative stimulus also requires the presentation of a second stimulus which is not correlated with the reinforcement, i.e., differential reinforcement (Terrace, 1966).

[2]A discriminative stimulus is often denoted as s^D and a time-out stimulus as s^Δ.

[3]Differential reinforcement may also be used to reinforce certain characteristics of a response, such as its intensity. This process is known as differentiation rather than discrimination.

is followed by an aversive stimulus. Both $S+$ and $S-$ usually remain constant during training. During the training period, the subject initially makes responses in the presence of both $S+$ and $S-$, but eventually responses are made primarily or only in the presence of $S+$.

The second technique, *errorless-discrimination learning*, involves the presentation of two or more very different stimuli, such as easily recognizable tones, that are gradually made more similar so that the differences between them are slowly faded out. During this latter technique, the subject makes very few errors; during the former technique, many errors may be made. If the discrimination is so easy, however, that no errors are made, learning may be slow. Because the error rate is low in errorless-discrimination learning, it has the advantage of producing less negative, emotional behavior than the traditional procedure.

Preliminary findings indicate that errorless-discrimination learning is superior to the traditional procedure both in the fineness of discriminations that can be achieved and in speed of learning (Terrace, 1963, 1966). Although studies with human subjects are few, they have confirmed these results with both retarded children (Sidman & Stoddard, 1967) and normal children (Moore & Goldiamond, 1964). In some cases, the errorless-discrimination procedure has produced fine discrimination before any discrimination was even observed in the traditional discrimination group (Powers, Cheney, & Agostino, 1970).

People as Discriminative Stimuli

A child's ability to determine when behaviors will be reinforced is an important aspect of early-childhood development. Although food is a primary reinforcer for a hungry child, he does not initially recognize the bottle as an antecedent to reinforcement. Later, the child will reach or begin sucking movements when the bottle comes into his sight indicating that he has associated the bottle with subsequent reinforcement. The bottle has become a discriminative stimulus. Because a child's parents are the most likely people to reinforce his behavior, they become discriminative stimuli for a variety of behaviors such as eating, crawling, and talking. If only the parents attend to the child, these behaviors may come under narrow stimulus control by the parents so that when they are absent a marked deterioration of behavior may occur. In short, the child "acts up" when the baby sitter arrives. This may also be seen in the child's verbal behavior which may become greatly reduced when strangers rather than parents talk to the child.

The importance of a person as a discriminative stimulus for the development of speech has been illustrated by the treatment of a schizophrenic adult who had been completely mute for nearly nineteen years (Isaacs, Thomas, & Goldiamond, 1960). The experimenter first shaped verbal behavior by holding a stick of gum before the patient's eyes, waiting until the patient noticed it, then giving it to him. After about six meetings, the subject would look at this gum as soon as it was presented. The experimenter then shaped looking at the gum, moving lips, and making a sound resembling a croak. The next step was shaping vocalizations approximating the word, gum. During the eighteenth session, the patient suddenly said, "Gum, please," and was able to answer simple questions regarding his name and age when asked by the experimenter. He would not, however, answer questions asked by others. To facilitate generalization, a nurse was gradually introduced into the sessions until he was able to talk with other hospital personnel.

It is clear that very fine discriminations can be developed in social situations which involve reinforcers that are important to the observer. Ferster (1963, p. 223) has described how a person speaking to another learns to attend to the listener's eye movements:

> The probability of reinforcement of broad classes of behavior depends very critically on the attention of the listener, and the position of the eyes, in general, determines whether or not or to whom the listener is attending. When we are in a group, a certain method for determining whether we have someone's attention is to ascertain whether his eyes are focused on us. If two potential speakers are close together, the difference in angular displacement of the eyes is of the order of a few degrees. The focus of the eyes determines where the listener's attention is. The contingencies of reinforcement in respect to eye focus are so important that most individuals in the community rapidly come under the control of these fine stimulus changes. The critical operation in the development of this stimulus control is that the behavior of the speaker goes unreinforced in the absence of the attention of the listener, and the attention of the listener is indicated by whether his eyes are focused on the face of the speaker. The exquisite control with which we attend to other aspects of facial expression depends upon the same kind of differential reinforcement for its development and maintenance.

The observer of another person can learn to observe very small movements or gestures that serve as discriminative stimuli for the observer's own reinforcement. For example, the pick-pocket can use subtle movements by the potential victim such as a tenseness in his shoulder or a slight turning of his head as "cues" that the potential victim is about to turn around or reach for his billfold. Sometimes pick-pockets have put up signs warning people to watch out for pick-pockets. Some of the people read the signs and then check to see that their billfolds and valuables are safe. This tells the pick-pocket where the valuables are hidden on the person and thus greatly facilitates his work. The movement, checking one's valuables to see that they are safe, serves as a discriminative stimulus for the pick-pocket because if the pick-pocket makes the correct (but illegal) response of reaching into the victim's pocket, he will often be reinforced by the victim's money. The procedures used by professional pick-pockets are quite complex and usually require the careful coordination of the actions between two or more criminals. Nevertheless, some delinquents will spend much time and effort to learn this skill because, unlike school and other forms of vocational training, there is an immediate pay-off (the victim's money) which reinforces the learning of correct discrimination.

Thus far, people or their behaviors have been referred to as stimuli. To some extent this simplifies too much the complexity of the total stimulus situation and overlooks the theoretically rich discussion of what precisely constitutes a stimulus. Guthrie (1935) and Hull (1943) tended to define a stimulus in terms of its effects on the nervous system. Similarly, Hebb (1958) referred to stimuli as events outside of the central nervous system which excite the neurons. On the other hand, Tolman (1951) emphasized the role of perception and memory. Regardless of theoretical preference, it should be recognized that the term *stimulus* generally refers to a pattern of environmental events. Furthermore, a person as a "stimulus" always appears to the observer within some social or historical context and this may have considerable effect upon the subject's behavior. Adaptation-level effects may also apply to people as stimuli— "absence makes the heart grow fonder" (cf. Gewirtz & Baer, 1958; Eisenberger, 1970).

The qualities that constitute a person as a stimulus object are many. One must consider not only the person's physical characteristics but also his behavior toward the observer, the environmental context of the person and observer, and the past reactions of the observer to the person. By observing and scoring items in these categories, Pascal and Jenkins (1960, 1961) have found the behavior of stimulus persons toward alcoholics and nonalcoholics to be significantly different.

Pascal (1959) has also suggested that some standard behavioral problems related to marital disharmony and school underachievement could be helpfully described in stimulus terms. For example, a young man comes to the clinic for help with his marriage. At home he complains and expresses discontent until his wife can no longer tolerate him and threatens to break up the marriage. His history indicates that his mother highly valued him and was constantly responsive to his wishes. After his marriage, his wife, by taking care of him, acquired some of the stimulus value of his mother and the patient has reverted to behavior appropriate to his mother. But because his wife is not as acquiescent as his mother and does not see herself in this role, their behaviors have become incompatible. Treatment in this situation would involve either changing the wife's behavior so that the patient's expectations attached to his mother will not be attached to his wife or changing the patient's perception of his wife by increasing his discriminative ability.

In bringing behavior under new discriminative-stimulus control, one can either increase the discriminative ability of the subject or change the situation so that a more accurate discrimination of previous stimuli is not required. The simplest example of the latter procedure is that of sending a person on a trip or otherwise changing his daily environment. The success of such a procedure often depends in part upon the extent to which new discriminative stimuli can maintain new behavior when the person returns to the original environment. The gradual return to the old environment and the elimination of discriminative stimuli for old responses may be important factors in maintaining the new behavior.

Stimulus Control of Sexual Activity

Another class of behaviors that may come under extensive stimulus control is that of sexual response. The appearance of the other person, mannerisms, and topics of conversation may serve as discriminative stimuli indicating the possibility of sexual activity. These discriminative stimuli may be "secret symbols" of a subculture. Not long ago, a particular type of pin worn by girls on a Midwest campus could be rotated to point in various directions to indicate the girl's availability for a date. As with all discriminative stimuli, the observer, in this case the boy, had to learn to attend to those aspects of the stimulus situation closely correlated with reinforcement. If not, the boy could spend much time attempting to meet a particularly attractive girl only to discover that she was already going steady as indicated by the position of her pin. Under these conditions of differential reinforcement, the boy may learn to make the necessary discriminations rather rapidly.

In their discussion of the early sexual growth and activity of preadolescent males, Kinsey, Pomeroy, and Martin (1948) describe a wide range of nonsexual stimuli that may become associated with a sexual response. These stimuli may be swimming, tests at school, fires, finding money, and looking over the edge of a building. They then comment (p. 165):

> Originally the pre-adolescent boy erects indiscriminately to the whole array of emotional situations, whether they be sexual or non-sexual in nature. By his late teens the male has been so conditioned that he rarely responds to

anything except direct physical stimulation of genitalia, or to psychic situations that are specifically sexual. In the still older male even physical stimulation is rarely effective unless accompanied by such a psychologic atmosphere. The picture is that of the psychosexual emerging from a much more generalized and basic physiologic capacity which becomes sexual, as the adult knows it, through experience and conditioning.

The details of this conditioning procedure are not discussed, but we may surmise that the sexual arousal that occurs in a social situation that does not permit further sexual activity, as while taking a test, is not as satisfying as sexual arousal that occurs in a situation that does permit sexual activity. Stimuli such as shapely female legs at a dance are, therefore, much more likely to become discriminative stimuli for arousal in older males than taking a test. On the other hand, if taking a test were required prior to sexual activity (as in computer-programmed dating?), taking a test might become a discriminative stimulus for older males. Whether the stimulus is a test or a leg, the basic process of differential reinforcement in the development of stimulus control is the same.

In a somewhat similar manner, one may consider the problem of fetishes as a problem of stimulus control. (Of course, what is considered a fetish and what is considered normal are largely matters of social custom.) An example of a stimulus that may approach the level of a fetish is a pair of high-heeled shoes on a scantily clothed girl. The reason the girl may appear more sexually attractive to some men with these shoes than without them is perhaps related to the men's past childhood experiences. If we may borrow from Freudian theory, these men may have learned that there are two types of women, some similar to their mothers who are "good" and sexually unapproachable and others who are "bad" and sexually satisfying. Because they are not likely to have seen their mothers walking around the house wearing only high-heeled shoes, but may have seen pictures or heard stories about "bad" girls who did dress in this manner, these shoes become a discriminative stimulus for sexual satisfaction. Some stimuli may also acquire a direct arousal capability. This seems more related to Pavlovian classical conditioning than operant-discrimination learning and will be discussed later in this chapter.

What Does a Discriminative Stimulus Mean to the Observer?

In a sense, this is an unfair question for us to ask because it is one that has been long debated and is too complex and difficult to be answered here. But, it does point to a persisting problem in psychology that cannot be easily wished away; namely, what is the usefulness of attributing to stimuli a meaning in the mind of the observer? Does a green traffic light mean "go"? We are inclined to say that it does, but when dealing with animals it seems rather useless to ask what a stimulus means because ultimately the "meaning" of the stimulus will have to be determined by a relationship of the stimulus to a response in a specific experimental situation. Not much predictive ability is gained by postulating an intervening mental process in an animal.

On the other hand, asking about meaning to understand human behavior seems somewhat more helpful, depending upon how meaning is defined. If meaning is considered to be a subjective report by an observer on possible relationships perceived by him, then it may be helpful to the experimenter because it can provide clues for the development of better empirical procedures (and theories) for demonstrating lawful relationships between observable events.

In a related discussion on the use of experimenter introspection in psychological research, Goldiamond (1962, pp. 310–311) points out:

> The significance of an experiment can . . . reside in the procedures, the variables, or the phenomena discovered. To deny use of subjective experiences of an investigator as clues for properly conducted investigation is to impose restraints not found in other areas of science. The adequacy of the empirical procedures governs the adequacy of the experiment and minimally demonstrates the competence of the scientist. He may apply these procedures to solve a problem created by a theoretical issue, by a procedural issue, by his own subjective experience, by accident, by mistake, by serendipity, or in some other way. To limit the source of problems to any one of these, or to exclude any of them as sources on the grounds of lack of rigor, lack of relevance to theory or to well-articulated systems, would seem to confuse the issue of problem source, where such objections are invalid, with the issue of procedural adequacy, where such objections may be valid.

Perhaps we may take the liberty of a further cautionary note. Within the broader view of epistemology, the meaning (if any) of a discriminative stimulus depends upon the context in which the question is asked. Experimental psychology is not the only route by which knowledge about human events can be obtained. For example, it has often been said that there are only two events about which we can be certain, taxes and death. When the tax collector arrives at our door with a bill, we know what he "means"—pay. And when death arrives, what we know may, or may not, have meaning. Thus, meaning may be in part determined by the context of event, but the event includes the stimulus that we are attempting to understand by giving it meaning.

ELICITING STIMULI

The concept of eliciting stimuli is closely associated with developments in physiology late in the nineteenth century. By 1852, it had been discovered by Biddern and Schmidt that merely teasing a dog with food produced a gastric secretion (cf. Ban, 1964). A related observation was made by Claude Bernard who noticed that after collecting gastric secretions from a horse several times, merely his entrance into the stable was enough to induce a secretion. Also, near this time, a Russian physiologist, Ivan P. Pavlov, conducted some experiments in sham feeding. Dogs were repeatedly shown bread and fed small portions of it until only the presentation of the bread without feeding produced salivation. Pavlov also noticed that if during this sham feeding a person entered the laboratory or rang a bell the gastric secretion would stop. But, by using the same procedure as in sham feeding, i.e., ringing a bell and then placing food in the dog's mouth, the bell alone could eventually elicit a gastric secretion. There was, in a broad sense, a "substitution" of the bell stimulus for the food stimulus in the production of saliva.

This *psychic secretion*, as Pavlov initially termed it, later became designated by him as a *conditioned reflex*. This reflex (a reaction always produced by a stimulus) was called "conditioned" because, unlike inborn reflexes characteristic of an entire species, it depended upon the specific conditions under which a particular animal was raised or treated. Conversely, an inborn reflex was called an *unconditioned reflex* (Pavlov, 1927).[4] The term *reflex* is now often, perhaps customarily, changed to the term *response*. Thus, in Pavlov's experiment, the salivary response produced by the bell was a *conditioned response* and the bell was a *conditioned stimulus*. The original salivary response was an *unconditioned response* and the food that produced it was an *unconditioned stimulus*.

This procedure of pairing two stimuli so that the one acquires the potential to elicit a response similar to the response elicited by the other is known either as *classical conditioning* or *respondent conditioning*. The difference between classical conditioning and operant (or instrumental) conditioning will be discussed later in this chapter.

Pavlov's work has not been nearly as popular or well known in the United States as operant-conditioning theory. However, the value of classical-conditioning concepts in describing behavior is sometimes quite striking. An example is provided in a study by Dekker, Pelser, and Groen (1957) of the classical conditioning of asthma attacks. In the routine

---

[4]Pavlov also suggested the terms *inborn reflexes* in contrast to *acquired reflexes*, or *species reflexes* in contrast to *individual reflexes*.

testing of the severity of asthmatic reactions to various allergens, an allergen is administered to a patient and the subsequent reaction of the patient is measured. This reaction is then compared to the patient's reaction to a neutral solvent. There is usually very little or no change in the pattern of respiration produced by the neutral solvent. But, if the procedure is reversed, some striking results may occur.

During a testing procedure, a thirty-seven-year-old housekeeper who suffered from serious bronchial asthma inhaled an aerosol of a neutral solvent prior to the inhalation of a solution of grass-pollen extract. The grass pollen produced a severe asthma which was terminated by the administration of isoprenaline. The next day the same procedure was repeated. The neutral solvent caused no reaction, but the grass-pollen extract produced another severe asthma attack. To explore the possibility that the patient might believe that the first solution given to her would always be neutral, she was given only grass-pollen extract the following day and four days subsequently. Asthma attacks were induced on all these occasions. When the next test was conducted four days later, the neutral solvent promptly produced an asthmatic attack.

To rule out the possibility of a reaction caused by contamination, the patient was given oxygen through new equipment. Again, an asthmatic attack occurred. Then to guarantee that no allergens were present in the oxygen, only the glass mouthpiece was placed between the patient's lips. Within five minutes, the patient had another asthma attack even though she was breathing air in the same room that she had just previously breathed without any adverse effects. During the next three sessions, asthma attacks were induced using only the mouthpiece and attempts to reassure the patient that the mouthpiece could not possibly be harmful as it was not connected to any equipment did not prevent additional attacks.

Using a similar procedure, the investigators conditioned asthma attacks which occurred upon the presentation of the mouthpiece in a second patient. These case studies would tend to confirm the popular story of a lady who was hypersensitive to roses and upon being shown a paper rose developed an attack of asthma (Vaughan, 1939, p. 128). Stories have also been reported of patients who, being allergic to dust or to horses, had asthma attacks merely upon seeing dust or a picture of a horse.

Some additional support for these rather implausible stories is provided by the case of one patient who reported the onset of asthma attacks immediately after seeing a goldfish in a bowl. When the experimenter later exposed the patient to a live goldfish in a bowl, severe asthmatic reactions did occur. In fact, the patient developed asthma attacks even when exposed to a toy goldfish in the bowl which she clearly recognized as a toy. The patient commented, "Fancy my choking because of that silly toy thing. It isn't even alive" (Dekker & Groen, 1956).

Metcalfe (1956) has reported a case in which a young patient was studied daily over a period of eighty-five days during which she had fifteen asthma attacks. Without any detectable allergen, the asthmatic attacks were associated at statistically significant levels with the patient's contact with her mother. Conditioned anxiety or fear may be a contributing factor in the production of some reactions (Turnbull, 1962). This could explain the sometimes successful reduction of asthmatic reactions by pairing relaxation with imagined respiratory difficulties and stress-provoking events (Moore, 1965).

Finally, for those who feel more intellectual security in experimental studies involving animals, asthma-like reactions have been classically conditioned in guinea pigs. By simultaneously pairing a sound with an aerosol of protein or histamine, the sound alone is able to elicit an asthmatic type of breathing (Justesen, 1971; Noelpp & Noelpp-Eschenhagen, 1952). Guinea pigs have also been conditioned to egg white, to the apparatus without any allergen, and eventually to their experimental chambers in which they had several daily asthma-like attacks (Ottenberg, Stein, Lewis, & Hamilton, 1958).

Clearly not all asthmatic reactions are conditioned responses. In fact, the conditioning of asthmatic attacks in patients, while it has been possible, has generally been difficult and has often failed. This situation, with its present ambiguities, is similar to many problems in the area of psychosomatic medicine that require further analysis.

A Note on Terms

As can be seen from the previous discussion, much emphasis in classical-conditioning theory is placed upon the environmental events (the conditioned and unconditioned stimuli) that precede the response. In operant conditioning, the emphasis is placed on the environmental events (reinforcers) that follow the response.[5] There are several terms commonly used to describe the temporal relationships between conditioned and unconditioned stimuli. These relationships are important because they determine, to a large extent, the nature of the resulting conditioned response.

Simultaneous conditioning refers to those cases in which the onset (initiation) of the conditioned stimulus is simultaneous with or precedes

---

[5] In operant-conditioning theory, it is customary to say that responses are emitted; in classical-conditioning theory, responses are elicited.

by a few seconds (no more than five seconds) the onset of the unconditioned stimulus. If the conditioned stimulus precedes the unconditioned
stimulus, it must also overlap the presentation of the unconditioned
stimulus so that at some point both the conditioned stimulus and the
unconditioned stimulus are being simultaneously presented. Although
conditioning may occur if the onset of the conditioned stimulus and the
unconditioned stimulus are strictly simultaneous (this is a matter of
debate), conditioning will usually occur more readily if the conditioned
stimulus briefly precedes the onset of the unconditioned stimulus.

Delayed conditioning refers to those cases in which the onset of the
conditioned stimulus precedes the onset of the unconditioned stimulus by
more than five seconds and overlaps it. Trace conditioning refers to those
cases in which both the onset and termination of the conditioned stimulus
precede the onset of the unconditioned stimulus so that the conditioned
and unconditioned stimuli do not overlap. Backward conditioning refers
to those cases in which the onset of the unconditioned stimulus precedes
the onset of the conditioned stimulus.

Generally, simultaneous conditioning is more effective in producing
conditioned responses than delayed conditioning, although some conditioning can occur with a fairly long interval (over ten seconds) between
the onset of the conditioned stimulus and the unconditioned stimulus
(Kamin, 1965; Ost & Lauer, 1965). The development of conditioned
responses is also usually slower by trace conditioning than by simultaneous conditioning. Backward conditioning is certainly not very efficient
and there is some question as to whether backward conditioning can
actually produce any conditioned responses beyond general sensitization
(Dykman, 1965).

In simultaneous conditioning, the conditioned response is elicited
within a short period of time between the onset of the conditioned
stimulus and the occurrence of the conditioned response, i.e., a short,
conditioned-response latency. In delayed conditioning, the conditioned
response initially occurs shortly following the onset of the conditioned
stimulus but over a large number of trials the response latency gradually
becomes longer and the conditioned response occurs later, although still
before the onset of the unconditioned stimulus. The same effect is found
in trace conditioning; the conditioned-response latency gradually becomes longer.

Two processes, excitation and inhibition, have been central in
Pavlov's theory of nervous system functioning. If, in addition to the
conditioned and unconditioned stimuli, another stimulus is introduced
into the experimental situation, it may change certain characteristics of
the response. Excitation occurs if this additional stimulus facilitates the

response as indicated by response characteristics such as increased magnitude or shortened latency. Inhibition occurs if the additional stimulus hinders the response. Pavlov (1927, p. 44) offers an example of the inhibition of a conditioned response.

> The following is a very simple case, and one of common occurrence in our earlier experiments. The dog and the experimenter would be isolated in the experimental room, all the conditions remaining for a while constant. Suddenly some disturbing factor would arise—a sound would penetrate into the room; some quick change in illumination would occur, the sun going behind a cloud; or a draught would get in underneath the door, and maybe bring some odour with it. If any one of these extra stimuli happened to be introduced just at the time of application of the conditioned stimulus, it would inevitably bring about a more or less pronounced weakening or even a complete disappearance of the reflex response, depending on the strength of the extra stimulus. The interpretation of this simple case does not present much difficulty. The appearance of any new stimulus immediately evokes the investigatory reflex and the animal fixes all its appropriate receptor organs upon the source of disturbance, pricking up its ears, fastening its gaze upon the disturbing agency, and sniffing the air. The investigatory reflex is excited and the conditioned reflex is in consequence inhibited.

Both processes of excitation and inhibition, according to the theory, tend to spread and interact within the cerebral cortex. This spreading or "irradiation" is illustrated by the observation that if one tone produces a conditioned response, other similar tones are also likely to produce the response. Or better, if a mild vibration at one point on the body produces a conditioned response, a similar mild vibration at another point on the body will also produce the conditioned response (Bass & Hull, 1934; cf. Pavlov, 1927, pp. 177–183). This effect has also been referred to as response generalization.

A similar effect may be seen for the process of inhibition. For example, if vibration at any one of four points on the body produces a conditioned response, the effectiveness of vibration at one of these points can be reduced or eliminated. This *extinction* is accomplished by repeatedly presenting the conditioned stimulus, in this case, vibration, without the subsequent presentation of the unconditioned stimulus. Once the conditioned response to vibration has been extinguished at one point, the response produced by stimulation at the other points will usually be reduced.

By limiting and confining each other, and by occasionally yielding paradoxical reactions, these processes of excitation and inhibition produce the dynamic equilibrium of the organism. The process of inhibition is much less stable than that of excitation and is more easily modified than the process of excitation. Although excitation and inhibition have not received a wide acceptance as suitable explanations for the physiological processes underlying the effects of conditioning, they have had some heuristic value in logically ordering the data from Pavlov's many experiments on the conditioned response.

Higher-order Conditioning

It is some of Pavlov's later work, particularly in *higher-order conditioning*, that has attracted the interest of American investigators concerned with behavior change. In higher-order conditioning studies, the unconditioned stimulus used in the experiment is a conditioned stimulus developed in a previous experiment. By pairing a neutral stimulus with this conditioned stimulus, the neutral stimulus may acquire the capability of eliciting the conditioned response. The neutral stimulus thus becomes a stimulus of the second order, and the response is a second-order response. Words, imagined stimuli, and probably music are examples of second-order (or third-order) stimuli.

The early experiments in the systematic desensitization of snake phobias, discussed in Chapter 2, involved pairing these second-order stimuli with either first-order or unconditioned relaxation responses to eliminate the phobia. Just as the first-order conditioned response may differ somewhat from unconditioned response in magnitude, duration, or topology, so also the second-order response may differ from the first-order conditioned response.

The observation that words can be conditioned stimuli of the first or second order has led to the development of a lie detector test that conditions a person to inform the examiner when he tells a lie (Golden, 1967). This is done by using essentially the following procedure. There is a conditioning and test period. In the conditioning period, the subject is told to lie every time his correct name is asked. At the same time as he verbally says, "No," he is to press a switch which sounds a buzzer. Thus, if the subject's name is John, he will be asked, "Is your name John?" and is to immediately answer "No" and press the switch. This training is continued until John will instantly press the switch to sound the buzzer when he is asked if his name is "John." He is also trained not to press the switch when he answers "No" to an incorrect name such as "Jim." Thus, he is taught to press the switch when he lies about his name but not to press it when he tells the truth about his name. The galvanic skin response (GSR) and other physiological characteristics of the subject are continuously monitored during the conditioning and test period.

With the expectation that this response (pushing a switch) will generalize to subject matter other than the subject's name, he is presented with questions such as the following (Golden, 1967, p. 387):

Is your name John?	(conditioning question)
Were you born in Illinois?	(irrelevant question)
Is your name John?	(conditioning question)
Do you live in Chicago?	(irrelevant question)
Is your name John?	(conditioning question)
Do you know who stole Mr. Smith's $100?	(relevant question)
Is your name John?	(conditioning question)
Did you steal Mr. Smith's $100?	(relevant question)
Before you were 21, did you ever steal anything at all?	(control question)
Is your name John?	(conditioning question)
Do you know where Mr. Smith's $100 went?	(relevant question)
Before you were 21, did you ever lie about anything important?	(control question)
Did you take any money from Mr. Smith's desk without his permission?	(relevant question)
Is your name John?	(conditioning question)

At first, it seems incredible that anyone would sound a buzzer to indicate that he was lying.[6] In fact, the initial purpose of the research was not to elicit the tone signal following a lie, but merely to create a stress situation in which the person would be confused as to the proper response to make following a threatening question. During large-scale testing, this stress as reflected in the galvanic skin response and other measures did occur and did help to indicate lying. Beyond this, however, 33 percent of the 795 persons diagnosed as untruthful pressed the switch to indicate that they were lying. (Presumably the subjects would not intentionally indicate their lying as these tests were conducted as a part of routine investigation rather than as a mock laboratory study.) Seventy-two percent of those subjects who pressed the switch in response to a relevant or control test question later confessed.

Although these findings require further study and analysis, they

---

[6]A somewhat similar pattern of conditioned verbal and motor responses was used to detect criminal offenders by Luria (1932). We may also recall the power of the conditioned stimulus to elicit an unwanted response as in the case of the conditioned asthma attack discussed earlier. These occurred even when the subjects knew that these responses were unreasonable or foolish.

point to the possible significance and influence of higher-order verbal conditioning in daily life. Just as words may elicit second-order physical responses, so also visual or physical stimuli can elicit second-order verbal responses (thoughts?). Higher-order conditioning may be involved when we suddenly meet an old friend on the street. His appearance may bring the rapid recall of old events. The same thing may happen when visiting old, familiar places. Jean Cocteau's visit to his childhood home in Paris, as recorded in his diary, *Journal d'un Inconnu* (1953, p. 165) illustrates this:

> I was looking with surprise at the trees in the courtyard where I divided the summer between riding my bicycle and decorating puppets when a suspicious caretaker, sticking her head out of a high dormer window, asked me what I was doing there. When I answered that I had come to take a look at my childhood dwelling, she said, "You really surprise me," left the window, and came down to meet me by the entrance, inspected me, wouldn't be convinced by any proof, practically chased me away, and slammed the main gate behind me awakening with the noise, like a distant cannonade, a swarm of new memories.
>
> After this failure, I fancied crossing the street, starting out at the rue Blanche, going over to number 45, closing my eyes, and running my right hand over the bridges and the street lights as I used to do coming home from school. When this experiment didn't yield anything, I counselled myself that in those days I was shorter and my hand was now higher and therefore didn't meet the same textures. I started the same thing over. Thanks to a simple change of level and by a phenomenon similar to the rubbing of a needle on the grooves of a phonograph record, I heard the music of memory. I rediscovered all: my hooded jacket, the leather of my book satchel, the name of the friend who was with me, the names of our friends, certain expressions I had used, the sound of my grandfather's voice, the smell of his beard, the smell of the material of my sister's and mother's dresses.

In the same manner, stimulation of the other senses may elicit past memories.[7] Music may evoke emotions, particularly those that were associated with the music at an earlier date. Thus, the concept of

---

[7]Hermann Hesse (1968, pp. 276–277) has described an experience of one of his characters, Goldmund: "His homecoming put him under a spell, so violent that he himself was astonished by t. . . . From every corner of his past, the scent of his early adolescence came toward him, sweetly and movingly. Love drove him to see everything again, to hear all the sounds again, the bells for evening prayer and Sunday mass, the gushing of the dark millstream between its narrow, mossy banks, the slapping of sandals on the stone floors, the twilight jangle of the key ring as the brother porter went to ock up. . . . But more than anything else the tinkling of the little school bell moved him. It was the moment when, at the beginning of recess, all the cloister students came tumbling down the stairs into the courtyard." What are these "flowers of memory," as Hesse once called them, that bloom out of sensory stimulation? Higher-order conditioned responses.

higher-order conditioning provides a convenient, theoretical approach to understanding some aspects of human emotion in a fairly objective, measurable manner.

DIFFERENCES BETWEEN DISCRIMINATIVE STIMULI AND ELICITING STIMULI

Stimulus control refers to the extent to which an antecedent stimulus determines the probability of the occurrence of a response. The greater the change in response probability following the presentation of the stimulus, the greater the degree of stimulus control. As seen from the previous discussion, the stimulus that precedes a response may operate in at least two ways highly correlated with response probability: as a discriminative stimulus or as an eliciting stimulus. The discriminative stimulus sets the occasion for reinforcement to follow the response whereas the eliciting stimulus elicits the response independently of the consequences that follow the response. With the sudden screeching of automobile brakes, we momentarily become rigid and look toward the source of the sound. If we happen to be standing in the street, this response could be quite inappropriate from both an operant-conditioning and a social point of view—we might not remain intact long enough to receive reinforcement for an escape response. The shy girl may blush when certain verbal stimuli are presented to her, even though she tries to avoid it. If we are being fingerprinted by the police, sweating palms might be operantly conditioned by our escape from apprehension, but they are not useful when we are making a speech. In short, it is difficult or impossible to describe all behavior only in terms of operant conditioning. Similarly, it is difficult or impossible to describe all behavior in classical-conditioning terms. At this point in our learning, both theories seem useful.

Whether we describe certain responses in terms of the stimuli that precede or follow them may depend upon the nature of the response and the personal preference of the observer. For example, in an autobiographical essay, Skinner (1956, p. 223) comments that "Pavlov had shown the way; but I could not then [as a graduate student], as I cannot now, move without a jolt from salivary reflexes to the important business of the organism in everyday life." It may be this "jolt" (perhaps a classically conditioned response) that evokes Skinner's enthusiastic citation of a story by George Bernard Shaw entitled *The Adventures of the Black Girl in Her Search for God* (1932). In this story, a little girl, while lost in a jungle of ideas, meets many prophets of truth. Among these prophets is an elderly man who bears a very close resemblance to Pavlov. The following excerpt quoted by Skinner (1953, pp. 50–51) occurs in the story just after the little girl has been frightened by a roar from the biblical prophet Micah.

"What am I running from?" she said to herself, pulling herself up. "I'm not afraid of that dear noisy old man."

"Your fears and hopes are only fancies" said a voice close to her, proceeding from a very shortsighted elderly man in spectacles who was sitting on a gnarled log. "In running away you were acting on a conditioned reflex. It is quite simple. Having lived among lions you have from your childhood associated the sound of a roar with deadly danger. Hence your precipitate flight when that superstitious old jackass brayed at you. This remarkable discovery cost me twenty-five years of devoted research, during which I cut out the brains of innumerable dogs, and observed their spittle by making holes in their cheeks for them to salivate through instead of through their tongues. The whole scientific world is prostrate at my feet in admiration of this colossal achievement and gratitude for the light it has shed on the great problems of human conduct."

"Why didn't you ask me?" said the black girl. "I could have told you in twenty-five seconds without hurting those poor dogs."

"Your ignorance and presumption are unspeakable" said the old myop. "The fact was known of course to every child; but it had never been proved experimentally in the laboratory; and therefore it was not scientifically known at all. It reached me as an unskilled conjecture: I handed it on as science. Have you ever performed an experiment, may I ask?"

"Several" said the black girl. "I will perform one now. Do you know what you are sitting on?"

"I am sitting on a log grey with age, and covered with an uncomfortable rugged bark" said the myop.

"You are mistaken" said the black girl. "You are sitting on a sleeping crocodile."

With a yell which Micah himself might have envied, the myop rose and fled frantically to a neighboring tree, up which he climbed catlike with an agility which in so elderly a gentleman was quite superhuman.

"Come down" said the black girl. "You ought to know that crocodiles are only to be found near rivers. I was only trying an experiment. Come down" (Shaw, 1932, pp. 20–21).

The elderly "Pavlov" of the story is unable to get out of the tree so the girl conducts another "experiment" by telling him that there is a tree snake crawling near the back of his neck. He is on the ground immediately. To this story Skinner (p. 51) adds the comment, "The black girl is undeniably a good behavioral engineer. In two very neat examples of stimulus control she induces clearcut responses in the elderly myop."

Whether the girl has used eliciting stimuli or discriminative stimuli is open to some debate. The differences between these two types of stimuli are not always clear. Sometimes the physical characteristics of the stimulus itself provides a clue, as when the stimulus is a drop of acid placed on the tongue. It is then likely to be an eliciting stimulus. But if the stimulus is a tone signal of a specific frequency and intensity, it may either elicit a response or set the occasion for operant reinforcement. If, however, one looks more broadly at the total stimulus situation, noting whether the tone signal is followed by another stimulus such as a drop of acid on the tongue, then the nature of the stimulus can often be inferred from the physical structure and operation of the subject's physical environment.

Another approach is also possible. One can classify the stimulus in terms of the type of behavior, respondent or operant, which follows the presentation of the stimulus. This is the more common method of classifying these stimuli, but it is not always completely satisfactory. It is sometimes difficult to determine if the behavior is respondent or operant, although some general guidelines do exist.

Verhave (1966) has well summarized some of the major differences often found between respondent and operant behaviors and the procedures used to produce these behaviors. For example, classical conditioning involves the formation of new stimulus-response relationships. Operant conditioning, on the other hand, modifies only those behaviors already displayed by the subject. Therefore, in operant conditioning the experimenter must wait for the desired response to be emitted or use a shaping procedure to obtain it. In classical conditioning, the behavior can be directly produced by the experimenter and is "involuntary" on the part of the subject.

Respondent behavior does not usually manipulate the environment. It more frequently changes the internal physiology of the organism.[8] Operant behavior characteristically manipulates the environment to produce a reinforcer. The autonomic nervous system, glands, and smooth muscles are more often involved in classical conditioning than in operant conditioning. Respondent behavior appears to be more sensitive to the magnitude of the stimulus involved than operant behavior. Response differentiation involving a change of the characteristics of a response, such as rate, is usually more difficult to obtain in respondent behavior than in operant behavior. Also, it might be noted, in classical conditioning the stimulus usually elicits only one response whereas in operant conditioning many responses may be emitted in association with the stimulus.

Although operant and classical conditioning may involve different

---

[8]By placing electrodes within the nerves of the sensory organs and on the posterior of the spinal cord in a paralyzed animal, a conditioned motor response can be developed without any additional involvement of the external environment (Gantt, 1966).

processes, the two processes can occur simultaneously in a situation.[9] A response elicited by classical conditioning can be operantly reinforced. To use an earlier example, when we suddenly meet an old friend, his presence may elicit the memory of past experiences and the mentioning of these experiences to him can be reinforced by his agreement or smiles. But let us consider a more troublesome analytical situation. Suppose that we have a friend who has a hearing problem and who is also somewhat forgetful. Sometimes when we meet him he is wearing his hearing aid and sometimes he is not. When he is wearing his hearing aid, conversation with him is very pleasant, when he is not, conversation is very difficult and unproductive. We now happen to see him in the distance and as we approach we notice that he is wearing his hearing aid. Does the hearing aid act as an eliciting stimulus, a discriminative stimulus, or both?

An analog to this problem can be found in a study by Ellison and Konorski (1964). During the early phases of this study, dogs were classically conditioned to salivate to the sound of a buzzer (eliciting stimulus) and operantly conditioned to press a lever only in the presence of a light (discriminative stimulus). During the next phase, the dogs were required to press the lever nine times in the presence of the light which then terminated the light and sounded the buzzer. After eight seconds food was presented. In this experiment, the dogs did not learn to salivate when the light was presented though they did press the lever. When the buzzer was presented, the dogs salivated but they did not press the lever. The light did not acquire the properties of the eliciting stimulus. Thus, the answer to the question about the hearing aid is that it probably acts as a discriminative stimulus and the conversation which follows acts as an eliciting stimulus.

For several reasons this answer is not a final one applicable to all situations. A stimulus may have several functions when it is a part of a complex chain of closely integrated behaviors or when it precedes, overlaps, and follows a response. A smile from the boss may elicit a pleasant feeling and it may also set the occasion for asking him for a raise.[10] In negative reinforcement, the onset of the aversive stimulus may elicit fear as well as set the occasion for escape. Finally, though there may be distinctions between operant and respondent behavior, the

---

[9]Some investigators have suggested that all behavior can be described in terms of classical conditioning. The reinforcement in operant conditioning, e.g., food, is an unconditioned stimulus and the response-produced sensations in the subject preceding the presentation of the food are conditioned stimuli (Sheffield, 1965). Conversely, some investigations have suggested that typical classical-conditioning experiments involve considerable operant conditioning (Gantt, 1967). Even if the underlying learning processes in operant and classical conditioning turn out to be identical, it might still be useful to use the terms operationally to describe the different experimental procedures.

[10]For a further discussion of social stimuli of this type called *evaluative reinforcers* see Hill (1968).

classification of responses seems to more nearly fit a continuum than a dichotomy.

TREATMENT OF ALCOHOLICS AND HOMOSEXUALS

The importance of stimulus control in the understanding and treatment of alcoholism and homosexuality is gaining increasing recognition. To some extent, the experimenters are only discovering what many people, like Shaw's little girl, already know.

It is a common observation that people while intoxicated often misplace or lose objects and then later, when they are sober, are unable to find them. But, sometimes when they are again intoxicated shortly thereafter, they can recall where they placed the missing object (like retracing one's steps?). This observation led to an experiment in which three groups of students were "intoxicated"[11] and compared on various memory tasks with a similar group of control subjects (Goodwin, Powell, Bremer, Hoine, & Stern, 1969). The experiment lasted over two days with all of the subjects. taking the same tests both days. One group was intoxicated both days, one group was intoxicated on day 1 and sober on day 2, one group was sober on day 1 and intoxicated on day 2, and one group remained sober both days.

In summary, although intoxication generally impaired performance, the group that was intoxicated both days remembered significantly more words mentioned in a word-association test on day 1 than the group that was also intoxicated on day 1, but sober on day 2 during the test. Also, the group intoxicated both days remembered some sentences better from day 1 than the group intoxicated on day 1 but sober on day 2. A picture-recognition task was not affected and on an avoidance test the group intoxicated both days made considerably more errors than the group that was intoxicated and then sober. Conversely, but not quite so clearly, the group that was sober both days performed better than the group that was sober and then intoxicated. The experimenters concluded (p. 1358), "Alcohol appears to produce 'dissociated' or state-dependent effects in man, but not all forms of memory are equally sensitive to the phenomena."

The observation that some information acquired in an alcoholic state may transfer better to a subsequent alcoholic state than to a sober state points to the possibility of stimulus control by the sensory or physiological effects of alcohol. To reduce excessive drinking that may be associated with the initial consumption of alcohol (the problem of the

[11]These subjects each consumed between eight to ten ounces of 80-proof vodka diluted in a soft drink within one hour and all showed signs of intoxication.

"first drink" that leads to prolonged intoxication), the sight or taste of alcohol can be paired with aversive stimuli.

Medieval writings contain examples of the addition of revolting substances, such as dead spiders, to the alcohol to produce disgust and reduce drinking (Franks, 1963). Assuming that the response to be eliminated is the drinking of the alcohol and that the dead spider is found in the bottom of the glass, this old arrangement could not be expected to be very effective from a classical-conditioning point of view. This would be a form of punishment rather than conditioning because the noxious stimulus (spider) follows the response to be eliminated (drinking). On the other hand, if the drinking itself is considered the stimulus that elicits the response of additional excessive drinking which is to be eliminated, then the discovery of the spider may be appropriately timed. As Franks (1966) suggests, difficulties or inconsistencies in the design of treatment procedures in regard to principles of learning may account for some of the poor and contradictory results among the various studies. It should be noted that unlike the usual classical-conditioning experiment in which the conditioned stimulus is originally neutral, the conditioned stimulus in this case (alcohol) is originally positive and the procedure attempts to "recondition" it so that it becomes associated with unpleasant conditions such as nausea. The procedure, therefore, cannot be directly equated with simple laboratory experiments.

The aversive stimuli used have usually been an electric shock or an emetic that produces nausea and vomiting.[12] Nausea has also been produced hypnotically or by asking the patient to imagine that he suddenly becomes sick (Anant, 1967, 1968; Cautela, 1967, 1970b). These different aversive stimuli probably do not produce similar responses. Electric shock may produce an anxiety response which operates differently from a nausea response produced by an emetic. The advantages of one stimulus over another, however, is not yet clearly determined. Although the use of electric shock has the advantage of allowing precise timing which is not possible with an emetic (Rachman, 1965), there may be some advantages to using an aversive stimulus which is in the same sensory modality as the response to be extinguished (Lazarus, 1968b).

The results are only moderately encouraging with chronic alcoholics regardless of the many types of treatment that have been attempted: disulfiram and LSD (Ditman, 1964), milieu therapy (Wallerstein, 1957), hypnosis (Gordova & Kovalev, 1962), conditioning (Franks, 1963; Regester, 1972; Thimann, 1949) and psychoanalytically oriented psycho-

---

[12]The possibility of treating alcoholism by conditioning procedures has been long recognized. As early as 1930, Kantorovich reported treating twenty alcoholics with "associated-reflex therapy" using electric shock.

therapy (Zwerling & Rosenbaum, 1959). The success of these various treatments ranges from a low of 15 percent to a high of about 93 percent. The 51 percent abstinence for a period of two years as reported by Lemere and Voegtlin (1950) for 4,096 patients using conditioning procedures seems fairly typical for established behavior-change procedures. The variation in treatment effectiveness may result in part from an uneven distribution of the physiological concomitants of alcoholism among the patients in various studies (Davis & Walsh, 1970; Myers, 1963); differences in the personalities, conditionability, and home environments of patients (Miller, Pokorny, & Valles, 1970; Wallerstein, 1957); and variation in the skill with which treatment is designed and conducted.

The conclusion of Rachman and Teasdale (1969, p. 22) seems appropriate:

> In our opinion, the most fair-minded interpretation which can be given to the evidence on chemical aversion therapy is as follows. There is a strong possibility that chemical aversion therapy is effective in the treatment of certain types of alcoholic patients. However, we have been unable to locate adequately convincing evidence to *prove* this possibility beyond any doubt. It must also be added that the treatment is, at best, somewhat inefficient. Furthermore, it appears that the best prospects for a satisfactory response to this treatment include adequate motivation and a stable personality and background.

Most of the studies of alcoholism emphasize complete abstinence from alcohol following treatment. A few researchers have suggested that it is possible for some alcoholics to avoid alcoholism after treatment even though they are not completely abstinent. Apparently the percentage of successful, nonabstinent patients is usually low, 15 percent or less (Davis, 1962; Reinhert, & Bowen, 1968), and the drinking may be of a social or controlled nature involving only an occasional glass of wine or beer. In most cases, the drinkers seem to protect themselves by drinking in carefully selected circumstances. This may eliminate those situations in which discriminative stimuli would be present for heavy or uncontrolled drinking.

There may also be eliciting simuli associated with the preliminary stages of intoxication that evoke heavy drinking. To increase the patient's awareness of these stimuli, he can be trained in a laboratory to make accurate estimates of his blood alcohol level by periodic feedback. Once he can make this discrimination, high levels of blood alcohol can be followed by electric shock as a part of social-drinking training programs (Lovibond, 1970). This training has been carried out in social settings such as the home and hotel lounges where excessive drinking would usually occur. Although the initial results of this research are encouraging, it should be remembered that a return to moderation rather than abstinence is the exception rather than the rule.

The treatment of male homosexuality has involved a similar but somewhat broader range of behavior-change procedures than the treatment of alcoholism. Some of these additional procedures such as systematic desensitization and assertive training are compatible with major psychoanalytic theories of the cause of homosexuality. Psychoanalytic theories may be roughly placed into three large categories (Ovesey, Gaylin, & Hendin, 1963): (1) the homosexual is driven into homosexual relationships because of his fear or anxiety about heterosexual activity. This is usually produced by excessively strict parental discipline regarding normal heterosexual behavior during early childhood. (2) The homosexual has an unconscious wish for the infantile dependency that previously existed between him and his mother. Parental intimidation during childhood inhibited the assertive behavior necessary for the masculine role. In symbolic fantasy, the homosexual compensates for his inadequacy by incorporating the penis orally or anally. (3) A nonassertive male may attempt to deny his weakness by acting dominant toward other males and forcing them to take a feminine role. This is based upon an early power struggle between the homosexual and his father (Oedipal rivalry) or his brothers.

In some cases of sexual deviance, such as male homosexuality, one can often find a history of reinforcement in which a socially inappropriate stimulus has become a discriminative stimulus. Such reinforcement, of course, usually occurs inadvertently and frequently. A very detailed case history is usually required to reveal the circumstances under which such reinforcement has occurred. Stekel (1952), a psychoanalyst, reports the case of a female transvestite who had her first sexual experience while wearing male clothing. This was followed by a series of similar experiences in male clothing extending over a fairly long period of time until the behavior became a stabilized pattern. It is unlikely that only one or a few deviant experiences could firmly establish a deviant pattern of behavior. This is confirmed in part by the failure to find any statistically greater rate of subsequent deviancy among those who as children have had a deviant sexual experience with adults than among those without such experiences (Stafford-Clark, 1964).[13]

The persistent pattern of reinforcement contingencies leading to

[13]Ironically, one of the major dangers in the seduction of the young may lie in the inadvertent labeling of the child as a victim. The child may come to believe that certain harmful effects will follow and may be treated accordingly by the parents. Thus, some of the unhappy consequences of the incident may be more the result of self-fulfilling prophecy than the result of the specific act (cf. Karpman, 1962).

stimulus control by same-sex persons or sex-related objects may be seen in a case reported by Robie (1963) of a young, married man who had occasional homosexual experiences. As a boy of about six, he recalls that he happened to sleep with his youngest brother's nurse, a girl of seventeen, who patted his buttocks while pretending to spank him. This gave him definite pleasure and occurred several times. At the age of thirteen and one-half years, he was visiting some relatives and slept in a large room which contained many mirrors. While undressing, he noticed that the sight of his body, particularly his buttocks, pleased him and on this occasion he had his first masturbatory experience. This was followed by many similar experiences until the age of fifteen when this made him feel guilty and he attempted to avoid all sexual thoughts.

At the age of eighteen, he entered college and participated extensively in athletics. While he was celebrating the end of his first football season with excessive drinking, he had his first sexual relationship with a woman. Following this, he engaged in sexual intercourse about once a month or more. His pleasure was heightened when he also had contact with the woman's buttocks. Although his activity was exclusively heterosexual, he occasionally had homosexual thoughts, particularly related to the buttocks of young boys.

The first of several homosexual experiences occurred following his college graduation. As might be expected, the occasion involved a young boy about fifteen years old. The young man has described this experience in an unusually frank letter to Dr. Robie (1963, pp. 194–195):

One night in Montreal, after I had returned from a three week's camping trip, I chanced to be one of a group of people who had gathered to witness a street accident. We were closely pressed together, and the person in front of me was a good-looking French Canadian boy of about fifteen. Impelled by a wave of sexual excitement induced by this close contact, I let my hand run gently over his buttocks. He turned around and smiled shyly, and I read in his dark eyes that this attention did not displease him. When the crowd dispersed, I engaged him in conversation, complimenting him on his looks. I was stopping in a small second-rate hotel (as I had just come from the woods and was still in my camping clothes), and as the evening was still early, I asked the lad if he would not accompany me to my room. He hesitated a moment, and then accepted the invitation. I had no ulterior motive when I issued this invitation, but immediately when we were in the room, the boy's dark eyes and fresh face made another wave of lust roll over me and I continued my attentions. . . . At the conclusion, I was almost overcome by shame. I think he also had something of this feeling. However, when he left, I kissed him without embarrassment, and he returned it in the same manner. I trust you will forgive the intimate details of this first homosexual affair.

The several subsequent homosexual incidents were all similar in nature and occurred at widely spaced intervals during which there were many visits to prostitutes and girl friends and finally marriage. This detailed description suggests some of the difficulty in broadly classifying a person as homosexual or heterosexual because of the frequent variability and complexity of sexual behavior. The case reported here may be similar to many others as indicated by the observations of Kinsey, Pomeroy, and Martin (1948) that at least 37 percent of American males had at least one homosexual experience.

The case study above points to the possibility that sexual responses may be classically conditioned responses. Rachman (1966) successfully induced sexual fetishism in three subjects by pairing a colored slide of knee-length, women's boots with colored slides of attractive, nude girls as unconditioned stimuli. After twenty-four to sixty-five trials, all the subjects showed conditioned sexual responses to the picture of the boots. The arousal potential of these boots cannot be attributed to any inherent quality that they might have. McConaghy (1970) has subsequently classically conditioned sexual responses to colored circles and triangles by pairing them with moving pictures of nude males and females. This procedure was similar to that used by Rachman. In natural settings, the conditioning seems to take place more slowly, perhaps because old conditioned stimuli are gradually replaced by the new conditioned stimuli through usually inadvertent but repeated circumstances. A series of case studies collected by McGuire, Carlisle, and Young (1965) show that stimuli associated with masturbation gradually became eliciting stimuli usually over a period of years.

The most common forms of behavioral treatment of male homosexuality have been based upon the assumption that an attractive male image serves as a stimulus for subsequent homosexual behavior. The treatment involves pairing this image with aversive stimuli, usually an emetic or electric shock. The procedure employed by James (1962) is fairly typical. Following an injection of apomorphine to produce nausea, the patient lies in a darkened room in which a light shines on several photographs of nude or near-nude men. As nausea occurs, the patient is asked to select one which he finds attractive and it is suggested that he re-create a pleasant experience he has had with a homosexual partner. Tape recordings are then played which describe in slow and graphic terms the adverse consequences of his homosexual activity ending with terms such as "sickening," "nauseating," and the sound of vomiting. Later, when not undergoing aversion treatment, he is presented with pictures of sexually attractive young women and encouraged to have sexual fantasies about them. Freund (1960) followed up forty-seven patients over three- and five-year periods who were similarly treated and found that approximately 51 percent of the patients showed no improvement, 14.9 percent showed temporary improvement, and 25.5 percent permanent improvement. (Adequate information could not be obtained on 8.5 percent.)

Electric shock, first suggested in 1935 for the treatment of fetishes (Max), is now being increasingly used. The advantage that electric shock offers in controlling onset and intensity has encouraged a more careful examination of the learning theory underlying the design of various treatment methods. In laboratory studies of learning, consideration of the temporal relationships between stimuli and responses has led to the development of several standard learning paradigms. *Escape learning* requires a behavior on the part of the subject to terminate the aversive stimulus; e.g., an animal standing on an electrified grid terminates the shock by pressing a lever. *Active-avoidance learning* requires a behavior on the part of the subject to avoid the onset of the aversive stimulus; e.g., the animal standing on the grid must press a lever to prevent the grid from being electrified. Typically, in this situation, a discriminative stimulus such as a light or tone signal, is presented prior to the onset of the aversive stimulus so that the subject will eventually initiate avoidance behavior with the onset of the discriminative stimulus.

Passive-avoidance learning or *punishment* initially involves the performance of a behavior by the subject which is reinforced, e.g. pressing a lever for food. Then, after this behavior is well established, it is followed by an aversive stimulus. Thus, when the subject attempts to receive reinforcement, an aversive stimulus is received which can be avoided by refraining from the previously reinforced behavior.

One additional learning paradigm should be mentioned, *conditioned suppression.* When a previously neutral stimulus such as a light is repeatedly followed by an aversive event, subsequent presentations of this stimulus will reduce the frequency of ongoing behavior. If a light has been paired with electric shock and the light is presented to a pigeon while it is responding normally on a reinforcement schedule, the responding will be reduced. If an ambulance siren (usually associated with unpleasant events) is heard while studying, the studying is likely to be temporarily reduced. Conditioned suppression is often equated with the concept of anxiety.

Some researchers consider the pairing of an aversive stimulus with a homosexuality-oriented stimulus as a form of conditioned suppression. However, conditioned suppression usually involves the pairing of an aversive stimulus with a neutral stimulus rather than with a stimulus closely involved in the behavioral sequence or response chain. Also, conditioned suppression is generally not as effective as passive-avoidance learning in reducing responses.

Exactly what response in the behavioral sequence leading to a homosexual relationship should be followed by an aversive stimulus is open to question. Pigeons that received mild shock following reinforcement by food (i.e., punishment) gradually increased their rate of response until it almost reached the level it had been prior to the initiation of the shock contingency (Azrin, 1960). Recovery (return to the original operant rate), however, can often be prevented by increasing the intensity of the aversive stimulus.

Suppression of the first response in a sequence is generally more effective in disrupting the sequence than the suppression of later responses. When the sequence involves an operant behavior (pressing a lever) and a consummatory response (eating), suppression of the operant behavior is more effective in disrupting the sequence than suppression of the consummatory response (Church, 1969). A closer analog to most treatment procedures, however, would involve pairing the sight of food with shock, and comparing response decrement under this contingency with that of shock following food.[14]

Mandel (1970) has suggested interrupting the response chain leading to homosexual behavior as soon as possible because an aversive stimulus following the initial presentation of a sexually pleasing stimulus might reduce the attractiveness of potential male partners, thus weakening the reinforcement value of the homosexual contact. Haynes (1970) and Lovibond (1970), however, have suggested using an aversive stimulus following the actual homosexual response.[15] Treatment using this passive-avoidance paradigm has showed both favorable (e.g., Blakemore, 1964; Marks & Gelder, 1967; McGuire & Vallance, 1964) and questionable results (e.g., Bancroft, Jones, & Pullan, 1966).

It is not experimentally clear what the comparative outcome of these different procedures would be. The issue of the appropriate learning paradigm remains unresolved largely because factors such as the onset of the stimuli and responses, the type of patients and their motivation, and objective criteria for follow-up are often not clearly enough described to make a meaningful comparison among studies possible. Also, attention should be paid to the thoughts and attitudes of the subjects toward sexual matters and the experiment (Barclay, 1970, 1971). Thoughts can greatly facilitate or inhibit sexual response (Henson & Rubin, 1971).

---

[14]Some distant and surely not conclusive evidence for the potential effectiveness of early intervention in the behavioral sequence is found in Sears, Maccoby, & Levin's finding (1957) that mothers who immediately stopped disapproved aggression have less aggressive children than those mothers who intervene later. See also Mowrer's (1960) theory of response inhibition.

[15]Haynes has also suggested the use of male partners rather than slides, an idea consonant with the frequent, increased effectiveness of *in vivo* therapy.

If the treatment of the homosexual patient is aimed at only decreasing the homosexual behavior, he may be left with no satisfying sexual alternative, a situation which increases the probability of subsequent homosexual behavior. In situations in which a previously reinforced response produces an aversive stimulus (punishment), the provision of an alternative, reinforced response greatly reduces the original response. Based on data from a series of experiments, Azrin and Holz (1966, p. 406) concluded, "The alternative response situation leads to a greater suppression by a given intensity of punishment than does a single response situation, whether the aversive stimulus is a period of time-out, an annoying noise, electrode shock or whether the subjects are human or pigeon."

The development of an alternative sexual response in the homosexual, namely a heterosexual response, has not been easy. Several approaches have been tried. One has been the use of systematic desensitization to reduce the fear or anxiety associated with heterosexual intercourse (Kraft, 1969). Systematic desensitization to heterosexual stimuli can be integrated with the avoidance procedures as described above (Levin, Hirsch, Shugar, & Kapche, 1968).[16]

Another approach is called aversion-relief therapy. In the early studies of therapy involving electric shock, it became apparent that the patients were considerably relieved when they were told that the treatment session was over. Thorpe, Schmidt, Brown, and Castell (1964) developed a program in which relief was paired with heterosexual words or images. Words associated with homosexuality were presented and followed by shock but words associated with heterosexuality were followed by a break or a termination of the treatment session. Feldman and MacCulloch (1965) modified this technique to a partial, active-avoidance procedure. In the first stage, a slide of an attractive male was presented to the subject for eight seconds. If the subject pressed a switch within this time, the stimulus was replaced by a slide of an attractive female and the subject avoided an electric shock. The subject soon learned to press the switch to avoid the shock. The subject was then changed to a schedule in which one-third of his attempts were not successful in eliminating the male slide stimulus and the shock, one-third were successful in immediately eliminating the stimulus and the shock, and one-third were successful in eliminating the shock only after a delay of varying intervals of time. Initial results look rather promising. A sample of forty-three patients followed up for one year has shown improvement or complete absence of homosexual behavior in 58.3

---

[16]An interesting aspect of this study is that one of the slides used in the avoidance learning was a picture of the patient's room-mate toward whom he felt attracted. Treatment successfully reduced the attraction, but it calls to attention the high personal cost of successful treatment.

percent of the patients, 25.6 percent failure, and 16.1 percent termination from treatment (cited in Rachman and Teasdale, 1969, p. 66).

A more direct approach to developing heterosexual responses is to encourage masturbation to heterosexual stimuli. The homosexual fantasies used by a homosexual might be gradually changed by pairing typical, heterosexual stimuli such as pictures or films with orgasm (cf. Davison, 1968; Herman, Barlow, & Agras, 1971; Marquis, 1970). Brain stimulation by electrodes has also been used to increase the sexual arousal of a homosexual to heterosexual stimuli (Moan & Heath, 1972). It may be helpful to develop these heterosexual responses before attempting to eliminate homosexual responses by aversive forms of conditioning.

Finally, if heterosexual behavior is to be developed and maintained in the community, special attention may have to be given to training the patient to perform the masculine role well so that anxiety can be reduced and positive social relationships can occur. This may be facilitated by the therapeutic use of female assistants (Moan & Heath, 1972) or the use of male assistants skilled in social interaction who serve as models of appropriate behavior (cf. Marshall, 1971). These possibilities are discussed in more detail in the following chapters.

Uniqueness of the Person in Classical Conditioning: "Effect of Person" and the "Freedom Reflex"

There is some tendency to consider classical conditioning as destructive of individuality. Surely this is true when conditioning is viewed as a procedure for manipulating the environment so that similar responses can be elicited involuntarily in a large number of people. But just as the fact that people generally walk upright and eat food does not destroy their individuality so a similarity in psychological processes among persons does not necessarily destroy their individuality. Rather, individuality can be determined only if there is a common pattern or background from which personal variations can be distinguished. Individuality is lost, at least conceptually, when attention is focused upon generalities rather than specifics.

Classical-conditioning theory has traditionally emphasized the careful study of each individual subject unlike, for example, sociology that categorizes subjects in the aggregate. Furthermore, the careful study of each subject has led to the recognition that there are often inherent, individual-subject characteristics that find no easy explanation in terms of external events, thus affirming the uniqueness of the individual. Two types of responses, *effect of person* and the *freedom reflex*, illustrate a considerable degree of individual variation in conditioning.

When Claude Bernard noticed that his entry into the horse's stable produced an effect on the horse, he was demonstrating the effect of the person. It was this influence of a person upon an experimental dog that greatly contributed to Pavlov's discovery of the conditioned response. Later, Pavlov demonstrated what he called *social reflexes* by introducing different experimenters into a room with a dog and measuring the dog's reactions (Pavlov, 1928, pp. 255–368). The response was labeled effect of person.

Gantt and his associates have confirmed the conclusion of Pavlov that a dog will have different heart rate responses to various persons (1966).[17] These effects will be produced even though the dog is equally familiar with the people. Gantt (1967, p. 148) notes that "one person, by merely appearing before a dog, will make its heart rate go up; another will make it go down, irrespective, as far as we can know, of anything the person has done to or with the dog." It is possible to use the effect of person as an unconditioned stimulus. By pairing this effect with a bell, the bell will acquire the potential to modify the heart rate in dogs.

When a person enters the room where a dog is being studied, the dog's heart rate usually increases (tachycardia), but when the animal is petted the heart rate usually decreases (bradycardia). Electric shock also tends to increase heart rate. Anderson and Gantt found that tachycardia could be reduced by petting the dogs during the presentation of shock. In the case of one neurotic dog, Nick, the effects of petting were so extreme that not only was bradycardia induced but there were occasional, brief cardiac arrests (Gantt, Newton, Royer, & Stephens, 1966).

Lynch and McCarthy (1969) have found a suppression of the usual tachycardia in dogs by the presence of the person and by petting when tachycardia is a conditioned response. Female dogs responded more to petting than male dogs. However, after two to three sessions, the influence of the petting began to diminish.

It is also possible to use a person as a conditioned stimulus. By pairing the presence of a person with petting or an electric shock, it is possible to produce markedly different responses in dogs when they merely see the person (Lynch & McCarthy, 1969). There is some tentative indication that different breeds of dogs may react differently to the presence of people (cf. Scott & Fuller, 1965).

The effect of person has also been demonstrated in other animals such as cats, rabbits, and monkeys (Gantt et al., 1966). The effects produced within people by other people are so common that they may be overlooked. As a popular analogy puts it, fish would be the last to

---

[17]As previously noted, George Bernard Shaw was not too favorably inclined toward Pavlov's work. In discussing Pavlov he is reported to have said, "Pavlov is the biggest fool I know; any policeman could tell you that much about a dog" (Gantt, 1941, p. 22).

discover water. Surely, the effect of person has not yet been adequately studied.

Individuality may find expression not only in personal effects but also in other patterns of reaction to external stimuli. Early in his work, Pavlov noticed the resistance of some animals to physical constraints. He has described his experience with one of these animals (Pavlov, 1927, pp. 11–12):

> In the course of the researches which I shall presently explain, we were completely at a loss on one occasion to find any cause for the peculiar behaviour of an animal. It was evidently a very tractable dog, which soon became very friendly with us. We started off with a very simple experiment. The dog was placed in a stand with loose loops around its legs, but so as to be quite comfortable and free to move a pace or two. Nothing more was done except to present the animal repeatedly with food at intervals of some minutes. It stood quietly enough at first, and ate quite readily, but as time went on it became excited and struggled to get out of the stand, scratching at the floor, gnawing the supports, and so on. This ceaseless muscular exertion was accompanied by breathlessness and continuous salivation, which persisted at every experiment during several weeks, the animal getting worse and worse until it was no longer fitted for our researches. For a long time we remained puzzled over the unusual behaviour of this animal. We tried out experimentally numerous possible interpretations, but though we had had long experience with a great number of dogs in our laboratories we could not work out a satisfactory solution of this strange behaviour, until it occurred to us at last that it might be the expression of a special *freedom reflex*, and that the dog simply could not remain quiet when it was constrained in the stand. This reflex was overcome by setting off another against it—the reflex for food. We began to give the dog the whole of its food in the stand. At first the animal ate but little, and lost considerably in weight, but gradually it got to eat more, until at last the whole ration was consumed. At the same time, the animal grew quieter during the course of the experiments; the freedom reflex was being inhibited.

Pavlov also noted (p. 12), "It is clear that the freedom reflex is one of the most important reflexes or, if we use a more general term, reactions, of living beings." We are reminded of some students who are still young and growing and for whom freedom has a special significance. Pavlov concluded his comments on the freedom reflex (p. 12): "Some animals as we all know have this freedom reflex to such a degree that when placed in captivity they refuse all food, sicken and die." Perhaps there is a lesson here of broad significance for those governments which would attempt to use coercion rather than positive reinforcement to develop social conduct.

SUMMARY

A discriminative stimulus is a stimulus in the presence of which a response will be reinforced and in the absence of which a response will not be reinforced. This discriminative stimulus, which "sets the occasion" for the reinforcement of a response, will generally increase the frequency of the response. Although the discriminative stimuli used in laboratory experiments are often lights or tone signals, in natural social settings people may be discriminative stimuli. They indicate the possibility of receiving desired reinforcements such as food, money, sexual activity, or social approval.

The basic procedure in classical conditioning is the pairing of two stimuli close together in time so that the second stimulus acquires the potential to elicit a response similar to the response elicited by the first stimulus. In Ivan Pavlov's early work in classical conditioning, a bell was rung just prior to placing food in a dog's mouth. The food, an unconditioned stimulus, could by itself produce salivation, an unconditioned response. After the bell was paired with the presentation of the food several times, it became a conditioned stimulus capable of eliciting salivation, a conditioned response, even when no food was present.

Classical conditioning theory places much emphasis upon the time interval between the onset of the conditioned stimulus and the onset of the unconditioned stimulus. In simultaneous conditioning, the onset of the conditioned stimulus is simultaneous with or precedes by a few seconds the onset of the unconditioned stimulus. If the conditioned stimulus precedes the unconditioned stimulus, it must also overlap the unconditioned stimulus so that both stimuli are at some time simultaneously presented to the subject. In delayed conditioning, the onset of the conditioned stimulus precedes the onset of the unconditioned stimulus by more than five seconds then overlaps it. In trace conditioning, the conditioned stimulus is begun and terminated before the onset of the unconditioned stimulus. Backward conditioning refers to those cases in which the onset of the unconditioned stimulus precedes the onset of the conditioned stimulus.

Variations in the time intervals between the conditioned stimulus and the unconditioned stimulus produce different time intervals between the onset of the conditioned stimulus and the occurrence of the conditioned response, i.e., the response latency. It is sometimes possible to use the conditioned stimulus developed in a previous experiment as the unconditioned stimulus paired with a neutral stimulus in a second experiment. If the neutral stimulus then acquires the capability of eliciting a response similar to the conditioned response in the first experiment, higher-order conditioning has occurred. Words, imagined stimuli, and probably music are examples of second-order (or third-order) stimuli. The elimination or extinction of a conditioned response often occurs if the conditioned stimulus is repeatedly presented without pairing it with the unconditioned stimulus.

Treatment procedures based upon principles of classical conditioning have been extensively used with alcoholics and homosexuals. The procedures generally attempt to pair the sight or smell of alcohol or a sexual response with a noxious stimulus such as electric shock or with nausea produced by an emetic drug. Although it is difficult to generalize from the present studies which often use different subject populations and experimental designs, it tentatively appears that the behavior-change results produced by these procedures are roughly similar to the results achieved by the more traditional, long-term psychoanalytic methods. Very much more research needs to be done, however, to determine the essential therapeutic elements of classical-conditioning procedures which sometimes appear to be remarkably effective and sometimes ineffective.

Chapter 6

Observational Learning

It was one of those common but unfortunate situations in which a patient discovers that a simple fear produces increasing social disability. The thirty-one-year-old woman had such an extreme fear of snakes that she was not only unable to be near snakes but was also unable to view pictures of snakes or watch movies which might contain pictures of snakes. Activities such as hiking or swimming were very infrequent because of her fear of encountering snakes.

She answered a newspaper advertisement requesting volunteers for an experimental study of the treatment of snake phobias at a well-known university. However, during the initial phase of this study when she was asked to enter a room which contained a caged, harmless snake, she became hysterical, cried uncontrollably, trembled, and asked to leave the study. She was then referred to a therapist at the university for more intensive, individual treatment.

During the first session with the therapist (Mahoney, 1971), she

expressed pessimism about the outcome of the therapy. She was reas-
sured and told that the treatment would be adjusted to her own pace and
ability to tolerate the fear. Training was then begun in muscular relaxation.

During the next two sessions in which systematic desensitization
was used, she made considerable progress in imagining without great fear
other people approaching snakes.

> At that point she requested moving on to the film hierarchy which consisted
> of 7 scenes of graduated interactions between adults and a 4-ft corn snake.
> Each scene was presented twice in conjunction with muscular relaxation. A
> frame-by-frame presentation of two of the scenes was initially required due
> to the client's fear of snake movements. Gradual increments in the speed of
> the film allowed movement scenes to be successively approximated. Four
> sessions were required to complete the film hierarchy.
>
> The live modeling phase consisted of the therapist interacting with a
> 4-ft corn snake while the client watched through a one-way mirror.
> Self-induced relaxation was employed and the live modeling was paced by
> client reports. After two sessions, the client graduated to participant
> modeling.[1] This technique involves a graduated sequence of modeling and
> guided participation by the client in the operations of the therapist. . . .
>
> Three sessions of participant modeling were employed. At the end of
> that time (Session 12) the client reported that she felt very comfortable in
> handling the snake and that her fear-related problems had been eliminated.
> She felt no distress at viewing pictures of snakes or at talking about them.
> At her request, a snake skin was obtained and she expressed the intention of
> framing it as a decoration for her apartment. A behavioral posttest indicated
> that she was able to pick up and handle the snake for several minutes. This
> performance was in marked contrast to her initial avoidance. She neither
> exhibited nor expressed discomfort when the snake's head was within 5 in.
> of her face. These therapeutic gains were still present at a four-month
> follow-up.

Many techniques were involved in this study: encouragement,
relaxation, systematic desensitization, and several forms of modeling.
Within the past few years, there has been a rapidly increasing interest in
the use of observational-learning procedures in the treatment of behavior
problems. In the area of phobias, observational learning, either alone or in
combination with other procedures, may be one of the most effective
techniques (Rachman, 1968). Before examining the therapeutic use of
observational-learning procedures in detail, it may be helpful to consider
some of the basic concepts of observational learning.

[1]Participant modeling will be discussed in more detail later in this chapter.

SOME BASIC CONCEPTS

The ability of one person to observe another and imitate him has been discussed at least since the time of Aristotle.[2] That imitation occurs is clear, but why it occurs is much less clear. In the early 1900s, imitation was viewed as a basic human instinct. This view then gave way to a notion that imitation was similar to a Pavlovian reflex. This view has now been replaced by a variety of theories that emphasize the positive reinforcement that follows an imitative response.

Most recently, attention has been focused upon the teaching of imitative skills as a method of understanding the process of imitation. Evidence indicates that young children do not spontaneously imitate other people but rather are taught how to imitate. In the traditional view, a child persistently repeated a sound or movement to himself because it was self-stimulating. Some years ago, it was suggested that if parents imitated the child while he was babbling, these imitations by the parents could become associated with, or substituted for, the babbling of the child (Holt, 1931). Later, when the child was quiet, babbling by the parents could evoke babbling by the child. Thus, the child learned to imitate by first being imitated.

In the past few years, the hypothetical child discussed above has been replaced by real children. Peterson (1968) has demonstrated a reliable technique for developing imitation. The experimenter shows the child a simple behavior, such as tapping the table, and then taking the child's hand, taps it on the table. This is followed by praise and food as reinforcers. After a few repetitions, the child will begin to tap his hand on the table if the experimenter merely pushes his hand toward the table and continues reinforcement. Finally, the child will tap immediately following the experimenter's tapping. The imitation of another simple behavior is then similarly demonstrated, prompted, and reinforced until the child readily imitates a variety of behaviors such as putting on a hat or ringing a bell. The general ability to imitate is thus learned.

In training procedures of this type, an interesting phenomenon has been noted: some behaviors performed by the experimenter which are not reinforced by him will nevertheless be performed by the child. This is known as *generalized imitation* (Baer, Peterson, & Sherman, 1967; Peterson, 1968). This has been difficult to explain by using conventional reinforcement theory.[3] But whether or not reinforcement is necessary to

---

[2]A historical survey of the major theories of imitation from the time of Aristotle to 1940 can be found in Miller and Dollard's book, *Social Learning and Imitation* (1941, pp. 289–318).

[3]Some explanations have been attempted. One explanation is that there is some inherently self-reinforcing quality in the imitative process. However, when reinforcement of all imitative behavior is discontinued (extinction), both previously reinforced and nonreinforced imitative behaviors rapidly

teach a child the general process of imitation, it is clear that some actions can be learned without practice or external reinforcement. A child can learn how to put together a simple puzzle merely by watching another person do it. He may not require any practice to do it. Bandura (1969, p. 133) suggests:

> When a person observes a model's behavior, but otherwise performs no overt responses, he can acquire the modeled responses while they are occurring only in cognitive, representational forms. Any learning under these conditions occurs purely on an observational or covert basis. This mode of response acquisition has accordingly been designated as no-trial learning (Bandura, 1965a), because the observer does not engage in any *overt responding trials,* although he may require multiple *observational trials* in order to reproduce modeled stimuli accurately. . . . According to the author's formulation, observational learning involves two representational systems—an *imaginal* and *verbal* one. After modeling stimuli have been coded into images or words for memory representation they function as mediators for subsequent response retrieval and reproduction.

To understand the processes of observational learning, it is important to distinguish between the acquisition of a response and the performance of a response.[4] A response can be learned, in the sense that it is "available," but not displayed. A person can read about hijacking an airplane; he can learn how to do it, but this does not guarantee that he will actually do it. In fact, if he happens to observe a hijacking during which the hijacker is fatally shot, the observer might be even less likely to hijack an airplane than before he observed the hijacking. According to Bandura and Walters (1963, p. 57), "The *acquisition* of imitative responses results primarily from the contiguity of sensory events, whereas response consequences to the model or to the observer have a major influence only on the *performance* of imitatively learned responses."

The effects of observing modeled behaviors can be placed into four broad categories. (1) The *modeling effect* occurs when the observer learns a new response that was not previously in his behavioral repertoire. (2) The *response-facilitation effect* refers to an increase in the frequency (or other characteristics) of a response which is already in the observer's

---

decline in frequency. Another explanation is that the child has not adequately discriminated between imitative behaviors which will be reinforced and those which will not be reinforced. Some support for this latter explanation may be found in the fact that non-reinforced imitative behaviors are acquired more slowly or are extinguished more rapidly than reinforced imitative behaviors, thus suggesting that the child may be in the process of making some discriminations (Zahn & Yarrow, 1968). However, not all studies show similar results. It appears that the minimal, necessary, and sufficient conditions for the production of imitation have not yet been determined.

[4]This distinction was clearly developed by Tolman (1951).

repertoire and which is not socially prohibited. (3) The *inhibitory effect* refers to a decrease in the frequency (or other characteristics) of a response which is in the observer's repertoire and which is socially prohibited. (4) The *disinhibitory effect* refers to an increase in the frequency (or other characteristics) of a response which is in the observer's repertoire and which is socially prohibited.[5] In the analysis of the response facilitation effect and inhibitory or disinhibitory effects, the term *response* can be used to refer to either a response identical with the one observed or one within the same general class as the response observed, e.g., color-preference responses or aggressive responses.[6]

MODELING EFFECT

Modeling has, of course, been used frequently to develop new physical skills in the observer. Tumbling (Harby, 1962), knot tying (Roshal, 1949), and the assembly of automobile parts (Maccoby & Sheffield, 1957) are typical of the types of physical skills taught by modeling. Modeling seems to be most effective if the observers rehearse the behaviors that are being modeled and are provided with information regarding the accuracy of their imitation. For some simple mechanical skills, well-prepared and properly used films may be nearly as effective, or equally as effective, as live models (VanderMeer, 1945; Harby, 1962).

It was previously mentioned in Chapter 3 that modeling may be more effective than operant shaping in producing some types of new behavior. Bandura (1969, pp. 143–144) makes note of this.

> Apart from the question of survival, it is doubtful if many classes of responses would ever be acquired if social training proceeded solely by the method of successive approximations through differential reinforcement of emitted responses. The technique of reinforced shaping requires a subject to perform some approximation of the terminal response before he can learn it. In instances where a behavioral pattern contains a highly unusual combination of elements selected from an almost infinite number of alternatives the probability of occurrence of the desired response, or even one that has some remote resemblance to it, will be zero. Nor is the shaping procedure likely to be of much aid in evoking the necessary constituent

---

[5]These four categories correspond to those suggested by Bandura and Walters (1963) and Bandura (1969) which have found general acceptance. The terms "inhibition" and "disinhibition" are roughly analogous to, but not identical with, these terms as used in classical-conditioning theory (cf. Chapter 5).

[6]Some investigators have suggested that the term *imitation* refers to the production of behavior which is similar to the observed behavior. The term *observational learning* refers to the production of behavior which is the result of observation but which may or may not be similar to the observed behavior (e.g., Rachman, 1972).

responses from spontaneously emitted behavior. It is highly doubtful, for example, that an experimenter could teach a mynah bird the phrase "successive approximations" by selective reinforcement of the bird's random squeaks and squawks. On the other hand, housewives establish extensive verbal repertoires in their feathered friends by verbally modeling desired phrases either in person or by means of recordings. Similarly, if children had no exposure to verbalizing models it would probably be impossible to teach them the kinds of verbal responses that constitute a language. In cases involving intricate patterns of behavior, modeling is an indispensible aspect of learning.

A study by Luchins and Luchins (1966) has compared the effectiveness of learning by a trial-and-error method with modeling. The subjects were required to learn a complex, social ritual that involved taking a book from a bookcase, walking around a table, and placing the book on the table in an unusual manner. This ritual had aspects that were sensible and useful and some that were not.

In general, this study indicated that modeling was far superior to merely informing the subject that he had correctly performed parts of the ritual. Use of a model while giving the subject information about the parts he performed correctly was more effective than modeling or information alone. Although a technically correct shaping procedure was not attempted in this study, in view of the other results, it would probably not have been as effective as modeling. As might be expected, actions that appeared to be sensible in terms of reaching the final goal were learned more rapidly than those that did not appear sensible. Without modeling, some of the subjects in the study (college students) never learned the required behaviors.

It is very likely that modeling is a more efficient procedure for producing some new behaviors than is shaping, especially if the new behaviors involve elements that are not often performed by the subject. But, when the subject is not cooperative or not interested in imitating the behaviors of the model, then a shaping procedure may be needed to obtain the necessary attention from the subject. In the case of shaping the attendance of delinquents for interviews at a church (Chapter 3), showing the delinquents how to calculate the needed time for travel and how to use the subway would not alone have been effective. These behaviors were already available to the delinquents but not integrated into a behavioral pattern or a smoothly functioning sequence of responses. To help accomplish this integration, shaping provided reinforcement and positive feedback for small increments of response integration.

It is possible to combine some of the characteristics of shaping with modeling. In learning how to lift weights, for example, the student may observe the instructor perform small segments of the behavior, then try himself. The instructor can immediately reinforce proper movements and provide additional guidance by modeling the difficult elements. A combined procedure somewhat similar to this has been used in the treatment of phobic behavior and will be discussed later in this chapter.

In social situations in which a person is uncertain of the new behavior required, imitation of an appropriate model may be very helpful in developing suitable behavior. The model the observer selects is, of course, crucial to his success in the situation. Writers on social etiquette usually advise the guest to watch the host or hostess at a dinner party to determine the appropriate use of silverware and finger bowls. Of course, not all of the behavior of the host is to be imitated, especially if the host makes a standing toast to the guests. Social roles often determine the boundaries of the behaviors to be imitated. The employee may imitate the hard work and enthusiasm of his employer but he may not write company checks without serious social consequences. In young children, imitation frequently occurs without social-role limitations as when the child calls his mother by her first name or attempts to discipline a sibling who is younger.[7]

The importance of imitation in learning the behaviors required in certain social roles is often illustrated by referring to the behaviors that a delinquent must acquire in order to be a good, middle-class student, employee, or patient. He must learn to keep appointments, to reply when spoken to, and to be polite. Equally important, he must avoid emitting some behaviors such as "cracking" his knuckles, carving his initials in the furniture, and using certain profanities. Some of these behaviors are apparent; the delinquent in these instances can merely be told what to do or what to avoid doing. Some of the required behaviors, however, are not so obvious, such as asking the employer for help or apologizing for a mistake. In situations that require these behaviors, modeling as well as instruction may be useful.

Although the image of a socially advancing, upwardly mobile delinquent may be pleasing to many of us, the importance of imitation might be better illustrated by a less common example of downward social movement. Behavior-change procedures should be equally applicable. Imagine the difficulty of a middle-class, suburban housewife attempting to place an illegal bet in a working-class neighborhood with the hope of

---

[7]Perhaps it should be noted here that there is uncertainty about the similarities or differences between imitation and identification. After reviewing the various criteria that have been used to define identification, Bandura (1969, p. 119) notes: "Indeed, if the diverse criteria enumerated above were seriously applied, either singly or in various combinations, in categorizing modeling outcomes, most instances of matching behavior that have been traditionally labeled imitation would qualify as identification, and much of the naturalistic data cited as evidence of identificatory learning would be reclassified as imitation."

winning some "easy" money. Her first problem is deciding whether she will put money on the horses, dogs, or sports events or whether she will play the "numbers" or "policy." If she decides to play the "numbers," she has to find out where to go to place her bet with a "writer." She will then have to know how the three numbers each day are selected and reported (e.g., the United States Treasury balance of clearinghouse totals or the total amount of money wagered by the pari-mutuel method on certain races at a specific track). Assuming that she gets this far in the process, she must then decide whether she wants to redeem her ticket or B/R slip at a cashier or by runner if she should happen to win (very unlikely). There are also problems such as when to go into town, what to wear, how to avoid verbal or physical abuse, and how not to appear as though she were a member of a state commission investigating organized crime. Without intensive on-the-job training, she would very probably fail and be regarded by the skilled bet makers as grossly inept. It would be very helpful if she had a successful and understanding delinquent as a model and guide.

In psychotherapeutic settings, the therapist often inadvertently models behavior that he would like the patient to display. It is generally recognized that in the course of successful treatment patients tend to acquire the values and mannerisms of their therapists (Rosenthal, 1955; Strupp, 1960). A likely mechanism of this learning is imitation. Mowrer (1966, p. 455) has commented, "Only in a situation in which the so-called patient is encouraged to become as much like the so-called therapist as possible can we look for maximally rapid and maximally enduring modification."

TREATMENT OF PHOBIAS

Although there is rapidly increasing recognition of the potential value of observational learning in the treatment of a variety of behavioral disorders, its most frequent use has been in the treatment of phobias. In this area it has shown exceptional effectiveness. Much of the present research follows the work of Geer and Turteltaub (1967) and Bandura, Grusec, and Menlove (1967). The study by Geer and Turteltaub involved three groups of high-fear subjects: one group observed a model who acted very calmly while approaching a snake, the second group observed a model who acted quite frightened, and the third group spent an equivalent amount of time alone in a room. The subjects who observed the calm model later approached the snake much more closely than the control-group subjects. The subjects who observed the frightened model approached the snake less closely than the control-group subjects.

In a similar study, but more extensive, Bandura, Grusec, and

Menlove (1967) assigned young children who were frightened of dogs to four different experimental procedures. One group observed a model who interacted with a dog in a fearless and increasingly direct manner. This observation took place in a very pleasant party context. The second group also observed the same graduated-modeled performance but in a neutral context. The third group observed the dog in a positive context but without a model, and the fourth group participated in pleasant activities but did not see the model or the dog. The children who observed the model later displayed significantly more approach behaviors toward the experimental dog (and also toward a dog they had not previously seen) than the children who had not observed the model. Modeling in a positive context was the most effective method.

In a subsequent study that sets a standard of excellence in research design, Bandura, Blanchard, and Ritter (1968) compared the relative effectiveness of modeling and systematic desensitization in the reduction of snake phobias in adolescent and adult subjects. During the initial phase of the study, the subjects were tested and assigned to one of four groups. In the first group, the subjects were exposed to a film of various models engaged in progressively closer interactions with a large snake. This treatment situation, labeled *symbolic modeling,* involved two additional features. The subjects were taught deep relaxation and they controlled the presentation of the film. When a modeled scene produced anxiety, they were instructed to reverse the film, reintroduce deep relaxation, and then review the scene. This was to be continued until all anxiety to the scenes was thoroughly extinguished.

The second group received a treatment known as *participant modeling* or *contact desensitization.*[8] The method used with this group has been described by Bandura (1969, p. 185):

> In the application of this method of the elimination of snake phobia, at each step the experimenter himself performed fearless behavior and gradually led subjects into touching, stroking, and then holding the snake's body with first gloved and then bare hands while he held the snake securely by the head and tail. If a subject was unable to touch the snake after ample demonstration, she was asked to place her hand on the experimenter's and to move her hand down gradually until it touched the snake's body. After subjects no longer felt any apprehension about touching the snake under these secure conditions, anxieties about contact with the snake's head area and entwining tail were extinguished. The experimenter again performed

---

[8]The meanings of the terms participant modeling and contact desensitization do not yet seem to be stabilized in the literature. As used here, participant modeling involves the demonstration of a behavior and the guidance of the observer through it. If it additionally involves physical contact between the model and observer, it is labeled contact desensitization.

the tasks fearlessly, and then he and the subject performed the responses jointly; as subjects became less fearful the experimenter gradually reduced his participation and control over the snake until subjects were able to hold the snake in their laps without assistance, to let the snake loose in the room and retrieve it, and to let it crawl freely over their bodies. Progress through the graded approach tasks was paced according to the subjects' apprehensiveness. When they reported being able to perform one activity with little or no fear, they were eased into a more difficult interaction.

The third group of subjects received a standard form of systematic desensitization in which deep relaxation was paired with a hierarchy of imaginal representations of snakes (see Chapter 2). The fourth group was a control group that did not receive any form of treatment.

To summarize the results, the subjects in the control group remained unchanged in their approach responses to a snake as measured by behavioral tasks such as looking at it, touching it, and holding it in their laps. Next in order of improvement came the systematic-desensitization group, the symbolic-modeling group, and then the participant-modeling (contact-desensitization) group. This latter group showed markedly more improvement than the other groups with snake phobias eliminated in 92 percent of the subjects.

The study was not yet completed, however. In order to determine whether the partial improvement shown in some subjects was a deficiency in the treatment method or the subjects, all persons who failed to complete the terminal task of handling the snake were given the live-modeling-with-participation treatment (contact desensitization). Within a few brief sessions, all of these subjects, regardless of the severity of their prior avoidance, were able to handle the snakes. The results are presented in Figure 6-1.

A follow-up assessment conducted one month later indicated that the therapeutic changes had been maintained and that the behavioral improvements had generalized to natural settings. For example, the subjects were now able to participate in recreational activities that were formerly limited because of their fear of snakes.

This study has led to a series of investigations aimed at determining the critical factors that account for the effectiveness of procedures that involve the joint participation of the subject and model. Ritter (1969a) compared the effectiveness of contact desensitization with demonstration-plus-participation (no physical contact with the therapist) and demonstration alone. In the contact-desensitization condition, the subjects who were severely fearful of heights were first shown the climbing task by the therapist who acted as a model. The therapist then assisted the subjects with response replication by providing whatever physical con-

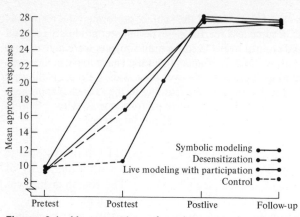

Figure 6-1 Mean number of snake-approach responses performed by subjects before and after (posttest) receiving different
treatments. Control subjects were subsequently administered symbolic-modeling treatment without relaxation. All subjects in the
desensitization, symbolic-modeling, and treated-control conditions
who failed to perform the terminal approach behavior were then
given the live modeling and guided participation treatment (post-
live). The snake-approach behavior of subjects in all four groups
was measured again in a follow-up study conducted one month
later. A. Bandura. *Principles of Behavior Modification.* New York:
Holt, 1969. P. 188.

tact was appropriate during the task, such as walking alongside the
subject with her arm around the subject's waist. Initially the subjects
could also hold onto a rail or wall, but gradually these supports as well as
therapist contact were faded out.

In the demonstration-plus-participation condition, the therapist first
demonstrated the climbing tasks then guided the subject verbally while
standing alongside or behind. There was no physical contact with the
therapist. In the demonstration-alone condition, the subject observed the
model and then performed the task. In all of these conditions, the pace of
the treatment was based upon the subjective feelings of the subject. A
new, more difficult task was not attempted until the subject felt fairly
comfortable in the assigned task.

Both the contact desensitization and the demonstration-plus-
participation groups improved significantly. The demonstration-alone
groups did not significantly improve. Contact desensitization was clearly
more effective than demonstration-plus-participation. There were no
significant changes, however, in the subjects' subjective ratings on a
fear-survey schedule. Both the failure to obtain changes on this subjec-
tive-measurement scale and the failure of the demonstration-alone proce-

dure to produce performance changes were attributed to the brevity of the treatment. Finally, it may be noted that unlike systematic desensitization procedures, there was no deliberate effort to induce relaxation as a part of the treatment method. This may also account for some of the failure to obtain significant changes on the fear-survey schedule.

Using a participant-modeling procedure similar to that developed by Bandura, Blanchard, and Ritter with snake-phobic subjects, Rimm and Medeiros (1970) specifically tested the importance of relaxation in participant modeling. They found that the effects of relaxation-plus-participation modeling did not differ significantly from the effects of participant modeling without relaxation, but that both of these procedures were significantly more effective than relaxation alone which was not significantly better than no treatment. The improvement in the subjects' performance remained stable over a one-month follow-up period. In a more clinically oriented, therapeutic setting, Piaget and Lazarus (1969) have successfully used a participant-modeling procedure which involves role playing and role reversal with a graded series of tasks by the patient and therapist.

It would appear that the prompting of demonstrated-approach responses by the therapist and the reinforcement of nonfearful responses are important factors in the success of this type of treatment (Callahan & Leitenberg, 1971). The presence of the therapist is also helpful (Barlow, Agras, Leitenberg, & Wincze, 1970). The effectiveness of participant modeling, however, cannot be completely attributed to the use of a graded series of tasks with reinforcement (Rimm & Mahoney, 1969) or to placebo (expectation) effects, or to the *demand characteristics*[9] of the experiments (Lick & Bootzin, 1970). Preliminary findings indicate that multiple models observed simultaneously or serially may be more effective than one model (cf. Bandura, 1969, pp. 179–180; Ritter, 1969a, b).

In an extensive survey of studies using observational learning techniques to reduce fear, Rachman (1972, p. 385) suggests:

> The main conclusions which one can draw from the data are: Symbolic modeling produces significant and lasting reduction of fear which generalizes to similar situations and stimuli. Supplementing the symbolic modeling by participant modeling increases the extent of fear reduction. . . .
>
> Next we turn to some tentative summary statements. The therapeutic modeling effect is facilitated by a combination of audio and visual presentations; repeated practice; prolonged exposure times (both within a session

[9]Demand characteristics are those elements of an experiment that induce expectations in the subjects in regard to how they should perform to please the experimenter (Orne, 1962). Subjects typically try to figure out what the experiment is about and then deliberately conform or sometimes refuse to conform to their guesses about the research hypothesis.

and overall); the use of multiple models, the use of multiple fear situations or stimuli. The supplementary use of participant modeling facilitates the generalization of improvements and the transfer from "internal" learning to manifest behavior change. The use of relaxation training prior to or during the modeling sessions, facilitates therapeutic change. Modeling procedures are capable of producing significant, generalized and lasting therapeutic improvements in psychiatric patients; they produce larger improvements in attitudes than other behavioral methods.

MODIFICATION OF SOCIAL BEHAVIOR

Some social behaviors are matters of public concern and are, therefore, either approved or prohibited. The frequency of a socially approved behavior can be increased through modeling effects if the behavior is not in the observer's repertoire or through a response-facilitation effect if the behavior has been previously performed by the observer. In the latter case, the model's behavior probably serves as a discriminative stimulus for the emission of similar behavior by the observer. If the behavior is socially prohibited, its frequency can often be decreased through an inhibitory effect when the observer sees the model experience aversive outcomes or increased through a disinhibitory effect when the model experiences positive outcomes. The following section will briefly examine how observational learning may produce these effects within several socially important categories of behavior.

Aggressive Behavior

There is considerable evidence that the modeling of a novel aggressive behavior can evoke that behavior in observers. In a well-known study by Bandura, Ross, and Ross (1963), children who watched models act aggressively toward a toy clown by striking it with a mallet displayed this novel response much more frequently than the children who were not exposed to the models. Lovaas (1961) found that children who watched an aggressive cartoon more frequently chose a toy that permitted aggression than those children who did not watch the cartoon.

In related studies by Berkowitz and Geen (1966, 1967), male college students were first made angry with an accomplice and then shown one of three films. One film showed a prizefight scene in which the person who received the beating was depicted in the accompanying story line as a "scoundrel." The aggression in this film might therefore be considered "justified." In the second film, the same prizefight scene was shown but the story line accompanying it portrayed the person who received the beating in a more favorable light. The aggression in this film might therefore be considered "less justified." The third film was an exciting but nonagressive track-race film. After viewing the films, the subjects were permitted to give electric shocks to the accomplice. In general, the subjects who watched the "justified" aggression film gave more shocks to the accomplice than those who watched the "less justified" aggression film. Those subjects who watched the nonaggressive film gave the fewest shocks to the accomplice.

Aggressive behavior by observers can also be increased by rewarding the model for aggressive behavior (Walters, Leat, & Mezei, 1963) or by encouraging the use of aggressive language by the observers (Loew, 1967). In some studies, aggressive verbal behavior has been increased either by direct social reinforcement or by allowing the subjects to observe the aggressive verbalizations of others. On the other hand, some studies have failed to show increased verbal aggression or assertiveness merely through the use of modeling techniques.

It has been shown that an artificially constructed group norm in a laboratory can be passed on from one group of subjects to another (Jacobs & Campbell, 1961) and that reinforcement by a peer group can maintain aggressive behaviors and direct the aggression toward specified target persons (Patterson & Anderson, 1964). A process similar to this that perpetuates the aggressive norms of behavior in delinquent groups may be occurring in natural settings on street corners.

Procedures for inhibiting aggressive behavior have not been so well defined or developed. Generally, four major types of procedures are used: punishment of an aggressive model, punishment of the subject, catharsis, and development of competing behaviors. Punishment of a model who displays aggressive behavior has been shown in some studies to inhibit similar aggressive behavior in the observer (e.g., Bandura, 1965b; Walters & Parke, 1964). Results do not seem to be quite as firm, however, as those studies showing the disinhibition of aggression. Rosekrans and Hartup (1967) have suggested that in daily life situations children may see aggressive responses both rewarded and punished. In a study conducted to determine the effects of this inconsistency, one group of children observed a model who was verbally punished following each aggressive response. Another group observed the model rewarded following each aggressive response. A third group observed the model rewarded following one-half of the aggressive responses and punished for the remainder. A fourth group did not observe the model.

The subjects who saw the rewarded model later displayed the largest number of imitative and partially imitative aggressive responses.

---

[10]As might be expected, studies have generally found significantly more aggressive verbalizations in the fantasy material of delinquent or antisocial youths than in the material of nondelinquent youths (Lesser, 1958; Mussen & Naylor, 1954; Purcell, 1956). An exception is a study by Schaefer and Norman (1967) in which no relationship was found.

Next in order of number of aggressive responses came the subjects who saw the inconsistently punished model, followed by the subjects who saw no model, followed by the subjects who saw the model consistently punished. [11] This would generally confirm the findings of previous studies and indicate that the inconsistent punishment of a model may result in more aggressive behavior than no model or a punished model.

Wheeler and Smith (1967) found that verbal criticism of a model for aggressive behavior, by a person whom the observer considered as having high status, inhibited the observer's subsequent aggression. This occurred even though the model continued to be aggressive following the censure. They also noted that the observers whose aggression was inhibited became significantly more depressed than they were prior to the experimental intervention. A similar transition from the expression of aggression to depression is commonly found using interview methods in the treatment of delinquents (Schwitzgebel, 1964). In these interviews, the therapist is quite likely to overtly or covertly censure the expression of aggression by both the delinquent and his friends who have served as aggressive models.

Another common method of dealing with aggression is to punish the aggressor. Although the short-term effect of this may be a temporary reduction of aggression (assuming, of course, that the punisher is more powerful than the aggressor), the long-term effect may be increased aggression. Children seem more likely to remember an act of punishment than the prohibition the punishment was intended to enforce. There is some evidence that the children of parents who are often physically aggressive are more likely to be aggressive than the children of less-aggressive parents (Gordon & Smith, 1965; Bandura & Walters, 1959; McCord, McCord, & Zola, 1959). If, in addition, threats to the person's present self-esteem are combined with extensive physical punishment, the likelihood of subsequent aggressive responses by him are even further increased (Feshbach, 1964; Gold, 1958).

This does not mean that all punishment of aggression is to be avoided. Punishment may take forms other than physical force such as verbal reprimand, withdrawal of reinforcement, and social exclusion. In institutional settings, the use of brief, "time-out" periods of social exclusion following aggressive behavior has effectively reduced this behavior (Tyler & Brown, 1967). The punishment was administered swiftly, fairly, and with a minimum of physical force and hostility. When

---

[11]No consistent effects of the four experimental conditions were shown on nonimitative aggressive responses. The modeling here involved a novel aggressive response and not those typically in the subjects' repertoires.

this punishment was experimentally discontinued, aggression increased and when the punishment was reintroduced the aggression was again reduced. Because this took place in an institutional setting, the control over the subject's behavior could be much more complete than in natural settings. However, aggressive behaviors can also be reduced by parental intervention in home settings (see Chapter 4; Hawkins, Peterson, Schweid, & Bijou, 1966). Much more study needs to be done in this area.[12]

Another procedure quite often used for the purpose of reducing aggressive behavior is *catharsis,* the overt expression of an emotion. The catharsis theory involves the assumption that the expression of aggression by the patient in one setting will reduce the patient's subsequent aggression in a different setting. The patient is therefore encouraged to act aggressively in specially constructed situations such as in play therapy when the child is encouraged to hit the "mother" doll when he feels hostility toward his mother. Adult patients may be encouraged to participate in aggressive forms of recreation. Therapists who use the catharsis technique with children typically warn the parents that the child may get worse before he gets better. The question is not so much whether the patient will get worse but whether he will get better. It should be noted that this use of catharsis in play therapy is a distortion of the classical, psychoanalytical use of catharsis in the treatment of acute hysterical symptoms such as blindness or paralysis. Catharsis as traditionally used also involved the simultaneous recall of traumatic experiences associated with the hysterical symptom, and even with this recall, catharsis was not considered to bring about permanent changes in personality structure.

There is at present considerable professional disagreement regarding the effectiveness of catharsis. In an often cited study by Feshbach (1955), an experimenter requested two groups of subjects to perform tasks and while doing so insulted them in regard to their motives and skill. One group was then allowed to express aggression verbally in stories about pictures that they were shown. The other group worked on tasks that did not allow verbal aggression. Following this, both groups were given a sentence-completion test. The group that was not permitted verbal aggression showed more aggression in the phrases they used to complete the sentences. They also openly expressed more dislike of the experimenter and were more reluctant to volunteer for additional experiments.

---

[12]The discussion here has focused on the punishment of aggressive behavior following its occurrence. It might also be possible to arrange aversive consequences before the display of aggressive behavior such as just prior to the subject's striking a person, or during threatening verbalizations, or during imagined aggressive scenes (Agras, 1967).

Feshbach (1961) also suggests that catharsis will not be effective if the aggression is not of an angry nature at the time of its expression.

In a study by Kahn (1960), however, students were exposed to an anger-arousing situation and then one group was allowed to talk with a sympathetic "physician" while another group merely sat for an equivalent period of time. The group that participated in the cathartic interview later expressed significantly more anger than the group that did not have the interview and showed more physiological arousal during the recovery period. This situation is closer in structure to the usual therapeutic situation than Feshbach's experiment and may, therefore, be more socially relevant. The free verbal expression of anger does not always lead to a subsequent reduction of aggressive responses as measured by projective tests (Pytkowicz, Wagner, & Sarason, 1967).

The issue of the effectiveness of catharsis is far from settled. The short-term effects may differ from long-term effects and these remain to be studied. Surely catharsis, as usually practiced in psychotherapeutic interviews, role playing, and child therapy is open to question (Berkowitz, 1970). Bandura and Walters (1963, p. 258) place the issue in an interesting perspective.

> While therapists, educators, and parents are frequently heard to defend the exposure of children to violent television and movie material, as well as children's participation in highly aggressive body-contact sports, on the grounds that aggressive impulses will thereby be reduced, few adults in North American society are likely to argue that vicarious participation in sexual activities will bring about a decrease in the observers' sexual responses. Indeed, considerable care is taken to exclude adolescents from "restricted admission" movies, presumably on the grounds that such exposure may generate sexual excitation and premature imitative sexual behavior.

Another method that has been used to inhibit aggressive behavior is the development of behaviors incompatible with aggression by modeling such behaviors. In a study by Chittenden (1942), children observed models who exhibited both aggressive and cooperative responses to a series of interpersonal conflicts. Aggressive responses by the models led to unpleasant consequences whereas cooperative responses were rewarded. The children who viewed this modeling displayed fewer aggressive behaviors than children who did not view the models. This difference was maintained in a one-month follow-up study.

These results are corroborated by Brown and Elliott (1965) who found that the aggressive behaviors of boys in a nursery-school class were successfully reduced by ignoring aggressive behavior while directly reinforcing socially helpful behaviors. In a home setting, it may be recalled from Chapter 4, "brat" behaviors could be markedly reduced when the child's mother combined the punishment of aggressive behavior with the reinforcement of socially acceptable behaviors (Bernal, 1969).

Deviant Behavior

When the family of a delinquent boy moves to a new neighborhood in order to get him away from "bad influences," they are probably attempting to place him in a social context that encourages contact with boys who can serve as models of prosocial behavior or who at least do not reinforce deviant behavior. Although it is difficult to find any general consensus on the cause of delinquency, there would probably be considerable agreement that the social environment is an important variable. Sutherland and Cressey (1960) have proposed that criminal behavior is learned within intimate personal groups and that this includes learning both the specific techniques of crime as well as the rationalization for crime. In their terms, "a person becomes delinquent because of an excess of definitions [associations] favorable to violation of law over definitions unfavorable to violation of law" (p. 78). This statement, known as the principle of *differential association*, points out that delinquency may result not only from an exposure to delinquent persons but also from nonexposure to persons who are not delinquents.[13] It is also implied here that there will be opportunities to perform the delinquent acts that have been learned (Cloward & Ohlin, 1960). Significant relationships have been found between the exposure to deviant role-models and the number of times drunk, poor school achievement, and court convictions among high school students (Jessor, Graves, Hanson, & Jessor, 1968).

Of course, not all persons will become delinquent by exposure to criminal models, even if this exposure occurs in a situation that allows the opportunity for deviance. If this were so, the famous biblical persons who "ate among the publicans and sinners" would soon have become sinners themselves. Likewise psychologists, psychiatrists, and social workers who treat seriously disturbed patients would be likely to become patients themselves. This sometimes happens, but generally the modeling of deviant behavior by a patient does not reliably produce deviant behavior in the therapist. Imitation is determined not only by the display of behavior and its consequences but also by the personal characteristics of the models. Thus, peer-group models are likely to have much more

---

[13]Differential-association theory includes variations in the frequency, duration, priority (age of the observer), and emotional intensity of the associations as factors in predicting the influence of association with others (Sutherland & Cressy, 1960).

influence on teenagers than adult models (Buehler, Patterson, & Furniss, 1966; Levin & Simmons, 1962).

In general, models who acquire prestige (Asch, 1948), display competence (Rosenbaum, Chalmers, & Horne, 1962), and reinforce the observer (Kanareff & Lanzetta, 1960; O'Connel, 1963) are more likely to be imitated than those who do not. Male models may be somewhat more effective than female models (Rosenblith, 1959), especially in modeling aggression. Perhaps this is because masculinity tends to be associated with aggression as well as prestige and resource allocation in our culture. It appears that the model who controls resources, i.e., has power, is more likely to influence the observer than the model who consumes or utilizes resources. Brown (1965, p. 401) has suggested that power is important "because power reliably implies the possibility of enjoying resources while the enjoyment does not so reliably imply control over them." Mental patients do not command many resources desired by social workers; psychiatrists do. Therefore, although social workers may spend more time with patients than psychiatrists, they are more likely to imitate the psychiatrists than the patients.

A study by Walters, Leat, and Mezei (1963) illustrates the disinhibition of prohibited behavior. Kindergarten children were assigned to three groups after they had seen a collection of attractive toys with which they were not allowed to play. One group saw a film in which a child played with the forbidden toys and was subsequently rewarded by his mother. The second group saw the model punished for playing with the toys, and the third group saw neither of these outcomes (control group). The children in all three groups were then tested for resistance to temptation by being placed in a room alone with the toys for fifteen minutes. Children who saw the model rewarded deviated most, the control group children were next in amount of deviation, and the children who saw the model punished deviated least. Behaviors contrary to the experimentally established norm were thus disinhibited by observation of the rewarded model.

More commonly accepted social norms, such as not looking at the breast or genital areas of others, have also been disinhibited in the laboratory. Male undergraduates were shown films of nude or almost nude males and females and told that a spot of light on the film indicated where a previous subject (model) had looked (Walters, Bowen, & Parke, 1963). For some of the subjects, the spot of light moved over the bodies of the subjects, particularly near the breast and genital areas. For other subjects, the light appeared in the background of the films to give the impression that the previous subject had avoided looking at the bodies. Following this, each subject presented to himself slides which were similar to those seen in the film and his eye movements were automatically rewarded. Subjects who were exposed to the supposedly sexually uninhibited model spent a significantly longer time looking at the nude and semi-nude bodies than did the subjects who had been exposed to the model who had avoided looking at the bodies.

In public settings, behavior contrary to social norms may also be disinhibited. Freed, Chandler, Mouton, and Blake (1955) placed three signs of varying inhibitory strength on the main door of a college building. The signs read: "Absolutely No Admittance—Use Another Entrance," "You Are Requested to Enter by Another Entrance," and "Absolutely No Admittance." The first sign was the most effective in preventing people from entering the building, the second sign was next in effectiveness, and the third sign was least effective. These signs were then tested using models who either obeyed the sign or disobeyed the sign by entering the building. The greatest frequency of entrance into the building by subjects occurred with the weakest sign and with a model "planted" just ahead of the subject who disobeyed the sign. The lowest frequency of entrance into the building occurred when the strongest sign was used and the model obeyed it.

Similar results were found by Lefkowitz, Blake, and Mouton (1965) who observed persons jaywalking against a "Don't Walk" sign. Less than 1 percent of the people waiting to cross the street violated the sign. When a model dressed as a low-status person wearing patched pants and a work shirt crossed the street against the light, violation increased to approximately 4 percent. When the model dressed as a high-status person crossed the street against the light, violation increased to approximately 14 percent. Comparable results were found by Kimbrell and Blake (1958) in a study of the effects of modeling upon students who were prohibited from using a water fountain.

The likelihood of a person speeding away from a stop sign can be greatly increased by a challenge to race from another driver (model) who thus indicates his approval of a speeding violation (Sechrest, 1965). Models in high-status cars are more effective than models in low-status cars. More effective disinhibition by high-status models may occur partially because similarity to a high-status person implies a lower probability of adverse consequences.

Prosocial Behavior

Prosocial behavior, which is closely linked with "helping" others or altruism, has had a troubled intellectual history in psychoanalytic psychology. It has been seen as a reaction formation to aggression or guilt (Freud, 1946), a manifestation of oral character traits (Glover, 1925), or the result of homosexuality and castration anxiety (Fenichel, 1945).

An antidote to this view can be found in studies by Peck and Havighurst (1960) which indicate that the parents of altruistic children tend to be warm and nonpunitive. However, some support for guilt as a possible motivating factor in altruistic behavior can be found in a study by Darlington and Macker (1966) in which subjects who believed that they had harmed another person were more willing than control subjects to donate blood to a local hospital.

Modeling may also facilitate some prosocial behaviors. Fourth and fifth grade students who saw a model give away a gift certificate which he had won were more generous than those who had not observed the model. The investigators in this study (Rosenhan & White, 1967) concluded that observation plus rehearsal in giving may be necessary for the internalization of the altruistic norm.

Other studies have shown that the number of people making a contribution to the Salvation Army in a street setting can be increased by using a model who places coins in the kettle (Bryan & Test, 1967). The interpersonal attraction between the donor and the solicitor of money seems to be an important variable. The amount of money given can be influenced by the amount that the subject believes other people have given (Blake, Rosenbaum, & Duryea, 1955).

The use of a model can also increase the number of people who volunteer for experiments (Rosenbaum, 1956), use turn signals while driving (Barch, Trumbo, & Nagle, 1957), and offer to help a girl fix a flat tire (Bryan & Test, 1967). In the latter experiment, an undergraduate female student stood by a car with a flat left-rear tire and an inflated spare tire leaning against the car. This was the control condition in the experiment. The model condition was similar except for another car which was positioned approximately one-quarter mile before the control car. This car was raised by a jack under the left-rear bumper and a girl was watching a man change the flat tire.

Out of 4,000 passing vehicles, thirty-five vehicles stopped in the control condition. In the model condition, fifty-eight vehicles stopped, a statistically significant difference in favor of the model condition. Virtually all of the offers of help were from men rather than women. The social meaning of the behavior that was modeled is not clear.

> Assuming the model effect to be real, one might still argue that it was not a norm of helping that was facilitated by the model, but rather that inhibitions against picking up helpless young ladies were reduced. That is, within the model condition, the passing motorists may have observed a tempted other and thus felt less constrained themselves regarding similar efforts. Indeed,

the insistence of some people to help in spite of the imminent arrival of other aiders suggested the operation of motives other than simply helping. Indeed, while the authors did not index the frequency of pick-up attempts, it was clear that a rather large number were evidenced (Bryan & Test, 1967, p. 402).

It may be noted that even with possible motives in addition to altruism only approximately 1.4 percent of the passing vehicles stopped in the model condition.

O'Conner (1969) has demonstrated the effectiveness of a film to increase the positive social interaction of socially withdrawn nursery school children. The film used multiple peer-group models and showed a sequence of scenes of increasing social interaction. The models were warmly reinforced for their social interactions and the film was narrated by the soothing voice of a woman who described the modeling in the film and the positive consequences that followed prosocial behavior.

Preliminary work with delinquents in developing their social skills has produced some positive outcomes (Sarason, 1968). Two models acted out a scene which had been carefully planned to illustrate important points about a problem area such as applying for a job or talking to a teacher. This was followed by a discussion and then the observers, a group of six delinquent boys, took turns role-playing the various parts they had seen. As in the previous study of modeled altruism, this procedure involved rehearsal as well as observation by the subjects. Also, the models in this study, two graduate students specially interested in the field of delinquency, were well liked by the delinquents and interacted informally with them between the modeling sessions, thus permitting reinforcement for the modeled behaviors even though this was not a formal part of the experiment. The delinquents who participated in this modeling-plus-role-playing showed changes in their behaviors and attitudes. In a controlled study using matched groups of delinquents, modeling-plus-role-playing produced the largest amount of positive change, role-playing-without-modeling produced the second-largest amount of change, and no participation produced the least amount of positive change.

SOCIAL IMPLICATIONS

It has often been said that "imitation is the sincerest flattery." This depends, of course, upon the social context and who is doing the imitating. Yerkes (1934) has reported that if an experimenter "noisily and with apparent satisfaction" chews on a piece of filter paper, chimpanzees will imitate him. Fortunately, since this discovery, considerably more progress has been made relating observational learning to significant social problems. Nevertheless, current research and application, though rapidly increasing, falls far short of its social potential.

Ritter (1969) has made the very useful suggestion that "schools" could be established which would offer "courses" specifically designed to modify behaviors such as phobias, obesity, and sexual perversions. The schools could produce films and provide in vivo treatment that would be difficult or impossible for the therapist to provide. Assistants and technicians could also be trained to do "on location" work when laboratory treatment would be less efficient as in the case of a fear of crossing streets. Therapists could refer patients to the school or they could apply directly.

The concept of a school is helpful because the social roles involved, such as instructor and student, aided by professional therapists or consultants (cf. Thorpe & Wetzel, 1969) can be closely integrated into the community without stigmatizing the students as they learn to function more adequately in the community. Professional therapists, scholars, and outstanding persons in the community could serve as consultants and models.

Observational procedures would seem ideally suited to this transitional, therapeutic situation as they can be readily used in natural settings. Beyond the therapeutic potential of observational-learning techniques in the treatment of behavioral deficits, there is the broader social possibility of utilizing or developing new social roles and models that may positively enhance the quality of contemporary life. Much of the entertainment and pleasure from social life is vicarious in the literal meaning of the word, i.e., the experience of the observed person produces a similar experience in the observer.

Berger (1962) has designed a noteworthy series of experiments using a classical-conditioning paradigm that indicates the possibility of the *vicarious conditioning* of emotional responses. The subjects watched a model supposedly receiving an electric shock (the unconditioned stimulus). A buzzer (the conditioned stimulus) was sounded immediately prior to the administration of the supposed shock and the subject quickly moved his arm (the conditioned response) as though he were avoiding a shock. When the subjects who had viewed this sequence were later exposed to the sound of the buzzer, they showed a significantly greater galvanic skin response to it than did the control groups.[14] Goffman (1967,

---

[14]Less dramatically, Roshal (1949) and other investigators have found that the teaching of simple tasks is improved if the model can show the observer the task from the same perspective as the observer would see it while he is performing the task. The greater effectiveness of this observer-oriented modeling also tends to support the theory of vicarious learning.

p. 269) has described some of the occurrences of vicarious experience in modern social life:

> When persons go to where the action is, they often go to a place where there is an increase, not in the chances taken, but in the chances that they will be obliged to take chances. Should action actually occur it is likely to involve someone *like* themselves but someone *else*. Where they have got to, then, is a place where another's involvement can be closely watched and vicariously enjoyed.

The delinquents, hippies, and other youths who provide vicarious adventures for observers are among the few groups in urban settings that have maintained a vigorous, self-conscious community where the participants interact directly on a face-to-face level. The intensity of the interactions, admittedly not always pleasant, provides an excellent source of vicarious experience as evidenced by the press and television coverage of events that would be trivial except for their ability to produce vicarious arousal. Yet, ironically, these people are often unknowingly or unwillingly constrained to live ultimately unsatisfactory lives because the observers of them do not provide adequate models and transitional roles for their change and entry into more conventional society.

The use of models in a broad social sense has perhaps not received adequate attention. The development of religions often relies upon models rather than the written or spoken word. A model, if participatory interaction is allowed, can facilitate not only new behaviors but also vicarious and direct experiences for the observer—a powerful combination. The philosopher, Martin Buber (1960), has called attention to the importance of models in providing the opportunity for the development of alternative life styles. In a short, imaginary conversation written by Buber, two men are discussing a mutual acquaintance (pp. 628–630):

> "A remarkable and charming man, your friend," said the professor; "but what does he really do? I mean . . . in the intellectual sphere?"
>
> "In the intellectual sphere . . ." I answered, "H'mmm . . . in the intellectual sphere . . . he is simply there."
>
> "How do you mean?"
>
> "Well, his occupation is not, in fact, of a very intellectual nature, and one cannot really assert that he makes anything out of his leisure time."
>
> "But his thoughts?"
>
> "He contents himself for the most part with images. When they want to combine and condense into a thought, he gladly helps them and is pleased if something real comes out of them. At times, in conversation, as just now, he also shares some of these clear and fulfilled images."
>
> "Then he does not write?"

"Oh, he once confessed to me, almost against his will, that occasionally, now and then, when his thoughts congeal, he enters a few lines in a secret book, in order, as he put it, to distinguish from then on what is actually won from what is merely possible."

"Then will he perhaps eventually publish something comprehensive?"

The answer to this question is no; he does not have any such project in mind. Nor are his friends persuading him to write because "his real unity lies in his personality and only there can it exist." Although books can help to educate others; "more powerful and more holy than all writing is the presence of a man who is simply and immediately present." The inquiring professor continues to ask questions about the man:

"Then all those who are not among the friends of such a man must remain excluded from his teaching?"

"Not at all, for those who are transformed through his teaching are forthwith, one and all, apostles—even though they do not repeat anything of it, nor even proclaim the name of the teacher; as transformed men, they are apostles through their existence, and whatever they do is done in apostleship, through the essence of his teaching which they express therein. In the life of his friends, in the life of all who meet him, and thus to distant generations, immediacy is transmitted."

The "use" of the person as a behavior-change or philosophical agent has not yet found any general acceptance in our culture. Some very preliminary attempts in this direction are being made in areas such as achievement-motivation training and self-directed change utilizing group processes. These and related procedures are considered next.

SUMMARY

There have been many theories proposed to explain imitation. At the present time, it appears that the ability to imitate is learned, perhaps through the reinforcement of imitative responses. Once a child has learned how to imitate he can observe simple, new behaviors and later imitate them without any prior practice or reinforcement. Thus observational learning can be a very rapid and efficient method of learning.

The observation of modeled behavior can produce at least four results. It can result in the learning of a new behavior which the observer does not have in his repertoire (modeling effect). It can increase the frequency of a behavior the observer already has in his repertoire which is not socially prohibited (response-facilitation effect). Observation can also decrease the frequency of a behavior in the observer's repertoire which is socially prohibited (inhibitory effect). Finally, observation can increase the frequency of a behavior in the observer's repertoire which is socially disapproved (disinhibitory effect). These different effects depend largely upon the conditions under which the behavior is observed and the consequences which the behavior has for the model being observed.

Observation seems to be a very important factor in the learning of social roles whether they are socially appropriate (e.g., middle-class housewife) or inappropriate (e.g., juvenile delinquent). Observational-learning procedures combined with positive reinforcement have also been very useful in treating behavior disorders, particularly phobias. The therapeutic procedures most frequently used have been participant modeling and contact desensitization.

In regard to social behaviors, it seems fairly clear that the observation of aggressive models can increase the observer's aggression by teaching him new aggressive behaviors or disinhibiting aggressive behaviors already in his repertoire. Conversely, the punishment of an aggressive model has been found in some studies to reduce aggressive behavior in the observer. It is also possible to inhibit aggression by modeling nonaggressive behavior. There is some consensus of opinion that the frequent physical punishment of an aggressive child may subsequently result in more aggression by the child rather than less aggression. Similarly, the overt verbal expression of aggression (catharsis) may increase rather than reduce aggression.

The use of observational procedures to facilitate prosocial behavior has not been extensively studied. Models have been used to increase behaviors such as donating to a charity, volunteering for an experiment, and using turn signals while driving. The broader implications of using prosocial models in natural settings to help solve social problems or to provide constructive directions for general social development needs to be studied.

Chapter 7

Achievement-Motivation Training[1]

The techniques of behavior change discussed thus far have been closely linked to the various learning principles of operant and classical conditioning. Although these principles do not emphasize the motivation of the organism, many learning theorists consider motivation to be one of the most important factors in learning. There is clear evidence that the deprivation of food, for example, will increase some activities of animals, particularly activities related to the acquisition of food.

The concept of motivation proposed by Hull (1943, 1951, 1952) was similar to, but not identical with, concepts of positive reinforcement. A stimulus such as food was assumed to be effective because it reduced a need or drive of the organism. Motivation was thus considered a form of

[1]We wish to thank Alfred S. Alschuler for his contributions to this chapter. Source material can be found in Alschuler, A. S., *The Achievement Motivation and Development Project: A Summary and Review*, Harvard University Graduate School of Education, 1967.

drive reduction.[2] *Achievement motivation* has expanded this Hullian view of motivation to include some of the psychodynamic motivational theories of Freud and his followers. To understand achievement-motivation training, it is helpful to first understand some of the basic characteristics of achievement motivation and how it has been measured.

HISTORICAL DEVELOPMENT

The hundreds of studies on achievement motivation, or *n* Achievement as it is technically called, are largely the result of the efforts of David McClelland who, in *The Achievement Motive* (1953), developed both this theory of motivation and a new means of measuring social motives through the use of projective tests. Prior to this work, there was a commonly accepted notion, especially among psychoanalytically oriented therapists, that human motivations were determined largely during childhood and remained fixed throughout the person's lifetime. In reviewing this work, McClelland (1965, p. 322) noted two unusual sources of behavior change that encouraged him to consider more carefully whether, in fact, motivations could be changed later in life.

> Oddly enough we were encouraged by the successful efforts of two quite different groups of "change agents"—operant conditioners and missionaries. Both groups have been "naive" in the sense of being unimpressed by or ignorant of the state of psychological knowledge in the field. The operant conditioners have not been encumbered by any elaborate theoretical apparatus; they do not believe motives exist anyway, and continue demonstrating vigorously that if you want a person to make a response, all you have to do is elicit it and reward it (cf. Bandura & Walters, 1963, pp. 238 ff).[3] They retain a simple faith in the infinite plasticity of human behavior in which one response is just like any other and any one can be "shaped up" (strengthened by reward)—presumably even an "achievement" response as produced by a subject in a fantasy test. . . . Like operant conditioners, the missionaries have gone ahead changing people because they have believed it possible. While the evidence is not scientifically impeccable, common-sense observation yields dozens of cases of adults whose motivational structure has seemed to be quite radically and permanently altered by the educational efforts of Communist Party, Mormon, or other devout missionaries.

[2]Because the food does not immediately satisfy the drive, Hull later modified his view somewhat by saying that the stimuli associated with food (e.g., taste) could evoke need-terminating responses. Needs or drives were conceived as intervening variables that could be used to explain the relationship between antecedent and consequent events.

[3]In this citation, Bandura and Walters discuss operant-conditioning studies which are similar to those discussed in Chapter 4 of this book.

McClelland is basically correct in his observations, but if the concept of achievement motivation is to be useful in behavior change it must be clearly measurable.

To measure achievement motivation, McClelland made a creative integration of Freudian and Hullian theories of motivation. According to Freud, motivation is evident in the fantasy lives of individuals. Dream interpretation is one principal method psychoanalysts use to discover a person's motivations, hidden conflicts, and wishes. Henry Murray's Thematic Apperception Test (TAT) is a second, widely used method of eliciting fantasies of individuals by having them make up stories to a set of ambiguous pictures. Both of these clinical approaches, however, lacked a rigorous quantitative method of determining the strength and extent to which motives were operating in a person's life. Here McClelland integrated the Hullian experimental perspective with the Freudian view. Consistent with the Hullian notion of drive-reduction, an attempt was made to quantify human motivation objectively as reflected in TAT responses.

The first task in devising a method of measuring motivation was to vary the intensity of a human motive and to measure its effects on imagination or fantasy. Just as Hull had experimentally manipulated drive states in animals (e.g., he increased the hunger drive by depriving animals of food for varying lengths of time), McClelland began by experimentally manipulating the strength of food motivation in humans. He obtained TAT stories from groups of Navy men who differed in the number of hours during which they had gone without food. The experiments, performed at the United States submarine base in New London, Connecticut, showed that different degrees of hunger were reflected in different amounts of food imagery in the TAT stories. In other words, fantasy TAT stories could be used to measure the strength of motivation (Atkinson & McClelland, 1948).

McClelland then used the same strategy to study achievement motivation. The intensity of achievement motivation was varied by giving different instructions to groups of individuals just before they wrote their TAT stories. One group was told that people who did well on the fantasy test were creative, intelligent leaders. It was assumed that these instructions would arouse achievement thoughts. The TAT responses of this group were compared to TAT responses of a group given "neutral" instructions and to a third group who were given "relaxed" instructions. The specific kinds of thoughts which were present in the achievement group TATs and absent in the "neutral" and "relaxed" set of TATs became the operational definition of achievement motivation (McClelland, Atkinson, Clark, & Lowell, 1953).

Subsequent research with this measure of achievement motivation indicated that individuals with high *n* Achievement showed certain consistent patterns of behavior:

1 These individuals preferred situations in which they had personal responsibility for the outcomes of events rather than situations, like gambling, where events were determined by chance (French, 1958; McClelland, et al., 1953).

2 They chose goals for themselves that were realistic but challenging as opposed to goals that were either too easy or too risky (McClelland, 1958; Atkinson & Litwin, 1960; Atkinson, 1958).

3 They sought situations where they could obtain immediate, concrete feedback to determine how well they were doing (French, 1958; Moss, & Kagan, 1961).

These findings, corroborated by other research in such diverse areas as child-rearing and management, began to indicate that high-achievement motivation was a key factor in the successful strivings for excellence which characterize the entrepreneur. Achievement motivation also appeared to influence task-oriented behavior. Lowell (1952) assigned subjects to two experimental groups depending upon whether they scored high or low in achievement motivation as reflected in six imaginary stories told by the subjects. The groups were then given the task of unscrambling and rearranging letters into meaningful words. The group that scored high in achievement motivation performed at a significantly higher level on this task than the group that scored low in achievement motivation.

The relationship between achievement motivation and entrepreneurship led McClelland to study the impact of achievement motivation on the broader problem of economic development. Weber (1904) had observed the relationship between the pervasiveness of the Protestant ethic and the rise of capitalism. McClelland suggested a social-psychological interpretation for Weber's hypothesis. The Protestant ethic represented a stress upon independence, self-reliance, and hard work—the achievement values which McClelland had shown to produce entrepreneurial activity. McClelland reasoned further that increases and decreases in these cultural values should herald subsequent increases and decreases in economic activity. Potentially, this hypothesis provided a psychological explanation for the economic flourishing and decay of nations throughout history.

The research documenting this interpretation of economic history has been presented in great detail in McClelland's book, *The Achieving Society* (1961). Only two key studies presented in this book will be described here. In the first, the average economic productivity of the twelve Protestant countries in the temperate zone was compared to the average economic productivity of the thirteen Catholic countries in the temperate zone. The measure used to compare economic productivity was the kilowatt hours of electricity consumed per capita. There was a striking difference in favor of the Protestant countries. In the second key study, McClelland obtained measures of the level of achievement motivation in twenty-two countries both in 1925 and in 1950 by counting the frequency of achievement themes in samples of third- and fourth-grade reading books. Three measures of the gain in economic productivity were obtained for the period 1925 to 1950: (1) change in national income as measured in international units per capita; (2) change in kilowatt hours per capita of electricity produced; and (3) a combination of the above two measures of change. Levels of achievement motivation in 1925 and 1950 were found to be correlated with the degree of deviation from expected economic gains. The level of achievement motivation in 1925 predicted the rate of economic development from 1925 to 1950.

This striking confirmation of achievement-motivation theory was extended in several subsequent research studies. Levels of achievement motivation were measured in the literature of Spain and England from the 1600s through the 1800s. In both cases, the rise and fall of achievement motivation preceded the rise and fall of economic productivity by about twenty-five to fifty years. Similar relationships were obtained for achievement-motivation levels and economic productivity in Greece from 900 to 100 B.C. and pre-Incan Peru from about 800 B.C. to A.D. 700 (McClelland, 1961, Chapter 4).

ACHIEVEMENT-MOTIVATION TRAINING FOR BUSINESSMEN AND POTENTIAL ENTREPRENEURS

The above findings raised an interesting theoretical issue with important practical implications. Was there a causal relationship between achievement motivation and entrepreneurial behavior; and if so, would it be possible to increase an individual's achievement motivation and thereby increase his entrepreneurial success? To answer this question McClelland and his coworkers set about the task of designing a training course to increase achievement motivation. Rather than rely on any single theory of behavior change in designing the course, they chose to draw their training techniques from a wide variety of psychological theories—learning theory, education, mass media research, theories of attitude change, motivation theory, and psychotherapy. Twelve propositions were drawn from these theories to describe how the course should be designed and run (McClelland, 1965). These propositions are summarized below under four major headings: Goal-Setting, Motive Syndrome, Cognitive Supports, and Group Supports.

Major Propositions

Goal-setting The three propositions in this group focus on inducing confidence, commitment, and the measurement of change in the attainment of goals. Proposition 1 states that the more reasons the person has in advance about the possibility and desirability of change, the more likely he is to change. This notion has wide support in the psychological literature: the Hawthorne effect (in business), the "Hello-Goodbye" effect (in therapy), "experimenter bias" studies (in experimental psychology), and prestige-suggestion studies (in attitude change), among others; all support the contention that belief in the possibility and desirability of change is influential in changing a person. Among the means used to create this belief in course participants have been the presentation of research findings on the relationship of n-Achievement to entrepreneurial success, the suggestive power of membership in an experimental group designed to show an effect, and the prestige of a university. This prestige "pitch" is given before the course proper begins. Later in the course, participants make a public commitment to seeking specific achievement goals.

Proposition 8 (numbered as in McClelland, 1965) states that the more an individual commits himself to achieving specific goals related to the motive, the more the motive is likely to influence his future thought and action. Proposition 9 states that motive change is more likely to occur if a person keeps a record of his progress toward his goal. Thus, in the course, reinforcement is built into the goal-setting procedure by having course participants establish methods of measuring just how well they are doing at any given time. This is the kind of regular, concrete feedback that is especially important to people with high achievement motivation and that fits well into operant-conditioning theory (cf. Chapter 4).

Motive Syndrome A *motive*, as defined here, is a pattern or cluster of goal-directed thoughts typically associated with certain action strategies. Because both thoughts and actions occur in specific, real-life contexts, the motive syndrome is the integration of thoughts, actions, and contexts. Proposition 3 states that the more an individual clearly conceptualizes the motive to be acquired, the more likely he will be to employ that motive. In the achievement-motivation courses, therefore, participants are given the TAT and then taught to score their own stories. In this way, they learn what the achievement motive is, and evaluate just how much of the motive they have upon entering the course. After learning the scoring system, participants are encouraged to use those labels in coding their own thinking in everyday situations. Similarly, participants learn the action strategies of people with high-achievement motivation through playing illustrative games, analyzing case studies and discussing everyday life situations as a group. This portion of the course is based upon two other propositions. The more a person can link the motive to related actions, the more likely it is that the motive will be acquired (Proposition 4). The more a person can transfer and apply the newly conceptualized motive to events in his daily life, the more likely the motive will be increased (Proposition 5). These propositions derive from experimental and educational research on the generalization and transfer of training.

Cognitive Supports   The research on attitude and opinion change demonstrates that thoughts and actions can be affected through rational discussion and dialogue. Thus, to increase a particular motive, it is also important to explore rationally how that motive is consistent with the demands of reality (Proposition 2), how it will be an improvement in a person's self-image (Proposition 6), and how it is consistent with the dominant cultural values (Proposition 7). The more a person sees these consistencies and possible improvements, the more likely it is that the motive will be increased. In the *n*-Achievement courses, these connections are fostered through an extensive presentation of the research showing the relationship between *n*-Achievement and entrepreneurial success; self-confrontation, meditation, and individual counseling; and group discussions of *n*-Achievement in relation to the folklore, religious books, and the expressed values of the culture.

Group Supports   Cognitive learning and practice alone are not sufficient to increase motivation; affective factors are important as well. Thus, the *n*-Achievement courses also encourage change in affect through several different procedures. Typically, the course leaders assume a nondirective, warm, accepting role consistent with the emphasis on warmth and support of client-centered therapists (Proposition 10). Although the instructors lead discussions and often present information, generally their role is to support open exploration by course members. The choice of whether or not to employ *n*-Achievement in one's own life is left to the participants.

In addition, this emotional, personal confrontation is encouraged by giving the course in "retreat" settings which dramatize the importance of self-study (Proposition 11). Finally, emotional group supports are fostered by encouraging the group members to continue group activities. In this way, the ideas and feelings are kept salient through the new reference group after the course has ended (Proposition 12).

Application

The first achievement-motivation training course was conducted for executives of a major American corporation. The course was five days long and was given to sixteen successful middle-level managers. At first blush, this seems like something akin to selling iceboxes to Eskimos because it is difficult to imagine individuals who should be more achievement motivated than successful executives in an exceptionally successful corporation. It was felt, however, that "even a moderate increase in the strength of achievement motivation would lead to more effective performance, which would be reflected by objective measures such as rate of advancement" (Aronoff & Litwin, 1971, p. 218). To test this hypothesis, the sixteen men who participated in the achievement-motivation training course were matched with sixteen other similar executives who participated in the corporation's regular four-week management-development course. Two years later the two groups were compared on an index of advancement in the company which ranged from -1 (demotion) to $+2$ (more than one promotion in the two-year period and/or a large salary increase). The achievement-trained group moved from an average advancement of 0.55 in the two years before the course to 0.88 in the two years after the course. The management-development group showed a decrease in the rate of advancement from .64 to 0.27 during this same period. Though these results must be interpreted cautiously because of the small sample size, it appears that the achievement training produced a marked increase in advancement for the course participants at a time when the careers of their peers seemed to be tapering off.

To test the theory of achievement motivation, entrepreneurship, and economic development further, a program of research on achievement-motivation training was initiated in developing countries. Training courses were run in Spain, Mexico, Japan, Italy, and India. The Indian training courses were given as part of a research design which allowed a scientific assessment of the impact of the training on entrepreneurial behavior and economic indicators (McClelland & Winter, 1969). Seventy-six businessmen running small businesses in the towns of Kakinada and Vellore participated in a ten-day achievement-motivation training course. Table 7-1 shows how the course affected the entrepreneurial activities of these trained businessmen in comparison to similar, untrained businessmen. (Percent "active" indicates how many men reported entrepreneurial activities such as promotions or salary increases above 25 percent, starting a new business, and/or expanding the business.) In all cases, the trained business groups showed substantial and significant increases in entrepreneurial activity in the two years after training while

Table 7-1   Percentage of Entrepreneurs Classified as "Active" (+2) During Two-Year Periods.

Type of group	Before course 1962–1964	After course 1964–1966
A. Kakinada—trained in n-Achievement (N = 51)a	18%	55%b
B. Kakinada—untrained controls (N = 22)	18%	18%
C. Rajahmundry—untrained controls (N = 35)	26%	31%c
D. Vellore—trained in n-Achievement (N = 25)	17%	44%d
E. Vellore—untrained controls (N = 16)	13%	19%e
X. All trained in n-Achievement (N = 76)	18%	51%f
Y. All untreated controls (N = 73)	22%	25%

aSlight variations in the N because of deaths, unavailability of data, and so forth.

bSignificant at p < .001 by chi square analysis, group A and B difference significant at p < .01.

cDifference between controls before and after, not significant. Significant difference compared to Kakinada trained entrepreneurs, p < .05.

dSignificant at p < .05.

eDifference between controls before and after not significant. Not significant versus Vellore trained.

fSignificant at p < .001.

gDifference between group X and Y, significant at p < .001.

Source: After McClelland, D., and Winter, D. G. *Motivating Economic Achievement.* New York: Free Press, 1969, p. 213.

the control groups remained near their initial levels. In addition, McClelland and Winter demonstrated that the trained businessmen achieved significant improvements in other aspects of entrepreneurial performance. They worked longer hours, made more definite attempts to start new businesses, and actually started more businesses. They also made more investments, employed more workers, and showed greater percentage increases in the gross income of their firms. Thus, by all measures they became better entrepreneurs than their untrained counterparts and more effective than they themselves were before they participated in achievement-motivation training.

In the United States, Timmons (1971) has reported similar positive results from the application of achievement-motivation training in two programs designed to stimulate black capitalism; one in Oklahoma and one in Washington, D.C. In both programs a one-week achievement-training program produced significant increases in business activity for course participants when they were compared to untrained counterparts in their respective communities six months after the training. Timmons makes the following comments about achievement-motivation training for entrepreneurs:

1 ... it appears that the training does not achieve such results by deep-seated transformation of the motivation or personality of the individual. Rather, in numerous instances, the training affects participants by stimulating, building on, or facilitating a latent potential for entrepreneurial activity.

2 The training program has an apparent catalytic effect of providing a basis for collaborative activities in the form of joint ventures and partnerships.

3 The unusual turnaround of a business ... suggests that persistent entrepreneurial behavior, in combination with the problem-solving techniques acquired in the training course, can appreciably help to overcome complex and stubborn internal management situations.

4 Entrepreneurial training is apparently effective in generating a common concern among the trainees for community betterment as a criterion for exploring or initiating a new venture (1971, p. 81).

ACHIEVEMENT-MOTIVATION TRAINING IN EDUCATIONAL SETTINGS

At the same time that achievement-motivation training courses were being conducted to increase the entrepreneurial activity of businessmen, similar courses were being conducted to see if achievement-motivation training could measurably improve the academic achievement of under-achievers and potential school dropouts. Although correlational studies between achievement motivation and academic achievement usually show only a small positive relationship (Atkinson, 1958; McClelland, et al., 1953; Uhlinger & Stevens, 1960), it seemed that achievement training might have a positive affect on the academic performance of the under-achiever. Kolb (1965) tested this hypothesis by giving an achievement-motivation training course to twenty high school boys who attended an Ivy League special six-week summer school for under-achieving students at a university. Thirty-seven boys at the same summer school served as control subjects. A year and a half later, the achievement-trained boys had improved significantly more in their grade average than had the other boys in the summer school. The amount of change as a result of achievement-motivation training, however, was very much a function of the boys' social class. High socioeconomic-status boys showed a great deal of improvement in grade average while low-SES boys did not (see Figure 7-1). This difference seemed due to the fact that high-SES boys lived in a class environment where achievement values

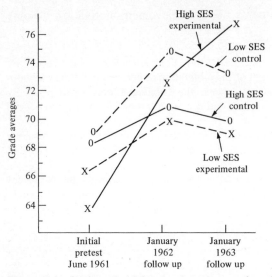

Figure 7-1 Changes in high school grades as a function of social class comparing achievement-motivation trained and control group subjects.

were encouraged while the class environment of lower-class boys did no encourage their newly acquired achievement orientation.

In a study by Alschuler (1967), two residential *n*-Achievemen courses were given to twenty-one high school juniors. These student were among a group of fifty-six students identified by school personnel a the "most difficult" students in school. Most of the students were potential dropouts and had a long history of discipline problems. Interest ingly, many of their characteristic behavior patterns were demonstrate during the residential course, to the dismay of the course leaders wh were less able to control the students than their high school teachers Given this unfavorable immediate feedback, the results of a one-yea follow-up study are particularly surprising. Only one student (4.7 percent in the experimental group dropped out of school while eight students (22. percent) in the matched control group of thirty-six dropped out of school The experimental group also showed a statistically significant increase i their average (mean) grade level. The grades of the experimental grou increased even though they tended to be taking more difficult courses tha before. No equivalent change in the level of aspiration was indicated i the course choices of the control group.

In discussing their new school and extra-curricular activities, mos of the boys who participated in achievement training described nev personal interests that led them into their activities. In contrast, very few of the boys in the control group attributed their new activities to their own motives. Instead, they cited the influence and pressure of others as reasons for their activities. Thus, they reflected a continued lack of internal motivation in contrast to the *n*-Achievement boys who showed a new sense of autonomy and control over their own lives.

SUMMARY

The achievement-motivated person is a hard-working person who seeks personal responsibility, who sets realistic but challenging personal goals and who seeks feedback about the effects of his efforts. As such he tends to do particularly well in those situations which allow for personal control and innovation, particularly entrepreneurial business situations. Historical studies have shown that the level of achievement concern in a nation's cultural values may be related to the rise and fall of the nation's economy. In Spain and England, for example, levels of achievement motivation as reflected by the nation's literature preceded the rise and fall of the country's economic productivity by about twenty-five to fifty years. On an individual level, businessmen in various countries who have received achievement-motivation training have shown significant improvements in their business performance as compared to businessmen who were not trained.

Achievement-motivation training involves an integration of individual and group tasks. The individual is asked to set clear goals of achievement for himself and is encouraged to develop confidence and commitment to these goals. He is also taught to think about achievement in everyday situations and to imitate and develop achievement strategies by reading case studies, playing illustrative games, and observing achievement-motivated role models. Much of this is done in a group context with leaders who are warm and supportive while the group encourages individual self-exploration and change.

In both business and educational settings, achievement training appears to be a workable technique for increasing achievement-oriented behavior. In these areas, motivation training has produced measurable changes in behavior that have been maintained over time. There are potentially great benefits to be gained from this approach to behavior change, both through the specific application of achievement-motivation training techniques and through the wider application of this general approach to behavior change.

Part Two

A Social-Psychological Perspective on Behavior Change

Chapter 8

Self-directed
Behavior Change

Two recent developments, one theoretical and one social, have led researchers to pay more attention to self-directed techniques of behavior change. From a social viewpoint, there is a growing demand for behavioral-science solutions to human problems. An increasing number of individuals are discovering that various forms of psychotherapy can provide viable solutions to their personal problems. In addition, social welfare agencies are seeking to change their role from that of policeman and distributor of government funds to that of an agent for individual and community development. This growing demand for the practical application of behavioral-science knowledge has made practitioners painfully aware of the fact that, using the existing techniques of behavior change which are so dependent on the change agent for their success, there can never be enough professionally trained personnel to meet this demand. So in desperation the practitioner is asking, "How crucial am I in the change process? Is it possible to develop change techniques that people can use themselves?"

Until recently, the theoretical answer was No. Therapeutic models of change, or perhaps more accurately, therapeutic custom, conceived of the patient as passive and reactive. In the tradition of the medical origins of psychotherapy, it was the doctor who was the active and curative agent in the therapeutic process. In an analysis of psychological journals, Allport (1960) found that psychologists predominantly used a reactive model of a man to interpret their results. In the psychologist's mind man was an animal who reacted to stimuli and who was controlled by his environment. The concept of will—man's ability to control and change his own behavior—was seldom found in respectable psychological theories. The idea of self-directed change appeared primarily in common-sense psychologies like those of Norman Vincent Peale and Dale Carnegie.

Currently, however, there are a great number of theorists who challenge the reactive conception of man. In 1947, Hartmann, Kris and Loewenstein and other ego psychologists began to reinterpret psycho-analytic theory by placing an increased emphasis on the power of ego processes in the rational direction and control of one's behavior. More recently, White (1961) detailed the research evidence for proactive, competence motivation in human beings—motives urging men and ani-mals to ignore safety and security, and to take on new, difficult, and challenging tasks. Of this group of men, it is perhaps Carl Rogers who has been most influential in applying the new growth-oriented theory of man to the practice of behavior change. He created a new theory and method of psychotherapy—client-centered therapy (1951). As the name implies, in *client-centered therapy* the client is the active and curative agent in the therapeutic relationship. The therapist's job is to create in a nondirective way the therapeutic conditions which will facilitate self-inquiry and personal growth in the client. By emphasizing man's creative and problem-solving abilities and his growth potential the proactive theorists imply that self-directed change is not only theoretically possible but that it occurs as a natural life process.

These two conflicting models of man pose something of a dilemma, for we cannot accept one and discard the other without doing an injustice to the data. Research evidence and common sense observations can be marshaled to support both theories—man is passive and controlled by his environment as well as creative and self-directing. The noted ethologist, Konrad Lorenz (1963, pp. 231–232) suggests, however, that this dilemma is an illusion. There is no contradiction, he maintains, between the fact that man's behavior is governed by causal stimulus-response-type laws and the fact that man strives toward goals and can modify his behavior by an act of will.

The appreciation of the fact that life processes are directed at aims or goals, and the realization of the other fact that they are, at the same time, determined by causality, not only do not preclude each other but they only make sense in combination. If man did not strive toward goals, his questions as to causes would have no sense; if he has no insight into cause and effect, he is powerless to guide effects toward determined goals, however rightly he may have understood the meaning of these goals. Increasing knowledge of the natural causes of his own behavior can certainly increase a man's faculties and enable him to put his free will into action.

Thus, in his integration of the two models of man, Lorenz suggests a methodology for self-directed change. If we can increase an individual's understanding of the psychological laws which govern his behavior, we can increase his capacity for self-direction.

INDIVIDUALLY DIRECTED CHANGE

Lorenz's suggestion has found application in the work of Goldiamond (1965). His approach is directed toward helping subjects develop self-control procedures by instructing them how to change the environments that control their behaviors. This also requires teaching the subjects some of the fundamental relationships between behavior and its environmental consequences.

Goldiamond's approach uses many concepts found in operant-conditioning theory combined with a careful consideration of the potential use of social reinforcement. The following case study by Goldiamond (1965, pp. 856–859) presents in detail many of the basic processes of self-directed change.

The husband in this case was a young man, 29, who was working on his master's degree. His wife was taking my course in behavioral analysis, and they both decided that he should come to see me about their marriage, which both wanted to maintain. The issue, as S told me, was that his wife had committed the "ultimate betrayal" two years ago with S's best friend. Even worse, it was S who had suggested that the friend keep his wife company while he was in the library at night. Since that time, whenever he saw his wife, S screamed at her for hours on end, or else was ashamed of himself for having done so and spent hours sulking and brooding. Since the events that led to the "betrayal" were an occasion for bringing home the first lesson on the consequences of behavior, we started from there.

Relation of Behavior to Its Consequences

Early discussions concerned the analysis of behavior in terms of its consequences. S's behavior provided stimuli for his wife's behavior. If he wished his wife to behave differently to him, then he should provide other stimuli than the ones which produced the behaviors he did not like. There was considerable analysis of such interactions. This conceptualization of behavior was apparently new to S, who took detailed notes; and I have discovered it to be new to many other Ss as well.

Stimulus Change

Altering the consequences of operant behavior will alter the behavior itself. However, this process may take a considerable amount of time. One of the most rapid ways to change behavior is by altering the conditions under which it usually occurs. This is called stimulus change, or the effects of novel stimuli. If the novel stimuli are then combined with new behavioral contingencies designed to produce different behavior, these contingencies are apt to generate the new behavior much more rapidly than they would in the presence of the old stimuli.

As part of the program of establishing new stimuli, S was instructed to rearrange the use of rooms and furniture in his house to make it appear considerably different. His wife went one step further and took the occasion to buy herself a new outfit.

Establishment of New Behavior

Since it was impossible for S to converse in a civilized manner with his wife, we discussed a program of going to one evening spot on Monday, another on Tuesday, and another on Wednesday.

"Oh," he said, "you want us to be together. We'll go bowling on Thursday."

"On the contrary," I said. "I am interested in your subjecting yourself to an environment where civilized chit-chat is maintained. Such is not the case at a bowling alley."

I also asked if there were any topic of conversation which once started would maintain itself. He commented on his mother-in-law's crazy ideas about farming. He was then given an index card and instructed to write "farm" on it and to attach a $20 bill to that card. The $20 was to be used to pay the waitress on Thursday, at which point he was to start the "farm" discussion which hopefully would continue into the taxi and home.

Stimulus Control

Since in the absence of yelling at his wife S sulked, and since the program was designed to reduce yelling, S's sulking was in danger of increasing. S was instructed to sulk to his heart's content, but to do so in a specified place. Whenever he felt like sulking, he was to go into the garage, sit on a special sulking stool, and sulk and mutter over the indignities of life for as long as he wished. When he was through with his sulking, he could leave the garage and join his wife. He was instructed to keep a daily record of such behavior and bring it to each session. The graph is presented in Figure 8-1. Sulking time had been reported as 7 hours on the preceding day, and, with occasional lapses, it was reported as dropping to less than 30 minutes before disappearing entirely. The reported reversals and drops were occasions for discussions.

Since the bedroom had been the scene of both bickering and occasional lapses, the problem was presented of changing its stimulus value when conjugality was involved. If this could be done consistently, eventually the special stimuli might come to control such behavior. The problem was to find a stimulus which could alter the room entirely and would be easy to apply and withdraw. Finally a yellow night light was put in, was turned on when both felt amorous, and was kept off otherwise. This light markedly altered the perceptual configuration of the room.

Records

Daily notes of events were kept in a notebook, as was the graph. S took notes of the discussions with E. These notes were discussed at each weekly session.

One of the notions which S held very strongly was that his wife's behavior stemmed from some inaccessible source within her, and that many of his own behaviors likewise poured out from himself. . . . A discussion on needs and personality ensued. "If by personality all that is meant is my behavior," he said, "then my personality changes from one moment to the next, because my behavior changes," he stated.

Figure 8-1 Graph kept of sulking behavior. I. Goldiamond. Self-control procedures in personal behavior problems. *Psychological Reports*, 1965, **17**, 851–868.

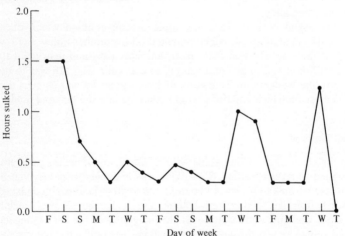

"I should hope so," I said.

"Well, what is my true personality; what is the true me?" he asked.

"Do you have a true behavior?" I asked.

He reported this as a viewpoint he had never considered; his previous training had been in terms of being consistent to his self, and of searching for "thine own self (to which he could) be true." He took extensive notes.

The next week he came in and stated: "I did something last week that I have never done before in my life. When I teach in classrooms I am able to manage my students, but when I talk to tradespeople I find I am very timid and allow myself to be cheated. Well, last week my carburetor gave out. I knew if I went to the garage they would make me buy a new one even though I have a one-year's guarantee. I sent my wife down to the garage instead. She is a real scrapper. She came back with a new carburetor. It didn't cost us a cent. Why should I have to be all things to all men? In school I control things, but with tradespeople I don't. So what?"

These weekly sessions continued during ten weeks of the summer term. After the initial training, S was assigned homework with his wife who was taking the course in behavioral analysis. The weekly discussions were centered around behavioral analysis and how it might apply to his problems.

During the course of one of the sessions, S started to talk about his childhood and was summarily cut off.

"Shouldn't I talk about this with a psychologist?" he asked. "Isn't this one of the things that interests you? Doesn't it affect me now?"

"Look," I said. "A bridge with a load limit of three tons opens in 1903. The next day, a farmer drives eighteen tons over it; it cracks. The bridge collapses in 1963. What caused the collapse?"

"The farmer in 1903," he said.

"Wrong," I said. "The bridge collapses in 1963 because of the cracks that day. Had they been filled in the preceding day, it would not have collapsed. Let's discuss the cracks in your marriage."

At the end of the period, there was no sulking in the garage and the partners were able to commune.

The above case illustrates several important aspects of self-directed change. Firstly, the change agent is a consultant to the subject, not a therapist—the subject should have the primary control over his attempts at behavior change. Goldiamond found that most of his subjects were surprisingly capable of this responsibility.

A second aspect of the procedure is the training of the subject to apply simple learning principles such as stimulus control to his own behavior. In effect, he becomes the experimenter in an attempt to control his own behavior using the principles of behavior change. There are, of course, many principles which might be selected. In a discussion of self-control, Skinner (1953) has suggested several commonly applied techniques. The person can employ physical constraint as jamming his hands in pockets to prevent nail-biting. He may change the stimulus situation by closing doors to eliminate distracting sounds or hide the box of candy. It is also possible to change motivational states such as could be done by skipping lunch so that a high state of deprivation could be developed prior to an evening dinner invitation. One can also use negative reinforcement (putting an alarm clock across the room to require getting up to turn it off), punishment (pulling one's belt very tight after overeating), or an incompatible behavior (talking about one topic to avoid another).

When arranging contingencies of *self-reinforcement*, subjects frequently make the mistake of requiring too much low-probability behavior such as studying before providing themselves with a reinforcing high-probability behavior such as eating. As in the shaping of behavior, the amount of behavior required should be gradually increased. Bandura and Kupers (1964) and Marston (1965) have shown that subjects may develop or modify their standards of self-reinforcement by observing models. Generally, those subjects who observe models setting low standards for self-reinforcement tend to be more self-reinforcing than those subjects who observe models with high standards of self-reinforcement. There is also some preliminary evidence that a subject's self-management of reinforcement contingencies may be more effective than imposed contingencies even when the magnitude of reinforcement remains the same (Lovitt & Curtiss, 1969).

A third aspect of self-directed change by an individual is the development of self-observation. This observation should include the measurement and recording of critical behaviors by the subject. To aid in this observation the subject can keep graphs and diaries which record his behavior over time and give him feedback about his progress toward his change goal. An independent person can also be used to make spot checks on the behavior to insure the accuracy of the recording. The observation of behavior is discussed in much further detail in Chapter 11.

A final important point about this process is that subjects in many cases are capable of successfully resolving what are very difficult and complex problems (e.g., marital problems) by proceeding from their own diagnosis of symptoms. Although many classic forms of psychotherapy still feel that a frontal assault on symptoms is ineffective, the evidence here suggests that, at least in some cases, the subject can, by beginning with his problem as he sees it, move toward a redefinition and resolution of that problem that brings him relief.

SELF-DIRECTED GROUPS

Another method of self-directed change involves the use of an automated form of group-sensitivity training (Berzon & Solomon, 1965; Berzon &

Solomon, 1966; Berzon, Reisal, & Davis, 1967).[1] In these groups, the trained professional leader is replaced by a tape-recorded program that guides the group members through exercises of self-exploration and self-improvement. The goal of the program, called PEER (Planned Experiences for Effective Relating), has been to develop therapeutic techniques which require little professional supervision so that therapy can become readily available to populations who have been unable to afford it.

PEER's general purpose is to help people learn to relate more fully and effectively to the world around them. To accomplish this, the program provides a series of structured opportunities for each participant to express more easily his genuine feelings and receive the genuine feelings of others; to inquire more actively into his own experience; and to try new behaviors in the group. These opportunities are to enable the individual to increase his awareness of the choices available to him, understand better his functioning in groups, and gain more control over interpersonal events.[2]

To make the best use of the resources that the participants bring with them, PEER guidelines emphasize personal strengths rather than weaknesses. The potentialities of the group members are discussed more than their deficiencies. The members of the group are to learn through the immediate, shared experience of the group to which all members contribute. Finally, the group is to conduct its own sessions using PEER guidelines, thus avoiding dependency upon a leader.

The program consists of ten one-and-a-half-hour sessions, each of which begins with tape-recorded instructions. The tape continues to run throughout the session to allow intervention with additional instructions during certain exercises. Several of the sessions are briefly described below:

Session 1—First Encounter Microlab

This session utilizes the concept of the compressed-time microlab, in which there are a series of short, timed meetings and a variety of activities designed to bring the participants into confrontation with one another. Activities include:

Impressions in which group members stand in a circle and, one at a time, each individual goes around the circle, stopping in front of each

---

[1]Only self-directed sensitivity groups are discussed here. Other forms of groups such as therapy groups, T-groups, and encounter groups are not discussed. Descriptions and discussions of these groups can be found in Cooper & Mangham (1971), Golembiewski & Blumberg (1971), Lubin & Eddy (1970) Bradford, Gibb, & Benne (1964), Schein & Bennis (1965).

[2]The PEER goals are based upon those defined by Warren G. Bennis (1962) in "Goals and Meta-Goals of Laboratory Training."

person. The instruction is to touch the person to make contact; look directly at him; and tell him your impression of him.

Break-in in which group members stand in a circle and one at a time each individual steps outside the circle and has to break in in some way—to become part of the in-group. The other group members are instructed to keep the person from breaking in.

Rolling in which the group members stand in a circle and one at a time each individual goes to the center of the circle, relaxes as completely as he can and allows himself to be passed around by the other group members—literally putting himself in their hands.

At the beginning of each of these activities, the narrator, on the tape, relates the activity to a personal growth issue, such as honesty, affiliation, trust, and so on.

After each of these activities, a timed discussion period is provided in which participants are encouraged to discuss their feelings about what they just did.

Session 2—Ground Rule

A ground rule is presented emphasizing the importance of expressing feelings, and of learning from the immediate, shared, "here and now" experience of the group. The rule is (a) to tune in to what is happening inside yourself and in the group and (b) to talk up about it. Examples of tuned-in and tuned-out groups are presented on the tape. Group members pair off to practice this kind of tuned-in interaction, then later reassemble as a total group to discuss what has happened.

Session 3—Feedback

Information is presented regarding the importance of giving and receiving feedback in the group. Definitions of facilitative and nonfacilitative feedback are given, and examples are given on the tape. Group members then practice giving and receiving facilitative feedback in a go-around exercise.

Session 4—Progress Report

Concepts presented in the three previous sessions are reviewed on the tape, and group members are asked to report to themselves on how they are doing relative to the ground rule, giving and using feedback, and so forth.

Session 7—Descriptions

Participants are asked to go around, one at a time, and describe the other group members metaphorically—as an animal, a piece of furniture, a car, etc. They are asked to tell everything they can about what they are describing, including how they feel about it. Examples of this kind of metaphorical description are given on the tape.

Session 9—Giving and Receiving

Participants are asked to select three people who have had the most trouble letting the other group members get close to them. These three people then go, one at a time, to the center of the circle. The other group members go, one at a time, to the person in the center and nonverbally express the positive feelings they have toward him. The person in the center is instructed to receive this expression without returning it—to have an undiluted experience of receiving, without giving back.

After the three people, and anyone else who wishes to, have taken their turn, the group members discuss what has happened and how they feel about it.

Session 10—Last Encounter Microlab

This session again involves a series of timed meetings, with varied activities. As in Session 1, the group members do impressions and rolling, each of which is followed by a discussion of what happened and how people felt about it. Opportunity is provided for participants to focus on how group members have changed in the PEER group. It is then suggested that they use the rest of the session to take care of unfinished business and to say good-bye to each other.

Early in the research on self-directed groups, professionals were quite concerned that groups without professional leaders might produce psychiatric casualties of one sort or another. As a result, early groups were carefully observed in one-way observation rooms (Berzon & Solomon, 1966). These observations and interviews with participants in the groups revealed that none of the self-directed group members were injured by the experience and several seemed to feel that they had learned from it. Rather than being more dangerous than professionally led sensitivity-training groups, the process of the self-directed groups seemed somewhat more tame.

To test more systematically the differences between professionally led and self-directed groups, an experiment was designed to assess the effects of the two types of groups. Members of six professionally led eight-man groups and six self-directed eight-man groups were compared on such variables as changes in psychological test scores and level of intrapersonal exploration. No differences were found between the two types of groups. Berzon and Solomon (1966, p. 492) concluded that "The presence or absence of professional leadership did not significantly effect the group's ability to establish facilitative conditions, nor the ability of most of its members to engage in the therapeutic work in a meaningful way." In a more recent study, participants in the PEER program have been compared to no-treatment controls (Berzon et al., 1967). The study was conducted with two different populations, law offenders in a county honor camp, and college students. The results indicated that PEER participants in both groups showed significant positive change in their self-concept while control subjects showed no change in self-concept during the same time period.

There is little doubt that the number of self-directed groups has rapidly increased during the past few years. Many self-help psychotherapy groups operate without the explicit use of recognized behavior-change principles and some groups appear to be effective in cases where professional treatment has failed (Hurvitz, 1970). Although the future direction of these groups is uncertain, they offer considerable potential for the development of new behavior-change techniques with broad, public applicability.

SELF-CHANGE THROUGH SELF-RESEARCH

Another approach to self-directed change was "invented" when a young fellow in a delinquency project (Schwitzgebel, 1967) approached the experimenter with a problem—he was overweight and as a result he was ignored by the girls and ridiculed by his peers. To make matters worse, he had an irresistible attraction to the ice cream parlor located conveniently on his path home from school. "How can I stop eating ice cream and lose weight?" he asked. Beleaguered by many other requests and demands on his time, the experimenter suggested that the boy try to change himself. He helped the boy set up a graph to record the results of his efforts. This involved plotting the amount of ice cream eaten each day. To everyone's surprise, the boy was quite successful in his efforts. In the course of three months, he controlled his ice-cream-eating habits and began to lose weight. His graph of the amount of ice cream eaten is shown in Figure 8-2. The dotted trend line shows the decline in amount of ice cream eaten over the course of the project.

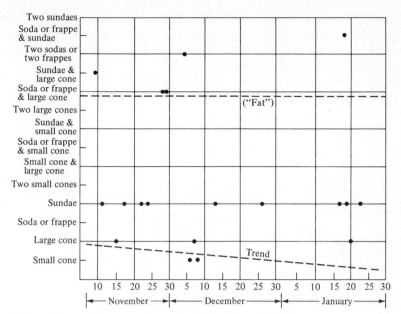

Figure 8-2 Incidence of ice cream consumption by one subject. R. K. Schwitzgebel, R. L. Schwitzgebel, W. N. Pahnke, & W. S. Hurd. A program of research in behavioral electronics. *Behavioral Science*, 1964, **9**, 233–238.

When shown the graph, the experimenter asked about the soda and sundae eaten on January 17. "That," he said, "was a celebration to show myself that I had beat the habit." The remark was indicative of the self-confidence that the boy seemed to gain from proving to himself that he could control his own behavior, a self-confidence that manifested itself in his relations with his peers. In many ways, the boy's general gains in self-confidence and self-control seemed much more important than his specific mastery of the ice cream habit. Successfully controlling one aspect of his behavior seemed to hold forth the promise of continued self-mastery and self-direction.

Intrigued by this rather dramatic and unexpected success, Schwitzgebel and Kolb began to encourage others to attempt self-directed change projects. A great number of cases were collected to document attempts to change sexual behavior, study habits, anxiety, shyness, smoking, and other behavior problems. (An analysis of some of these cases is reported in Schwitzgebel, 1964.) In many cases, subjects reported some degree of success with the self-research method and in some cases the method seemed totally successful. These case studies seemed to support two principles. The first principle: under proper conditions, proactive forces emerge in individuals, permitting experimentation with new behavior and striving toward new goals. Evidence for proactive motivation has been presented by White (1959), Harlow (1953), Rogers (1951), and others. Maslow (1954) has suggested that motives for personal growth and self-actualization emerge when lower-order physiological, safety, relatedness, and ego needs are satisfied to a reasonable degree. It appears that conditions can be created that allow some individuals to set goals for themselves and to achieve these goals.

The second principle: changes in behavior are most likely to be permanent if the process of change is seen by the individual to be under his own control. The individual should feel that he, and not some external agent of change, is responsible for the change that occurs. It is generally believed that true psychotherapeutic change does not occur until the patient works through his dependence upon the therapist and achieves self-direction. Experiments on cognitive dissonance provide some evidence for the importance of self-direction in attitude change. These experiments indicate that attitude change is greatest and most enduring when the person feels that he has freely chosen to alter his point of view (Secord & Backman, 1964). Recognizing the importance of self-direction in personality change, self-help societies like Alcoholics Anonymous and Synanon (for narcotics addicts) have made the principles of personal responsibility and voluntary commitment to change a central part of their ideology.

To examine these principles and to understand more about the dynamics of self-directed change, a series of experimental investigations have been conducted. In the first study by Zachs (1965), one half of the college students who responded to a "Do you want to stop smoking?" ad in the newspaper recorded on a graph the number of cigarettes they smoked each day and reported their results each week to the experimenter. These students' results were compared to the other half of the respondents to the ad who were told to try to stop in any way they wanted. At the end of eleven weeks, students using the self-research graph showed a significant 53 percent decrease in number of cigarettes smoked while the control subjects (those who did not record smoking) showed only a 17 percent decrease. A one-year follow-up showed that the students using the self-research method were still smoking significantly less than control students. This study suggested that systematic goal-setting and the recording of progress facilitated goal achievement.

Further studies of self-directed change were conducted with students participating in sensitivity training groups (Kolb, Winter, & Berlew 1970; Winter, Griffith, & Kolb, 1968; Kolb & Boyatzis, 1970). As part of his participation in these groups, each student was encouraged to reflect on his own behavior and to select a limited and well-defined goal which he would like to achieve. He then kept a continuing and accurate assessment of his behavior in the area related to the change goal. This assessment generally took the form of a graph which measured progress toward the goal day by day. In some cases, ratings by peers or objective counts (e.g., "number of times I spoke today") were plotted on the graph; in other cases, the students simply rated their progress on a 1 to 10 scale. At the end of the training period, each student wrote a final report that analyzed how successful he was in achieving his goal. The training-group leaders also rated each student on his success in achieving his goal. By comparing students who were successful and unsuccessful in achieving their change goal according to these two criteria, three critical aspects of the self-directed change process were identified: (1) the personality of the individual who undertakes the self-directed change project, (2) the process of goal-setting, and (3) the information feedback he receives about his project.

Personality Factors   The ideal self-concept and real self-concept of successful and unsuccessful changers was assessed by analyzing two essays written by each subject describing "How I would like to be" and "How I am now." The ideal self-descriptions of successful changers were characterized by a pattern of thinking which indicated a statement of personal goals coupled with the recognition that these goals were not yet achieved. This pattern was called *conditional desire* since its most common manifestation was statements in the conditional tense; e.g., "I would like to be a leader." The ideal self-descriptions of unsuccessful subjects, on the other hand, showed little of this pattern of thinking. Instead, these essays were characterized either by current self-descriptions ("I am a leader") which involved no projection of an ideal state or by statements of an ideal state which implied no recognition that the state might not be achieved ("I will be a leader"). This pattern was called *description of essence.*

The real self-concept essays of unsuccessful changers indicated a pattern which was called *identity diffusion* after Erikson (1959). This pattern was characterized by: (1) concern with reality, (2) feelings of playing a role, (3) vagueness about others' perception of oneself, and (4) indecisiveness and lack of conviction. This pattern was not present in the real self essays of successful changers.

These findings were interpreted in terms of congruity theories of attitude change (Brown, 1965) which suggest that the motivation for self-directed change comes from the dissonance between one's current self-image and one's ideal self-image. Unsuccessful changers do not think about goals in a way that allows them to experience this dissonance and thus they do not strive to reduce it. In addition, the identity diffusion of unsuccessful changers produces a lack of clarity about the self at the present time which would tend to reduce felt dissonance.

The Process of Goal-Setting   A number of characteristics of the initial goal-setting process have been identified as important for success-ful self-directed change.[3] The very process of consciously setting a goal seems to facilitate goal achievement. Individuals change more in those areas of their self-concept that are related to change goals they set for themselves than they do in those areas which are unrelated to their goal. This difference is not due to the choice of a goal that is easy to achieve. Once a goal has been set, an individual's success in achieving it seems to depend on his commitment to that goal. The individual's initial rating of his commitment to his change goal is positively related to his eventual success. In addition, experimental attempts to increase initial commit-ment by emphasis on goal-setting increased the percent of successful changers in one study from 44 percent to 61 percent (Kolb, Winter, & Berlew, 1970). The individual's level of awareness also influences the process of self-direction. Successful changers show a greater initial awareness of factors influencing their change projects than do unsuccess-ful changers. Also, successful changers have higher initial expectations of success than unsuccessful changers who are often pessimistic about their ability to achieve their goal.

Successful changers tend to define their goal in such a way that progress can be measured, while unsuccessful changers defined their goals in a way that is general and vague. They also define their goals in such a way that they maintain the responsibility for evaluating their own progress. Standards of evaluation are internal rather than external. Finally, successful changers, in general, evidence a higher level of psychological safety. They indicate feelings of confidence and security at the time of goal-setting while unsuccessful changers show lack of confidence and insecurity during initial goal-setting.

Feedback   In order to be successful in his self-directed change project, the individual must receive information feedback about his progress toward his goal. Zachs' (1965) study of individuals who were trying to control their smoking suggests that feedback in the form of systematic records of progress (i.e., a daily record of number of cigarettes

[3]Self-directed procedures have been developed for helping individuals to set goals, measure them, and receive feedback in small-group settings suitable for use in educational and business organizations (Kolb, Rubin, & McIntyre, 1971).

smoked) facilitates goal achievement. In another study (Kolb et al., 1970), the opportunity to receive feedback in the training group related to one's change goal increased successful goal achievement from 5 percent to 44 percent. There is also a positive relationship between the total amount of feedback received from fellow training-group members and goal-achievement although this relationship is strongest in the last half of the change project. This last finding has been interpreted to mean that the quality as well as the quantity of information feedback is important. Feedback in the last half of the training period should be more helpful because it is perhaps better understood since group members know one another better and have learned what kind of feedback is helpful to others in the group.

   Although the data in these experiments are not sufficiently quantified to allow tests of the interrelationships among those variables identified as important characteristics of the self-directed change process, the results suggest some tentative outlines for a cybernetic model of behavior change. Nearly every student of personality and behavior change has recognized that human personality is a dynamic feedback system with self-sustaining and self-reinforcing qualities. Sullivan, for example, sees this aspect of personality (which he calls the self-system) to be the major stumbling block to constructive personality change. Hall and Lindsey (1957, p. 139) describe his concept of the self-system this way:

> The self system as the guardian of one's security tends to become isolated from the rest of the personality; it excludes information that is incongruous with its present organization and fails thereby to profit from experience. Since the self guards the person from anxiety, it is held in high esteem and protected from criticism. As the self system grows in complexity and independence it prevents the person from making objective judgments of his own behavior and it glosses over obvious contradictions between what the person really is and what his self system says he is.

   Because individuals tend to act in accord with their self-system, threats to the self-system will cause a person's activities to become more and more inappropriate and rigid leading to further failure and insecurity, which in turn leads to further distortions in the self-system and so on. The characteristics which have been found to be associated with successful self-directed change give some clues about the nature of the intervening variables in this process. Figure 8-3 shows how these characteristics fit into a cybernetic model of the change process. Interrelationships among the variables are simplified to show the dominant feedback loop. For purpose of illustration, the characteristics in Figure 8-3 describe an unsuccessful change process beginning with low psychological safety.

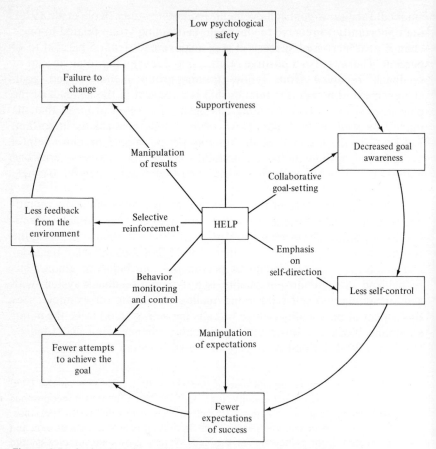

Figure 8-3 A simple cybernetic model of behavior change and helping interventions.

Low psychological safety can lead to decreased awareness. This decrease in awareness would in turn lead to a decreased sense of self-control which would lead to fewer expectations of success. Low expectations of success would produce few attempts to achieve the goal which would in turn produce fewer opportunities for feedback from the environment. All this would tend to produce failure in achieving the goal. The failure feelings thus aroused would tend to further decrease psychological safety producing an amplification of this positive feedback loop.

IMPLICATIONS FOR HELPING INTERVENTIONS

This cybernetic model of the behavior-change process suggests several intervention strategies that may serve to create more effective helping relationships with individuals who are seeking change. Since feedback loops are composed of elements which need not have either a prior or hierarchial causal order, helping interventions can be directed to the point or points in the feedback loop where they will be most effective in producing change. As Phillips and Weiner (1966, p. 96) put it:

> Within the cybernetic framework, although not unique to it, variables are selected and regulated in the feedback chain which are most amenable to manipulation and control. In structured therapy, elusive causes are not sought that might operate to produce a disordered system: the therapist goes directly to the element (information) in the feedback loop that has a meaningful coefficient of efficiency in maintaining the loop, and he proceeds immediately to try to insert the change.

Thus, cybernetic models of the change process hold forth the promise of an eclectic approach to the choice of helping strategies based on research which identifies those elements in the feedback loop having the highest "coefficient of efficiency."

The simplified model of change in Figure 8-3 suggests seven types of intervention which may prove effective in breaking into the self-defeating cycle of failure.

1 Supportiveness Rogerian theory has been based primarily on the supportive strategy of increasing the client's security and self-confidence through the therapist's unconditional positive regard, accurate empathy, and genuineness (Rogers, 1961). Truax and his associates (e.g., Truax & Carkhuff, 1964) have shown that these three therapist characteristics are related to constructive personality change in both Rogerian and other forms of therapy. In addition, they find that the presence of these variables in the therapist is positively related to intrapersonal exploration on the part of the client. This suggests that supportive interventions aimed at increasing psychological safety have a relatively high coefficient of efficiency because they produce positive change and gains in another element in the feedback loop—awareness (intrapersonal exploration).

2 Collaborative Goal-Setting Attempts to increase awareness of personal-improvement goals through an explicit process of collaborative goal-setting have not often been a part of behavior-change programs. There are, however, some notable exceptions. Homme, et al. (1969), have described procedures of "contingency contracting" in which the therapist and patient explicitly develop agreements in regard to when and how behaviors will be reinforced. A collaborative, goal-setting approach has also often been used in achievement-motivation training programs, in organization-management programs (Likert, 1967; Kay, French, & Myer, 1962), and in research on self-directed behavior change. The results suggest that goal-setting procedures may be a highly effective intervention method. As previously indicated, studies of the personality pattern of those who are unsuccessful in achieving their self-directed change goals indicate that intervention techniques which help the individual define his current self-image and help him to recognize and commit himself to personal improvement goals may be an effective means of increasing motivation to change.

A careful examination of behavior-therapy methods of change suggests that in addition to applying, for example, the principles of reciprocal inhibition (cf. Chapter 2), the therapist is also leading the patient through a process of explicit goal-setting. By asking the patient to define and rank in order the fear-evoking situations in his life, then helping him to relax while visualizing the weakest fear situation until he masters it, then proceeding to the next weakest and so on, the therapist is in effect helping the patient to set realistic goals and work to achieve them in a way that is quite similar to the self-directed change method. At this point, research evidence is not clear as to the extent of the contribution that collaborative goal-setting makes to the therapeutic success of reciprocal inhibition. Similar questions can be raised about other behavior-therapy methods.

3 Encouragement of Self-Direction Although few therapeutic systems place a heavy emphasis on self-control of the change process in their methodology, it is commonly accepted that enduring changes following treatment will require self-direction. The preliminary success of some self-directed change procedures may well point toward the greater use of self-directed change techniques in the future which greatly reduce the patient's dependence on the therapist. The finding that successful self-directed change is facilitated by a goal definition which emphasizes self-evaluation focuses new attention on Rogers' (1961, p. 55) observation about effective helping relationships.

> I have come to feel that the more I can keep a relationship free of judgment and evaluation, the more this will permit the other person to reach the point where he recognizes that the locus of evaluation, the center of responsibility, lies within himself. The meaning and value of his experience is in the last analysis something which is up to him and no amount of external judgment can alter this.

4 Manipulation of Expectations In addition to the findings in self-directed change projects, there are a number of psychotherapy studies that have shown the influence of an individual's expectations on his own chances for successful change (Goldstein, 1962; Frank, 1963). As yet, few direct attempts have been made to directly increase individuals' expectations of success. A significant exception is the previously cited work on achievement-motivation training. That manipulation of expectations can produce change has been shown in a study by Rosenthal and Jacobson (1968). Grade school children were given intelligence tests and assigned to their new teachers at the beginning of the school year. The names of a randomly selected group of these children were given to their new teachers who were told that these children could be expected to show unusual gains of intelligence during the year. Subsequent intelligence tests showed a significant increase in the intelligence test scores of those children whose teachers expected a gain. This research, while not conclusive, suggests that helping interventions that increase expectations of success may be a useful method of breaking the cycle of failure.

5 Behavior Monitoring and Control Behavior-change techniques often attempt to evoke behaviors that are consistent with the subject's personal change goals. Two commonly used techniques previously discussed are stimulus control and modeling. In stimulus-control methods, environmental events can serve as discriminative or eliciting stimuli to increase or decrease the frequency of specified behaviors. For example, a student can move his study area away from his bed to help prevent his falling asleep while studying. Modeling provides the systematic opportunity for observing the behavior of others which presents cues for appropriate behavior to the observer (Brayfield, 1968). This can facilitate a similar response by the observer if the modeled responses are reinforced or decrease similar responses by the observer if the modeled responses are punished (see Chapter 6).

In self-directed behavior-change projects, another method has been successfully used to repeatedly evoke goal-directed behavior—behavior monitoring. By keeping continuous records of progress toward their goals, subjects are constantly reminded of the goal they are trying to achieve, thus producing more attempts to achieve that goal (Zachs, 1965; Goldiamond, 1965; Schwitzgebel, 1964). The fact that successful subjects in self-directed change projects give more attention than unsuccessful subjects to how their progress can be measured provides additional evidence for the efficiency of behavior-monitoring procedures.

6 Selective Reinforcement One of the best documented strategies for producing behavior change is the manipulation of environmental feedback through the use of selective reinforcement. The methods of operant shaping and scheduled reinforcement have been used to alter such insignificant behaviors as use of pronouns and such major behavioral patterns as delinquent behavior and schizophrenic symptoms (see Chapters 3 and 4). As discussed earlier, research on self-directed change suggests that the quantity and quality of information feedback may also be related to change.

   7 Manipulation of Results   A final intervention method which deserves consideration is the manipulation of results of change. Although this method has not been used systematically as a therapeutic intervention, it is a common device in experimental research. For example, the literature on level of aspiration is replete with examples of the artificial manipulation of performance results, which show measurable changes in future goal-setting and performance (Lewin, et al., 1944; Festinger, 1942; Frank, 1941). Although there are obvious problems of credibility and honesty when using such artificial distortions of reality, this method may prove to be a promising intervention strategy.

   As can be seen from the above discussion, elements of the goal-setting process that are crucial for successful goal achievement can be modified by helping interventions. The task for future research is to determine how effective these interventions, taken singly or in combination, can be in changing the cycle of insecurity and failure to one of psychological safety and success. The most-effective intervention strategy may well prove to be some behavior-change methods in combination with the goal-setting procedures of self-directed change.

SUMMARY

The rapidly growing demand for behavioral-science solutions to human problems has made practitioners increasingly aware of the fact that there are not enough professionally trained personnel to meet this demand now or in the foreseeable future. This has encouraged researchers to look for new ways in which patients can actively assist in their own behavior-change programs.

   The therapist or change agent can serve as a consultant to the patient to assist him in developing the plans and skills necessary to change his behavior. The patient can, for example, be taught how to apply the principles of contingency management to his own behavior. He can also develop the ability to observe his own behavior and plot his progress toward clearly specified goals. This self-directed behavior change can sometimes be enhanced by participation in carefully structured group situations.

   It appears that under proper conditions, proactive forces can emerge in individuals allowing them to experiment with new forms of behavior. Changes in behavior are most likely to be permanent if the process of change is seen by the individual to be under his own control. The person should feel that he, not some external agent, is producing the change. Change can also be facilitated if the person sets goals which he wants to reach to improve his self-concept and if he can receive feedback about his progress toward his goals.

A cybernetic model of behavior change suggests several types of intervention which may be helpful in breaking into a patient's self-defeating cycle of failure. Among these interventions are supportiveness, collaborative goal-setting, encouragement of self-direction, manipulation of expectations, behavior monitoring and control, selective reinforcement, and manipulation of results. Further study is required to assess the behavior-change potential of these interventions used singly or in combination.

Chapter 9

Behavior Change in Transitional Roles

The study of behavior change cannot depend upon the theories of individual psychology alone. It must also focus on the social role changes that can result from individual behavior change or, conversely, that can cause individual behavior change. If we are to understand and improve the effectiveness of techniques which attempt to produce behavior change, we must understand the social as well as the psychological impact of interventions. The individual who enters psychotherapy is not only being subjected to a particular set of experiences within the therapeutic context, he is also, by the very act of entering therapy, experiencing an alteration of his social role. The new role of "patient" creates, at the very least, changes in others' expectations of him. The individual finds that by entering the patient role he has acquired new privileges (odd behaviors may now be excused because he is "sick"), new stigmas (others may not trust his opinions), and new responsibilities (he should begin to show improvement).

The goal of this chapter is to understand the effect of this social role of "person-who-is-changing" on the process of behavior change. To accomplish this goal, we will examine not only the patient as he moves from sickness to health but also the other roles that people enter to make the transition from one status to another. There are a great number of these *transitional roles* in contemporary American society ranging from the universal and much-discussed period of adolescence to the highly specialized position of medical student. Perhaps the two largest categories of these positions are student roles and patient roles. (Patient roles are broadly construed to include medical patients, psychotherapy patients, clients of guidance and marriage counselors, as well as all recipients of help in "helping relationships.") Other, more specific transitional roles are the parolee, the apprentice, the engaged couple, the initiate, and the victim of brainwashing.

To the student of behavior change, these transitional roles constitute natural laboratories in which natural experiments can be conducted to test the effectiveness of techniques for bringing about behavior change and maintaining it in the social environment with a minimum of emotional hazard. By the examination and comparison of these transitional roles, their successes and failures, we may perhaps gain some understanding about how behavior change is produced in the social environment and how role characteristics lead to successful or unsuccessful transitions.

USE OF TRANSITIONAL ROLES

Sociologists have long emphasized the forces in the social system which operate to insure stable patterns of interaction and expectation. Our actions are predicted and controlled by our associates and we likewise demand that others fulfill our expectations. It is, in fact, through these stable and mutual patterns of expectation that we are able to function in a highly developed and specialized society. Individual behavior change can seriously disrupt these mutual expectation and interaction patterns. If changes in behavior are to be maintained, the social environment must be altered to integrate the new behavior and reestablish the equilibrium which allows others to predict the person's actions and empathize with his feelings. The social environment can influence and can be influenced by changes in behavior ranging from the alteration of insignificant habits to the total reorganization of personality. A typist who finally masters the typewriter makes it inappropriate for her boss to vent his frustrations by ordering much-erased letters to be redone. A former drug addict, if his abstinence is to be maintained, must develop a new circle of associates who will lead him to the nonaddict world of a steady job and to a life with the "squares" he formerly despised. Changes such as these in the behavior and desires of individuals are potentially disruptive to social interaction, and can create emotionally hazardous situations for both the changing individual and his associates. An ex-addict will undoubtedly be quite uncomfortable in a middle-class suburban neighborhood. Inquiring neighbors who learn of his past will fear for their children, and the so-called "pusher" will fear for the safety of his disguised identity which the new responsible citizen may divulge.

The major function of transitional roles is to provide a social position which will aid and protect an individual as he changes from one social role to another; whether it be from sickness to health, as in the patient role; or from prison to the outside, as in the role of the parolee; or from childhood to adult as in adolescent rites of passage. To perform this function adequately, the transitional role must accomplish two important tasks. First, the individual must acquire the necessary knowledge, skills, and values to accept the status to which he aspires. It is important to note that in most cases this involves more than acquiring the physical ability to perform each distinct behavior required of an occupant of the terminal status. Mere imitation or rote learning without personal application are superficial and relatively meaningless changes. Changes in behavior that are maintained must be organized into a personally meaningful and self-directed pattern of living. It is the peculiar characteristic of transitional roles that they are successful, for the individual and for the society, only if the occupant leaves them to acquire a new status. But, the occupant cannot leave unless he has developed, independently, some principles for dealing with the ongoing events of the new status he wants to acquire. The successful psychotherapy patient must not be completely dependent upon the therapist for advice, but must be helped to develop his own principles and methods for interpreting and creating experience.

Secondly, the people with whom the transitional-role occupant will associate in his terminal status must be prepared to accept him as a legitimate occupant of his new position. If other people's expectations are not modified to accept and integrate the individual into his new status, effective role performance becomes difficult. Young doctors often have difficulty with patients who are mistrusting because they doubt the doctor's experience (Becker, Geer, Hughes, & Strauss, 1961). Marriage counselors have found it very difficult to bring about change in one marriage partner when his spouse has a strong investment in maintaining the old expectations about the relationship (Haley, 1963; Hurwitz, 1967). One empirical example of the influence of social environment is contained in the previously cited study of the effectiveness of achievement-motivation training on the grades of under-achieving high school boys

Kolb, 1965). In this study, upper-class boys were able to increase their grades quite markedly after training, while lower-class boys were apparently unable to break those old expectations which continued to determine study habits and teacher evaluations. Furthermore, Kahl (1962) has shown that academic success is not determined by social class alone but by the expectations that a boy's social acquaintances, especially his parents, hold about him. In his study of intelligent, lower-middle and working-class boys, he found "the evidence showed that if the parents were pushing toward college, in eight out of nine cases the boy responded appropriately, but if the parents were indifferent about college, in eleven out of fifteen cases the boy was uninterested" (p. 288).

Because the transitional-role occupant's future associates in most cases are not involved in specific training designed to help them make transitions in their expectations, the legitimization of the individual's new status is often accomplished by conferring on the individual in transition the symbols, both formal and informal, of the terminal status. Thus, as the young medical student acquires the experience of a long period of training, he gradually adopts a restrained, cool, professional attitude with his patients; and the medical community identifies him as a legitimate and competent doctor by giving him a medical diploma. All of these symbols and rituals serve to create the proper role expectations in his prospective patients.

To understand transitional roles, it is important to realize that transition involves not only the acquisition of a future status but also the phasing out and/or integration of a former status.[1] The acquisition of a new status must be accompanied by the integration of old habits, attitudes and desires with the new style of life thus giving that sense of continuity and meaning which we call a "sense of identity" (Erikson, 1962). Failure to accomplish either the integration of the past or the articulation of the future can only lead to difficulties in transition. Different transitional roles have emphasized various aspects of this dimension. Psychotherapy has been primarily concerned with the acceptance and understanding of the past and has often been criticized for its failure to articulate the goals of health and normality. Many student roles, on the other hand, have been more concerned with preparation for future performance than with helping the individual to make sense of his past experience and his present abilities, desires, and fears. The recent rapid growth of the school-guidance movement marks the educator's growing awareness of the importance of the student's past and present experiences.

[1]For a discussion of the relationships between role and social status, see Linton (1936) and Merton (1965, pp. 368–386).

An Example: The Medical Student

Before examining and comparing the general characteristics of transitional roles, it may be useful to examine one case in detail. The process of initiating medical students into the medical profession has received a great deal of attention from sociologists (see, for example, Parsons, 1951; Merton, et al., 1957; Becker, et al., 1961) and, as a result, is ideal for our purpose. The training of medical students is a particularly enlightening example of transitional roles because of the great technical skill and responsibility required of the physician. As we will see later, there are many similarities between this system for changing behavior and other systems which we more commonly recognize as involving techniques of behavior change. In his book, *Boys in White*, Howard Becker and his associates report a carefully documented field study of the training of medical students. Their analysis of medical training at the University of Kansas Medical School will form the basis of our portrait of the medical student.

In the lay culture, the physician occupies a position of tremendously high prestige (following only Supreme Court Justices and United States Senators according to a government survey in 1965). The profession is thought to be an extremely difficult one, requiring great skill and intelligence. A high amount of commitment and dedication to becoming a doctor is required of the young college student who aspires to this profession. In many cases, a prospective medical student must forsake a wide liberal arts background in college to prepare himself in the sciences needed to master medical school. The number of positions in medical schools is far exceeded by the numbers who desire to occupy them. Thus the student must, in most cases, demonstrate his commitment to the profession by an outstanding record of performance.

As a result, the freshman medical student arrives highly committed to his occupational choice and willing to endure the trials of the next years in order to become a doctor. His view of the medical profession is, at this point, idealistic. His major goal is serving his fellow man, and he becomes quite angry and upset when others suggest that doctors are out only for the big fees that medicine offers. Surprisingly, Becker finds that most students, even those whose close relatives are doctors, initially have quite a vague idea of what a doctor's actual work is like and little idea of the alternative specialities within the medical profession. The freshman medical student thus finds himself totally dependent on the faculty and the administration for definition of his future professional role; and more importantly, dependent upon the faculty's definition of essential skills that will focus the student's effort in his acquisition of knowledge.

This dependency is further increased in the freshman and sophomore years by the student's comparative isolation from professional role models. In these years, the student is acquiring the general knowledge on which his future practice will be based—intensive freshman courses in gross anatomy, microanatomy, neurology, psychiatry, and, in the sophomore year, courses on pathology, microbiology and pharmacology. His professors are academicians and scientists, generally not practicing physicians. Visits to hospitals and clinics are short and infrequent.

Time for learning the shortcuts of practical experience will come later in the clinical years. Now, in the freshman year, the student feels that he must attempt to learn everything, for the ideal doctor must know everything about medicine. When the work overload makes this attempt unfeasible, the student begins to "psych out" the professors—to learn what the professors want him to learn and what he will be tested on. A few students do not accept this norm and try to master only that material which they think will be useful to them as doctors. But, it soon becomes apparent that they do not know what is important because they are not yet aware of what doctors do. So, these students end up "giving the professors what they want."

But the faculty does not make this easy by responding with aid and comfort to the students depending on them for defining what is important. The faculty still acts as though everything is important and gives no clues as to what is unnecessary to the practicing doctor.

It is the student who remains responsible for choosing what of the mass of material will go unlearned. The student must make his best guess as to what is important at the expense of possibly being "caught" on the exam. To make these guesses, the students band together in a student "culture," a culture whose main function is to define what they will learn and work on in order to please the faculty. Once a successful definition is reached, student resentment of the faculty decreases and initial tensions of medical school are reduced.

The junior and senior clinical years mark a turning point in the student's training. The locus of his activities moves to the hospitals and clinics where he dons a white jacket and white pants like those worn by the staff doctors and residents. In this new setting, the student becomes less a student and more an apprentice. Students are given limited responsibility to diagnose and treat incoming patients under supervision. At last they are in the real world of real patients. Yet, even here they still remain dependent on their faculty, men who are now experienced, practicing doctors. For in the clinical years there is a marked shift in the standards of knowledge from "book learning" to practical, clinical experience. The status system of the hospital is based on experience, and responsibility is granted largely on this basis. As a result, the student has no recourse to the authority of a textbook as he did in his first two years. He must accept what his superior says because his superior "knows from experience."

The student comes to realize that to gain status he, too, must acquire experience, the experience of acting as a responsible doctor. Acquiring this experience requires an almost total commitment of time and energy. Because they are at the bottom of the hospital hierarchy, they work odd hours and do most of the dirty work. The price they pay for the experience of attending during a difficult operation is cleaning up afterwards. During the clinical years, their whole life is involved with the hospital. They are at work or on call nearly all of the time; often they sleep in the hospital overnight. There is little free time to associate with anyone but the people at the hospital; even spouses get little attention.

In all of their work, the students find that the faculty's standard of evaluation is ever-present but increasingly vague. There are still formal exams but they are less frequent. They are now being judged by their performance with patients on the ward. It becomes less clear what things will "please the faculty." More and more their major concern is solving the problems they face in their work as apprentice doctors. Standards of evaluation are becoming internalized and problem-centered.

During this time, the students are also acquiring a style of dealing with patients through a supervised practice. The experiences related to this are difficult and often embarrassing. Patients are often nervous when they find that their young doctor is only a student. Intimate physical examinations, especially of women, are difficult for both doctor and patient. The student's response is a mixture of the feelings and attitudes of the layman, doctor, and student. Yet, through it all the student is developing the personal professional style which will serve in his future practice.

At the conclusion of his senior year, the medical student has still not reached his goal. Ahead are periods of more responsible apprenticeship, an internship and perhaps a residency. There are still choices to be made—whether to be a specialist in a hospital or a general practitioner, a researcher or a teacher. But by now the course is set—the student will soon reach the long-anticipated termination of his formal training.

THE CHARACTERISTICS OF TRANSITIONAL ROLES

The Transitional Culture—A Moratorium

Because so much time has been devoted to Becker's study of the medical student, it may be well to begin our analysis with his central thesis about transitional roles. Becker takes issue with scholars like Huntington (1957) and Fox (1957) who seem to imply that the process of transition from one status to another is a straight line progression, a gradual, steady acquisition of a new status while the old status is steadily relinquished. To Becker, this represents a simplification of the process which leaves out an important factor, the culture which develops during the transition. His study documents how medical students form a culture to decide on how effort should be directed to meet the challenges and pressures of medical school work. He finds that students are not as concerned with acting like doctors as they are about finding some way of coping with the day-to-day demands of the student role.

The notion of a *transitional culture* is important because it highlights the fact that the process of change creates for the individual immediate situational demands to which he must in some way adapt. The changing person can never be left in a nonexistent limbo where he no longer occupies one status and has not yet acquired another. Yet, in many cases, the society responds to these persons as if this were the case.

The classic example is the adolescent. "No longer a boy and not yet a man," he is placed by his society in a position of role conflict, a situation with antagonistic demands and expectations. His response, much like that of the medical student, is to withdraw into a culture of peers—a culture which James Coleman calls "the adolescent society" (1961). Here the group creates strategies for coping with these conflicting demands and, in the process, defines which goals are important and to what status members of the culture will aspire. When the society at large (usually the school) fails to make identification with the adolescent culture attractive and gratifying by providing symbols which are meaningful indicators of the transition to adult status, students are led to premature seizure of these symbols or to apathetic withdrawal. For example, Stinchcombe (1964) has found that when satisfactory identification with the adolescent culture as created by the school is lacking, rebellion results.

Given the necessity of the transitional culture, we must now ask what form it would take when bringing about successful transitions. To continue the example of adolescence, Erikson (1958, 1962) suggests that a kind of moratorium is important in the formation of personal identity—a period of relative isolation and freedom from the daily demands of life. Other transitional roles also place the individual in a situation where he is somewhat isolated and protected from the pressures of "real life." We have seen how the medical student's life is enclosed in the early years by the academic environment and later by the demands of hospital work. In addition, the student role generally provides both special privileges and special restrictions which serve the function of relieving problems of earning a living and having to bear adult responsibilities before training is complete. Students can get scholarships and special government loans to support themselves. They are not expected to fill adult roles and, in fact, restrictions like child labor laws specifically prohibit this.

Parsons (1951), in his analysis of the patient role, finds similar restrictions and privileges for the person who is sick. The patient is exempted from fulfilling his normal duties and, in many cases, receives special services and attention as long as he is willing to be defined as sick. As will be discussed later in the section on responsibility, the handling of this *secondary gain* that the patient receives from the sick role constitutes a major issue in the process of psychotherapy.

In addition to relieving outside expectations and pressures, the moratorium has implications for the structuring of rewards and punishments within the transitional role. Anselm Strauss describes this process as it exists in coaching relationships (1964). In Strauss' terms, a coaching relationship occurs in most transitional roles. He suggests (p. 410) that a coaching relationship exists whenever "someone seeks to move someone else along a series of steps, when those steps are not entirely institutionalized and invariant, and when the learner is not entirely clear about their sequences (although the coach is)." The moratorium has been described by him as follows (p. 415):

> It is as if there were a kind of moratorium, during which effort is great, but during which both sides ceremonially ignore negative performances. Of course, such a moratorium and such make-believe run all through the coaching process, perhaps particularly during new phases in cycles of learning, when the person is particularly sensitive to criticism and must be encouraged and must encourage himself to chance endeavors.

Moore (1960) has developed this notion further in what he calls *autotelic folk models.* He maintains that in order for socialization to take place, the culture must provide situations which teach individuals the skills required for survival in the society, while at the same time allowing exploratory trial-and-error performances which do not "count" either for the individual's survival or the society's. Puzzles, games, and the creation of aesthetic objects are examples of these situations which occur in most societies. Moore has developed a special kind of autotelic teaching device by which he taught "pre-school children to the point where they were reading and writing first grade stories, and typing on an electric typewriter with correct fingering within a matter of weeks" (p. 212). The same device has since proven useful in cases of retarded and schizophrenic children. Moore's (1959, pp. 206–207) requirements for autotelic folk models, listed below, may well serve as an ideal design for transitional culture.

1 They must be "cut off," in some suitable sense, from the more serious aspects of the society's activity—those aspects connected with immediate problems of survival and well-being. If a child is learning the intricacies of interaction by experience, the activity in which he is experiencing or practicing interaction *must* allow him to make many mistakes without endangering the lives or futures of those around him. Similarly, such rewards as he receives from the activity must not be too expensive to those around him—or again the activity may have just those serious consequences which the teaching devices must avoid.

2 But in spite of the fact that the teaching device must avoid these serious consequences, some motivation must be built into the activity, else the learner may lose interest. If we rely on the distinction between activities that are *intrinsically* rewarding, and those that are rewarding only as a means, or *extrinsically* rewarding, we may say that the rewards in the learner's activities must be intrinsic, or inherent in the activity itself. Such activities we call *autotelic*: they contain their own goals and sources of motivation.

3 And finally, they must help a child to learn the relevant techniques. Indeed, this whole discussion began with the assumption that people in a society *do* cope with interactional, noninteractional and affective problems —all of which require study, practice and experience, if solutions are to be found.

It should be mentioned in passing that the educational practice of using grades as a cumulative index of ability and worth and the practice of making transitional evaluations of progress "count" in the individual's later life, are direct violations of Moore's first criterion. It may also be noted that the suggestions made here in regard to coaching and motivation fit well with the use of observational-learning techniques, such as imitation, to produce behavior change (see Chapter 6).

In the approaches of both Strauss and Moore, the notion of play is central, play in the sense of involved, intrinsically motivated exploration of situations which do not "count" for survival. Sarbin (1954, p. 226) points out why this kind of play is so important in a child's development:

At least two resultants follow from the play acting of children: (a) the acquisition of roles (truncated, of course, because of maturational limitations), and (b) the acquisition of skill in shifting roles. In play, the child can shift from role to role without observing the formal logic of the adult. This movement from role to role leads to oscillatory shifting of sets, thus enabling the child to take both his own role and the role of the other.

Thus, it is through play that a person can acquire the experience of a new role and others' response to him in it without his being committed to meet the real-life expectations that the role entails. In a transitional role where this special kind of play is allowed, the individual can step into the role for which he is preparing, practice it awhile, step out of the role to examine his performance with the "coach," and begin again.

Goal-Setting—Commitment, Articulation, and Reserved Judgment

Individuals in transition, if they are to be successful, must value highly the status to which they aspire. A primary goal of transitional roles that require membership (e.g., the parolee or, to a lesser extent, the student) is to "unfreeze" the person in transition and to generate commitment to achieving the terminal status. The very nature of the process of change makes it important that the goal be a firmly fixed, unchangeable ideal, a stable point of orientation to guide one through the morass of conflict and ambivalence which inevitably accompanies the process of transition. The change goal can be positive, as in the case of the medical student who desires to be a doctor, or negative, as in the case of the psychotherapy patient who is trying to relieve the anxieties of his former status. In either case, one would predict that the importance of the goal to the individual would be positively related to his chances for a successful transition. Evidence for this hypothesis is found in a study by Luborsky (1964) which indicates that high anxiety is associated with improvement in psychotherapy. Similarly, Zachs (1965) found that the ability to stop smoking is positively related to the individual's commitment to reach this goal. As noted in Chapter 8 on self-directed behavior change, the relationship between commitment and success in achieving personal change goals has been illustrated by Kolb, Winter, and Berlew (1970) in a study which shows that commitment to a personal change goal is related to achievement of that goal in self-analytic groups. In a subsequent study, these researchers (Winter et al., 1968) found that the degree of goal achievement was also positively related to the subject's awareness of his motivation to change.

Thus, another important aspect of the goal-setting process is the degree to which the individual in transition has an articulated awareness of his terminal role. Those who have a poor notion of the nature of their goal will, undoubtedly, be less willing to endure the anxieties of change for some vaguely defined future state. Educational research provides us with examples of this fact. Research on school dropouts suggests that an important reason for failure to complete school is the absence of adult role models—role models which give an empathic notion of what adult life is like (Thomas & Pattison, 1963). Stinchcombe (1964) finds that one of the major factors leading to rebellion in high school is poor articulation of future career possibilities.

It should be noted, however, that while both high commitment and high articulation of the change goal are important, the latter may be less so, and may, in some cases, actually inhibit the change process. A case in point is the medical-student example discussed earlier. Here the positive, idealistic conception of the medical profession may have been a result of the student's relatively poor idea of what a doctor actually does. Too vivid an image of the trials and tribulations of a doctor's life may frighten the student and reduce his commitment. Problems appear infinitely difficult until one has acquired the tools to solve them.

For this reason, the future goal is often set aside once the individual has committed himself to the transitional role. In the early stages of transition, the future is left for private thoughts and fantasies. Before progress toward the new goal can be considered, a break must be made with the old role and the basic principles of the new role must be acquired. This is the case in the first two "academic" years of medical school; so also in the early sessions of psychotherapy.

The principle of suspended judgment is described most explicitly by the author of a self-improvement book (Maltz, 1960, p. xv):

> Do not allow yourself to become discouraged if nothing seems to happen when you set about practicing the various techniques outlined in this book for changing your self image. Instead reserve judgment—and go on practicing—for a minimum period of twenty-one days . . . . During these twenty-one days do not argue intellectually with the ideas presented, do not debate with yourself as to whether they will work or not. Perform the exercises even if they seem impractical to you.

Involvement

Transitional roles require a high degree of personal involvement. They require that the individual commit a great deal of his resources (time, money, effort, emotional and intellectual facilities) to the process of acquiring a new status. This enforced involvement is obvious in the example of the medical student. In psychotherapy, investment is both emotional and financial. Here, as in other transitional roles, investment is cumulative. At the end of one session, the patient has spent twenty dollars, at the end of two sessions, forty dollars, at the end of ten sessions, two hundred dollars. This discourages turning back.

Often the transitional role requires not only a great deal of effort, but also a certain number of rather unpleasant duties. Apprentices usually use the broom as much as the tools of their trade. Haley (1963, p. 55), in his analysis of psychotherapy, says, "It is possible to describe any form of therapy as a self-punishment for the patient. After all, it is difficult to go and discuss one's weaknesses and inadequacies with a therapist (who ostensibly has none). To be successful, therapy must in some sense be an ordeal." By making the transition require great effort and some pain, the individual's valuation of his goal may be increased, thus enhancing the probability of a successful transition. The individual will reduce cognitive dissonance by saying, "If I'm suffering through all this, the goal must be really worth it." In an experimental initiation rite situation, Festinger and Freedman (Festinger, 1964) found just this result. Sarbin (1954, p. 235) expands this notion:

> In *rites de passage*, the role of the celebrant is characterized by high organismic involvement. The manifest purpose of the intense role behaviors of the ritual is to signify the change from one position to another in the society: the effect of the intensity of role enactment is to modify the participant's self concept so that the new role, e.g., adult, may not be incongruent with the self. If, for example, strength is an expected property of the adult person, and the rites of passage from adolescent to adult includes passing a test of strength, then the successful completion of the test allows the person to add the adjective "strong" to his self description. Thus he is better equipped to occupy the position of adult, not only because others know he has strength, but because he conceptualizes the self as strong.

Acquisition of the Terminal Status—Personal Responsibility

As was pointed out earlier, a successful transition involves not only the acquisition of the basic skills required in the terminal status, but also the organization of these skills into an independent self-concept which can successfully interpret and organize experiences in the new status. The individual must adopt a proactive, as opposed to reactive, orientation to his experience; i.e., he must originate actions and create situations rather than respond to the actions of others and react to situations created for him. The student situation is, for the most part, reactive. The student responds to questions asked by the teacher. He reads and writes what he is assigned. From this role, he will grow into adulthood where he must choose an occupation important to him. He must decide what interests him and what doesn't and how he will spend his time.

Haley (1963, p. 32) suggests how this change may be accomplished:

> If one defines the behavioral goal of psychotherapy, it would seem to be this: the therapist must induce a patient to voluntarily behave differently than he has in the past. It is unsatisfactory if a patient behaves differently

because he is told to do so: he must initiate the new behavior. Yet, an essential paradox lies in this goal of therapy: one cannot *induce* someone to *voluntarily* behave differently. Such a paradox can only be resolved if it is seen that in non-directive therapy the patient is directed in such a way that the direction is denied and therefore his changed behavior is defined as spontaneous.

Haley's solution involves the use of "double bind" communications to control the patient's behavior; i.e., the therapist must tell the patient what to do while at the same time creating a situation which makes it appear as though the patient is voluntarily doing what he, the patient, wants.

This rather complicated process is well illustrated in the case of the medical student. As we have seen, the students first tried to learn either everything or material selected according to their notion of what doctors need to know. When these ill-informed strategies failed, they reverted to a reactive approach—learning what the professors wanted them to know. But the professors never acknowledged this dependency by defining a few masterable areas as important. Thus, the students remained responsible for their choices while the professors kept control of what was learned. In effect, a pseudo-choice situation is created by the work overload, since in the best of all worlds, all the material should be mastered.

The development of a sense of personal responsibility is brought about in yet another way. The individual in transition often earns symbols of his progress toward the terminal status. The student earns a diploma, the prospective doctor earns his white coat and stethoscope. All these symbols serve the function of announcing to the society that this particular individual is qualified to fill a particular position. In response to these symbols, people will treat the individual as though he were a legitimate and responsible occupant of the position. In effect, they demand that he be responsible.

Stinchcombe (1964, p. 108) illustrates this process by comparing a case where these symbols are abundant, an apprentice, with a case where they are lacking, the non-college-bound high school student.

    1   Perhaps the most striking difference between the ritual situations of the apprentice and the future worker in high school is that the apprentice is supposed to be working for a status that not everybody can achieve. Rather than being negatively defined as "leftovers," apprentices are positively identified as future journeymen.

    2   Among the mechanisms of this positive identification are the progressive allocation to the apprentice of work defined (in trade union jurisdictional provisions) as too skilled for unskilled workers. The greater

command over the skills of the trade is made meaningful by a progressive approach to the wages of skilled craftsmen, relatively soon exceeding the wages of unskilled labor.

   3 A second mechanism of positive identification of the apprentice is the progressive accumulation of personal capital equipment. The carpenter's apprentice builds a tool kit, buys a set of carpenter's overalls, and so on. . . . The high school student graduates with a diploma rather than with a kit of tools.

   4 The culminating ritual of apprenticeship is an examination or other test of competence, and the award of a journeyman's card. This is a certificate to future employers of the skill of the workman, and a symbol to the journeyman of the labor market rights he has gained by apprenticeship.

Interpersonal Relationships—Status and Solidarity

It is through interpersonal relationships that the person in transition acquires the knowledge, skills, and values necessary for him to be successful in his terminal status. Although education has its books, exercises, and demonstrations; the apprenticeship, its tools and machines; the behavior therapist, his schedules and techniques for reinforcement; the teaching and learning essential to the transitional process generally occur through human interactions.

   The aim in this last section is to understand the complex dynamics of human interactions in transitional roles. It is a further goal to determine how these interactions facilitate or hinder transition to the terminal status as measured by two criteria for successful transition: (1) acquisition of the knowledge, skills, and values necessary for legitimate occupation of the terminal status and (2) the integration of these into a meaningful self-directing sense of identity.

   To accomplish these tasks, we first need a conceptual framework for the analysis of interpersonal dynamics. Brown (1965) offers such a framework in his suggestion that interpersonal relationships can be described in terms of two dimensions—status and solidarity. The *status dimension* refers to the tendency for interpersonal relationships to be arranged in a superior-subordinate hierarchy. Behavior on this dimension arouses the need for power and is related to influencing and controlling others and being influenced and controlled. The *solidarity dimension* refers to the tendency for interpersonal relationships to be arranged on a dimension of proximity and remoteness. Behavior on this dimension arouses the need for affiliation and is related to intimacy, similarity of views, and frequent interaction or the lack of these. More detailed descriptions of the characteristics of solidarity and status are given in Table 9-1.

Table 9-1 Aspects of Solidarity and Status

	Personal characteristics	Spatial relations	Sentiments	Behavior	Symbols
Symmetrical relations	Solidarity marked by similarities of taste, attitude, fate, age, sex, occupation, income, and so on.	Solidarity marked by proximity (being near).	Solidarity marked by liking, sympathy, trust, and other pleasant sentiments.	Solidarity marked by frequent interaction, confiding in one another, beneficent actions, self-disclosure, and so on.	Solidarity marked by any perceptible similarity, proximity, or intimacy.
	Nonsolidarity marked by differences.	Nonsolidarity marked by remoteness (being far).	Nonsolidarity marked by indifference or dislike which are not pleasant sentiments.	Nonsolidarity marked by infrequent interaction and little intimacy.	Nonsolidarity marked by any perceptible difference, distance, or formality.
Asymmetrical relations	Status differences marked by differences in valued characteristics such as age, sex, occupation, income, and so on.	Status differences marked by being above or below, in front or behind.	Status differences marked by agreeable sentiments of superiority and by disagreeable sentiments of inferiority.	Status differences marked by influence, control, power, etc.	Status differences marked by any perceptible differences in valued characteristics, by "superior" and "inferior" spatial positions, or by influence and control.

Source: Brown, R. *Social Psychology*. Glencoe, Ill.: Free Press, 1965. p. 72.

Given these two dimensions, it is possible in a specific social environment to draw a psychological "map" of a person's interpersonal relationships. Every individual in the focal person's environment is placed on the map according to two coordinates—the extent to which the focal person perceives the individual to have influence and control over him and the amount of affection and intimacy the focal person shares with the individual. The result of this mapping is the distribution of the people with whom the focal person interacts into four quadrants—those people seen as highly influential and highly intimate, those highly intimate but with low influence, those with high influence and low intimacy, and those who are seen as neither influential nor intimate.

If we draw a psychological map for the occupant of a transitional role, we can begin to conceptualize the effect of his relationships on his movement through the system. To illustrate this analysis and to provide a specific case for discussion, we have drawn such a map for one rather special transitional role situation—a wilderness survival camp whose aim is to foster the character development of high school and college boys. This program, known as Outward Bound (Katz & Kolb, 1967), is a twenty-six-day camping experience that provides instruction in sailing, mountain-climbing, survival techniques, and other experiences designed to stretch a boy's conception of his abilities. The program is rugged and intensive and many boys report dramatic personal changes as a result of the experience.

The map shown in Figure 9-1 is drawn for an Outward Bound boy in one student group (known as a Watch at this particular ocean sailing school). It shows the relationships between this boy and all other people at the camp in terms of how much power he thinks these people have over him and how intimate he is with them. Note that the boy's fellow students fall in quadrant I while most of the teachers and staff of the camp are scattered through quadrants III and IV.

What effects do the individuals in each of these different quadrants have on the boy's process of transition? Are authorities more effective when they occupy quadrant III or when they occupy quadrant IV? For answers to these questions we must look to theories which seek to explain the effect of interpersonal relationships on behavior change. The most comprehensive theory in this area is Schein's elaboration of Lewin's classic unfreezing-moving-refreezing model of the change process (Bennis, Schein, Berlew, & Steele, 1964).

In Schein's model, change occurs through the assimilation of new information. This new information results in the cognitive redefinition of situations and new ways of perceiving the world. These new personal constructs then lead to changes in attitudes and behavior. The primary

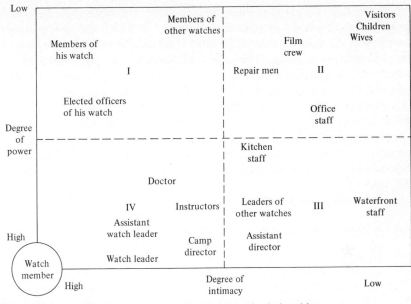

Figure 9-1 A typical watch member's interpersonal relationships at Outward Bound.

sources of information for changes in attitudes and behavior are other people. The individual in transition can either receive information from a single person through a process of observational learning labeled by Schein as *identification* or he can acquire information from a wide array of other sources via a process which Schein calls *scanning*.[2] These two processes mark the ends of a continuum where the scanning end implies attention to the content of the message regardless of the person, and the identification end implies attention and emotional reaction to the person at the expense of some of the content.

When an individual is scanning, his primary concern is about the usefulness of available information for solving his particular problem and about the expertness of the people who are the sources of information. He is not influenced by others about what is useful and who is expert and, therefore, the information that he voluntarily accepts or rejects is more likely to become integrated into his personality.

When the individual in transition acquires information through identification, it is the object of identification who determines what information is relevant and useful. There are two ways of identifying with

[2]"Identification" as used here refers to the behavioral consequences produced by models and not a global personality orientation.

others; defensive identification and positive identification. *Defensive identification* generally implies a relationship in which the change agent operates as the primary source of unfreezing (i.e., he provides the bulk of the disconfirming cues). The observer responds to this situation by becoming preoccupied with the change agent's position or status which is perceived to be the primary source of the change agent's power. This preoccupation with the position, in turn, implies a limited and often distorted view of the identification model. The observer tends to pay attention only to the power-relevant cues, tends to have little or no empathy for the person actually occupying the position, and tends to imitate blindly and often unconsciously only certain limited portions of the model's behavior.

According to Bennis et al. (pp. 376–377):

> *positive identification*, by contrast, tends to be person rather than position oriented. . . . The model's power or salience is perceived to lie in some personal attributes rather than in some formal position. . . . He [the observer] will tend to have empathy for the model and genuinely assimilate the new information obtained from seeing the world through the model's eyes rather than directly imitating his behavior. Thus, the target's new behavior and attitudes may not actually resemble the model's too closely. The whole process of identification will be more spontaneous, differentiated, and will enable further growth, rather than be compulsive and limiting.

Returning now to the map of the Outward Bound boy's interpersonal relationships (Figure 9-1), we can see that the boy will tend to use these three processes of acquiring information for behavior change differentially, depending on how much influence and intimacy he perceives others to have. Individuals who are low on intimacy and high on influence (quadrant III) will tend to elicit defensive identification. These are the formal authorities who have the power to make the boy obey, but their lack of intimacy with the boy precludes any empathic relationship. As a result, behavior changes coming from this relationship tend to be superficial imitations or mere compliance. The boy obeys because "It's the rules and if I don't, I'll be punished." In the classroom this type of formal-authority teacher tends to produce students who work for grades at the expense of learning.

The high-influence, high-intimacy individuals in quadrant IV will tend to elicit primarily positive identification. The boy will tend to know these people very well and trust them. This relationship provides a situation where the boy can explore the implications of new information for his own personality by exploring the implications it has for the model. Mutual trust and understanding provide a mechanism for the modification of general principles and rules to fit the individual case. As can be seen in Figure 9-1, many of the Outward Bound watch leaders elicited positive identification from their boys. Many changes in the boys' self-confidence came from sharing vicariously the confidence of their leader on a particularly difficult climb or rappel. Many private fears were alleviated by the leader's admission that he too once felt fear and had then mastered it. The leader and boys knew one another well enough to be mutually aware of times when the boy was really challenging himself and when he was "slacking off." General requirements for completing the course existed, but the intimacy between instructor and boy allowed for individualized evaluation.

Changes in behavior through positive identification are often directed to becoming liked by the model. Changes that do occur in this situation are more likely to be maintained than are behavior changes in the defensive-identification–formal-authority situation. Nonetheless, it is possible that the boy may change his behavior just to please the admired authority and will revert to old behavior patterns when he thinks that the authority no longer cares about him or will not know what he is doing (Kelman, 1961).

As the perceived influence of individuals in the boy's interpersonal relations decreases, information is increasingly gathered through the process of scanning. Thus, those individuals in quadrants I and II who have little generalized influence become sources of information only when the boy, on the basis of his current attitudes and values, decides that they are "experts" in regard to the particular information he needs. However, because he spends more time with, and is more similar to, those with whom he shares a high degree of intimacy, in this case his peers (see Table 9-1), most of his scanning targets will lie in quadrant I. Behavior changes resulting from the scanning process are very likely to be maintained by the individual because they are based on information chosen to coincide with his own knowledge and values; i.e., the process of behavior change is *self-directed*. However, because the peer group requires similar attitudes and behavior to maintain solidarity, the range of information available to the individual will be limited.

Boulding (1961, pp. 73–74) describes the role of the peer-group scanning process in changing attitudes and behavior in this way:

It is not by ceremonial and formal instructions alone, however, that value images are created. In our consideration of the dynamics of the value image we must not forget the extreme importance of the small face-to-face group, especially the group of the individual's peers. In every society, there seems to be a ceremonial value image which is transmitted by the official and formal institutions of the society; there seems to be, however, an informal value image which is often much more important in governing the actual behavior of an individual. It is this informal image which is transmitted by the peer group and also very often by the family. The value system of the schoolboy, of the street-corner society, of the soldier, or the executive is often markedly different from that which is involved from the rostrum or sounded from the pulpit. The sanctions of the peer group, however, are usually much more effective on the individual than the sanctions of superiors. This is the basic explanation of the persistence of crime in the face of preaching. *We rapidly learn to order our images in the way that the gang orders them because of the extremely low value we place on exclusion and loneliness. We can bear everything except not to be borne by others* (emphasis added).

Thus, we see that the process of scanning among peers is limited not by power but by the tendency to maintain similarity among intimates. The peer group tends to reinforce a common set of attitudes and behaviors which often run counter to those sanctioned by authorities.

This raises a problem for those formalized transitional institutions like schools whose task it is to socialize the young. In Schein's words, "The dilemma of socialization . . . is how to balance the greater power of potentially countercultural change agents (the peer group) against the more functional learning to be obtained from change agents who have less chance of becoming influential" (Bennis, et al., p. 380).

One typical solution to this dilemma has already been presented in the example of the training of medical students. Faculty members occupy their high-power–low-intimacy quadrant in students' eyes and elicit from students the kind of compliant, defensive identification that has been described. But by creating a work-overload problem and by making impossible demands, the faculty creates a double-bind situation which forces the peer culture to develop its own norms about what is important and to become responsible for behavior resulting from these norms. This strategy forces a student to scan among his peers for experts on "how to beat the system" and to choose for himself a strategy for learning, thus increasing the probability that changes in behavior and attitudes will be congruent with his personality.

A critical problem with this solution is that it requires a highly integrated and intimate peer group to be successful. In Becker's analysis of medical students, it was shown that academic success seemed to be related to the amount of peer-group organization; i.e., fraternity students did better than independents.

Hall (1966) has further documented this finding in an experimental examination of the role of authorities and peers in academic role transition. He studied science and engineering Ph.D. candidates at the

Massachusetts Institute of Technology and measured their degree of successful role transition in two ways, by their performance on general exams and by the degree to which their self-image increased in similarity to their perception of an admired professorial role model. Quite surprisingly, he found that amount of faculty contact was unrelated to either of these measures of success. Peer interaction, as measured by the number of sociometric links, however, was strongly related to both of these measures of successful role transition. In addition, the correlation between exam performance and peer interaction was shown to be independent of cumulative grade average. An illustration of the relationship between peer interaction and exam performance is shown for the nuclear engineering department in Figure 9-2. It may be noted that all the outstanding scores occur in the center group of high interconnecting and interacting students, while the failing students appear to be isolated in closed dyadic interactions.

This research on the importance of the peer group in bringing about change has great implications for the design of behavior-change programs. The growing concern in university administrations about the social "climate" of student living and the emergence of student-controlled experimental universities both point to a greater role for the student culture in the educative process. A similar trend is occurring in the field of psychotherapy in which increasing emphasis is being placed on group psychotherapy that emphasizes the importance of helping relationships among peers. As previously seen in Berzon's (1966) work with self-directed groups, peers can effectively help one another even when there is no formal leader.

Some very preliminary efforts are now being made to restructure experimentally peer groups to utilize behavior-change techniques. For example, Patterson, Shaw, and Ebner (1969) have used grade school students as "peer coaches" in changing academic and social behavior. In one case, a student who was the most popular boy in the class and the best student, was assigned to help modify the behavior of a student who often fought with the other children and frequently failed to attend to his lessons. The peer coach or model was a natural change agent with quick praise for others and a warm smile. Each day he helped the failing student by offering assistance in arithmetic and reinforced correct responses with social reinforcement and with points which led to special events (a contingency-management program). Within a few weeks, the failing student's aggressive behaviors became very infrequent and often none were observed. The frequency of his nonattendance fell below that of the mean for the other boys in the classroom. These results were maintained over the six-month follow-up period.

The findings of studies such as those cited above point to the

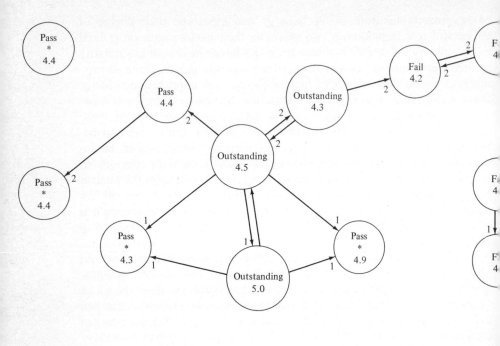

* These students did not
  complete the sociometric
  rating form.

Figure 9-2 Performance on Ph.D. general examination as a function of peer group interaction in a nuclear engineering department.
D. Hall. Peer and authority relationships during the transition from
student to scientist. Unpublished doctoral thesis, Massachusetts
Institute of Technology, 1966.

importance of social context in which behavior-change techniques are
applied. The two concepts of intimacy and status seem to be helpful in
understanding how the social environment influences the behavior of the
person in transition.

SUMMARY

A person who enters psychotherapy may experience a change of role as
he becomes labeled a "patient." When the patient later moves from

sickness to health, he may make transitions from one role to another. Typical transitional roles in our society are student, adolescent, parolee, the engaged person, and the apprentice. Transitional roles are successful, for the individual and for society, only if the occupant of the role leaves it to enter a new role.

One of the characteristics of transitional roles is that they may relieve the occupant of some responsibilities and impose others. The individual in the transitional role may be somewhat isolated and protected from the pressures of "real life." In the case of the adolescent, he is given a moratorium from the demands of the adult world and associates with his peers in the adolescent subculture. Also, the adolescent is allowed to practice adult behavior often without bearing the full consequences of his mistakes or failures. Similarly, the patient, student, or trainee needs to be given an opportunity to practice those behaviors which will be required of him in the new role into which he is moving.

Transitional roles often require the occupant to commit a large amount of his resources in learning new skills and developing values which are compatible with his final role. Many of these skills and values are learned in the context of interpersonal relationships which can be described in terms of status and solidarity. Individuals in transition tend to receive information from one person through a process of identification or from a wide array of sources through a process of scanning. If the identification is defensive, the observer pays attention primarily to the power aspects of the change agent. If the identification is positive, the observer is concerned with the personal aspects of the change agent and has empathy toward him. Changes through positive identification are more likely to be maintained than those produced through defensive identification.

Because of the importance of the peer group in either hindering or promoting change, some preliminary experiments have been conducted to restructure peer groups. An outstanding student, for example, can be a "coach" or model for a failing student and can reinforce the success of the student by using social reinforcement or secondary reinforcers in a contingency-management program. Increasing recognition is being given to the importance of the social context in facilitating and maintaining changes in behavior.

Chapter 10

Problems in the Assessment of Behavior Change

One of the essential characteristics of behavior-change programs is the accurate measurement of the behavior to be changed. But, like balancing a checkbook to determine if the bank is correct, this is more easily said than done. How the measurement is to be made and how the results are to be interpreted are not always clear. In fact, research on behavior change presents some of the most complex and difficult methodological problems in the behavioral sciences. Attempts to solve these problems inevitably raise basic issues of scientific inquiry. This chapter will explore the implications of some of these issues for behavior-change research.

As previously mentioned, the criticism of the therapeutic effectiveness of psychoanalytically oriented treatment methods by Eysenck (1952, 1955, 1961) resulted in much controversy. In a survey of studies measuring the outcome of treatment, he concluded (1961, p. 720):

> With the single exception of the psychotherapeutic methods based on learning theory, results of published research with military and civilian

206

neurotics, and with both adults and children, suggest that the therapeutic effects of psychotherapy are small or non-existent, and do not in any demonstrable way add to the non-specific effects of routine medical treatment or to such events as occur in the patients' every day experience.

This challenge to the conventional forms of therapy met with counterchallenge,[1] praise,[2] and methodological inquiry.[3] It is hazardous to make overall conclusions about the effects of psychotherapy, either positive or negative. This is not to say that there are no good studies on the effects of psychotherapy. The problems arise when one makes conclusions about the general effects of all forms of therapy on patients in general. Before statements of this sort can be made, it is necessary to control certain sources of error which up to this time has been a very difficult task. Many factors or variables, in addition to the therapy itself, may be responsible for a failure to find positive results, such as the use of criteria not relevant to the therapy, the improper comparison of experimental and control groups, and the use of tests that are insensitive to change.

PROBLEMS OF RESEARCH DESIGN
Design Structure

Meehl (1955) has suggested some minimum requirements for outcome studies in psychotherapy. These involve the use of an experimental and a control group, pretherapy and posttherapy observation or testing, and a follow-up study of both groups which may be repeated once or several times. If O_1 represents the first observation of the experimental group which receives treatment (T) and O_2 represents the first observation of the control group that receives no treatment and so on, then the design structure proposed by Meehl looks something like this:

$$O_1 \quad T \quad O_3 \quad O_5 \quad (O_7)$$
$$O_2 \quad \quad O_4 \quad O_6 \quad (O_8)$$

By comparing the changes in the treatment group before and after treatment (the difference between O_1 and O_3) with changes, if any, in the

---

[1]"There is no particular harm in pointing out to the Eysenckians that their simple-minded physiological etiologies and methods of treatment cannot be ascribed to them as a virtue" (Glover, 1965, p. 161). See also Chapter 2.

[2]"Curiously, though, we have only the most sparse scientific support for this faith [of psychoanalysts] in psychotherapy. Indeed, any demand for proof of its effectiveness is viewed with the shocked surprise that would greet an Englishman who asked for proof that Britain needs a queen. . . . I have not seen any study of comparable size or validity which neutralized Eysenck's conclusions" (Davidson, 1965, p. 172).

[3]Cf. Bergin (1963), Strupp (1965), Schuldt & Truax (1970) Garfield & Bergin (1971).

control group (the difference between O_2 and O_4), some notion of the effectiveness of the treatment can be obtained. Ignoring for the moment additional follow-up studies ($O_{5,6,7,8}$), it may be helpful to consider this basic *pretest—posttest control-group design*. This design has stood for many years as the model for outcome research in nearly every area— from opinion polling to therapy research. It serves well because it provides potentially adequate control for many factors which could cause changes in the experimental group independent of the treatment. Campbell (1957) has listed some of the more important of these factors. They may be briefly summarized as follows:

History   During the time between the observations of the subjects, many events may occur to them unrelated to the experimental treatment. Some of these events, such as a national crisis or a personal achievement, may provide alternate explanations of what appear to be treatment effects.

Maturation   Subjects change systematically from pretest to posttest; e.g., the child in therapy grows out of his problems.

Testing   Here Campbell makes the distinction between "reactive" and "nonreactive" tests. Reactive tests are those which influence the subject; e.g., the subject is interviewed about his psychological complaints. Nonreactive tests are those of which the subject is essentially unaware; e.g., ratings of the subject made by his employer. Without control subjects, it is difficult to say whether a reactive pretest or the treatment caused the change in the treatment group. An obvious example would be IQ tests given before and after therapy.

Instrument Decay   The most common examples of this variable are found in the use of rating scales. From pretesting to posttesting, judges can become more experienced or more fatigued, thus introducing systematic differences in preratings and postratings.

Statistical Regression   Many times groups are selected for a particular treatment on the basis of extreme scores on O_1. In this manner, extreme high scorers on the MMPI neurotic triad might be selected for psychotherapy. The natural trend for extreme scores is to regress toward the mean on a retest.

Selection The initial selection of the experimental and control-group members might be inadvertently biased.

Experimental Mortality Even if the experimental and control groups were equivalent and control groups were equivalent at O_1 and O_2, some subjects may drop out of treatment or be unavailable for subsequent testing. These subjects may be a group of persons with special characteristics that interact positively or negatively with the treatment. This is a typical problem in making inferences about changes in the attitudes of college freshmen and seniors because those students adversely affected by college may not be available for testing.

In addition to these seven factors that threaten the validity of experimental studies, Campbell and Ross (1968) and Campbell (1969) have recently suggested two more: *instability* (unreliability of measures often resulting from wide fluctuations in the data) and *selection-maturation interaction* (selection biases producing differential rates of maturation among the subjects).

To control adequately these threats to validity, all subjects should come from the same population and be randomly assigned to experimental and control groups. This, however, is an ideal which is seldom realized. Some of the reasons for this will be discussed later. One of the values in spelling out the factors that threaten validity is that alternative designs can be used to control for the most threatening factors when the design cannot be perfect. For example, in a study of personality change after client-centered psychotherapy by Rogers and Dymond (1954), each patient was compared with himself before and after treatment (the patient was his own control) to eliminate factors such as motivation for change and unique personal histories, and an independent control group was used to control for history and maturation.

Even if the logic of the experimental design proposed by Meehl could be perfectly fulfilled; in some cases, it would still need to be extended. When the pretest is reactive (and nearly all tests are to some degree) we are faced with an interaction effect between the test and the treatment. For example, if the patient is given a test that measures his self-ideal discrepancy before therapy, he may become aware of the discrepancy between what he is and what he wants to be. This awareness may increase his motivation to be helped and he may thus profit more from therapy than a person who has not had this same pretest.

Solomon (1949) has developed a modification of the basic control-group design which permits the reactive pretest effect to be measured and partialed out. This is known as the *Solomon four-group design.* Its structure has been described by Campbell (1957) in the following manner:

$$O_1 \quad T \quad O_2$$
$$O_3 \qquad\quad O_4$$
$$\qquad\quad T \quad O_5$$
$$\qquad\qquad\quad O_6$$

Here all four groups are assumed to come from the same population. There are two equivalent experiment-treatment groups and four equivalent control groups. Standard statistical analysis can be used to determine both treatment effects and pretest effects. This design has become a new standard for the outcome research, but its complexity makes one wonder at its practical use in research, especially when Meehl (1955) notes that in a perusal of over two hundred journal articles and a dozen books only one paper approximated the comparatively lenient criteria he suggested for an adequate outcome study.

Campbell (1957) has mentioned another design which can control the above-mentioned factors and also avoid the pretest problem. This design involves random assignment of subjects to experimental and control groups at some point before treatment begins (A) and elimination of all pretesting:

$$A \quad T \quad O_1$$
$$A \qquad\quad O_2$$

If assignment to groups is truly random, then any differences between O_1 and O_2 are attributable to the treatment. The major problem with this design is that it is less precise and less sensitive to change; but it does offer a possible alternative to pretest designs.

Turning to questions of follow-up in outcome research, Meehl (1955) has indicated the desirability of one or more follow-up studies of both the experimental and control groups so that remission rates can be estimated and curves extrapolated. The practical problems involved in follow-up studies, however, appear almost insurmountable. Sargent (1960) has discussed patient attitudes which hamper accurate reporting in the follow-up interview. Most patients want to forget the time when they were sick and are likely to see continuing follow-up as an invasion of their privacy. Attempts to interview friends and associates of the patient are likely to be even more offensive. In addition, there is likely to be a good deal of "selective forgetting" in reporting information.

On another level, there is the more basic problem of finding a person after he leaves treatment. Results at the Phipps Psychiatric Clinic, Johns Hopkins (Frank, 1958) are typical. One year after therapy, the investigators were able to contact fifty-three out of fifty-four patients; at two years, forty-eight out of fifty-four. "Since then attrition has been marked." It is doubtful whether meaningful exacerbation and remission curves could be extrapolated. Also, as one might expect, there are indications of systematic biases in patients who are not contacted in the follow-up years (Frank, 1969). It has been found that in questionnaire follow-up studies the group which returns the questionnaires is likely to be very different from the group which does not return the questionnaires (cf. Speer & Zold, 1971). The "successful" patients are the ones most likely to reply.

If we consider the reactive pretest problem, other complications arise. Since the posttest will act as a pretest for the follow-up, a continuation of the logic of Solomon's design would require the addition of four groups for each follow-up period. In the random-assignment–no-pretest design by Campbell, two additional groups would be required for each follow-up. Add to these difficulties the fact that few researchers are particularly interested in waiting for two to four years to complete their projects—and the follow-up problem appears to be one that allows no easy solution.

Control Procedures

The concept of "controls" seems almost synonymous with "control groups." But as indicated earlier, it might be more useful to work with factors or variables to be controlled—what Rogers and Dymond (1954, pp. 21–22) call "control phenomena." In their words:

> The important concept regarding controls is not so much the concept of *control groups* as the concept of *control phenomena*—that is, the importance of controls lies in adequate accounting for variables presumed to be relevant to therapy. Such controls can be instituted in many ways. Sometimes it means using separate control groups. At other times the best controls may come from using different measures of the same person, that is, the "own control" method. In still other instances controls lie in data not in people. For example, if one wishes to describe those points in therapy which counselors characterize as deep, an essential part of such a description comes out of a comparison of such points with randomly selected passages. Finally, effective control methods lie in statistical controls as a supplement to experimental controls. For example, if one wishes to institute controls when continuous measurement is involved (e.g., recognition time in a perception experiment), a method of choice may be analysis of covariance where the effects of initial differences between experimental and control groups are partialed out and the groups equated by statistical means.

In addition to the above control techniques, it is useful to further divide Rogers and Dymond's "separate control" groups into three types:

Random-assignment Control Groups. Subjects from the same general population are assigned randomly to experimental and control groups.

Stratified Sampling Controls. In this design, relevant variables are controlled by having them occur in the same proportion in both the experimental and control groups.

Matched Controls. In this design each experimental subject is matched with a control subject on relevant variables.

The last two designs present an interesting dilemma. Although this control of relevant variables increases precision by making the two groups more similar on the matched variables, the matching procedure violates the principle of random assignment and increases the probability that the two groups may be significantly different on other variables (Selltiz, Jahoda, Deutsch, & Cook, 1959).[4] Frank (1959) questions whether it is worth the trouble to match controls because research in psychotherapy is in such a preliminary stage that the relevant variables are not known. He cites the previously unrecognized effect of social class on the therapeutic process as an example (But see Luborsky, Chandler, Auerbach, Cohen, & Bachrach, 1971). Brunswik (1956) also makes an important point in this regard. Most psychological variables, he notes, are tied to other variables (e.g., social class with delay of gratification, IQ, and so forth). The manipulation of one variable manipulates other known and unknown variables in unclear and perhaps unnatural ways. For this reason, the matching of subjects not only makes generalization difficult, but also may manipulate variables the researcher has not considered, which will in turn cause differences which he may attribute to the known variable manipulated in the matching process. These considerations do not invalidate matching methods, but do suggest great caution in using them.

In addition, there are problems in selecting variables on which to base the choice of the experimental and control groups. There is a similar problem in specifying the variables involved in the treatment condition. Failure to specify carefully can lead to erroneous generalizations. Eysenck (1961) lists four types of variables which may be peculiar to the

[4]This, of course, need not be so if the experimental and control subjects are selected randomly from a large sample of people who are matched on the variable—a highly impractical procedure.

experimental group. None of these is covered in most theoretical discussions of what occurs in therapy. These variables include the medical treatment of minor illnesses, long periods of rest in an institution, a more nutritional diet, and attempts by the therapist to change the attitudes of the family. Although these variables do not confound all studies, Eysenck's point is well taken. Overemphasis on unvalidated theories about the process of change may cause us to overlook other important aspects of the treatment process.

Another phenomenon which may work to produce differences in the treatment condition, regardless of the treatment, is the therapy dropout. With all control methods but the own-control design the person who drops out of therapy constitutes a major biasing factor toward a *type I error*, i.e., finding a positive result when in fact there was none. (*Type II error* would occur when no positive result was found when in fact there was one.) The dropouts are likely to be self-selected and represent therapeutic failures (assuming that they do not improve). If these failures are not included in the experimental group totals—they cannot be included if the dropout is before the posttest—then the experimenter has excluded a group of persons of low change potential, thus artificially increasing the apparent amount of change in the experimental group. Further, it is not clear which subjects should be removed from the control group to counter this bias or how they should be selected. Some research efforts have been directed toward identifying abrupt terminators from therapy so that administrative and research problems associated with dropouts can be reduced (e.g., Affect & Mednick, 1959; Barron, 1953).

Assignment of Control Subjects

If the control procedure selected involves the use of subjects as controls, there are several possible methods for designing the control groups. Perhaps the most common one used in studies of psychotherapy is the *waiting-list control method.* This method requires the random assignment of patients on a waiting list to therapy and control groups. Random assignment is necessary to contravene several biasing tendencies that would otherwise operate in the construction of the control group. For example, without random assignment, interviewers will sometimes select for therapy those who appear to be the sickest and in the greatest need. This would appear to create a clear bias toward a type II error. We cannot, however, be certain of the direction of the bias in the light of Luborsky's (1962) findings that anxiety and discomfort are positively related to improvement in therapy.

On the other hand, there is a growing body of research suggesting that therapists tend to prefer patients who have characteristics which will help them improve, e.g., higher IQ, higher ego-strength, psychological-mindedness, higher social class, and so on. Thus, there may be a selection factor in treatment assignments which gives therapy to those patients who will get well anyway. This would introduce a type I error (see Levinson, 1962; Schaffer & Myers, 1954; Saenger, 1970).

Even when random assignment is used, there are still problems. Very disturbed and uncomfortable people on the waiting list often do not wait. They seek help elsewhere. Sometimes they remain in the research project and sometimes they leave altogether. Either event biases the results toward a type II error; in the first instance controls are receiving therapy, in the second the most disturbed members of the control group are not included in the sample. Finally, there is some question whether the waiting list is really a no-treatment control. It would seem that interviewing, testing, and so forth may in fact have therapeutic value (Goldstein, 1960). This possibility will be discussed in more detail subsequently.

The *own-control method* (e.g., Rogers & Dymond, 1954) nicely avoids the aforementioned problems of the waiting-list control and some others such as the differential motivation for therapy. In the own-control method, each patient is compared with himself before and after treatment. Unfortunately, this method has some problems of its own. There is the possibility of reactive pretests and critical events before therapy begins. Also, a painful waiting for therapy may increase the perceived value of the therapy and the expectation that it will help. The patient becomes the aspiring knight who must do penance before entering the sacred shrine (cf. Frank, 1959). If there is anything at all to these speculations, then we are faced with a problem of logical explanation. If the patients improve more in therapy than in waiting under these conditions, are we justified in saying that the therapy alone is more effective than no treatment?

A second problem with the own-control method is more obvious. It provides no control for events that occur during the course of therapy. For example, Frank (1958) suspects that neuroses may get better during the summer months. He uses the drop-off in intake percentages during summer months as data. Similarly, it appears that neuroses may go into remission after about a year (Eysenck, 1961). Thus, a patient may "hit the bottom" near the end of the waiting period or at the beginning of therapy and gradually improve after that. In the same way, young patients may grow out of their difficulties.

Finally, to control for passage of time, the waiting period should be as long as the therapy. This raises two very difficult problems. The first is the ethical one of depriving persons of help who need it. Whether in fact there is an unfair or unreasonable deprivation depends in part upon whether available treatment facilities are being withheld. Very often all treatment facilities are in use, the demand for treatment cannot be met, and the problem is better considered one of allocation of limited resources rather than deprivation. The second problem is one that has already been mentioned. Disturbed persons do wait for long periods of time for therapy.

A third type of control is the use of *population base rates.* Proper use of this control permits generalizations of the following type: treatment X shows more (or less) improvement than the base rate of improvement in the absence of that treatment. Although from a practical point of view this method provides a very effective practical score-keeping device, it is not as useful from a purely scientific view as some other types of control. The basic problem lies in the specification of the nature and causes of the base-rate improvement (spontaneous remission). In other words, in most cases one cannot specify the nature of the "treatment" given to the base-rate controls.

Denker's attempt to give base rates for recovery from neurotic disorder can serve as an example of the difficulties in this specification (reported in Eysenck, 1961). Denker studied 500 consecutive disability claims due to psychoneurosis, taken from the files of the Equitable Life Assurance Society of the United States. These patients were treated only by general practitioners, not psychotherapists. He found that 45 percent of the patients recovered after one year, another 2 percent after two years, another 10 percent after three, another 5 percent after four, and another 4 percent after five years.[5] His criteria for improvement were: "a) return to work, and ability to carry on well in economic adjustments for at least a five-year period; b) complaint of no further or only very slight difficulties; c) making of successful social adjustments" (Eysenck, 1961, p. 710). Even if we accept these criteria as reported—and there is perhaps question about bias in reporting to one's insurance company—there is certainly a question as to what caused the return to health. Eysenck seems content to call it spontaneous remission and leave it at that. A critique of Denker's study by Cartwright (1955), however, does not make the remission appear spontaneous. Cartwright points out that Denker's neurotic patients were selected at the peak of the Depression, the follow-up carrying over to the early 1940s. Since one of Denker's major criteria was employment, it would seem reasonable to attribute remission

[5]More recently, Eysenck (1969) has reviewed a German study by Cremerius (1962) of 523 neurotic patients followed up for a period between eight and ten years. The abolition of symptoms was found in 21 percent of those treated by psychoanalytically oriented methods, 12 percent in those treated by verbal discussion, and 7 percent in those treated by hypnosis. Some initial selection was made of patients likely to be benefited by the various treatment methods.

of these patients to increasing employment opportunities after the Depression. In addition, it is unreasonable to think that these patients went without "therapy." Even the most "general" practioner is willing to hear a patient's troubles. Similarly, there are always friends, relatives, ministers, and so on who can help when the need arises.

Special Effects—Spontaneous Remission, Expectation, the Placebo Effect

It may be helpful to consider briefly a set of related factors that tend to produce errors in outcome research. Barron and Leary (1955) have provided an example. In a pre and post study with 150 psychoneurotic patients who had applied for treatment, eighty-five received group therapy, forty-two received individual therapy, and twenty-three were placed on waiting lists to serve as controls. Criteria for improvement in this study were changes in scores on a standard psychological test, the Minnesota Multiphasic Personality Inventory (MMPI). At the posttest conducted after approximately eight months, the therapy patients showed significant decreases on the depression, hysteria, hypomania, and lie scales of the MMPI (both individual and group therapy patients). In addition, group-therapy patients decreased significantly on paranoia and psychasthenia. Both therapy groups showed significant increases on the ego-strength scale. The control patients also showed improvement. Depression, psychastenia, and hysteria scales decreased slightly more for the controls than for the therapy groups. Ego-strength scores of the controls increased significantly.

Barron and Leary concluded that, for the most part, the changes were in the same direction for the therapy and control groups and of about equal magnitude. They further suggested that the mere act of commitment to therapy may help to break the neurotic pattern and that the initial interview and psychological testing may themselves be therapeutic events.

This study was one of the first that called attention to the possibility of a so-called placebo effect in psychotherapy research (cf. Campbell, 1957; Rosenthal & Frank, 1956). A placebo generally refers to an inert substance given to a patient as a medicine which produces a therapeutic effect (Shapiro, 1960). A common example is the administration of "sugar pills" to patients to eliminate headaches (Lasagna, Laties, & Dohan, 1958). Not only may psychotherapy produce a placebo effect, but so also may initial interviews, testing, and placement on a waiting list.

The placebo effect is of concern to outcome-research strategy because it seriously challenges the possibility of a "no-treatment" control. The previous discussion of controls was based on the assumption that the control group received no treatment. It was seen, however, that untreated patients are usually involved in some kind of therapy-type interactions with friends, relatives, etc. It now appears that the very act of setting up a control group may be a kind of therapy. As Frank (1959) points out, a good deal of the change in the patient may be a result of the patient's expectation of change and his perception of the potency of the therapeutic institution.

Goldstein (1960) has listed several control-group activities which could be "pseudotherapeutic": intake interview, initial psychological testing, social-work interview, periodic and/or post-wait-period psychological testing, post-wait psychiatric interview, and interviews with a patient's relatives or friends. Controls have often participated in one or more of these activities. Goldstein has given a formula for control-group improvement which is similar to Frank's. Improvement is a function of the patient's degree of favorable expectation of improvement from psychotherapy and the extent to which he receives professional attention via nonspecific placebo-like activities. Conversely, it can be argued that waiting may make some patients more difficult to treat as their symptoms become more firmly established. Sufficient evidence on the influence of control-group activities and waiting has not yet been obtained.

To overcome this problem, a shift in research strategy is required. It is helpful to think in terms of comparing one type of therapy with another rather than comparing therapy with "nothing" (Campbell, 1957; Frank, 1958; Goldstein, 1960). The recognition that therapy is only one of many types of potentially therapeutic dyadic interactions represents a major research breakthrough. It opens the door to the study of within-therapy variables such as patient and therapist expectations, length of therapy, and the theoretical orientation of the therapist as they influence outcome. In an extensive review of research on the effectiveness of psychotherapy (Fiske, Luborsky, Parloff, Hunt, Orne, & Reiser, 1970, p. 729) the authors suggest:

> It is impossible to conceive of a true (i.e., untreated) control group which can be precisely implemented in such research. A group not explicitly treated (in some way) as part of the study is likely to suffer serious attrition or to seek treatment elsewhere. Also, withholding therapy is itself a treatment. Patients in an own-control group who wait a period of time before treatment are affected by that waiting (e.g., they may become less amenable to the treatment they subsequently receive). Hence, the comparison must be between levels of a single type of treatment (e.g., time-limited versus unlimited) or between qualitatively different treatments.

Another source of bias lies in the differential evaluation of experimental and control groups by experimenters resulting from the therapy given to the experimental groups. A study by Walker and Kelly (1960) is illustrative. A group of newly admitted schizophrenic patients in a Veterans' Administration hospital were given short-term psychotherapy and compared with a control group who did not receive treatment. No differences in improvement were found, except that significantly more patients in the control group were discharged from the hospital than the patients in the therapy group. The researchers suggested that apparently higher therapeutic goals were set for the treatment group than the control group. No follow-up differences were found between the two groups.

Here is an instance in which a relatively objective criterion for improvement, discharge from a hospital, was biased so as to show no positive effects or negative effects for the experimental group. It is possible that therapists, in their desire to help patients, keep them in the hospital longer and thus make them appear worse than untreated patients. One cannot help but wonder if this phenomenon does not occur in other criteria for improvement. We may very well have here a particular instance of what White (1961) has called "relative deprivation." This is the phenomenon in which people who have had very little of a commodity raise their level of aspiration very high when they are given a small quantity of the commodity. White notes that this phenomenon has led to dissatisfaction and unrest in underdeveloped countries.

The same may be true of the prospect of receiving therapy. Having made a therapy contract, the patient may feel a certain amount of relief. He may now begin to want new comfort, to be more perfect, or "normal." He will most likely become more conscious of his faults and more painfully honest about himself; his self-ideal and his perceived-self correlation will decrease; in short, he will tend to see himself negatively. The therapist may also then perceive him more negatively. Thus, it may be that even though control patients and experimental patients do not differ on objective criteria, the experimental patients may be more "honest" and use more stringent subjective criteria (e.g., Barron and Leary found significant decreases in the MMPI lie scores for the therapy groups, but not for the control group).

One way out of this problem is to use evaluation scales in which the patient (relative, therapist, ward personnel, and so forth) defines his evaluation criteria for the researcher. In this way, changes in the criteria used for evaluation can be noted.

EVALUATION OF OUTCOME—THE CRITERION PROBLEM

The development of suitable outcome criteria is perhaps one of the most pressing problems in behavior-change research. It is not the purpose of this section to review the various kinds of outcome measures; this has been done quite adequately in a number of other articles (Cohler, 1963; Eysenck, 1961; Forsyth & Fairweather, 1961). Instead, the emphasis is placed once again on methodological problems in defining the criterion and the resulting strategy of research. The selection of criterion variables inevitably involves consideration of some basic strategic alternatives in the process of scientific inquiry. Three of these will be considered.

Naturalistic versus Hypothesis-testing Research

The issue here is whether it is best to observe as many changes as possible and then try to interpret them, or whether one should formulate specific hypotheses and interpretations in advance and then test them by gathering relevant data. The advantage of the first strategy is that it is very sensitive to change—it can pick up changes which existing theories do not predict. The disadvantage is that it becomes difficult to specify what variables produced the change. The second strategy improves the ability to isolate variables but increases the probability that some changes will not be detected because the theory does not predict them. Thus, the statement that psychotherapy does not produce any change in patients is not completely justified. It could just as well be that the theories we have about what happens in psychotherapy are not able to predict the changes that do occur (cf. Edwards & Cronbach, 1962; Campbell, 1957; Strupp, 1971).

Most researchers, however, agree that this is not an issue of either/or but a matter of sequence. They point out as do Butler, Rice, and Wagstaff (1962) that the development of all science is from naturalistic observation to hypothesis testing. The question then becomes, "When have we observed enough to begin testing hypotheses and formulating variables?" It is only in the face of rather dismal and oftentimes negative results (e.g., Eysenck, 1961, 1969) that we are beginning to shake off oversimplified preconceptions and face the tremendous complexity of the therapeutic dyad.

Nomothetic versus Idiographic Approaches to Evaluation

This decision refers to strategy in selecting dimensions on which to measure change. Should one use variables derived from general personality theories (variables which we assume to operate in all individuals in general, lawful ways) or should one consider variables which seem primarily relevant to the individual patient? The nomothetic approach has the advantage of giving comparable scores, while the idiographic approach presumably gives only qualitative differences. The danger of the nomothetic approach is its potential insensitivity to change. It is very difficult for a person to change on a dimension that is not relevant to him (Krech, Crutchfield, & Ballachey, 1962). In addition, it is difficult for a person to report how he has changed if he is not asked the right questions.

Since idiographic methodology has only recently gained acceptance by psychological researchers, it may be useful to describe the idiographic approach to personality assessment in some detail and to describe some specific idiographic-research methods. Much confusion surrounds the idiographic-nomothetic controversy. The source of this confusion lies in the fact that other similar, but conceptually distinct, issues break along the same lines as the idiographic-nomothetic issue. As a result, idiographic and nomothetic tend to be defined in terms of these associated issues which have often been discussed in psychology. Idiographic has been associated with subjectivism and intuition while nomothetic has been associated with objectivism and positivism. William James referred to "tender-minded" and "tough-minded" researchers. Allport (1962) referred to the unique versus the general while Brunswik (1956) distinguishes between the naturalistic method and the experimental method. The list of contrasting conceptualizations can probably be extended indefinitely.

Although there is undoubtedly some "truth" in all of these definitions, the ambiguity that arises from them renders the idiographic-nomothetic distinction relatively useless for scientific purposes. Though it is perhaps arbitrary, we can, for the purposes of this discussion, define the idiographic approach in terms of two principles: (1) The idiographic approach is concerned with studying the patterning of components within a single individual, as opposed to studying the correlates of a particular component or group of components across individuals; (2) The idiographic approach attempts to minimize theoretical and methodological distortions of the subject's naturalistic behavior.

The implications of these two principles can best be seen in the research strategy which results from them (cf. Katz, 1962). The individual's behavior should be assessed in varied situations. The range and variation of the stimuli presented to the person should be such that the person is encouraged to respond throughout the range of his response capacity in a way representative of his natural behavior patterns. The individual should be allowed to respond in ways which best communicate his reactions to the situation. In many cases, one cannot best express his opinion by answering true or false. No matter how much care is taken to observe these principles just mentioned, all is lost if "unnatural" statistical methods combine the data in artificial ways or if the data are "trimmed" to fit into neat compartments of existing theory.

A collaborative effort between the researcher and the subject or patient may also be helpful. Rollo May (1958, p. 5) has quoted Strauss as saying, "The unconscious ideas of the patient are more often than not the conscious theories of the therapist." In order to avoid making the subject a projective test of his theory, the researcher should attempt to gain the subject's point of view. A joint agreement of collaboration may be useful in preventing a description of the behavior which is exclusively researcher oriented. Finally, both parties should attempt to gain a full understanding of the situation in which the behavior occurs.

Some impression of the use of idiographic methods in behavior-change research may be provided by the following examples of test instruments. The *self-anchoring scale* by Kilpatrick and Cantril (1960) is one of the better-known idiographic methods. It is an excellent example of the use of the response-freedom principle without the loss of nomothetic-comparison power. Whereas ordinary rating scales dictate for the subject the variable they are rating (e.g., self-respect) and assume the meaning of the variable to be the same for all subjects, Kilpatrick and Cantril ask the subject to give as complete a definition as he can of both ends of the continuum represented by the variable. Thus, in psychotherapy research we might ask the patient to describe the best person he can imagine and the worst person. Then by showing him a 10-point rating scale, the ends of which are defined by his two descriptions, we can ask him to rate his present self, his self five years ago, his ideal self, etc. Two kinds of data are obtained here—a description of the person's salient concerns which define the variable (these definitions can be content analyzed to get an empirical definition for a large population) and a rating on the variable which is comparable across individuals.

Shapiro (1961) has developed a *personal-questionnaire method* to measure changes in psychiatric patients which utilizes the joint decisions of the psychologist and patient to construct the questionnaire. Following an interview in which the patient discusses his problem, the psychologist produces a list of symptoms in the patient's own words. These are then clarified by further discussion and a trial questionnaire is constructed in which each symptom statement is supplemented by an improvement statement and a recovery statement. These three statements are then scaled along a continuum of pleasant-unpleasant. The questionnaire is then administered at various times during the patient's treatment.

In Kelly's Role Construct Repertory Test (Rep Test), the subject is given a list of roles three at a time, such as mother, father, girl friend (Kinne, 1963). His task is to tell how two of them are alike and how they are different from the third. After a number of these constructs are obtained, the subject is then asked to tell which roles are described by the various constructs he has developed. The resulting role-construct matrix is then subjected to a nonparametric factor analysis. The major factors can then be extracted, as well as the subject's perceptions of the various role members, his identification figures, and many other useful variables. The chief advantage of this and other methods of single-case factor analysis is that they permit the assessment of changes in the saliency, the intensity, and the structure of relationships among the different variables.

Objective versus Subjective Change

This last decision to be made in selecting outcome criteria turns on the assumed validity of subjective report. Most attempts to find relationships between objective behavioral indices and subjective report fail to find consistent results (Forsyth & Fairweather, 1961; Kelman & Parloff, 1957; Parloff, Kelman, & Frank, 1954). Outcome research which uses both objective and subjective criteria often shows change on one type of criteria and not on the other. A particularly good example of this is an experiment done by Heller and Goldstein (1961). To measure changes in dependency during therapy, they gave patients a subjective measure of dependency (the Edwards Personal Preference Schedule Scales) and a behavioral measure of dependency (a role-playing form of the Rozensweig P-F test). The posttherapy results indicated that patients had changed in subjective report of dependence but on the behavioral measure of dependence, there was no change. Rogers and Dymond (1954) have found similar results. Some of this discrepancy between objectively measured behavior can be accounted for by factors that bias subjective reports.

Two factors which can influence subjective report have already been discussed—relative deprivation and constraints placed on the subject by the experimenter so that he can obtain nomothetic data. An additional group of factors can be subsumed under the heading of *reciprocal-role expectations*. The classic formulation here is Hathaway's "hello-goodbye effect" (1948). His general notion is that the patient, in his statements and evaluations, tries to legitimize his relationship with the therapist by acting out his perception of the therapist-patient role relationship. Specifically, the patient applying for therapy immediately presents problems in order to justify the contact. He is likely to make the problems seem fairly serious, even though there is no necessary relationship between the problems he presents and his real reason for entering therapy. Later, as therapy draws to a close, the patient will begin to summarize, wrap up old topics and hesitate to bring up new ones. The patient will imply that topics of conversation have been adequately treated; perhaps saying he feels better. In short, the patient will, to some degree, say what he thinks the therapist wants to hear. Here one may recall the embarrassment of Freud when he discovered that his patients had made up stories of childhood seduction, perhaps to please him. There is a cautionary lesson here.

Frank (1959) has suggested that some of the supposed recovery from symptoms of persons on a waiting list for therapy might be accounted for by variations in their verbal reports. If persons on the waiting list decide against treatment, they may minimize their symptoms; those who continue to want treatment may emphasize them. There is the additional possibility that if a patient says he feels better or worse than he actually does, his feelings may change to correspond to his statement. His statement may or may not accurately correspond with his behavior.

One approach toward a solution to these problems of subjective report lies perhaps in the interpretation of subjective reports as a function of the situation in which the report is made. Kelman (1961) has developed a theory related to this approach. He distinguishes three levels of attitude change—*compliance, identification,* and *internalization.* In compliance, the attitude change is demonstrated only under surveillance of the influencer (e.g., the therapist). In identification, the change is demonstrated when the situation is of salience to the influencing agent (i.e., when the therapist is likely to find out by testing the patient). In internalization, the change is demonstrated in situations where it is relevant to issues of concern to the person (i.e., the patient demonstrates change in his everyday life). It is this last level of change which is the objective of therapy. But for the most part, change has been tested only at the first two levels. To test the last level, testing needs to be done by persons whom the patient does not perceive as related to the therapy.

The so-called objective (e.g., multiple choice) tests can also be biased by the person taking them. Kelly (1955) has neatly presented the dilemma in psychological testing by noting that in projective tests the experimenter attempts to determine what is on the subject's mind, while in objective tests the subject attempts to determine what is on the experimenter's mind. The experimenter may also bias the outcome by using idiosyncratic definitions of variables or unusual rating scales.

A more subtle problem is that of rater bias. A study showing improvement with electro-shock therapy can serve as an illustration (Brill, Crumptom, Eiduson, Grayson, Hellman, Richards, Straussman, & Unger, 1957). This study attempted to determine some of the specific factors associated with improvement produced by electro-shock therapy by systematically eliminating important variables. This was done with successive groups of patients. For example, in one group, the experimenters conducted the usual treatment procedure but did not administer the shock. In another group, strapping the patient down and administering the shock was eliminated. In another group, the muscle relaxation shot was eliminated, and so on. One of the criteria used was ratings by ward personnel. Results, in general, indicated no significant differences in the amount of improvement between groups, except in extreme cases. One of the difficulties in making generalizations from this study is the fact that it is difficult to tell whether ward personnel changed their ratings because of actual differences produced in the patients or because of their expectation that patients would improve after electro-shock treatment. (This expectation should have been constant for all groups.) The addition of another control group might test this hypothesis. Nurses could be asked to rate untreated patients whom they were told had received electro-shock on the previous shift. This might give an estimate of the effect of expectation. Another method would be to obtain independent estimates of the nurses' belief in the effectiveness of electro-shock treatment and correlate these estimates with their improvement ratings. The expectation effect could then be removed by partial correlation.

Another issue in behavior-change research is the use of objective personality tests constructed by the method of contrasting groups. There is some question whether change scores on these tests, such as the Minnesota Multiphasic Personality Inventory and the California Personality Inventory, are meaningful. Although the scales themselves are highly validated, there are disappointingly few demonstrations that correlate changes on these scales with meaningful changes in the behavior of the treatment population. There are, of course, some exceptions (e.g., Jacobson & Wirt, 1969). In general, however, changes on scales of this type are not often predictably associated with specific changes in observed behavior. This points to the need to relate theories of behavior change more closely to observable behavior. This is discussed in the following chapter.

SUMMARY

Research on the effectiveness of psychotherapy and behavior-change programs present many difficult methodological problems. One of the most frequently used research designs includes a treatment and a control group, pre- and posttherapy observation or testing, and a follow-up study of both groups. This basic design can be modified, often through the use of additional treatment and control groups, to control for factors which might produce apparent therapeutic effects when in fact there are none (type I error). Alternatively, a poor research design may fail to reveal therapeutic effects which actually exist (type II error).

One factor which can produce a change in the experimental group independent of the treatment received by the group is the occurrence of a significant event between the initial and final observation of the group. Such an event might be a national crisis or personal achievement (i.e., the history of the group). Other factors can be the sensitization of the group by pretesting, the maturation of the subjects and the biased selection of subjects for the study. Additional matters to be considered are statistical regression, instrument decay, mortality or dropout rate, instability, and selection-maturation interaction. A research design which can control for all these factors can seldom be developed because of the many practical, social, and economic limitations. It is, however, not always necessary to control experimentally for all of these factors. It is sometimes possible to account for the possible influence of these factors through logical or statistical procedures. It is important nevertheless to consider these factors in some ambiguity of inferences made about the effects of behavior-change programs.

There are several control methods commonly used in psychotherapy research. One is the waiting-list control method in which prospective patients are randomly selected to receive treatment or to be placed on a waiting list. Because there appears to be a tendency for therapists to select patients with characteristics such as high intelligence and high socioeconomic status, which are positively related to therapeutic success and the remission of symptoms, random assignment is needed to avoid biasing a study in the direction of positive findings for therapy. Another control method is the own-control procedure in which each patient is compared with himself before and after treatment. A third control method involves the use of population base rates in which the rate of improvement in the therapy group is compared with the rate of improvement in an equivalent population.

Another difficult problem in assessing therapy programs is the selection of appropriate outcome criteria for measuring the effects. One approach is to formulate specific hypotheses and test them very carefully in a laboratory experiment. A different approach is to observe the therapeutic interactions between patients and therapists as they naturally occur and then attempt to measure as many relevant changes as possible. Each approach has advantages and disadvantages and each may be used at different stages in the development of new treatment techniques.

Outcome criteria can be selected which are assumed to reflect change in all of the patients (a nomothetic approach) or outcome criteria can be selected which seem particularly relevant to one individual patient (an idiographic approach). Although nomothetic procedures have most often been used in assessing behavior-change programs, some idiographic methods have also been developed. Outcome criteria can also be selected which will measure either objective or subjective changes. Discrepancies between objectively measured behaviors and the subjective reports of patients are sometimes produced by factors which bias the subjective reports of the patients. The social situation in which subjective reports are made can considerably influence the content of the reports. Increased attention needs to be given to both the validity and reliability of subjective reports and to the development of better methods for objectively recording behavior.

Part Three

Research Issues

Chapter 11

Observation and Recording of Behavior

The accurate observation and recording of human behavior is essential if behavior is going to be understood and effectively changed. Behavior should be observed both in the experimental laboratory under special conditions and in natural, daily-life situations. The famous psychoanalyst, Carl G. Jung, was very emphatic about the need for therapists to observe and experience the social world of their patients. His advice was extreme (1912, p. 238):

> The man who would learn the human mind will gain almost nothing from experimental psychology. Far better for him to put away his academic gown, to say good-bye to the study, and to wander with human heart through the world. There in the horrors of the prison, the asylum, and the hospital, in the drinking-shops, brothels, and gambling halls, in the salons of the elegant, in the exchanges, socialist meetings, churches, religious revivals, and sectarian ecstasies, through love and hate, through the experience of passion in every form in his own body, he would reap a richer store of knowledge than text-books a foot thick could give him. Then would he know to doctor the sick with real knowledge of the human soul.

The noted behaviorist, John B. Watson, made a similar plea for observation in natural (non-laboratory) settings on the first page of his famous book, *Psychology from the Standpoint of a Behaviorist* (1919). "Everyone agrees that man's acts are determined by something, and that, whether he acts orderly or not, there are sufficient grounds for his acting as he does act, if only these grounds can be discovered. In order to formulate such laws, we must study man in action—his adjustments to the daily situations of life, and to the unusual situations which may confront him." More recently, Berk and Adams (1970, p. 110) have suggested that, "The investigator should be prepared to observe, unencumbered by his personal values and those of middle class society, the whole spectrum of human behavior from the most common to most deviant."

It is clear that the observation of behavior is helpful, if not absolutely essential, for developing effective methods of behavior change.[1] The following sections will discuss the need for observation, observational procedures, instrumentation, and public policy.

INADEQUACY OF INTERVIEW AND QUESTIONNAIRE DATA

Because people can observe their own behavior, it is tempting for the researcher just to ask people how they behave. This is particularly true regarding behavior that is not readily observable by a researcher. The results of asking are, however, disappointing.[2] For example, although it is unlikely that respondents will forget serious legal convictions, a community survey in a small, western town found that sixteen out of forty-five persons with criminal records (35.5 percent) denied in the survey having a record.

Even when the behavior is not generally considered to be very sensitive, marked discrepancies may be found between self-report and objective measures. In regard to the simple matter of the frequency of toothbrushing much inaccuracy of reporting has been found (Evans, Rozelle, Lasater, Dembroski, & Allen, 1970). More seriously, Bancroft (1940) found the inaccuracy of interview responses by 1,595 unemployed

---

[1]Some therapists (May 1953) have argued that we also need to understand inner, invisible events. In contrast to this view, Krasner (1965b, p. 22) has succinctly suggested, "Even if man's behavior is determined by internal mediating events such as awareness, or thinking, or anxiety, or insight, terms which we are all so reluctant to give up because myths die slowly, these events can be manipulated by outside stimuli so that it is these stimuli which basically determine our behavior." One is reminded of Sir Charles Sherrington's (1955, p. 261) comment about the mind. "Mind, for anything perception can encompass, goes therefore in our spatial world more ghostly than a ghost. Invisible, intangible, it is a thing not even of outline, it is not a 'thing.'"

[2]See Denton, 1964; Jenkins & Corbin, 1938; Kahn & Cannell, 1957; Weiss, Davis, England, & Lofquist, 1961; and Wenar, 1961.

persons ranging from 8 percent to 75 percent on standard biographical questions. Hyman (1944) found that out of large numbers of persons interviewed, 17 percent denied having redeemed their United States War Savings Bonds when records showed that they had, 42 percent claimed to have a poster on display which inspection showed that they did not, and 4 to 27 percent claimed they were at work when in fact they were not.

When married college men were asked whether they used cream and sugar in their coffee, there was 22 percent disagreement between their responses and those of their observer wives (Pinneau & Milton, 1958). Not even a college cafeteria could be run efficiently on the basis of such data—surely the behavioral sciences should be no less exacting in their requirements.

Thus far we have considered the *validity* of interview data, i.e., the agreement of interview data with data collected from a source other than the respondent's statements. Interview *reliability*, the agreement between two or more statements made by a respondent, has also sometimes been found to be quite poor. For example, much of developmental child psychology depends upon the reports of mothers regarding their children's attitudes and activities. Wenar and Coulter (1962) interviewed twenty-five mothers about their nursery school children twice, at three- to six-year intervals. They found only 57 percent agreement between first and second statements regarding the developmental histories of the children. Forty percent of the statements that were different contained extreme changes. For example, the mothers during the second interview tended to report starting toilet training much later; the mean discrepancy was eight months. Studies by other investigators have also shown poor reliability in regard to parental recall of child-rearing practices (e.g., McCord & McCord, 1961; Pyles, Stolz, & Macfarlane, 1935; Robbins, 1963; Burton, 1970).

Many of the same inadequacies of validity and reliability that have been reported for interview data have also been reported for questionnaire data (e.g., Pascal & Jenkins, 1961). On the other hand, some studies have claimed satisfactory validity and reliability for interview and questionnaire data (e.g., Keating, Paterson, & Stone, 1950). What is considered "satisfactory" is a matter of opinion. Ball (1967) reports satisfactory validity for interview procedures based upon data from fifty-nine narcotic addicts. Validity, as measured by the percentage of agreement with FBI reports, ranged from 82.8 percent on the question of the age of the respondent at the time of the interview to 54.4 percent on the question of the age of first arrest. This can also be interpreted as 17.2 and 45.6 percent error. In regard to number of arrests, if one includes the respondents' report of more arrests as well as fewer arrests than the number shown by FBI reports (Ball excludes the report of more arrests from his calculation), then the validity of this item is 32.7 percent and this can be interpreted as 67.3 percent error.

Two studies by Walsh (1967, 1968) purporting to show the adequate validity of questionnaire and interview data are instructive. In their first study, several hundred college students at two midwestern universities were presented a series of questions regarding their academic performance and their responses were checked against records at the university. Questions such as "How many courses have you received an 'A' in at SUI?" were presented to randomly selected students either in an interview or in the form of a questionnaire. These three different forms of inquiry did not produce any clear differences in response. The percentage of accurate self-reports for each question ranged from 100 percent ("How many courses have you failed at OSU?") to 49 percent ("What is your OSU over-all cumulative ' grade point average?"). A majority of the questions showed a percentage of accuracy in the range of 70 to 80 percent.

In the second study (1968), which also involved the incentive of future participation in a pleasant and well-paying project depending upon the answers given, college males had only 36 percent accurate self-reports on the question regarding grade-point average. Although Walsh (1968, p. 186) concluded that "In general, the interview and questionnaire methods of collecting self-report data show evidence of validity under varied conditions for biographical information"; other investigators might reach the opposite conclusion. This depends upon what the investigator considers adequate validity for his particular study.

Perhaps, it would be more useful to consider the validity of particular items or types of items in questionnaires and interviews rather than the validity of interview or questionnaire techniques in general. Weiss and Davis (1960) found that in the total sample of information obtained from a group of counselors and job applicants the median error was 16 percent. The validity varied according to the type of information requested from 100 percent correct responses (sex of the subject) to less than 50 percent correct responses (prior assistance from the agency). In general, the level of error appeared to be positively related to social acceptability of the replies.

A study by Braginsky and Braginsky (1967) demonstrated that schizophrenic patients were able to manipulate evaluation interview situations to present themselves as healthy or sick depending upon their immediate goals.[3] In a treatment project which involved the comparison

---

[3]Also, when experimental subjects are properly instructed, they can learn to introduce systematic biases into questionnaire responses to distort results (Azrin, Holz, & Goldiamond, 1961).

of alcoholics' statements about their drinking and their arrests for drunkenness over a one-year period, Blane (1964) found a near-zero correlation between the two. If the statements of these alcoholic patients had been accepted at face value, there would have been a large but spurious difference between the treated and the nontreated group in favor of the treated group.

To study home influences, delinquents were asked on a questionnaire if they received allowances and, if so, how much and from whom. Delinquents often reported receiving allowances from their fathers when in fact their fathers were absent from home or unknown (Schwitzgebel, 1964). Although delinquents are not generally known for their exceptional honesty, some investigators continue to develop theories of delinquency based upon questionnaire data of doubtful validity and reliability. Perhaps some of these "questionnaire theories" of delinquency account for the wide discrepancy between social theory and effective behavior-change programs.

In addition to error introduced deliberately or inadvertently by the respondent, error may also be introduced by the interviewer. As used here, *interviewer bias* refers to certain systematic distortions induced by the interviewer. *Interviewer error* is a broader term and includes nonsystematic or random influences. There is in addition, of course, just simple mechanical error. In Guest's (1947) study of interviewer error, a recorder was placed in a respondent's home. A series of interviewers questioned this respondent and, by comparing their interview reports with the recordings of the interviews, many errors of both omission and commission were found. In a later comparison of tape-recorded interviews with reports written from memory immediately after interviews, Payne (1949) found that 25 percent of the statements attributed to a respondent were clearly incorrect. Roth (1966) has provided some excellent case studies of "hired-hand research" in which the assistants introduced error and bias into interview and coding procedures. He quotes an assistant (p. 191):

> One of the questions on the interview schedule asked for five reasons why parents had put their child in an institution. I found most people can't think of five reasons. One or two—sometimes three. At first I tried pumping them for more reasons, but I never got any of them up to five. I didn't want (the director) to think I was goofing off on the probing, so I always filled in all five.

Roth then suggests that cheating, carelessness, and the distortion of data are not the result of temporary lapses in ethical behavior or supervision but that "such behavior on the part of hired data-collectors and processors is not abnormal or exceptional, but rather is exactly the kind of behavior we should expect from people with their position in a production unit" (p. 191).

Interviewer attitude may also be a source of considerable bias, particularly when the interviewer may have expectations regarding the probable attitudes of the respondent (Cantril, 1944). By using a "planted" respondent, Smith and Hyman (1950) have nicely demonstrated the biasing effect of interviewer expectations on survey results. Although the respondent gave exactly the same answers to the questions asked by a series of interviewers, the interviewers reported markedly different answers. Bias can be introduced by varying the racial background of the interviewer (Athey, Coleman, Reitman, & Tang, 1960; Katz, 1942). Also, the age (Riesman & Ehrlich, 1961), sex (Benney, Riesman, & Star, 1956), and social class (Lenski & Leggett, 1960) of the interviewer have biased results.

Data obtained from official records and the direct observation of behavior can be used to verify and supplement the data obtained from interviews and questionnaires (e.g., Kinsey et al., 1948). The following section discusses some of the procedures that have been used to observe behavior in natural social settings.

OBSERVATIONAL PROCEDURES

Beyond the experimental laboratory and the therapeutic clinic lies almost the entire domain of human activity virtually unexplored and unobserved by scientific procedures. Unlike many of the natural sciences, psychology does not yet have extensive records of the patterns of the daily behavior of man. To a considerable extent, psychology has bypassed, perhaps not successfully, this typical step in the development of the natural sciences—the observation of relevant, naturally occurring phenomena.

In biology, data from the observation of animals in their natural habitats is frequently used to help formulate theories and confirm or disconfirm hypotheses. There are bird-watching organizations that collect and store useful information. The latest sightings of specific birds can be verified and then disseminated to others by prerecorded telephone messages. Most people, at least, would consider people to be more important than birds, yet there is no well-established social equivalent in psychology to the bird watcher in biology. There are very few social observers and perhaps no organized groups of layman collecting information on human behavior in a systematic manner.

The various behavioral-science disciplines appear to differ markedly in their methods of collecting the data they use to test hypotheses. To examine this difference in more detail, seventy journals in anthropology, sociology, psychology, and psychiatry (excluding psychoanalysis) which were published in 1965 were randomly selected for study (Schwitzgebel, 1967c). This sample included nearly all the major, official journals published by these disciplines as well as many lesser known publications. From these journals, 1,608 articles were randomly selected, read, and coded according to the sources of data used by the authors of these articles.[4] Five major sources of data were coded: (1) questionnaire, (2) interview, (3) direct observation—including behavior in laboratory settings, (4) statistical—including data from records such as voter registration lists, and (5) tests—both objective and projective instruments. In addition, each data source was coded as to whether the author collected the data himself (primary source) or relied upon data previously published by others (secondary source).

In summary, there were many highly significant differences among the disciplines. Anthropology used direct-observation sources most frequently and differed significantly from sociology which used these sources least frequently. Psychology and psychiatry occupied a middle position between sociology and anthropology in the use of direct observation. Test data were most frequently used by psychology, followed by the use of data from direct observation (usually laboratory studies), statistical records, questionnaires, and interviews. Sociology most often used statistical records and data previously published by others.[5]

The historical development and conceptual framework of the disciplines appear to influence the data sources predominantly used. Anthropology, which has traditionally used direct observation in the formulation of theories, currently shows the most frequent use of direct observation. The influence of anthropologists such as Malinowski and Radcliffe-Brown who were intrepid observers may still be strong. In contrast, sociology depends greatly upon the use of data from statistical sources such as the United States Bureau of the Census, a procedure similar to that employed by the classical sociologist, Durkheim, in his famous study of suicide.

---

[4]Articles on business matters, professional training, convention activities, and related topics were excluded from the study. The remaining articles were then assigned to one of the four disciplines according to the major disciplinary orientation of the journal in which it was published. For example, articles in *Behavioral Science* and the *Journal of Genetic Psychology* were classified in psychology; articles in the *American Sociological Review* and the *Public Opinion Quarterly* were classified in sociology.

[5]Comparable results were reported by Riley (1964) in an analysis of eighty-eight sociological articles. Although the selection and coding criteria are not given, she reports that "only 7 studies were based on data from observation and five of these combined the observation with questioning" (p. 1004).

Observation in Natural Settings

Barker and Wright (1954), noted for their studies of human behavior in natural settings, have frequently stressed the need for what they call "psychological ecology." They have expressed the view (pp. 2–3):

> Psychologists know little more than laymen about the frequency and degree of occurrence of their basic phenomena in the lives of men—of deprivation, of hostility, of freedom, of friendliness, of social pressure, of rewards and punishments. Although we have daily records of the behavior of volcanoes, of the tides, of sun spots, and of rats and monkeys, there have been few scientific records of how a human mother cared for her young, how a particular teacher behaved in the classroom and how the children responded, what a family actually did and said during a mealtime, or how any boy lived his life from the time he awoke in the morning until he went to sleep at night. . . . Moreover, the lack of field data limits the discovery of some of the laws of behavior. It is often impossible to create in the laboratory the frequency, the duration, the scope, the complexity, and the magnitude of some conditions that it is important to investigate. In this, psychology has much in common with meteorology. Some of the principles of the whirlwind and the thunderbolt can be studied in the laboratory, but to extend the curves into the high values, and to include all complicating factors, it is necessary to go to the plains and to observe these events as they occur under natural conditions. In principle, the same is true in psychology for studies of conditions which are frequent in daily life, but which are difficult to create experimentally. This should not be discouraging. Experiments in nature are occurring every day. We need only the techniques and facilities to take advantage of them.

If an observer of human behavior attempted to follow Jung's suggestion to wander with human heart through the world and experience passion in every form, and if he survived the local police and professional ethics committee, he would still face serious methodological problems such as inadequate sample size and the biased selection of observed events. Nevertheless, as McClelland (1955, pp. 37–38) has noted, "The fact that one cannot produce some of these phenomena [such as 'falling in love'] in the laboratory does not mean that they cannot be observed and studied scientifically as they are found in nature. The biologist would be quite seriously limited if he had to confine his study of living organisms to those he could produce in the laboratory. Yet, no one declares him less of a scientist because he cannot. What the psychologist working in the field of personality has needed is the improvement of techniques for studying the complex processes of human nature as they occur naturally." This suggestion needs to be taken seriously. Some studies (cf., Raush, Dittman, & Taylor, 1960) indicate as much variation in behavior between different social settings with similar subjects as between different subjects within similar social settings.

It is not possible here to discuss in detail the many possible types of observational procedures that might be used in natural settings. Rather, three types will be briefly presented to illustrate the potential range and variety of these procedures. These are *participant observation, self-observation*, and *instrumentation*. Common to all of these procedures are the requirements of validity, reliability, a theoretically suitable classification of the observed events, and the development of satisfactory techniques of data storage and retrieval.

The continuous *stream of behavior*, as Barker (1963a) has termed it, must somehow be divided into conceptually isolated events. These events may be classified, i.e., assigned a unity, by applying any common set of identifiable characteristics. Just as an apple and a car may be placed in a category of "red," smashing a toy and hitting a teacher may be classified as "aggression." The latter classification may be said to represent a *functional unity*, in contrast to a superficial similarity of events, if the events vary concomitantly, or are interdependent, or are causally related (Peak, 1953).

This functional unity is usually determined by a concomitant variation of the observed events which is determined by statistical procedures involving correlation or factor analysis. These methods for determining unity require the making of certain assumptions about the nature of the observed events and statistical techniques which are largely matters of judgment or faith. Some investigators have suggested that the difficulties here can be reduced by selecting behaviors that are classifiable by external or time-space characteristics.

The temporary "simplification" of observed events may not be entirely regressive for the behavioral sciences. Barker (1963, p. 24) in his Kurt Lewin Memorial Award address commented: "Psychology has been so busy selecting from, imposing upon, and rearranging the behavior of its subjects that it has until very recently neglected to note behavior's clear structure when it is not molested by tests, experiments, questionnaires, and interviews." There must, of course, still be units of observation. Units such as "taking off her shoes," "sitting closer to the big girls," "putting on her shoes," are termed by Barker as *behavior episodes* and are not considered to be arbitrarily imposed dimensions of the behavior continuum.

The categories into which observed behavior is coded may be quite broad, such as those suggested by Barker, or extremely small. In a study by Condon and Ogston (1965), the interaction of the subjects was filmed and each subject's movements were analyzed during each frame of the movie which was filmed at twenty-four frames per second. In another film, changes in bioelectric activity from scalp electrodes on each of the two participants was studied in relationship to their speech and movement during each frame. Speech, body motions, and bioelectric activity appeared to be synchronous.

The optimal size of the categories of behavior being used by an observer depends in part upon the subject matter being studied. Small categories tend to have a higher validity than large ones. On the other hand, large categories which do not require a very great amount of inference on the part of the observer may provide somewhat better reliability. Reliability may also be increased by specifying whether the observers are to include the intent of the acts of the subjects and the social context in which the behavior takes place. Also, the categories should generally be mutually exclusive.

Although the observer may attempt to record each occurrence of a specified behavior, the more-typical procedure involves a sampling of the behavior on a specified time schedule. The periods of observation may be arranged to take place at fixed (usually evenly spaced) intervals, such as during the first minute of each quarter hour or the periods of observation may be randomly determined. Before determining a sampling schedule, it may be necessary to observe the behavior for a long period of time to determine its frequency and duration.

Participant Observation

One of the early, systematic studies of behavior by participation occurred as a response to social criticism. Nels Anderson, concerned about the inhumane treatment of the poor in the early 1900s lived for awhile as a tramp. His book, *The Hobo: The Sociology of the Homeless Man* (1923), was widely read and his technique became known as participant observation (Lindeman, 1924). The procedure did not, however, gain widespread use although there were some notable exceptions such as Whyte's study of delinquents in *Street Corner Society* (1943). More recently, under the influence of "participation" sociologists, such as Becker (1963), Goffman (1967), and Polsky (1969), there has been renewed interest in participant observation.

A major advantage of participant observation is that the behavior in question may be observed directly and extensively. In some cases there may be only a little disturbance of typical behavioral patterns, but in other cases the addition of a participant observer may markedly change the social system and thus may introduce either random or nonmeasurable systematic error. If the observer takes a role that is already an integral part of the social system, his presence is probably less likely to affect the rest of the system than if he uses a novel role such as psychologist or observer (Madge, 1953; Junker, 1960). It is, of course, impossible for the observer to completely escape his past or future, and he therefore cannot become identical to the subjects.

Not long ago the newspapers reported the attempted robbery of a bank by a college girl in Massachusetts. The reason: she was writing a paper on bank robbers for a psychology class and wanted to understand the robber's viewpoint. Apparently neither the robbery nor the paper was very successful. Likewise, an experimenter cannot become a twelve-year-old child in order to participate in group games, nor is it likely that he will become an alcoholic in order later to join Alcoholics Anonymous. The observer is often recognized as an observer and should be honest with those he is observing (Berk & Adams, 1970).

Another advantage of participant observation is that the observer is close to the behavior being studied; yet views it from a perspective different from that of the other actors. This different perspective can be quite valuable when compared with the actors' perspective. On the other hand, the use of an observer different from the subjects may, as noted above, influence the behavior being observed.

The nature and extent of this influence is unclear. Deutch (1949) and Willems (1965) have suggested that the initial influence of an observer gradually decreases until it is not an important factor. The minimal influence of an observer following the "habituation" of subjects to his presence has been a frequently suggested idea (e.g., Jersild & Meigs, 1939). Conversely, other investigators (Polansky, Freeman, Horowitz, Irwin, Papania, Rapaport, & Whaley, 1949) have reported a situation in which the observer became increasingly less accepted by the subjects in a camp situation over a period of three weeks.

Suggestions to correct for this influence have varied from becoming the personal friend of the subject (cf. Kinsey el al., 1948) to Peak's suggestion (1953, p. 414) that "the observers will do best, barring any special conditions . . . by showing all of the external signs of a piece of furniture." In one study (Sherif & Sherif, 1953) an observer disguised himself as a laborer on the grounds of a summer camp to observe gang activities.

Another strategy has been to train a member of the group to be observed in observational procedures. An early, carefully designed study using this type of participant observer was conducted by the Tavistock Institute of Human Relations. An ex-coalminer was employed as a member of the research team to help the investigators determine some of the social and psychological effects of a new method of coal mining (Trist & Bamforth, 1951). In a somewhat similar manner, delinquents have been employed as "experts" in describing and reducing certain aspects of crime (Slack, 1960; Schwitzgebel, 1964).

Occasionally, investigators who are not members of the observed group disguise their intentions and become a member of the group. In a study of approximately one hundred bars in the San Francisco area, Cavan (1966) attempted to determine some of the stable patterns of behavior in public drinking places by becoming a "typical patron."

One of the most extensive and remarkable examples of participant observation is a study by Laud Humphreys (1970). This study, reported in the book *Tearoom Trade: Impersonal Sex in Public Places*, involved the observation of illegal homosexual acts in public rest rooms. This involved the inspection of over ninety public rest rooms in the parks of a large metropolitan area, of which twenty were used as locales for sexual games. In one phase of the study, 134 homosexual acts were observed on a time-sampling basis. Systematic observation included noting factors such as time and place, description of participants, weather, design of the rest room, movements of participants, and details of the sexual act.

Observation of this illegal activity which would ordinarily be completely eliminated by the presence of an "outside" observer was made possible by taking a role that was already a part of the subcultural social system. This has been described by Humphreys (1970, pp. 27–28):

> The very fear and suspicion encountered in the restrooms produces a participant role, the sexuality of which is optional. This is the role of the lookout ("watchqueen" in the argot), a man who is situated at the door or windows from which he may observe the means of access to the restroom. When someone approaches, he coughs. He nods when the coast is clear or if he recognizes an entering party as a regular.
>
> The lookouts fall into three main types. The most common of these are the "waiters," men who are waiting for someone with whom they have made an appointment or whom they expect to find at this spot, for a particular type of "trick," or for a chance to get in on the action. The others, the masturbators, who engage in autoerotic behavior (either overtly or beneath their clothing) while observing sexual acts, and the voyeurs, who appear to derive sexual stimulation and pleasure from watching the others. In terms of appearances, I assumed the role of the voyeur—a role superbly suited for sociologists and the only lookout role that is not overtly sexual. On those occasions when there was only one other man present in the room, I have taken a role that is even less sexual than that of the voyeur-look-out: the straight person who has come to the facility for purposes of elimination.

By linking the participants with specific automobiles and tracing the license numbers, many of the participants could be later interviewed. But, how the interviews could be conducted initially presented a problem. "Clearly, I could not knock on the door of a suburban residence and say, 'Excuse me, I saw you engaging in a homosexual act in a tearoom last year, and I wonder if I might ask you a few questions.' Having already been jailed, locked in a restroom, and attacked by a group of ruffians, I had no desire to conclude my research with a series of beatings" (p. 41). The problem was overcome by including them as an unidentifiable part of a larger sample in a different, ongoing study (p. 42):

> This strategy was most important—both from the standpoint of research validity and ethics—because it enabled me to approach my respondents as normal people, answering normal questions, as part of a normal survey. They *are* part of a larger sample. Their being interviewed is not stigmatizing, because they comprise but a small portion of a much larger sample of the population in their area. They were not put on the spot about their deviance, because they were not interviewed as deviants.

Finally, fifty of the subjects who were interviewed in this manner (there was a 13 percent refusal rate and 22 percent attrition from other factors in the original sample) were matched with fifty randomly selected control subjects. Thus, the personal and social characteristics of those engaged in public homosexual acts could be compared with a control group without undue risk or embarrassment to the subjects.[6]

Even when observation is appropriately and skillfully conducted, there remains the problem of recording and interpreting the data. Every direct observation is subject to the perceptual biases of the observer. Observation is also cognition. As Kaplan (1964, pp. 133) notes, "Data are always *data for* some hypothesis or other," and the behavior must be "mapped" into data.

The hypotheses which permit the gathering of data, which in fact make the data meaningful within the discipline, may also influence the perceived and reported content of the behavioral event. This may then lead to an unwarranted confirmation or disconfirmation of the hypothesis. It has been rumored (Wooster, 1959) that physicians who were asked to

---

[6]One of the noteworthy results of this study was the finding that the subjects observed in the rest rooms were more conservative on matters such as civil rights, economics, and police practices than the control subjects. "Social conservatism is revealed as a product of the illegal roles these men play in the hidden moments of their lives" (p. 139). In fact, many were moral crusaders in favor of more vice squads. One subject commented; "They should be more strict. I can think of a lot of places they ought to raid" (p.141).

classify several hundred patients as obese, normal, or underweight showed systematic error. The lean physicians classified more patients as obese than did the heavy physicians.

Letemendia and Harris (1959) have effectively demonstrated the bias of observers. The subjects in their study were divided into two groups of fourteen subjects each. Subjects in the experimental group were given nicotinic-acid capsules each day which caused a slight flushing; subjects in the control group were given lactose placebo capsules each day. The nursing staff was informed in very general terms that a clinical trial of drugs was being conducted and was asked to report on all of the patients during the nine-week experimental period. During the first three weeks, the staff correctly reported flushing effects only in the experimental group receiving the nicotinic acid. But from the fourth to the ninth week, flushing effects were also reported for the subjects in the control group. It should be noted that this is not an example of bias produced by an observer but bias in the observer's perception of the subject's unchanged behavior.

Rosenthal and Halas (1962) have experimentally demonstrated observer bias in a matter as simple as observing the number of turning and contraction responses of planaria (flatworms) in a well-controlled laboratory setting. Rapp (1965) asked eight pairs of observers to describe objectively the behavior of one child. One member of the pair of observers was led to believe that the child was feeling "under par" while the other observer was led to believe that the child was feeling "above par." Seven of the eight pairs of observers wrote descriptions that were clearly biased in favor of the suggestions given prior to the observation.

The bias introduced by observers which is a result of their direct influence upon the subjects or their perceptual distortions can sometimes be reduced by using self-observation and instrumentation. These techniques may be used alone but are usually more valuable when used in combination with other data-collection techniques such as observation, testing, or interviewing.

Self-Observation

The ship's log book and the personal daily diary are very old and common methods of recording self-observations. Although there is much variety and meaning in the information recorded in this manner, it is seldom systematic enough to permit the usual behavioral or statistical analyses. Some of this difficulty can be overcome by asking people to record their behaviors according to predetermined rules or schedules.

The behaviors can be recorded each time they occur or a sampling procedure can be used. Accuracy of the recording can be increased by using a small, portable counter on which the behavioral event is recorded immediately after it is observed. These counters can be the wrist-worn type used to keep score during golf games or small pocket-sized adding machines which allow the recording of several behaviors simultaneously (cf. Lindsley, 1968; Schwitzgebel, 1964). Two examples of behavior graphs can be found in Chapter 8. One is a graph of the numbers of hours of sulking behavior by a subject involved in marital discord (Goldiamond, 1966). The subject was instructed to sulk whenever he wished but to keep a daily record of it and bring it to the treatment sessions. The other example is a graph of a subject who wanted to lose weight by reducing the amount of ice cream he ate.

In a study by the authors, subjects kept daily records of a wide variety of behaviors such as smoking, eating, asthmatic attacks, nervous mannerisms, studying, sexual activity, phone calls, and exercise. Both cumulative frequency and sampling techniques were used. The time period of observation ranged from a week to over five years, with a typical period of one or two months. A typical behavior graph is presented in Figure 11-1.

The graph in Figure 11-1 was developed by a college student who was concerned about the number of words which he would skip over while reading when he was uncertain about their meaning. He attempted to change this behavior (at point indicated by arrow) and was successful during the following thirty-five days. The subject commented, "Very rarely did I ever use the dictionary. In spite of the latter fact, I found it fairly easy to change my behavior. It would have been even easier if on some days I didn't have so many words to look up. Incidentally, I never

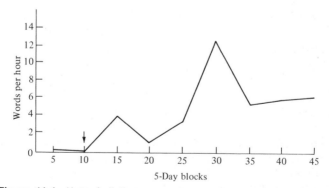

Figure 11-1 Use of dictionary as measured by the number of words looked up per hour of reading reported by the subject.

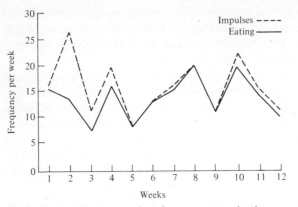

Figure 11-2 Impulses and eating responses in the presence of fattening foods per week reported by the subject.

would have believed that I could have come across even 10 words in a day that I didn't know, let alone 35, 37, or 45!"

A not-so-successful attempt to reduce weight by reducing the number of times a "fattening" food was eaten is presented in Figure 11-2. Each day for three months the subject recorded the number of times a fattening food was desired and the number of times it was eaten. Weight was also determined each day. The graph indicates that on most occasions when a fattening food was desired it was eaten. The subject considered it best for her morale to allow at least one fattening food each day rather than feel "completely deprived." There was no significant weight loss.

Sometimes the subject can use information sources not readily available to the experimenter, such as cigarette packages, mileage on an automobile or bicycle odometer, or business records to construct a behavior graph. The graph in Figure 11-3 was based upon information contained in telephone bills. The initially high cost of long-distance phone calls was related to subject's engagement for marriage late in October and telephone calls to her family and friends. The subject noted that "the graph did not change my behavior more because I was not sufficiently interested in changing. I realized that $65 was an exorbitant amount to spend on calls for one month, but apparently I am perfectly willing to spend $20–30 each month on the calls."

Self-observation surely does not completely eliminate bias on the part of the subject (cf. Simkins, 1971a, 1971b) but it may make the bias more obvious than usual to the subject and researcher and help to eliminate errors of memory. The subject cannot, for example, easily report only data favorable to himself with the rationalization of a loss of memory, because the data are to be immediately recorded. A persistent failure to record an event is likely to become obvious. The accuracy of behavior graphs should be checked when possible against information obtained by direct observation of the subject or from secondary sources such as spouses, room-mates, and public records.

The self-recording of a behavior may have a marked effect upon the behavior (see Broden, Hall, & Mitts, 1971). For example, the graph in Figure 11-4 was produced by recording the number of times each day the subject bit her lips as a nervous mannerism (a problem of several years' duration) and the number of times she stopped her behavior immediately upon becoming conscious of it. This illustrates some of the behavior-change potential of self-observation which was previously discussed in the chapter on self-directed change (Chapter 8).

The subject, a twenty-four-year-old graduate student, has described in considerable detail the effect of the observation procedure upon her behavior:

> The first significant outcome of recording the lip-biting behavior along with the number of times I tried to stop was that I became much more conscious of the activity itself, and of the fact that I really did have the power to stop if I so desired. Even when I was not biting my lips the thought would sometimes flash through my mind: "Well, I'm not biting my lips now."
>
> At first, I could see by the graph that I was biting my lips a great deal and not making much of an effort to stop biting them. But I was able to cut down very much towards the end of November. Two reasons—seeing that I had cut down a great deal (and, therefore, could now relax my efforts) and a return to studying—caused a large rise in the number of times I bit my lips.

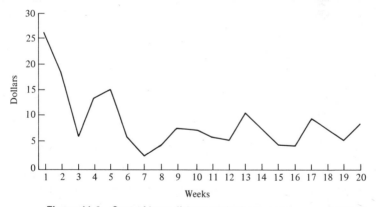

Figure 11-3 Cost of long distance telephone calls per week based upon telephone bills received by the subject.

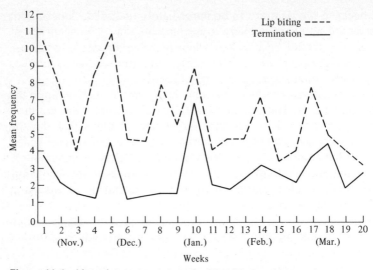

Figure 11-4 Mean frequency per week of lip biting and its termination immediately upon becoming conscious of it, as reported by the
subject.

When I saw how the graph had shot up, I made a more determined effort to
stop. The number of times I *stopped* biting my lips began to approach the
number of times I *started* to bite them. When this happened, the level of the
graph went down. That is, I began to bite my lips much less.

This pattern shows up again in the following month, January. . . . A
slight rise in lip-biting at the beginning of February was again followed by an
increased effort to stop and a consequent rise in the number of times I
stopped biting my lips. As before, the general level of lip-biting was
reduced. This pattern appears for the fourth time at the beginning of
March. . . .

On the whole, the amount of lip-biting was considerably reduced from
November to March. Recording the behavior had a great deal to do with this
reduction. In the first place, I became more aware of the behavior. In the
second place, my efforts to stop biting my lips were influenced by the
appearance of the graph: when the upper line became too high, I increased
my effort to stop.

The possible influence of the subject's self-observation upon the
frequency or rate of the observed behavior, while not necessarily
invalidating the observation, does nevertheless make it hazardous to
assume that the behavior was the same prior to the self-observation as
during it. This change in behavior can sometimes be considered a
therapeutic effect.

One subject wrote the following comment in regard to his behavior graph:

> It is a very strange and sometimes fearful experience to record one's own behavior over an extended period of time. When the graph . . . sloped in a downward direction, I had a feeling of triumph, almost conquest over something. But when the graph sloped upward, I reacted with a feeling of disgust with myself—"Am I going to let this habit get the best of me?"—and sometimes, also, I felt like giving up entirely.

An experimental study by McFall (1970) on the effects of self-observation on cigarette smoking indicated that self-observation significantly affected the amount of smoking done by the subjects as recorded by observers. Self-observation has also been used to change study behavior (Johnson & White, 1971). As Kanfer (1970) notes, there is a problem of *reactivity* here—the measuring operations affect the observed event. The degree of reactivity can be determined to some extent if the self-observation data are compared with external, observable events such as a loss of weight (Orne, 1970) and thus their validity or accuracy can in a general way be determined (Nelson & McReynolds, 1971).

The recording of events in this manner, when suitable validity and reliability are established, produces records of behavior that may reveal important cyclical trends or short-term variations that might otherwise be missed by the subjects in the usual treatment situation. The data also become suitable for use with some of the newer techniques of statistical inference based on the single case (Chassan, 1960, 1967; Edington, 1967; Holtzman, 1963).

The reactivity of self-observation is in a curious way both a "problem" and an "opportunity." The fact that self-observation can change the behavior being observed can be looked upon as a procedure which biases research data. It is a "problem" because it interferes with the collecting of accurate data. On the other hand, the fact that self-observation can change behavior can be looked upon as an aid to therapy or an "opportunity" to enhance other behavior-change procedures.[7]

To increase the accuracy of their recording, the subjects can use various forms of instrumentation. Subjects, for example, may film their own behavior. In one project (Schwitzgebel, 1964), delinquents were asked to help film various aspects of their daily life. The delinquents were loaned 8 mm. movie cameras and film was inexpensively purchased from

---

[7]This is particularly true in newly developed self-directed behavior-change techniques in which self-observation and self-reinforcement are important elements (Kanfer, 1970).

the project. After exposing the film, the boys sent it to a processing laboratory and it was returned directly to them. The boys then decided what portion of the film they wished to sell to the project. In this way, they remained in control of the filming process and there was no unobserved or unwanted intrusion by the researchers. The use of other forms of instrumentation is discussed below.

Instrumentation

The process of observation in the behavioral sciences is easily confounded since human beings are both the observers and the subjects of observation. There is no way of avoiding this "group introspection" which is, epistemologically speaking, a closed system. However, certain phases of man's self-observation may be standardized or automated in a manner to confine or reliably measure probable error. This realization combined with recent advances in technology has produced a rapidly developing interest in the use of instrumentation to measure or change human behavior.[8]

Some of the devices used can be as simple as a turnstile or a pedometer to measure large movements of the legs or arms. Larsen (1949) has used pedometers in the treatment of obesity. Special gravity-sensitive watches have been used to measure hyperactivity with measurement confirmed by records of oxygen consumption (Schulmann & Reisman, 1959). Small, ultrasonic speakers worn on the wrist were used by Goldman (1961) to measure body movement. Investigators have also measured body movement by modifying furniture such as desks (Foshee, 1958), beds (Cox & Marley, 1959), and chairs (Haring, 1968). Webb, Campbell, Schwartz, and Sechrest (1966) have provided a very useful guide to this and related types of equipment in their book, *Unobtrusive Measures: Nonreactive Research in the Social Sciences.* Special "automated analysis toys" have been developed (Friedlander, 1966) that record babies' play responses in the home. Cigarette cases can also count the number of cigarettes removed and shock the user (Powell & Azrin, 1968).

Since the early use of the magnetic-tape recorder and movie camera, some notable advances have been made. For example, rather than continuously filming behavior, a time-lapse camera can be used which will automatically sample events at preset intervals such as every six minutes (Sanders, Hopkins, & Walker, 1969). This eliminates observer bias in the selection of events to be recorded and afterward allows several ob-

---

[8]Reviews of instrumentation currently used in the behavioral sciences can be found in Sidowski (1966), a special issue of the *American Psychologist* edited by Sidowski & Ross (1969), Schwitzgebel (1968, 1970) and in Schwitzgebel & Schwitzgebel (1973).

servers to look at the filmed event and code it. Cameras can also be remotely activated by voice keys which detect the subject's speech (Dawe, 1966). Closed-circuit television can be used to transmit ongoing events to observers (Stoller, 1967). The person filmed or taped can later observe his own behavior (Gaier, 1952; Nielsen, 1964).[9] Special equipment has been designed to facilitate the efficient search and analysis of large amounts of information that may be stored on film without lengthy review or editing (Ekman & Friesen, 1969).

The effects of the presence of the camera on the subject have not yet been clearly determined. Some investigators suggest that the camera is not distressing or disruptive of therapy (e.g., Haggard, Hiken, & Isaacs, 1965). The customary view is that there is a gradual adaptation to the camera (Sternberg, Chapman, & Shakow, 1958). Other investigators suggest, however, that the camera produces more favorable self-references (Roberts & Renzaglia, 1965). Problems such as this might be overcome in the future in some settings by utilizing advances in infrared technology (cf. Haith, 1969; Woodward & Williams, 1967).

Some very helpful developments have been made in the instrumentation of self-report which eliminates the bias and error of an observer. Lindsley (1963, 1969) and others (McGuire & Stigall, 1967; Nathan, Schneller, & Lindsley, 1964) have developed a two-way closed-circuit television system which requires the patient to push a foot switch at a predetermined minimal rate in order to continue to see and hear the therapist. If the patient fails to maintain the required operant rate, there is a progressive and simultaneous deterioration of the picture quality and sound intensity at the patient's television receiver. The therapist's audio and video reception of the patient, however, remains unaffected. This creates an operant measurement of the patient's view of (and perhaps interest in) the therapist.

With new equipment, it has become increasingly feasible to record automatically discrete behavioral events and corollary physiological events without the presence of an outside observer. This often tends to increase reliability as well as guarantee the anonymity of the subjects. An example is the development of instruments to assess the "smoothness" of driving (Safren & Schlesinger, 1964) and the eye movement, perceptual field, respiration, and heart rate of drivers under actual road conditions (Michon & Koutstaal, 1969). Several different devices have been developed to measure sexual arousal in male subjects (e.g., Freund, 1963; Barlow, Becker, Leitenberg, & Agras, 1970).

---

[9]Subjects have also been presented with video tapes of themselves under various conditions of therapist-assisted self-confrontation or feedback (Kagan, Krathwohl, & Miller, 1963; Rogers, 1968).

In 1963, a pioneering study in the use of telemetry was conducted by Soskin and John. A major objective of the study was to determine whether subjects could adjust to the continuous monitoring by a radio transmitter of their public and private conversations. Two husband-wife couples at a resort served as subjects. Soskin and John (1963, pp. 234–235) concluded:

> It is difficult to ascertain how much and under what circumstances behavior was influenced by consciousness of the transmitter. Both pairs of subjects reported afterward that they were aware of such influence at some times and not at others. Both also reported that self consciousness diminished with the passage of time. We do not know how "representative" is the behavior of our subjects, but for the purposes at hand it need not be representative of anything but the behavior of a young couple wearing transmitters on a summer vacation. There are no data presently available by which to determine how their behavior among strangers, in an unfamiliar setting, when neither had any work responsibilities, might differ from their behavior at home among friends, in their more customary patterns of living. Such comparisons remain as tasks of the future. Nevertheless, the present tapes do contain recordings of a violent argument, of tender expressions of love, of petty behavior, of sober soul-searching, and sheer exuberant pleasure.

Similar research involving children at school and simultaneous observer ratings has been conducted by Herbert and Swayze (1964).

This work has been further extended by the research of Purcell and Brady (1966). Thirteen young adolescent boys and girls at a residential treatment center for asthma wore small, cigarette-package-size FM transmitters. Thirteen other subjects wore similar "dummy" transmitters. These transmitters were worn for one hour on ten consecutive days during evening snack time before bedtime. During the first to third days there was a marked decrease in the subjects' verbal references to the transmitters. House parents were not able to guess accurately which children wore the "live" transmitters and which wore the "dummy" transmitters. The house-parent ratings of the children's behavior prior to wearing the transmitters and behavior ratings while wearing the transmitters showed no statistically significant differences. Also, there were no significant changes in the amount of talking or in the types of interpersonal behavior between the subjects and others except for "showing off" the transmitters which consistently and significantly decreased over time.

Many other forms of data have also been remotely monitored. Heart rhythms (EKG) have been transmitted from emergency vehicles to a hospital (Huszar & Haloburdo, 1969) and over shorter distances brain-wave patterns (EEG) have been transmitted and recorded from freely moving patients (Delgado, Mark, Sweet, Ervin, Weiss, Bach-y-Rita, & Hagiwara, 1968).[10] The geographical locations of subjects within a several-block area in a city have been continuously monitored every thirty seconds as an alternative to imprisonment (Harvard Law Review, 1966; Schwitzgebel, 1968a, 1969b, c). Low-power transmitters have also been ingested by human subjects to measure physiological responses (Mackay, 1969).

PRIVACY

The observation of human behavior raises several very important ethical and policy considerations. Some of the ethical considerations are discussed in Chapter 12; here attention is focused upon issues related in a general way to the concept of "privacy."

In a noteworthy article by Ruebhausen and Brim (1965) entitled "Privacy and Behavioral Research," a concept of privacy is proposed that involves the right of a person to determine when and to what extent information about himself will be shared or withheld from others. Ironically, it is a technological invention very closely related to observation which led to the development of the early legal concepts of privacy. This invention was that of "instantaneous photography" which used flash powder.

Photography, it may be recalled, originally required long periods of exposure so that it was necessary to go through a time-consuming procedure of "sitting" for a portrait. It was difficult to take a person's picture under these conditions without his awareness and cooperation. Flash powder changed this, for photographs could then be taken "instantaneously" without the subject's cooperation. Pictures thus taken were sometimes displayed in the newspapers for the amusement of readers and this led to the writing in 1890 of the first legal article on privacy by Samuel D. Warren and Louis D. Brandeis (later a Justice of the United States Supreme Court). In this article, privacy was defined largely in terms of "the right to be left alone."

A somewhat more detailed concept of privacy may be useful in formulating policy in regard to modern observational techniques. A distinction can be made between the method of acquiring observational data and the type of data acquired. Data may be obtained in such a manner that the subjects involved are not personally identifiable; that is,

---

[10]This equipment also included the capability of remotely transmitting electrical signals into the brain to alter behavior, a process known as intracerebral radio stimulation.

they remain individually unknown or anonymous. Or, the subjects might be partially identifiable, such as being members of a small, specific group. Or finally, the subjects might be uniquely identified as particular individuals. Data thus obtained could be categorized along a dimension ranging from subject anonymity to unique subject identification. Another dimension that might be helpful in categorizing observational data is that of personal-public. Certain information is conventionally considered available to the public, such as marital status and occupation; other information, such as financial status or sexual conduct, is considered private.

These two dimensions may be used to define four commonly found categories of data. There is category A in which the data from the subjects are anonymous and the information lies clearly within the domain of public knowledge. Data on topics such as parking behavior and consumer preferences would generally fall into this category. Category B would involve public information in which the subject could be uniquely identified. An example here would be the collection of data from library lists or petitions. Category C would include personal information in which the subject could be uniquely identified. Data in this category are often obtained in the form of clinical or observational case studies. Finally, category D would include data of a personal but anonymous nature, such as is frequently found in published case studies or in broader descriptive studies of socially embarrassing or disapproved behavior. The issue of privacy is mostly, but not exclusively, relevant to category C, the collection of data about personal behavior in such a way that the subject is uniquely identifiable.

The categorization of data suggests two methods the researcher can use to safeguard privacy: (1) avoid the observation of personal behavior or (2) establish anonymity for the subject or obtain his informed consent. The first method is most readily advocated by the popular press, perhaps because it is the easiest and most straightforward. Prompted by mass-media hysteria, legislation can be written sharply curtailing investigation of specified types of behavior. This is an easy solution, but perhaps in the long run the most expensive one in terms of human welfare. The alternative to psychological investigation and study is ignorance which has, in historical perspective, contributed much to human suffering. The safeguarding of privacy through guaranteed subject anonymity may be more difficult to obtain than proscriptive legislation but perhaps eventually most beneficial to both society and the individual.

The more risk there is for the subject, the more it would seem necessary to guarantee his anonymity, or obtain his informed consent, or both. A Public Health Service memorandum of December 12, 1966, noted:

[A] major class of procedures in the social and behavioral sciences does no more than observe or elicit information about the subject's status, by means of administration of tests, inventories, questionnaires, or surveys of personality or background. In such instances, the ethical considerations of voluntary participation, confidentiality, and propriety in the use of the findings are the most generally relevant ones. However, such procedures may in many instances not require the fully informed consent of the subject or even his knowledgeable participation. In such instances full and specific documentation is necessary for the record.

This would generally seem to be the proper approach (cf. Westin, 1967). The use of instruments to "observe or elicit information" would presumably, in many instances, not require fully informed consent as long as the anonymity of the subjects was fully protected. If equipment were used, however, to change personal behavior deliberately and experimentally, some form of consent or indication of voluntary participation would probably be needed (Schwitzgebel, 1970b).

Once a subject has knowingly and voluntarily disclosed some personal information about himself, the investigator is still obligated to prevent, as much as he reasonably can, any subsequent misuse of the information that might harm the subject. In some states, the investigator may use special statutes that provide confidentiality for research information of a sensitive nature (Schwitzgebel, 1969a). Also, special procedures, such as on-line testing by a computer, may be developed to help safeguard anonymity or confidentiality.

Basic policy aimed at safeguarding the privacy and other rights of subjects is still in the process of formulation. Behavioral scientists need to exercise imagination and leadership in this area to combine long-term research goals with a sensitivity to the personal experience of subjects. An open, collaborative effort between the investigator and the subject may sometimes be most productive for both. An approach to research ethics based upon social agreements of this kind is discussed in the following chapter.

SUMMARY

The accurate observation of human behavior in experimental laboratories and natural social settings is essential for the continued development of behavior-change techniques. One reason why the direct observation of behavior is necessary is that interview and questionnaire procedures produce information about behavior which is often not adequately valid or reliable. In addition to errors which may be introduced into interview data by respondents, errors and biases may be produced by interviewers through factors such as interviewer behavior, attitudes, age, and socio-economic class.

Some human events such as child rearing, political rallies, and "falling in love" cannot be confined to the experimental laboratory for observation and study. Procedures need to be developed to study these events in their natural settings. Among the many possible types of observational procedures that can be used to study these events in natural settings, three have received special attention within the past few years. These are participant observation, self-observation, and instrumentation. All of these procedures require the demonstration of adequate validity and reliability, a theoretically suitable classification of the observed events, and the development of satisfactory techniques of data storage and retrieval.

During participant observation, behaviors can be studied directly and extensively over a long period of time. The participant observer may have a perspective different from the perspectives of the other participants and a comparison of these different perspectives can be valuable. There is the danger that the participant observer may unknowingly influence the behavior he is observing.

It is possible for people to record their own behaviors according to predetermined rules or schedules. Behaviors and internal feelings can be thus recorded which would be difficult or impossible for another person to observe. Subjects can, of course, bias or distort the information reported by such a procedure as they can in questionnaires and interviews but these biases or distortions may be more readily noticed by the subject or researcher. There is some indication that self-observation can change some types of behavior being observed. Depending upon the purpose for which the self-observation data are to be used and the setting of the research, this influence of self-observation upon the observed behavior can be considered a factor which interferes with collecting accurate data or an aid in changing behavior. The validity of self-observation data can be indirectly established by comparing it with clearly observable, related events.

Some of the problems of participant observation and self-observation can be overcome through the use of instrumentation. Such instrumentation can include devices such as counters, recorders, cameras, and transmitters. Use of automated information-storage systems, increased recognition of ethical obligations, and the development of appropriate legislation can help to preserve subjects' privacy by providing anonymity and safeguarding the confidentiality of research information.

Chapter 12

Toward an Ethic for Research on Human Behavior

with Kenneth J. Gergen[1]

Within the past few years there has been a rapid increase in the number of discussions about the ethics of research. Surely, some research activities require careful examination and perhaps censure. For example, in one study:

> The investigators took special precautions to keep subjects ignorant of the fact that their remarks were being recorded. To this end, they concealed themselves under beds in students' rooms where tea parties were being held, eavesdropped in dormitory smoking rooms and washrooms, and listened to telephone conversations (p. 230).

The researchers report that the "unwitting subjects were pursued in the streets, in department stores, and in the home."[2]

Those who think that such a research practice illustrates the recent decline of research ethics may be surprised to learn that this study took

[1]Chairman, Department of Psychology and Education, Swarthmore College.

[2]Henle & Hubble (1938). In 1930, French, Carter, & Koenig monitored telephone conversations. We thank Webb, Campbell, Schwartz, & Sechrest (1966) for citing these studies in their excellent book on unobtrusive measures.

place in 1938. Although past errors do not justify present ones, some caution is needed before assuming that we have reached a new state of ethical impropriety in research. Rather, some ethical problems in research appear to be long-standing and persistent. Ethical guidelines for research in the behavioral sciences have been slow and uneven in their development. The development of guidelines seems to take place primarily when public concern has been evoked by some dramatic, widely publicized impropriety.

There are, of course, some good reasons for the slowness in developing appropriate guidelines. The behavioral sciences are sufficiently wed to the pragmatic tradition that ends, in terms of scientific progress, tend to justify whatever "reasonable" means may be utilized.[3] In addition, concern with the ethical grounds of an experiment may threaten the investigator with the possibility that his proposed research will not be executed—often a threat to his professional identity. Finally, as a result of findings within the behavioral sciences themselves, investigators are well apprised of the cultural relativity of ethics. Few can thus respect "ethical absolutes" as having relevance to their lives—in or out of the profession.

In spite of the lack of concern about the ethical standards of research, theory and data of relevance to human ethics are constantly being generated within the behavioral sciences. Not only is much known about the ethical systems of various cultures, but there is also an increasing amount of information being obtained about the conditions that foster prejudice, interpersonal exploitation, aggression, cooperation, and so on. It is possible that advantage may be taken of such knowledge in developing an ethic of both general and specific utility for carrying out research within the behavioral sciences themselves. In effect, an opportunity is presented for the creation of an *indigenous ethic*. The complete form of such an ethic is clearly many years in the future, and it will depend to some extent on the development of the sciences themselves. As the sciences evolve, so can the ethic. The aim of the present chapter, however, is a modest one: to outline one approach to the problem of an indigenous ethic, an approach of special relevance to experimental work in the area of behavior change.

CURRENT INFLUENCES

At present, ethical considerations relevant to experimentation with human subjects are heavily influenced by two traditions: the medical and

[3]See, for example, some of the principles suggested by the ad hoc Committee on Ethical Standards in Psychological Research of the American Psychological Association (Cook, Kimble, Hicks, McGuire, Schoggen, & Smith, 1971).

the humanistic. Each of these traditions deserves attention. In particular, consideration needs to be given to the capacity of each to furnish adequate guidelines for behavioral research.

Medical Influence

The impact of organized medicine has largely stemmed from the historical fact that the medical profession has held eminent domain in matters of illness or abnormality. When psychological investigation was conducted in these areas, it was largely considered an extension of the medical sciences. The profession of psychiatry and the position of clinical psychologists within hospital settings are vestigial forms of the assumption of medical preeminence. Other indications would include Beecher's (1958) small but influential book, *Experimentation in Man*, in which the entire ethical stance is developed from a medical perspective. In other literature, experimental techniques in the behavioral sciences are often listed as subtechniques of medical investigation. For example, research on mental disorder, personal adjustment, perception, counseling, and psychotherapy are all the designated responsibility of the medical branches of the armed services.

The guidelines set forth by the medical tradition take two forms. The archaic form is derived from the Hippocratic Oath, which stresses such vague principles as using good judgment in providing benefit to others and avoiding mischief and corruption. A more timely code governing human experimentation was proposed by the Judicial Council of the American Medical Association in 1946. It suggested three prerequisites for experimentation: (1) voluntary consent of the subjects, (2) the assessment of danger through means of animal experimentation prior to human experimentation, and (3) the performance of experiments under proper medical protection and management.

As one examines the ethical stance supplied by the medical profession, it becomes apparent that more problems may be created than answered. This is hardly unexpected, as experiments in the behavioral sciences differ in a number of important ways from those conducted by the medical profession. It may be helpful to consider briefly several of these differences.

An obvious difference between research conducted in the medical rather than behavioral sciences is that in the former, the subject's knowledge about the experiment can have relatively little influence on the experimental outcome. Although a patient may be aware that an experimental procedure is being attempted in the repair of a broken bone, his knowledge is not likely to change the placement of the bone. By contrast, a subject's awareness of the intent of a study in behavior change may considerably influence his behavior. Such effects were demonstrated as early as 1920 when workers at the Hawthorne plant were found to improve their work habits simply because of the special attention they received as experimental subjects (Rothlisberger, 1950). This effect became known as the *Hawthorne effect*. More recently, Orne (1962) discussed the *demand characteristics* in psychological experiments, those cues in the experiment which convey experimental hypotheses to the subjects. The power of these demand characteristics was demonstrated in an experiment in which subjects were asked to add numbers on sheets filled with 448 random digits. Each subject was given 2,000 sheets to complete, a clearly impossible task. Also, following the completion of each sheet of problems, the subject was instructed to tear the sheet into a minimum of thirty-two pieces and then complete the next sheet of problems.

Contrary to expectations that the subjects in this experiment would stop when they discovered that the task was meaningless, the subjects continued to work at the task for several hours with little sign of overt hostility. Postexperimental inquiry indicated that the subjects viewed the experiment as an endurance test or something related to it. Rosenthal (1966) has demonstrated that research hypotheses can greatly bias the results of psychological experiments. Psychologists are sufficiently aware of such effects that may intentionally falsify the aims of their study in order to obtain uncontaminated results. This in turn raises an ethical question about the use of deceit in psychological research, a topic which will be considered later.

Pathology versus Normality

Medical experimentation is largely based on understanding and correcting pathological conditions. In fact, the very existence of the medical profession is dependent on man's aversion for pain and death. On the other hand, much research in the behavioral sciences is devoted to understanding normal behavioral processes. It does not always seek to change these processes or their outcomes, but merely to understand their existence and to develop the tools which could produce change if necessary. For example, Verplanck's (1955) early study on unconscious verbal conditioning in informal relationships was not based on the assumption that informal relationships needed correction, nor was he primarily interested in the change that may be effected in a person's use of personal pronouns. Rather, he attempted to demonstrate a rather subtle aspect of ongoing relationships, and how one might systematically alter the features of interaction through conditioning procedures and without the apparent awareness of the subject.

Of course, this issue of pathology versus normality raises important questions concerning the ethical criterion of having "proper medical protection and management." Experiments in observational learning that are aimed at increasing the contribution of persons to a worthy cause (Byran & Test, 1967) or increasing the use of turn signals by drivers (Barch et al., 1957) are clearly inappropriate for medical supervision. Even when a subject may have his behavior or ways of viewing the world profoundly altered, there may be some question about the appropriateness of medical attention. The dangers here are of a considerably different nature than those found in typical medical experiments. In a study by Bramel (1962), for example, subjects were extensively exposed to information which indicated they had strong homosexual leanings. Although each subject was assured at length at the close of the experiment that the information was false, the long-term self-doubts which may have been created by such a method were left unexamined. Whether a postexperimental interview in this case constituted proper protection and management is doubtful, but the medical ethic offers no appropriate solution.

Biology versus Human Distinctiveness

If one looks at biological aspects alone, there is a clear continuity between the features of the human being and those of lower organisms. This continuity is best represented, of course, in the concept of the phylogenetic scale. Such a view is quite central to the medical profession, and thus to its ethics for research. Within this ethic, man is looked at as the apex of the evolutionary scheme, and for his benefit all other forms of life are expendable. Thus, the recommendation can be made that the danger of each experiment be investigated by means of animal experimentation. We have already alluded to the difference between the medical and behavioral science definition of "danger." The matter of preliminary animal studies is also problematic.

The principal difficulty hinges on the fact that many aspects of human behavior that engage the interests of behavioral scientists are distinctly human in character. Verbal behavior is but one example. There are also no direct analogs in animal behavior for studies of social perception, attitude change, interpersonal attraction, conformity, suicide, juvenile delinquency, and so on.

This distinction may initially seem less apparent in the area of behavior change than in other areas. Many of the principles utilized in work on behavior change have been developed from work with animals. Without the dog, the rat, and the pigeon our knowledge of learning processes could have been set back three decades. It is also easier to accept biological continuities if one remains on the level of overt behavior than when one begins to specify internal processes. On the other hand, many of the phenomena discussed in the later chapters of this book would be extremely difficult to pursue with animal studies. Animal studies provide some useful information for the development of hypotheses about behavior change. They are not meant to describe completely and adequately the processes of behavior change in humans as can be seen clearly in regard to topics such as observational learning (Chapter 6), achievement motivation training (Chapter 7), or self-directed change (Chapter 8).

Simple versus Multiple Values

Generally, medical experimentation works toward gaining knowledge that will aid in serving the physical health of human beings. Such an aim receives almost universal sanction and support. In the behavioral sciences, universal support for an undertaking is almost never available. In studying international relations, there are some who feel that war is the optimal state; in experimenting with the reduction of race prejudice, there are a few who feel that prejudice is justified. Research has been described in previous chapters which involves the early release of convicted law breakers. Such a goal has many critics. There are also many who view all methods of behavior change as immoral because such methods may permit the manipulation of one person by another.

Even if the values within a society predominantly supported a given research undertaking, behavioral scientists have the additional problem of dealing with relative values across cultures. A good illustration is provided by an experiment undertaken in 1952 to increase the motivation and living standards of the inhabitants of Vicos, a small community in Peru. As a result of this experiment, the economic situation of the community was vastly improved, starvation diminished, crime rates reduced, and the segregation of classes prohibited at public meetings (Holmberg, 1965). In short, the experiment was a striking success from the standpoint of contemporary American values. From the point of view of the local power elite, the project was much less positively regarded. When the research group attempted to transfer land titles back to the local inhabitants, the workers were accused of being pawns of American capitalism, and spies for the American government. Even such a "progressive" organization as the Rotary Club of Huaraz soundly denounced the project, and accused its field director of being an agent of Communism. Matters were settled only after intervention by the President of the Institute of Indigenous Affairs, United States government officials in Peru, and the Public Benefit Society.

In essence, while the general goals of medical research are seldom questioned, research in the behavioral sciences exists in a context of mixed values (cf. Mann, 1965). Universal sanction allows one to avoid many problems of ethical subjectivity. In cases where one's research is controversial, matters of ethical judgment become much more complex. The need for an ethic which grows out of the peculiar problems faced by the behavioral scientist is thus all the more apparent.

Humanistic Influence

The humanistic viewpoint, and it is probably erroneous to speak of it in the singular, has appeared in many forms. If any ethic were to spring from the behavioral sciences at the present time, it would most likely be of the humanistic form. The core of this tradition seems generally to be composed of a confluence of several themes. Most basically, the view maintains that the highest goal is the worldly happiness, freedom, and prosperity of all men. The individual should be allowed active self-direction and self-expression as his reason, foresight, and emotional commitments dictate. Humanistic ethics are derived from human experience itself, and tested within the social context. Scientific laws governing human behavior may be an adjunct to this quest inasmuch as they may help the person to understand both himself and others to a greater extent, and thus to be able to live harmoniously within the larger society.

It should come as no surprise that these various emphases have captured the enthusiasm of many behavioral scientists. They do not depend on absolutist or mystical principles that are found to exist in such highly variegated forms throughout the world. Nor do they point to another world as the goal of all present human endeavor. Rather, they settle for the finite, the concrete, and the pragmatic; and cause man to be the center of his own concern. Most importantly, they see the scientific method as the major tool for carrying out this concern on a legitimate and rational basis. The question remains, however, as to whether the humanistic viewpoint provides sufficient grounds for establishing an ethic to guide investigation in the behavioral sciences. In the main, it seems that it would not.

First, humanistic philosophy is far too abstract at the present time to be especially useful in many concrete instances. Most men would agree that happiness, freedom, and progress are worthy goals, but what various individuals mean by these abstract concepts may be quite different, if not contradictory. The ascetic happiness of one may be anathema to another's libertinism, and the prosperity that some feel urban renewal represents may be considered by others a major assault on community cohesiveness. The problems of applying the viewpoint in instances of actual research undertakings seem hopelessly beyond the pale of present resolution.

Second, while the humanistic tradition does develop a set of ideal end-states, the problem of means has received short shrift. Milgram's (1963) study of social obedience, in which subjects were coerced by an experimenter to administer electric shock to another person until it appeared that the victim might have been killed, is a case in point. Inasmuch as the study was an attempt to lay bare processes that might cause one man to slay another out of obedience to an authority (e.g., Eichmann in World War II), it was in the best humanistic tradition. At the same time, whether the outcomes of the study merited the mental suffering which the subjects were caused to experience has been a heated issue among psychologists.

Thus far two dominant influences upon the development of ethical guidelines have been discussed, the medical and the humanistic. In each case, it has been found that important shortcomings exist and that such traditions are inadequate for providing an ethical cornerstone. It has been seen, however, that each of these domains raises a number of critical issues which an adequate set of guidelines would have to encompass. It would be presumptuous, of course, to pretend that the discussion below can meet all such issues in a completely satisfactory way. Rather, the intent is to outline what may be a promising approach to the problem—an approach that makes use of behavioral science to build its own ethical guidelines. Based on this framework, we will strike off—perhaps only to go a stride or two—in the direction of a preliminary skirmish with some of the issues treated above.

RESEARCH ETHICS IN BEHAVIOR EXCHANGE

In *The Social Psychology of Groups*, Thibaut and Kelley (1959) have developed a conceptual framework with widespread implications. As they suggest, it is possible to view the behavior of any two interacting persons in matrix form. In Figure 12-1, for example, person *p* may give an expensive gift (behavior A) or an inexpensive gift (behavior B). The other person *o* may choose to accept the gift (behavior C) or reject it (behavior D). Further, behaviors A and B may have differential value (utility or hedonic consequences) for *p*. In spite of the increased expense involved, he might generally prefer to give expensive gifts (A). Likewise, *o* may generally prefer to receive gifts (C) than to refuse them (D), although he gains some slight satisfaction from refusing. By placing options in a matrix form, one can consider the values of the respective individuals for joint positions in the various possible combinations of behavior.

If *p* gives an expensive gift and *o* chooses to receive the gift, hedonic

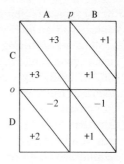

Figure 12-1 Interaction matrix.

outcomes might be placed at a numerical value of let us say +3. At the same time, *o* experiences pleasure equivalent to +3 in receiving an expensive gift. Both receive less pleasure at giving and receiving a less expensive gift. On the other hand, should *p* give an expensive gift and *o* refuse, *p* might experience considerable displeasure (−2), while *o* would be somewhat gratified (+2). Both would experience less intense feelings when the smaller gift was refused (+1, −1).

Given this basic paradigm, it is initially a simple matter to apply it to the experimental situation in psychological research. Assume for a moment that *p* is an experimenter and *o* his subject. The situation is clearly one where the exchange of payoffs is at a premium. In the pure research setting, *p* (the experimenter) might wish to elicit a behavior of a certain kind from *o* (subject). The experimenter might wish the subject to participate in a certain type of operant-conditioning experiment and to react without a deliberate attempt to bias the results. The subject's participation thus has a reward value for the experimenter. At the same time, the subject's participation may have certain costs attached to it from his point of view. At a minimum, his time and effort are required. When behavior-change techniques are applied for therapeutic reasons, the relief of suffering may be the subject's (patient's) goal, and as a result he will desire behavior of a certain class from the experimenter (therapist). On the other hand, the therapist may receive various rewards, such as financial gain, research data, or gratification of humanistic desires. In general, there is a variety of behaviors in which experimenter and subjects may engage. Each of these behaviors may have a certain reward value and certain costs attached, and these rewards and costs will largely depend on the combination of behaviors emitted by both participants.

In the form outlined thus far, this social-exchange orientation is purely descriptive and has no prescriptive implications for the ethics of research. If, however, we make one further distinction, and three preconditions, the ethical implications become manifest. Initially, we must distinguish between the matrix initiator and the respondent—the individual proposing the exchange in behavior and the person to whom the proposal is being made. This is simply to point out that in defining ethical responsibility, the researcher and object of his research may be subject to differing demands. The three preconditions are: (1) the respondent is allowed a choice of alternatives within the matrix throughout the interaction sequence; (2) the respondent is to remain at all times aware of the matrix contingencies; and (3) the behavioral commitments of the initiator at any point are binding. The first precondition should ensure that the respondent has free access to response alternatives and allows him at all times in the sequence the choice of not participating at all. The second precondition insures him of sufficient information upon which to base a decision. The third precondition transforms the descriptive system into a contractual agreement.[4]

One can view these preconditions in several additional ways. For example, there are parallels for each within the legal realm, namely, the responsibility of the individual for actions performed without duress, the close relationship between foreknowledge of action and responsibility for its consequences, and the binding nature of contractual agreements. The various preconditions also have parallels in the humanistic tradition. Free access to behavioral alternatives can help to maximize the dignity of the individual. He is not reduced to infrahuman status through the enforcement of participation. Knowledge of the matrix coincides with the value placed on informed decision making as opposed to irrational behavior. The final stipulation emphasizes the experimenter's human responsibility and devalues duplicity. On a third level, the system lends itself to thinking in the metaphor of the game. In these terms the stipulations insure that the invited participant has the choice of whether to play or not, that he is aware of the rules, and that his opponent will not break them.

Given these broad stipulations, the task remains of spelling out various concrete implications, and to indicate a number of advantages of the system. The preconditions are dealt with in the order presented above.

Respondent Choice

As suggested above, a major alternative for the subject in the matrix is whether to participate or not.[5] There are two immediate implications of this precondition that suggest departures from current standards of practice.

---

[4]See principles (1.521, 1.524); (1,411, 1.412, 1.413, 1.421); (1.61, 1.62) suggested by Cook, Kimble, Hicks, McGuire, Schoggen, & Smith (1971). Veatch (1972) has proposed a contractual model for medical ethics.

[5]The widely recognized Nuremberg Code (United States Adjutant General's Department, 1947) asserts in its first principle that the voluntary consent of the subject is absolutely essential. Various forms of this principle can also be found in the Declaration of Helsinki (1964) and in the standards promulgated by the American Psychological Association (1967; 1973), the American Medical Association (1946), and the United States Public Health Service (1966).

The first implication is that subjects not be conscripted for psychological experiments in a way that jeopardizes their initial status as unencumbered decision-makers. Widespread research practices in both university and medical settings often violate this condition. The most pervasive technique of conscription is to attach requisites for experimental participation to academic courses in psychology. Such requirements are typically justified by the assumption (often erroneous) that participation will improve the student's knowledge of the field. Within the matrix, the "improvement" would appear as a value attached to one of the behaviors contributed by the experimenter (should the subject choose to participate). In this sense, the increment of knowledge should produce an increment in the subject's payoff for participation. On the other hand, the potential subject has little room to reject this alternative, should he feel that the positive "payoff" in knowledge was not worth the negative consequences produced by subjecting himself to the experiment.

One could counter by saying that the subject does have choice of a kind—he can participate to earn academic credit, or he can forego credit by not participating. However, in this case the researcher is taking advantage of the matrix offered by the educational system. That is, under the guise of providing knowledge to the subject, the experimenter is also obtaining the right to subject students to procedures of little academic merit which provide him data for his noneducational pursuits. These are not outcomes which the student customarily agrees to provide simply by his matriculation in the educational system.

A similar situation often exists in medical settings where patients may be required to subject themselves to research procedures of no benefit to their health (mental or physical) by virtue of their desiring entrance to the hospital. Blanket statements are often secured at admission causing the patient to forego his right of choice. In academic and medical settings, as well as others, thought needs to be given to alternative practices. In academic settings, other methods of obtaining knowledge about the manner in which research is conducted might be offered along with opportunities for participating as experimental subjects. In the medical setting, rather than requiring blanket permission, agreement might be sought for each individual project.

A second concrete implication of the choice requirement is that the subject be allowed to choose not to participate in the research at any point during the procedure. Typically an investigator cannot outline all of his activities (all matrix contingencies) prior to requesting participation. As a result, the subject learns more and more about what may be required of him as the investigation progresses. The necessity, however, is that the subject be allowed to withdraw from participation as the contingencies become more manifest and his payoffs are altered (Schwitzgebel, 1968).

After acquiring a subject's agreement to participate in a study of problem solving, it may be unwarranted then to hold him responsible for continuing in the research when he discovered that certain of his actions would be accompanied by electric shock, for example.[6] This issue will be discussed in more detail below in the context of matrix awareness.

Research with legally constrained persons, such as mental patients and prisoners, raises some very special and difficult problems. Morris (1966) has suggested a principle of "less severity" in research within correctional settings. This principle states that the experimental treatment should be regarded by the community at large as less severe than the treatment or condition against which it is being compared. Thus, prison inmates could be experimentally released from prison but offenders already in the community could not be experimentally placed in a prison for treatment. The nature of the permissible behavior-change procedures used in settings such as these may also be legally limited by constitutional and legislative provisions (Schwitzgebel, 1970a).

One further implication of respondent choice, if such choice is genuinely voluntary and informed, requires attention. Traditionally, the research scientist has been held entirely responsible for any negative outcomes occurring to a subject in a psychological experiment. In many instances, however, an experimenter cannot gauge all the consequences of the stimulus events to which a subject is exposed, and in perhaps a good many cases, the subject himself is in a better position to gauge whether or not participation would be a harmful experience. A person who is worried about his abilities should realize that a study involving complex tasks and competition might be upsetting. A neurotic volunteering for behavior-change procedures that might ameliorate his condition should realize the possibility of failure or negative consequences.

It is also important to recognize that investigators may not be held responsible for all possible consequences to their subjects, particularly those risks "extrinsic" to the experiment that are not under their direct control and that are not ordinarily foreseeable in the course of the research (Wolfensberger, 1967). Subjects themselves may be viewed as sharing the responsibility of various risks of research. However, the degree to which responsibility is shared is roughly commensurate with the amount of choice the subject is given in participating. Only if the subject is allowed free access to alternatives throughout the procedure does he acquire joint responsibility.

[6]As with all general formulations, there may be exceptions. In some therapeutically oriented experiments, the right of an extremely disturbed patient to withdraw from an apparently beneficial program and to choose a more severe treatment of prolonged deprivation might be questioned, especially if physical harm would result (American Medical Association, 1966).

In regard to risks such as the subject's expenditure of time, money, and effort, the term "research" should not magically increase the ethical obligations of the researcher over those of the practitioner. Kanfer and Phillips (1970, p. 545) ask the following questions:

Does "informed consent" require that patients receiving shock therapy or insight psychotherapy first be told the discouraging figures on the effectiveness of such treatments? If psychotherapy does not alter the rate or extent of recovery from neurosis as many investigations suggest, then is it improper to accept a client's trust, time, and money for psychotherapy, or to train students in inefficient procedures?

They appropriately conclude (pp. 545–546):

Although very few clinicians may be willing to take such an extreme position, increasing skepticism about the efficacy of traditional psychotherapies and consequent reluctance to rely upon them has resulted in greater openness to experimentation with alternative methods and some feeling of urgency in designing more powerful and conclusive research.

Matrix Awareness

The second of the preconditions suggested above was that the subject be informed at all times of the contingencies of the matrix.[7] He should first be aware that he may choose either to participate or not to participate, and then of what behaviors he might expect from the experimenter should he choose one or another of the alternatives. A similar point has been made by Alumbaugh (1972, pp. 897–898) in a rousing criticism of some proposed ethical guidelines by an ad hoc Committee of the American Psychological Association:

Roughly 500 years ago, Pope Innocent XIII commissioned two Dominican monks, Heinrich Kramer and James Sprenger (Summers, 1951), to define witchcraft, to determine how witches could "successfully be annulled and dissolved," and to establish proper judicial proceedings. Specific incidents of how witches "inflict every sort of infirmity" were included to aid in both their identification and eradication. Though their exposé on carnal practices of witches led ultimately to much genocide, little criticism could be mounted

---

[7]This stipulation is not unlike the clause in the Nuremberg Code that points out the necessity for the subject's knowing "the nature, duration, and purpose of the experiment, the method and means by which it is to be conducted; all inconveniences and hazards reasonably to be expected; and the effects upon his health or person which may possibly come from his participation . . . " (United States Adjutant General's Department, 1947).

against the monks, who were protected by the moral authority of the church.

To my knowledge, no one other than a few existentialists has suggested that researchers be burned at the stake; yet, the recently proposed ethical principles for research (Cook, Kimble, Hicks, McGuire, Schoggen, & Smith, 1971) "hammers" at issues similar to blows delivered by the original malleus. Namely, how can those investigators be identified that exploit innocent, naive participants in research? . . .

My fundamental disagreement with the Committee centers around their assumption that subjects "willingly participate" in experiments. . . .

The issue that should be explored centers around the disclosure of all contingencies that affect subject participation. If contingencies are discussed comprehensively, theoretically the probable behavior will evolve which is most rewarding to the potential subject. Thus, a potential subject may "willingly consent" to participate because the alternative behavior of nonparticipation is simply less reinforcing. It is difficult to see, therefore, the rationale for Principles 1.5111, 1.5112, or 1.5142. In all three of these Principles, the primary obligation of the investigator is to restrict the use of reinforcers.

It is assumed in the present discussion that the subject is mature and not a child or mentally incompetent. The subject may be considered, in a sense, a type of "collaborator" who is entitled to direct information about ethical codes and practices (Baumrind, 1971). By being aware of the social limits of the situation (including perhaps the possibility of certain forms of deception?), he can make a rational decision about his participation. This decision can be based upon what he knows about the experiment and also upon what he knows he does not know.

The one immediate problem with this specification of matrix awareness may appear to be the fact that in order to carry out much human research it is often impossible to inform the subject of all contingencies prior to his participation. However, not all contingencies must be laid out at the beginning of the experiment. In particular, it does not seem necessary that the experimenter outline all that might happen to the subject if he chooses to participate. On the contrary, he could say to the subject that he is able to tell him very little about what might occur. Insofar as the subject is able to choose not to participate under these circumstances, the experimenter's obligation would be fulfilled. Clearly, in this type of case, few subjects would volunteer to participate. Purely on pragmatic grounds, the experimenter might need to increase the information which he provided about the experiment. He might inform the subject, for example, that the study would last only thirty minutes, it would involve innocuous procedures, and that it would net the subject a certain fee for his participation. In this case, a greater number of subjects might choose to participate. They might ask for further information, but the experimenter is not thus obliged to provide it to them. He has essentially specified the "rules of the game," and the normally competent subject has assumed at least some responsibility for outcome if he agrees to "play" with less information than he might otherwise prefer to have.

It is possible that the experimenter might wish to expand or fill in the matrix in greater detail as the experiment proceeds. While a subject might volunteer for a study of systematic desensitization in a therapeutic setting, he might find, after beginning the procedure, that the experimenter asks him about issues he wishes to keep private. The experimenter is not at fault in making more manifest the contingencies involved in participation. However, the initial stipulation would play a crucial role at this juncture. The subject should be allowed to curtail his participation at this point in the experiment. When new information is made available, a new choice point is essentially established.

To avoid the situation in which subjects consent only once without an adequate understanding of the experiences produced by an experimental procedure, arrangements should be made for repeatedly requesting the consent of the subjects throughout the duration of an experiment. In one experiment, which employed delinquents as experimental subjects over a period of several months, the receipts signed by the subjects in return for payment were also release forms reminding the subject in simple language of his right to quit (Schwitzgebel, 1964). In this way the subject was clearly given the opportunity of terminating his participation as he became increasingly familiar with the experiment. At the same time the experimenters were quite sure that in the absence of duress they were receiving valid, voluntary consents repeatedly affirmed.

As can be seen, this point of view also makes it unnecessary to debrief a subject at the end of every experiment. Revealing the purposes of the investigation could be added explicitly as a payoff for the subjects as spelled out in the original matrix. Subjects could be told that if they participate they would be able to learn about the research design and other matters at the close of the procedure. However, if providing this information is not made part of the initial agreement, the subject has no claim to access. On the other hand, if the subject desires this information, he would be permitted to make his participation contingent upon receiving it.

The precondition of matrix awareness does have certain restrictive features. There is a widespread tendency among psychologists to assume that because a person has volunteered or has agreed to participate for money, then he is obligated to continue the experiment until its conclusion—no matter what distasteful schemes the experimenter has in mind for the subject. If a subject agrees to participate on the basis of the minimal information provided to him at the outset, experimenters often deal with him as if he has agreed to any new details of the matrix which might later be revealed. From the present viewpoint, the experimenter in such cases is unfairly taking advantage of the subject's initial commitment. The subject has agreed to play one game, and the experimenter is using that commitment to hold him responsible for playing a second but different game.

The Agreement as Binding

The third of the preconditions specified above simply holds the experimenter responsible for acting in good faith; i.e., he is required to make good on the contingencies as he sets them forth. This precondition guarantees that he will play by the rules. Although such a requirement, on the face of it, would seem to be a minimum, it is also clear that there are many instances in psychological experimentation in which this has not been done. There are numerous experiments in the literature, for example, in which subjects have been promised expensive gifts, sizeable amounts of money, valid appraisals of themselves, a scientifically matched date, or information on the study itself, in which no valid payoff was ever made. Subjects under such conditions have a justifiable complaint, and the ethical currency of psychological experimentation is reduced accordingly.

There is, however, a more subtle issue which can be raised in this context. In order to maintain rigor and to manipulate variables effectively, it appears necessary in many experiments to cause the subjects to undergo a procedure of which they have not been made specifically aware. It is not so much that the experimenter fails to make good on his promises; rather, he causes the subject to experience certain events that do not appear to be under his control . Research on prosocial behavior in a time of crisis is a good case in point (e.g., Darley & Latane, 1968). The investigators are often interested in those factors that cause a person to render more or less aid to another in distress. In order to get at these factors, it is necessary to create situations in which it appears that someone requires help. If the initial matrix were to include information regarding a developing crisis, clearly the subsequent manipulation would lose all potency.

Numerous other examples could be cited; the primary feature in each case being that the subject must feel that what befalls him has not been under the experimenter's influence. Can the experimenter's behavior in such cases be considered appropriate on ethical grounds? The answer is difficult. Kelman (1968, pp. 209–210) has dealt with the issue of "deception" experiments in the following manner:

> It is easy to "view with alarm," but it is much more difficult to formulate an unambiguous position on this problem. As a working experimental social psychologist, I cannot conceive the issue in absolutist terms. I am too well aware of the fact that there are good reasons for using deception in many of our experiments. There are many significant problems that probably cannot be investigated without the use of deception, at least not at the present level of development of our experimental methodology. Thus, we are always confronted with a conflict of values. If we regard the acquisition of scientific knowledge about human behavior as a positive value, and if an experiment using deception constitutes a significant contribution to such knowledge which could not very well be achieved by other means, then we cannot unequivocally rule out the experiment. The question for us is not simply whether it does or does not use deception, but whether the amount and type of deception are justified by the significance of the study and the unavailability of alternative, that is, deception-free, procedures.

Inasmuch as some studies may have considerable payoff for science and the society at large, it seems wise to consider possible affirmative resolutions.

One possible approach to this issue, and an approach which might be used in other cases in which ambiguity pervades, is to establish an ethics advisory group. A group of representatives from the subject population in question might be established, and might act in an advisory capacity on ethical matters (Schwitzgebel, 1967b, 1968b).[8] These representatives of the subject population might judge the extent to which the intended manipulations violated ethical suppositions under which a typical subject might participate. Being made aware of the methodology of the experiment, the subject's probable state of mind, and his probable reaction to the manipulation, they might indicate where ethical improvements should take place from their point of view.[9] In the above case, for example, if a subject were not being caused pain or mental anguish as a result of the manipulation, and the behavior of the experimenter or the contingencies

---

[8]Since the major share of psychological experimentation involves college students, departments of psychology might be wise to establish panels of undergraduates who would review the ethical issues relevant to all research to be conducted in their culture. Review by such panels would not only aid in meeting ethical requirements made by minor granting agencies, but might provide valuable pretest information to the investigator in addition to solving various ethical dilemmas.

[9]It has also been suggested that in these circumstances the subject should be allowed to withdraw his data from the study if he so wishes (Cook, Kimble, Hicks, McGuire, Schoggen, & Smith, 1971).

of the experiment were not being grossly misrepresented, the end might justify the chosen means.

IMPLICATIONS

Any system of ethics is necessarily based on a number of arbitrary assumptions. In this sense, there is little to recommend the present system over other proposals in the same domain (cf. Kelman, 1965; Shils, 1959; Wolfensberger, 1967). To be sure, there is much overlap between the present system and much that has been said by others. Yet, there are emphases and proposed restrictions that do separate the present proposal from others. Much greater weight is placed on the subject's own responsibility in the experimental setting. Typically, the subject is treated as a defenseless creature whose fate is entirely in the hands of the scientist. This conception may be inappropriate and potential subjects might well be apprised of their continued right to action. This "right to action" or "right to informed participation" is buttressed by the experimenter's presentation of behavioral alternatives, as suggested above. Without such a presentation, the subject loses his status as an independent decision maker.

The present system also differs from others in its position on the issues of individual privacy and informed consent. In the present view, individual privacy is not sacrosanct, nor does the scientist have the right to access. Rather, volunteering of intimate information is considered a behavioral alternative in the matrix. The subject is free to provide such information, depending on his assessment of the benefits that he might derive from the experiment. In essence, the experimenter is developing an agreement in order to receive the needed information. In the same way, a subject need not know all of the details as to what may happen to him within reasonable limits of risk. The subject, however, may demand this information, and if the experimenter is unwilling or unable to provide it, the subject should be free to sever his relationship with the investigation.

Given many varying ethical orientations, how might one choose among them? Personal taste and inclination may ultimately win out. However, behavioral scientists do have the opportunity of dealing with the problem empirically. In effect, varying ethical systems have differential effects on subjects, scientists, and the public at large. Subjects may feel variously violated, scientists variously encumbered, and society variously skeptical. We are in an ideal position to test these differential effects, and might well give attention to ways in which this might be done. Cox and Sipprelle (1971), for example, conducted a preliminary study which indicated that an experiment run with "coerced" subjects (students required to participate as a part of a psychology course with an increase in the final grade) produced results different from a similar experiment conducted with true volunteer subjects. The suggestion, then, is that an ethic might ultimately be based upon both pragmatic as well as utilitarian grounds.

SUMMARY

The behavioral sciences have contributed much to an increased understanding of the ethical systems of various cultures and have provided valuable information about matters such as aggression, interpersonal exploitation, and cooperation. Advantages may be taken of this knowledge in developing an ethic for guiding research in the behavioral sciences themselves.

Although ethical guidelines used in medicine have traditionally been very influential, they are in several ways inappropriate to the special conditions of research in the behavioral sciences. The results of studies in the behavioral sciences can often be more easily influenced by subjects' knowledge, expectations, or attitudes than the outcomes of traditional medical studies. The Hawthorne effect is one well-known consequence of subject awareness, but there are many other behavioral effects which can be produced by the demand characteristics of behavioral studies. In addition, medical research is largely based upon understanding and correcting pathological conditions whereas research in the behavioral sciences is often devoted to understanding normal psychological and social pressures which may be directed toward broad, social objectives. Also, the medical objective of aiding physical health is a value which finds wide acceptance, whereas the diverse goals of the behavioral sciences often find less general acceptance.

It is possible to view the behavior of any two interacting persons in a matrix in which there can be a mutual exchange of rewards and costs. The behaviors of the persons may have differential value (utility or hedonic consequences) for the other. When placed in matrix form, it is possible to consider and assess the values of the individuals in regard to various possible combinations of behavior. This basic paradigm can be applied to the experimental situation in which one person is considered to be the experimenter and the other the research subject. In such a situation there may be an exchange of value.

This social exchange orientation has no prescriptive implications until some preconditions are set. Three preconditions are suggested: (1) the respondent (the person who is asked to participate in the research) is allowed a choice of alternatives within the matrix throughout the interaction sequence; (2) the respondent is to remain at all times aware of the matrix contingencies; and (3) the behavioral commitments of the initiator at any point are binding. There are several immediate ethical implications. One is that subjects should not be conscripted for psychological experiments in a way that jeopardizes their status as unencumbered decision makers. Another is that subjects may share some of the responsibility of certain intrinsic risks of the research. It is also clear that the experimenter is to act in good faith by following the contingencies as he has presented them to the subject.

General principles cannot settle the many complex issues arising from human research nor can the overall risks and benefits to science and the subjects often be readily determined. Ethics advisory groups, including representatives of the subject populations, might be helpful in providing guidance. Also, it is possible to conduct research to assess the effects of various experimental procedures upon subjects and experimenters. This could provide data upon which to construct a pragmatic and utilitarian ethic of research.

REFERENCES

Addison, R. M., & Homme, L. E. The reinforcing event (RE) menu. *National Society for Programmed Instruction Journal*, 1966, **5**, 8–9.

Afflect, D. C., & Mednick, S. A. The use of the Rorschach test in the prediction of the abrupt terminator in individual psychotherapy. *Journal of Consulting Psychology*, 1959, **23**, 125–128.

Agras, W. S. Behavior therapy in the management of chronic schizophrenia. *American Journal of Psychiatry*, 1967, **124**, 240–243.

Allen, K. E., Hart, B. M., Buell, J. S., Harris, F. R., & Wolf, M. M. Effects of social reinforcement on isolate behavior of a nursery school child. *Child Development*, 1964, **35**, 511–518.

Allport, G. W. *Personality and Social Encounter.* Boston: Beacon Press, 1960.

Allport, G. W. The general and unique in psychological science. *Journal of Personality*, 1962, **30**, 405–422.

Alumbaugh, R. V. Another "malleus maleficarum"? *American Psychologist*, 1972, **27**, 897–899.

American Medical Association. *Cases on Consent to Treatment.* Washington, D. C.: American Medical Association, 1966.

American Psychological Association. *Casebook on Ethical Standards of Psychologists.* Washington, D. C.: American Psychological Association, 1967.

American Psychological Association, Ad hoc Committee on Ethical Standards in Psychological Research. *Ethical Principles in the Conduct of Research with Human Participants.* Washington, D.C.: American Psychological Association, 1973.

Anant, S. S. A note on the treatment of alcoholics by the verbal aversion technique. *Canadian Psychologist,* 1967, **8**, 19–22.

Anant, S. S. Treatment of alcoholics and drug addicts by verbal aversion techniques. *The International Journal of the Addictions,* 1968, **3**, 381–388.

Anderson, H. H. Domination and integration in the social behavior of young children in an experimental play situation. *Genetic Psychology Monographs,* 1937, **19**, 341–408.

Anderson, N. *The Hobo: The Sociology of the Homeless Man.* Chicago: University of Chicago Press, 1923.

Anderson, S. L., & Gantt, W. H. The effect of person on cardiac and motor responsivity to shock in dogs. *Conditional Reflex,* 1966, **1**, 181–189.

Arnoult, M. D. The specification of a "social" stimulus. In S. B. Sells (Ed.), *Stimulus Determinants of Behavior.* New York: Ronald, 1963. Pp. 16–30.

Aronoff, J., & Litwin, G. H. Achievement motivation training and executive advancement. *Journal of Applied Behavioral Science,* 1971, **7**, 215–229.

Asch, S. E. The doctrine of suggestion, prestige, and imitation in social psychology. *Psychological Review,* 1948, **55**, 250–276.

Ashem, B. The treatment of a disaster phobia by systematic desensitization. *Behaviour Research and Therapy,* 1963, **1**, 81–84.

Athey, K. R., Coleman, J. E., Reitman, A. P., & Tang, J. Two experiments showing the effect of the interviewer's racial background on responses to questionnaires concerning racial issues. *Journal of Applied Psychology,* 1960, **44**, 244–246.

Atthowe, J., Jr., & Krasner, L. The systematic application of contingent reinforcement procedures (token economy) in a large social setting: A psychiatric ward. Paper read at the American Psychological Association meeting, Chicago, September 1965.

Atkinson, J. W. (Ed.) *Motives in Fantasy, Action and Society.* Princeton, N.J.: Van Nostrand, 1958.

Atkinson, J. W., & Litwin, G. H. Achievement motive and test anxiety conceived as motivation approach success and motive to avoid failure. *Journal of Abnormal and Social Psychology,* 1960, **60**, 52–63.

Atkinson, J. W., & McClelland, D. C. The projective expression of needs II. The effect of different intensities of the hunger drive on thematic apperception. *Journal of Experimental Psychology,* 1948, **38**, 643–658.

Ayllon, T. Discussion in reinforcement therapy: A supplement to the film "Reinforcement Therapy." Philadelphia: Smith Kline & French Laboratories, 1966.

Ayllon, T., & Azrin, N. *The Token Economy: A Motivational System for Therapy and Rehabilitation.* New York: Appleton Century Crofts, 1968.

Ayllon, T., & Haughton, E. Control of the behavior of schizophrenics by food. *Journal of the Experimental Analysis of Behavior,* 1962, **5**, 343–352.

Ayllon, T., & Michael, J. The psychiatric nurse as a behavioral engineer. *Journal of the Experimental Analysis of Behavior,* 1959, **2**, 323–334.

Azrin, N. H. Sequential effects of punishment. *Science,* 1960, **131**, 605–606.

Azrin, N. H., & Holz, W. C. Punishment. In W. K. Honig (Ed.), *Operant Behavior: Areas of Research and Application.* New York: Appleton Century Crofts, 1966. Pp. 388–447.

Azrin, N. H., Holz, W. C., & Goldiamond, I. Response bias in questionnaire reports. *Journal of Consulting Psychology,* 1961, **25**, 324–326.

Azrin, N. H., & Lindsley, O. R. The reinforcement of cooperation between children. *Journal of Abnormal and Social Psychology,* 1956, **52**, 100–102.

Baer, D. M., Peterson, R. F., & Sherman, J. A. The development of imitation by reinforcing behavioral similarity to a model. *Journal of the Experimental Analysis of Behavior,* 1967, **10**, 405–416.

Baer, D. M., & Sherman, J. A. Reinforcement control of generalized imitation in young children. *Journal of Experimental Child Psychology,* 1964, **1**, 37–49.

Ball, J. C. The reliability and validity of interview data obtained from 59 narcotic addicts. *American Journal of Sociology,* 1967, **72**, 650–654.

Ban, T. A. *Conditioning and Psychiatry.* Chicago: Aldine, 1964.

Bancroft, G. Consistency of information from records and interviews. *Journal of the American Statistical Association,* 1940, **35**, 377–381.

Bancroft, J. H. J., Jones, H. G., & Pullan, B. R. A simple transducer for measuring penile erection, with comments on its use in the treatment of sexual disorders. *Behaviour Research and Therapy,* 1966, **4**, 239–241.

Bandura, A. Vicarious processes: A case of no-trial learning. In L. Berkowitz (Ed.), *Advances in Experimental Social Psychology.* Vol. II. New York: Academic Press, 1965. Pp. 1–55. (a)

Bandura, A. Influence of models' reinforcement contingencies on the acquisition of imitative responses. *Journal of Personality and Social Psychology,* 1965, **1**, 589–595. (b)

Bandura, A. *Principles of Behavior Modification.* New York: Holt, 1969.

Bandura, A., Blanchard, E. B., & Ritter, B. The relative efficacy of desensitization and modeling approaches for inducing behavioral, affective, and attitudinal changes. Unpublished manuscript, Stanford University, 1968. [Cited in Bandura, A., *Principles of Behavior Modification.* New York: Holt, 1969. Pp. 182–189, 204.]

Bandura, A., Grusec, J. E., & Menlove, F. L. Vicarious extinction of avoidance behavior. *Journal of Personality and Social Psychology,* 1967, **5**, 16–23.

Bandura, A., & Kupers, C. J. Transmission of patterns of self-reinforcement through modeling. *Journal of Abnormal and Social Psychology*, 1964, **69**, 1–9.

Bandura, A., & McDonald, F. J. Influence of social reinforcement and the behavior of models in shaping children's moral judgements. *Journal of Abnormal and Social Psychology*, 1963, **67**, 274–281.

Bandura, A., & Menlove, F. L. Factors determining vicarious extinction of avoidance behavior through symbolic modeling. In press, 1967.

Bandura, A., & Rosenthal, T. L. Vicarious classical conditioning as a function of arousal level. *Journal of Personality and Social Psychology*, 1966, **3**, 54–62.

Bandura, A., Ross, D., & Ross, S. A. A comparative test of the status envy, social power, and secondary reinforcement theories of identificatory learning. *Journal of Abnormal and Social Psychology*, 1963, **67**, 527–534.

Bandura, A., & Walters, R. H. *Adolescent Aggression.* New York: Ronald, 1959.

Bandura, A., & Walters, R. H. *Social Learning and Personality Development.* New York: Holt, 1963.

Barch, A. M., Trumbo, D., & Nagle, J. Social setting and conformity to a legal requirement. *Journal of Abnormal and Social Psychology*, 1957, **55**, 396–398.

Barclay, A. M. Urinary acid phosphatase secretion in sexually aroused males. *Journal of Experimental Research in Personality,* 1970, **4**, 233–238.

Barclay, A. M. Information as a defensive control of sexual arousal. *Journal of Personality and Social Psychology*, 1971, **17**, 244–249.

Barker, R. G. (Ed.), *The Stream of Behavior.* New York: Appleton Century Crofts, 1963. (a)

Barker, R. G. On the nature of the environment. *Journal of Social Issues*, 1963, **19**, 17–38. (b)

Barker, R. G., & Wright, H. F. *The Midwest and Its Children: The Psychological Ecology of an American Town*, Evanston, Ill.: Row, Peterson, 1954.

Barlow, D. H., Agras, W. S., Leitenberg, H., & Wincze, J. P. An experimental analysis of the effectiveness of "shaping" in reducing maladaptive avoidance behavior: An analog study. *Behaviour Research and Therapy*, 1970, **8**, 165–173.

Barlow, D. H., Becker, R., Leitenberg, H., & Agras, W. S. A mechanical strain gauge for recording penile circumference change. *Journal of Applied Behavior Analysis*, 1970, **3**, 73–76.

Barrett, B. H. Reduction in rate of multiple tics by free operant conditioning methods. *Journal of Nervous and Mental Disease*, 1962, **135**, 187–195.

Barron, F. An ego-strength scale which predicts response to psychotherapy. *Journal of Consulting Psychology*, 1953, **17**, 327–333.

Barron, F., & Leary, T. Changes in psychoneurotic patients with and without psychotherapy. *Journal of Consulting Psychology*, 1955, **19**, 239–245.

Bass, M. J., & Hull, C. L. The irradiation of a tactile conditioned reflex in man. *Journal of Comparative Psychology*, 1934, **17**, 47–65.

Bateson, P. P. G. Ethological methods of observing behavior. In L. Weiskrantz (Ed.), *Analysis of Behavioral Change*. New York: Harper & Row, 1968. Pp. 389–399.

Baumrind, D. Principles of ethical conduct in the treatment of subjects: Reaction to the draft report of the Committee on Ethical Standards in Psychological Research. *American Psychologist*, 1971, **26**, 887–896.

Beck, S. The science of personality: Nomothetic or idiopathic? *Psychological Review*, 1953, **60**, 353–359.

Becker, H. S. *Outsiders*. New York: Free Press, 1963.

Becker, H., Geer, B., Hughes, E., & Strauss, A. *Boys in White*. Chicago: University of Chicago Press, 1961.

Beecher, H. K. *Experimentation in Man*. Springfield, Ill.: Charles C Thomas, 1958.

Beh, H. C., & Barratt, P. E. H. Discrimination and conditioning during sleep as indicated by the electroencephalogram. *Science*, 1965, **147**, 1470–1471.

Belson, W. A. Tape recording: Its effect on accuracy of response in survey interviews. *Journal of Marketing Research*, 1967, **4**, 1–12.

Benney, M., & Hughes, E. C. Of sociology and the interview: Editorial preface. *American Journal of Sociology*, 1956, **62**, 137–142.

Benney, M., Riesman, D., & Star, S. Age and sex in the interview. *American Journal of Sociology*, 1956, **62**, 143–152.

Bennis, W. G. Goals and meta-goals of laboratory training. *NTL Human Relations Training News*, 1962, **6**, 1–3.

Bennis, W. G., Schein, E. V., Berlew, D. E., & Steele, F. I. *Interpersonal Dynamics*, Homewood, Ill.: Dorsey, 1964.

Bentler, P. M. An infant's phobia treated with reciprocal inhibition therapy. *Journal of Child Psychiatry*, 1962, **3**, 185–189.

Berger, S. M. Incidental learning through vicarious reinforcement. *Psychological Reports*, 1961, **9**, 477–491.

Berger, S. M. Conditioning through vicarious instigation. *Psychological Review*, 1962, **69**, 450–466.

Bergin, A. E. The effects of psychotherapy: Negative results revisited. *Journal of Counseling Psychology*, 1963, **10**, 244–250.

Bergin, A. E. The evaluation of therapeutic outcomes. In A. E. Bergin and S. L. Garfield (Eds.), *Handbook of Psychotherapy and Behavior Change: An Experimental Analysis*. New York: Wiley, 1970.

Berk, R. A., & Adams, J. M. Establishing rapport with deviant groups. *Social Problems*, 1970, **18**, 102–117.

Berkowitz, L. Some aspects of observed aggression. *Journal of Personality and Social Psychology*, 1965, **2**, 359–369.

Berkowitz, L. Experimental investigations of hostility catharsis. *Journal of Consulting and Clinical Psychology*, 1970, **35**, 1–7.

Berkowitz, L., & Geen, R. G. Film violence and the cue properties of available targets. *Journal of Personality and Social Psychology,* 1966, **3,** 525–530.

Berkowitz, L., & Geen, R. G. Stimulus qualities of the target of aggression: A further study. *Journal of Abnormal and Social Psychology,* 1967, **5,** 364–368.

Bernal, M. E. Behavioral feedback in the modification of brat behaviors. *Journal of Nervous and Mental Disease,* 1969, **148,** 375–385.

Bernal, M. E., Duryee, J. S., Pruett, H. L., & Burns, B. J. Behavior modification and the brat syndrome. *Journal of Consulting and Clinical Psychology,* 1968, **32,** 447–455.

Bernal, M. E., Young, S., & Shannon, G. Application of a procedure for modification of brat behaviors. Unpublished manuscript, University of California, Neuropsychiatric Institute, Los Angeles, 1970.

Bersh, P. J. The influence of two variables upon the establishment of a secondary reinforcer for operant responses. *Journal of Experimental Psychology,* 1951, **41,** 62–73.

Berzon, B., Reisel, J., & Davis, D. P. An audio tape program for self-directed small groups. Unpublished paper, Western Behavioral Sciences Institute, La Jolla, Calif., 1967.

Berzon, B., & Solomon, L. N. The self-directed group: A new rehabilitation resource. Paper presented at the meeting of the American Psychological Association, Chicago, 1965.

Berzon, B., & Solomon, L. N. The self-directed therapeutic group: Three studies. *Journal of Counseling Psychology,* 1966, **13,** 491–497.

Bevan, W. The contextual basis of behavior. *American Psychologist,* 1968, **23,** 701–714.

Bevan, W., & Adamson, R. Reinforcers and reinforcement: Their relation to maze performance. *Journal of Experimental Psychology,* 1960, **59,** 226–232.

Bevan, W., & Turner, E. D. Vigilance performance with a qualitative shift in verbal reinforcers. *Journal of Experimental Psychology,* 1966, **71,** 467–468.

Birnbrauer, J. S., Bijou, S. W., Wolf, M. M., & Kidder, J. D. Programmed instruction in the classroom. In L. P. Ullmann and L. Krasner (Eds.), *Case Studies in Behavior Modification.* New York: Holt, 1965. Pp. 358–363.

Blake, R. R., Rosenbaum, M. E., and Duryea, R. Gift-giving as a function of group standards. *Human Relations,* 1955, **8,** 61–73.

Blakemore, C. B. The application of behaviour therapy to a sexual disorder. In H. J. Eysenck (Ed.), *Experiments in Behaviour Therapy.* New York: Macmillan, 1964. Pp. 165–175.

Blakemore, C. B., Thorpe, J. G., Barker, J. C., Conway, C. G., & Lavin, N. I. The application of faradic aversion conditioning in a case of transvestism. *Behaviour Research and Therapy,* 1963, **1,** 29–34.

Blane, H. Personal communication, Massachusetts General Hospital, 1964.

Block, J. The assessment of communications: Role variations as a function of interactional context. *Journal of Personality,* 1952, **20,** 273–286.

Bookbinder, L. J. Simple conditioning versus the dynamic approach to symptoms and symptom substitution: A reply to Yates. *Psychological Reports*, 1962, **10**, 71–77.

Booth, C. *Life and Labour of the People of London.* London: Williams and Norgate, 1889.

Bond, I. K., & Hutchinson, H. C. Application of reciprocal inhibition therapy to exhibitionism. *Canadian Medical Association Journal*, 1960, **83**, 23–25.

Bostow, D. F., & Bailey, J. B. Modification of severely disruptive and aggressive behavior using brief time-out and reinforcement procedures. *Journal of Applied Behavior Analysis*, 1969, **2**, 31–37.

Boulding, K. *The Image.* Ann Arbor, Mich.: Ann Arbor Press, 1961.

Boulougouris, J. C., Marks, I. M., & Marset, P. Superiority of flooding (implosion) to desensitization for reducing pathological fear. *Behaviour Research and Therapy*, 1971, **9**, 7–16.

Bradford, C. P., Gibb, J., & Benne, K. *T-Group Theory and the Laboratory Method.* New York: Wiley, 1964.

Brady, J. P. Brevital-relaxation treatment of frigidity. *Behaviour Research and Therapy*, 1966, **4**, 71–77.

Braginsky, B. M., & Braginsky, D. D. Schizophrenic patients in the psychiatric interview: An experimental study of their effectiveness at manipulation. *Journal of Consulting Psychology*, 1967, **31**, 543–547.

Bramel, D. A. A dissonance theory approach to defensive projection. *Journal of Abnormal and Social Psychology*, 1962, **64**, 121–129.

Brayfield, A. Human resources development. *American Psychologist*, 1968, **23**, 479–482.

Breedlove, J. L., & Krause, M. S. Evaluative research design: A social casework illustration. In L. A. Gottschalk and A. H. Aurbach (Eds.), *Methods of Research in Psychotherapy.* New York: Appleton Century Crofts, 1966. Pp. 456–477.

Breger, L., & McGaugh, J. L. Critique and reformation of "learning theory" approaches to psychotherapy and neurosis. *Psychological Bulletin*, 1965, **63**, 338–358.

Brill, N. Q., Crumpton, E., Eiduson, S., Grayson, H. M., Hellman, L. I., Richards, R. A., Straussman, H. D., & Unger, A. A. Investigation of the therapeutic components and various factors associated with improvement with electro-convulsive treatment: A preliminary report. *American Journal of Psychiatry*, 1957, **113**, 997–1008.

Broden, M., Hall, R. V., & Mitts, B. The effect of self-recording on the classroom behavior of two eighth-grade students. *Journal of Applied Behavior Analysis*, 1971, **4**, 191–199.

Brown, B. M. Cognitive aspects of Wolpe's behavior therapy. *American Journal of Psychiatry*, 1967, **124**, 854–859.

Brown, C. C., & Katz, R. A. Operant salivary conditioning in man. *Psychophysiology*, 1967, **4**, 156–160.

Brown, P., & Elliott, R. Control of aggression in a nursery school class. *Journal of Experimental Child Psychology*, 1965, **2**, 103–107.

Brown, R. *Social Psychology.* Glencoe, Ill.: Free Press, 1965.

Bruce, M. Tokens for recovery. *American Journal of Nursing,* 1966, **66,** 1799–1802.

Bruning, J. L. Direct and vicarious effects of a shift in magnitude of reward on performance. *Journal of Personality and Social Psychology,* 1965, **2,** 278–282.

Brunswik, E. *Perception and the Representative Design of Psychological Experiments.* Berkeley: University of California Press, 1956.

Bryan, J. H., & Test, M. A. Models and helping: Naturalistic studies in aiding behavior. *Journal of Personality and Social Psychology,* 1967, **6,** 400–407.

Buber, M. Productivity and existence. In M. R. Stein, A. V. Vidich, & D. M. While (Eds.), *Identity and Anxiety: Survival of the Person in Mass Society.* Glencoe, Ill.: Free Press, 1960.

Buehler, R. E., Patterson, G. R., & Furniss, J. M. The reinforcement of behavior in institutional settings. *Behaviour Research and Therapy,* 1966, **4,** 157–167.

Buell, J., Stoddard, P., Harris, F. R., & Baer, D. M. Collateral development of accompanying reinforcement of outdoor play in a preschool child. *Journal of Applied Behavior Analysis,* 1968, **1,** 167–173.

Burchard, J. D., & Tyler, V. O. The modification of delinquent behavior through operant conditioning. *Behaviour Research and Therapy,* 1965, **2,** 245–250.

Burton, R. V. Validity of retrospective reports assessed by the multitrait-multimethod analysis. *Developmental Psychology Monograph,* 1970, **3,**(3) pt. 2.

Butler, J., Rice, L. N., & Wagstaff, A. K. On the naturalistic definition of variables: An analogue of clinical analysis. In H. H. Strupp, & L. Luborsky (Eds.), *Research in Psychotherapy.* Vol. II. Baltimore: French-Bray, 1962. Pp. 178–205.

Callahan, E. J., & Leitenberg, H. Reinforced practice as a treatment for acrophobia. Unpublished paper, University of Vermont, 1971.

Campbell, B. A., & Church, R. M. (Eds.) *Punishment and Aversive Behavior.* New York: Appleton Century Crofts, 1969.

Campbell, D. T. Factors relevant to the validity of experiments in social settings. *Psychological Bulletin,* 1957, **54,** 297–312.

Campbell, D. T. Reforms as experiments. *American Psychologist,* 1969, **24,** 409–429.

Campbell, D. T. & Ross, H. L. The Connecticut crackdown on speeding: Time-series data in quasi-experimental analysis. *Law and Society Review,* 1968, **3,** 33–53.

Canter, R. R., Jr. The use of extended control-group designs in human relations studies. *Psychological Bulletin,* 1951, **48,** 340–347.

Cantril, H. *Gauging Public Opinion.* Princeton, N.J.: Princeton, 1944.

Cantril, H., & Williams, F. The use of interviewer rapport as a method of detecting differences between "public" and "private" opinion. *Journal of Social Psychology,* 1945, **22,** 171–175.

Cartwright, D. S. Effectiveness of psychotherapy: A critique of the spontaneous remission argument. *Journal of Consulting Psychology*, 1955, **17**, 290–296.

Cautela, J. R. Covert sensitization. *Psychological Reports*, 1967, **20**, 459–468.

Cautela, J. R. Covert reinforcement. *Behavior Therapy*, 1970, **1**, 33–50. (a)

Cautela, J. R. The treatment of alcoholism by covert sensitization. *Psychotherapy: Theory, Research and Practice*, 1970, **7**, 86–90. (b)

Cavan, S. *Liquor License: An Ethnography of Bar Behavior.* Chicago: Aldine, 1966.

Chassan, J. B. Statistical inference and the single case in clinical design. *Psychiatry*, 1960, **23**, 173–184.

Chassan, J. B. *Research Design in Clinical Psychology and Psychiatry.* New York: Appleton Century Crofts, 1967.

Chein, I. (Ed.) Consistency and inconsistency in intergroup relations. *Journal of Social Issues*, 1949, **5**, No. 3.

Chittenden, G. E. An experimental study in measuring and modifying assertive behavior in young children. *Monographs of the Society of Research in Child Development*, 1942, **7**, No. 1.

Church, R. M. Response suppression. In B. A. Campbell, & R. M. Church (Eds.), *Punishment and Aversive Behavior.* New York: Appleton Century Crofts, 1969. Pp. 111–156.

Clark, D. F. Behavior therapy of Gilles de la Tourette's syndrome. *British Journal of Psychiatry*, 1966, **112**, 771–778.

Cloward, R. A., & Ohlin, L. E. *Delinquency and Opportunity.* New York: Free Press, 1960.

Cocteau, J. *Journal d'un Inconnu.* Paris: Grasset, 1953.

Cohen, B. B. The desensitization of social anxiety. *Pennsylvania Psychiatric Quarterly*, 1965, **5**, 31–36.

Cohen, H. L. Behaviour architecture: New thinking for new universities. In H. L. Cohen, I. Goldiamond, J. Filipczak, & R. Pooley (Eds.), *Training Professionals in Procedures for the Establishment of Educational Environments.* Silver Spring, Md.: Educational Facility Press, 1968. Pp. F3-1–F3-11.

Cohen, H. L., Filipczak, J. A., Bis, J. S., & Cohen, J. E. CASE project: Contingencies applicable for special education. Report, Institute for Behavioral Research, Inc., Silver Springs, Md., 1966.

Cohen, H. L., Goldiamond, I., Filipczak, J., & Pooley, R. *Training Professionals in Procedures for the Establishment of Educational Environments.* Silver Spring, Md.: Educational Facility Press, 1968.

Cohler, B. The use of environmental demographic variables in epidemiological studies of mental illness. Unpublished manuscript, Harvard University, 1963.

Coleman, J. S. *The Adolescent Society.* Glencoe, Ill.: Free Press, 1961.

Conant, M. B. Conditioned visual hallucinations. Unpublished manuscript, Stanford University, 1964.

Condon, W. S., & Ogston, W. D. A segmentation of behavior. *Journal of Psychiatric Research*, 1965, **5**, 221–235.

Cook, S. W., Kimble, G. A., Hicks, L. H., McGuire, W. J., Schoggen, P. H., & Smith, M. B. Proposed ethical principles submitted to the APA membership for criticism and modification (by the) ad hoc Committee on Ethical Standards in Psychological Research. *APA Monitor*, 1971, **2**, 9–28.

Cooke, G. Identification of the efficacious components of reciprocal inhibition therapy. Unpublished doctoral dissertation, University of Iowa, 1966. (a)

Cooke, G. The efficacy of two desensitization procedures: An analog study. *Behaviour Research and Therapy*, 1966, **4**, 17–24. (b)

Coombs, C. H. Some hypotheses for the analysis of qualitative variables. *Psychological Review*, 1948, **55**, 167–174.

Cooper, C. L., & Mangham, I. L. *T-Groups: A Survey of Research.* New York: Wiley, 1971.

Cowles, J. T. Food-tokens as incentives for learning by chimpanzees. *Comparative Psychology Monographs*, 1937, **14**, No. 71.

Cox, D. E., & Sipprelle, C. N. Coercion in participation as a research subject. *American Psychologist*, 1971, **26**, 726–728.

Cox, G. H., & Marley, E. The estimation of motility during rest or sleep. *Journal of Neurology, Neurosurgery and Psychiatry*, 1959, **22**, 57–60.

Crawford, M. P. Cooperative behavior in chimpanzee. *Psychological Bulletin*, 1935, **32**, 714.

Cremerius, J. *Die Beurteilung des Behendlungsverfolges in de Psychotherapie.* Berlin: Springer, 1962.

Cressey, D. R. Social psychological foundations for using criminals in the rehabilitation of criminals. *Journal of Research in Crime and Delinquency*, 1965, **2**, 49–59.

Crisp, A. H. "Transference," "symptom emergence," and "social repercussion" in behavior therapy: A study of fifty-four treated patients. *British Journal of Medical Psychology*, 1966, **39**, 179–196.

Cumming, W. W. A bird's eye glimpse of men and machines. In R. Ulrich, T. Stachnik, & J. Mabry (Eds.), *Control of Human Behavior.* Glenview, Ill.: Scott, Foresman, 1966. Pp. 246–256.

Daniel, W. J. Cooperative problem solving in rats. *Journal of Comparative Psychology*, 1942, **34**, 361–369.

Darley, J., & Latane, B. Bystander intervention in emergencies. *Journal of Personality and Social Psychology*, 1968, **8**, 377–383.

Darlington, R. B., & Macker, C. E. Displacement of guilt-produced altruistic behavior. *Journal of Personality and Social Psychology*, 1966, **4**, 442–443.

Davidson, H. A. Discussion of "The effects of psychotherapy." *International Journal of Psychiatry*, 1965, **1**, 171–173.

Davis, D. L. Normal drinking in recovered alcohol addicts. *Quarterly Journal of Studies on Alcohol*, 1962, **23**, 94–104.

Davis, V. E., & Walsh, M. J. Alcohol, amines, and alkaloids: A possible biochemical basis for alcohol addiction. *Science,* 1970, **167**, 1005–1006.

Davison, G. C. A social learning therapy programme with an autistic child. *Behaviour Research and Therapy,* 1964, **2**, 149–159.

Davison, G. C. The influence of systematic desensitization, relaxation, and graded exposure to imaginal stimuli on the modification of phobic behavior. Unpublished doctoral dissertation, Stanford University, 1965. (a)

Davison, G. C. Relative contribution of differential relaxation and graded exposure to *in vivo* desensitization of a neurotic fear. *Proceedings of the Psychological Association,* Chicago, 1965, 209–210. (b)

Davison, G. C. Elimination of a sadistic fantasy by a client-controlled counter-conditioning technique: A case study. *Journal of Abnormal Psychology,* 1968, **73**, 84–90. (a)

Davison, G. C. Systematic desensitization as a counterconditioning technique. *Journal of Abnormal Psychology,* 1968, **73**, 91–99. (b)

Davison, G. C. Noncontiguous presence during treatment sessions of relaxation and imaginal aversive stimuli: A reply to Nawas, Mealiea, & Fishman. *Behavior Therapy,* 1971, **2**, 357–360.

Davison, G. C., & Valins, S. Maintenance of self-attributed and drug-attributed behavior change. *Journal of Personality and Social Psychology,* 1969, **11**, 25–33.

Dawe, P. G. A transistorized voice-operated key. *Quarterly Journal of Experimental Psychology,* 1966, **81**, 82–84.

Dekker, E., & Groen, J. Reproducible psychogenic attacks of asthma: A laboratory study. *Journal of Psychosomatic Research,* 1956, **1**, 58–67.

Dekker, E., Pelser, & Groen, J. Conditioning as a cause of asthmatic attacks: A laboratory study. *Journal of Psychosomatic Research,* 1957, **2**, 97–108.

Delgado, J. M. R., Mark, V., Sweet, W., Ervin, F., Weiss, G., Bach-y-Rita, G., & Hagiwara, R. Intracerebral radio stimulation and recording in completely free patients. *Journal of Nervous and Mental Diseases,* 1968, **147**, 329–340.

Denton, J. C. The validation of interview-type data. *Personnel Psychology,* 1964, **17**, 281–287.

Deutsch, M. An experimental study of the effects of cooperation and competition upon group processes. *Human Relations,* 1949, **2**, 199–231.

Dichter, E. *The Strategy of Desire.* New York: Doubleday, 1960, chapter 5.

Ditman, K. S. Alcoholism. *American Journal of Psychiatry,* 1964, **121**, 677–681.

Dollard, J., & Miller, N. E. *Personality and Psychotherapy: An Analysis in Terms of Learning, Thinking, and Culture.* New York: McGraw-Hill, 1950.

Donner, L., & Guerney, G. G., Jr. Automated group desensitization for test anxiety. *Behaviour Research and Therapy,* 1969, **7**, 1–13.

Doubros, S. G., & Daniels, G. J. An experimental approach to the reduction of overactive behavior. *Behaviour Research and Therapy*, 1966, **4**, 251–258.

Dulany, D. E. Awareness, rules, and propositional control: A confrontation with S. R. behavior therapy. In T. R. Dixon, & D. L. Horton (Eds.), *Verbal Behavior and General Behavior Theory*. Englewood Cliffs, N.J.: Prentice-Hall, 1968. Pp. 340–387.

Dunlap, K. *Habits: Their Making and Unmaking*. New York: Liveright, 1932.

Dykman, R. A. Toward a theory of classical conditioning: Cognitive, emotional, and motor components of the conditional reflex. In B. A. Maher (Ed.), *Progress in Experimental Personality Research*. Vol. 2. New York: Academic Press, 1965. Pp. 229–317.

Edgington, E. S. Statistical inference from N=1 experiments. *Journal of Psychology*, 1967, **65**, 195–199.

Edwards, A. L., & Cronbach, L. J. Experimental design for research in psychotherapy. *Journal of Clinical Psychology*, 1962, **8**, 51–59.

Efran, J. S., & Marcia, J. E. Treatment of fears by expectancy manipulation: An exploratory study. *Proceedings, 75th Annual Convention*, American Psychological Association, 1967, 239–240.

Eisenberger, R. Is there a deprivation-satiation function for social approval? *Psychological Bulletin*, 1970, **74**, 255–275.

Ekman, P., & Friesen, W. V. A tool for the analysis of motion picture film or video tape. *American Psychologist*, 1969, **24**, 240–243.

Ellison, G. D., & Konorski, J. Separation of the salivary and motor responses in instrumental conditioning. *Science*, 1964, **146**, 1071–1072.

Ellson, D. G. Hallucinations produced by sensory conditioning. *Journal of Experimental Psychology*, 1941, **28**, 1–20.

Erikson, E. H. *Young Man Luther*. New York: Norton, 1958.

Erikson, E. H. Identity and the life cycle. *Psychological Issues*, 1959, **1**, 1–171.

Erikson, E. H. Youth: Fidelity and diversity. *Daedalus*, 1962, Winter, 5–27.

Erikson, K. T. A comment on disguised observation in sociology. *Social Problems*, 1967, **14**, 366–373.

Evans, R. I., Rozelle, R. M., Lasater, T. M., Dembroski, T. M., & Allen, B. P. Fear arousal, persuasion, and actual versus implied behavioral change: New perspective utilizing a real-life dental hygiene program. *Journal of Personality and Social Psychology*, 1970, **16**, 220–227.

Eysenck, H. J. The effects of psychotherapy: An evaluation. *Journal of Consulting Psychology*, 1952, **16**, 319–324.

Eysenck, H. J. The effects of psychotherapy: A reply. *Journal of Abnormal and Social Psychology*, 1955, **50**, 147–148.

Eysenck, H. J. The effects of psychotherapy. In H. J. Eysenck (Ed.), *Handbook of Abnormal Psychology: An Experimental Approach*. New York: Basic Books, 1961. Pp. 697–725.

Eysenck, H. J. *Handbook of Abnormal Psychology: An Experimental Approach*. New York: Basic Books, 1961.

Eysenck, H. J. Editorial. *Behaviour Research and Therapy*, 1963, **1**, 1–2.

Eysenck, H. J. The effects of psychotherapy. *International Journal of Psychiatry*, 1965, **1**, 99–144.

Eysenck, H. J. Relapse and symptom substitution after different types of psychotherapy. *Behaviour Research and Therapy*, 1969, **7**, 283–287.

Feather, B. W. Human salivary conditioning: Effect of unconditioned stimulus intensity. *Journal of Experimental Psychology*, 1967, **74**, 389–392.

Feldman, M. P., & MacCulloch, M. J. The application of anticipatory avoidance learning to the treatment of homosexuality: I. Theory, technique and preliminary results. *Behaviour Research and Therapy*, 1965, **2**, 165–183.

Fenichel, O. *The Psychoanalytic Theory of Neurosis.* New York: Norton, 1945.

Ferster, C. B. Intermittent reinforcement. In J. I. Nurnberger, C. B. Ferster, & J. P. Brady, *An Introduction to the Science of Human Behavior.* New York: Appleton Century Crofts, 1963. Pp. 239–263.

Ferster, C. B. The environmental control of behavior. In J. I. Nurnberger, C. B. Ferster, & J. P. Brady (Eds.), *An Introduction to the Science of Human Behavior.* New York: Appleton Century Crofts, 1963. Pp. 222–238.

Ferster, C. B. Reinforcement and punishment in the control of human behavior by social agencies. In H. J. Eysenck (Ed.), *Experiments in Behaviour Therapy.* New York: Macmillan, 1964. Pp. 189–206. (a)

Ferster, C. B. Positive reinforcement and behavioral deficits of autistic children. In A. W. Staats (Ed.), *Human Learning: Studies Extending Conditioning Principles to Complex Behavior.* New York: Holt, 1964. Pp. 425–442. (b)

Ferster, C. B. An evaluation of behavior therapy with children. Paper presented at the meeting of the American Psychological Association, Chicago, 1965.

Ferster, C. B., & DeMyer, M. K. The development of performance in autistic children in an automatically controlled environment. *Journal of Chronic Disease*, 1961, **13**, 312–345.

Ferster, C. B., & Skinner, B. F. *Schedules of Reinforcement.* New York: Appleton Century Crofts, 1957.

Feshbach, S. The drive reducing function of fantasy behavior. *Journal of Abnormal and Social Psychology*, 1955, **50**, 3–12.

Feshbach, S. The stimulating vs. cathartic effects of a vicarious aggressive activity. *Journal of Abnormal and Social Psychology*, 1961, **63**, 381–385.

Feshbach, S. The function of aggression and the regulation of aggressive drive. *Psychological Review*, 1964, **71**, 257–272.

Festinger, L. A theoretical interpretation of shifts in level of aspiration. *Psychological Review*, 1942, **49**, 235–250.

Festinger, L., & Freedman, J. L. Dissonance reduction and moral values. In P. Worchel, & D. Byrne (Eds.), *Personality Change.* New York: Wiley, 1964.

Findley, J. D. Programmed environments for the experimental analysis of human behavior. In W. K. Honig (Ed.), *Operant Behavior: Areas of Research and*

Application. New York: Appleton Century Crofts, 1966. Pp. 827–848.

Fine, B. J., & Sweeney, D. R. Socio-economic background, aggression, and catecholamine excretion. *Psychological Reports,* 1967, **20,** 11–18.

Fiske, D. W., Luborsky, L., Parloff, M. B., Hunt, H. F., Orne, M. T., & Reiser, M. F. Planning research on effectiveness of psychotherapy. *American Psychologist,* 1970, **25,** 727–737.

Folkins, C. H., Lawson, K., Opton, E. M., Jr., & Lazarus, R. S. Desensitization and the experimental reduction of threat. *Journal of Abnormal Psychology,* 1968, **73,** 100–113.

Forsyth, P. P., & Fairweather, G. W. Psychotherapeutic and other hospital treatment criteria: The dilemma. *Journal of Abnormal and Social Psychology,* 1961, **62,** 598–604.

Foshee, J. G. Studies in activity level: I. Simple and complex task performance in defectives. *American Journal of Mental Deficiency,* 1958, **62,** 882–886.

Fowler, H. Suppression and facilitation by response contingent shock. In R. Brush (Ed.), *Aversive Conditioning and Learning,* New York: Academic Press, 1971. Pp. 537–604.

Fox, R. Training for uncertainty. In R. K. Merton, G. G. Reader, & P. L. Kendall (Eds.), *The Student Physician.* Cambridge, Mass.: Harvard, 1957. Pp. 207–241.

Frank, J. D. Recent studies of the level of aspiration. *Psychological Bulletin,* 1941, **38,** 218–226.

Frank, J. D. Problems of controls in psychotherapy as exemplified by the psychotherapy research project of the Phipps Psychiatric Clinic. In E. A. Rubenstein, & M. B. Parloff (Eds.), *Research in Psychotherapy,* Vol. I. Washington, D. C.: American Psychological Association, 1958. Pp. 10–26.

Frank, J. D. The dynamics of the psychotherapeutic relationship: 1. Determinants and effects of the therapist's influence. *Psychiatry,* 1959, **22,** 17–39.

Frank, J. D. *Persuasion and Healing.* New York: Schocken Books, 1963.

Franks, C. M. Behavior therapy, the principles of conditioning and the treatment of the alcoholic. *Quarterly Journal of Studies on Alcohol,* 1963, **24,** 511–529.

Franks, C. M. Conditioning and conditional aversion therapies in the treatment of alcoholics. *The International Journal of Addictions,* 1966, **1,** 61–98.

Franzen, R. Scaling responses to graded opportunities. *Public Opinion Quarterly,* 1950, **14,** 484–490.

Freed, A., Chandler, J. P., Mouton, J. S., & Blake, R. R. Stimulus and background factors in sign violation. *Journal of Personality,* 1955, **23,** 499 (Abstract).

French, E. G. Effects of the interaction of motivation and feedback on task performance. In J. W. Atkinson (Ed.), *Motives in Fantasy, Action and Society.* Princeton, New Jersey: Van Nostrand, 1958. Pp. 400–408.

French, J. R. P., Jr. Experiments in field settings. In L. Festinger and D. Katz (Eds.), *Research Methods in the Behavioral Sciences.* New York: Dryden, 1953. Pp. 98–135.

French, N. R., Carter, C. W., & Koenig, W. The words and sounds of telephone conversations. *Bell System Technical Journal,* 1930, **9,** 290–324.

Freud, A. *The Ego and the Mechanisms of Defence.* New York: International Universities Press, 1946.

Freud, S. Analysis of a phobia in a five-year-old boy (1909). In *Collected Papers*, Vol. III. London: Hogarth, 1956. Pp. 149–289.

Freud, S. An autobiographical study, *The Problem of Lay-Analyses* (J. Strachey, translator). New York: Brentano's, 1927. Pp. 189–316.

Freud, S. *Collected Papers*, Vol. V. London: Hogarth, 1956.

Freund, K. Problems in the treatment of homosexuality. In H. J. Eysenck (Ed.), *Behaviour Therapy and the Neuroses*. Oxford: Pergamon, 1960. Pp. 312–327.

Freund, K. A laboratory method for diagnosing predominance of homo- or heteroerotic interest in the male. *Behaviour Research and Therapy*, 1963, 1, 85–93.

Friedlander, B. Z. The effect of speaker identity, voice inflection, vocabulary, and message redundancy on infant's selection of vocal reinforcement. University of Wisconsin, Department of Behavioral Studies, 1966.

Friedman, D. A new technique for the systematic desensitization of phobic symptoms. *Behaviour Research and Therapy*, 1966, 4, 139–140.

Gaier, E. L. Selected personality variables and the learning process. *Psychological Monographs*, 1952, 66, No. 349, 1–25.

Gantt, W. H. Introduction. In I. P. Pavlov, *Conditioned Reflexes and Psychiatry* (Volume 2 of Lectures on Conditioned Reflexes). Edited by W. H. Gantt, New York: International Publishers, 1963. Pp. 11–35.

Gantt, W. H. Reflexology, schizokinesis and autokinesis. *Conditional Reflex*, 1966, 1, 57–68.

Gantt, W. H. Pavlovian, classical conditioned reflex—A classical error? *Conditional Reflex*, 1967, 2, 255–257.

Gantt, W. H., Newton, J. E. O., Royer, F. L., & Stephens, J. H. Effect of person. *Conditional Reflex*, 1966, 1, 18–35.

Garfield, S. L., & Bergin, A. E. Personal therapy, outcome and some therapist variables. *Psychotherapy: Theory, Research and Practice*, 1971, 8, 251–253.

Gebhard, P. H., Gagnon, J. H., Pomeroy, W. B., & Christenson, C. V. *Sex Offenders: An Analysis of Types*. New York: Harper & Row, 1965.

Geer, J. H. & Turteltaub. Fear reduction following observation of a model. *Journal of Personality and Social Psychology*, 1967, 3, 327–331.

Geis, G. L., Steffins, W. C., & Ludin, R. W. *Reflex and Operant Conditioning: The Study of Behavior*. Vol. I. New York: Appleton Century Crofts, 1965.

Gelder, M. G. Desensitization and psychotherapy research. *British Journal of Medical Psychology*, 1968, 41, 39–46.

Gelder, M. G., Marks, I. M., & Wolff, H. H. Desensitization and psychotherapy in phobic states: A controlled enquiry. *British Journal of Psychiatry*, 1967, 113, 53–73.

Gelfand, D. M., Gelfand, S., & Dobson, W. R. Unprogrammed reinforcement of patients' behavior in a mental hospital. *Behaviour Research and Therapy*, 1967, 5, 201–207.

Gericke, O. L. Practical use of operant conditioning procedures in a mental hospital. *Psychiatric Studies and Projects*, 1965, 3 (5), 1–10.

Gewirtz, J. L., & Baer, D. M. The effect of brief social deprivation on behaviors of a social reinforcer. *Journal of Abnormal and Social Psychology*, 1958, **56**, 49–56.

Gibbs, D. N. Reciprocal inhibition therapy of a case of symptomatic erythema. *Behaviour Research and Therapy*, 1965, **2**, 261–266.

Girardeau, F. L., & Spradlin, J. E. Token rewards on a cottage program. *Mental Retardation*, 1964, **2**, 345–351.

Glover, E. Notes on oral character formation. *International Journal of Psycho-analysis*, 1925, **6**, 131–154.

Glover, E. Discussion of "The Effects of Psychotherapy." *International Journal of Psychiatry*, 1965, **1**, 158–161.

Glynn, J. D., & Harper, P. Behavior therapy in a case of transvestism. *Lancet*, 1961, **1**, 619–620.

Goffman, E. *Interaction Ritual: Essays in Face-to-Face Behavior*. Chicago: Aldine, 1967.

Gold, M. Suicide, homicide, and the socialization of aggression. *American Journal of Sociology*, 1958, **63**, 651–661.

Golden, R. I. A conditioned reflex technique in lie detection. In S. A. Yefsky (Ed.), *Law Enforcement Science and Technology*. London: Academic Press, 1967.

Goldfried, M. R. Systematic desensitization as training in self-control. *Journal of Consulting and Clinical Psychology*, 1970, in press.

Goldiamond, I. Perception. In A. J. Bachrach (Ed.), *Experimental Foundations of Clinical Psychology*. New York: Basic Books, 1962. Pp. 280–340.

Goldiamond, I. Self-control procedures in personal behavior problems. *Psychological Reports*, 1965, **17**, 851–868.

Goldiamond, I. Modification of disordered behavior. In R. Ulrich, T. Stachnik, & J. Mabry (Eds.), *Control of Human Behavior*. New York: Scott, Foresman, 1966. Pp. 114–127.

Goldman, J. A look at measurements in industry. In L. E. Slater (Ed.), *Interdisciplinary Clinic on the Instrumentation Requirements for Psychophysiological Research*. New York: Fier, 1961.

Goldstein, A. J. Separate effects of extinction, counterconditioning and progressive approach in overcoming fear. *Behaviour Research and Therapy*, 1969, **7**, 47–56.

Goldstein, A. P. Patients' expectancies and non-specific therapy as a basis for (un)spontaneous remission. *Journal of Clinical Psychology*, 1960, **7**, 180–184.

Goldstein, A. P. *Therapist-patient expectancies in psychotherapy*. Oxford: Pergamon, 1962.

Golembiewski, R. T., & Blumberg, A. *Sensitivity Training and the Laboratory Approach*. Itasca, Ill.: Peacock, 1971.

Goodson, F. E., & Brownstein, A. Secondary reinforcing and motivating properties of stimuli contiguous with shock onset and termination. *Journal of Comparative and Physiological Psychology*, 1955, **48**, 381–386.

Goodwin, D. W., Powell, B., Bremer, D., Hoine, H., & Stern, J. Alcohol and recall: State-dependent effects in man. *Science*, 1969, **163**, 1358–1360.

Goorney, A. B. Treatment of aviation phobias by behaviour therapy. *British Journal of Psychiatry*, 1970, **117**, 535–544.

Gordon, J. E., & Smith, E. Children's aggression, parental attitudes, and the effects of an affiliation–arousing story. *Journal of Personality and Social Psychology*, 1965, **1**, 654–659.

Gordova, T. N., & Kovalev, N. K. Unique factors in the hypnotic treatment of chronic alcoholism. In R. B. Winn (Ed.), *Psychotherapy in the Soviet Union*. New York: Grove Press, 1962. Pp. 136–140.

Gormezano, I. Classical conditioning. In J. B. Sidowski (Ed.), *Experimental Methods and Instrumentation in Psychology*. New York: McGraw-Hill, 1966. Pp. 385–420.

Graubard, P. S. Use of indigenous grouping as the reinforcing agent in teaching disturbed delinquents to learn. *Proceedings, 76th Annual Convention, American Psychological Association*, 1968.

Graziano, A. M., & Kean, J. E. Programmed relaxation and reciprocal inhibition with psychotic children. *Proceedings, 75th Annual Convention*, American Psychological Association, 1967.

Griffin, J. H. Is this what it means to see? In W. Burnett (Ed.), *The Spirit of Man*. New York: Hawthorn, 1958. Pp. 50–64.

Gruber, R. P. Behavior therapy: Problems in generalization. *Behavior Therapy*, 1971, **2**, 361–368.

Guest, L. A study of interviewer competence. *International Journal of Opinion Attitude Research*, 1947, **1**, 17–30.

Guthrie, E. R. *The Psychology of Learning*. New York: Harper, 1935.

Guttman, E. S. Effects of short-term psychiatric treatment. *Research Report, No. 36*, State of California, Department of Youth Authority, 1963.

Haggard, E. A., Brekstad, A., & Skard, A. G. On the reliability of the anamnestic interview. *Journal of Abnormal and Social Psychology*, 1960, **61**, 311–318.

Haggard, E. A., Hiken, J. R., & Isaacs, K. S. Some effects of recording and filming on the psychotherapeutic process. *Psychiatry*, 1965, **28**, 169–191.

Haith, M. M. Infrared television recording and measurement of ocular behavior in the human infant. *American Psychologist*, 1969, **24**, 279–283.

Haley, J. *Strategies of Psychotherapy*. New York: Grune and Stratton, 1963.

Hall, C. S., & Lindsey, G. *Theories of Personality*. New York: Wiley, 1957.

Hall, D. Peer and authority relationships during the transition from student to scientist. Unpublished Doctoral thesis, Massachusetts Institute of Technology, 1966.

Hall, J. F. *The Psychology of Learning*. Philadelphia: Lippincott, 1966.

Harby, S. F. Evaluation of a procedure for using daylight projection of film loops in teaching skills. Paper available from Pennsylvania State College Instructional Film Research Program, 1962.

Hardt, R. H., & Bodine, G. E. *Development of Self-Report Instruments in Delinquency Research*. Syracuse, New York: Youth Development Center, Syracuse University, 1965.

Haring, N. G. Equipment listing with examples of application. University of Washington, Experimental Education Unit, 1968 (mimeo).

Harlow, H. F. Mice, monkeys, men, and motives. *Psychological Review*, 1953, **60**, 23–32.

Harris, F. R., Wolf, M. M., & Baer, D. M. Effects of adult social reinforcement on child behavior. *Young Children*, 1964, **20**, 8–17.

Hartmann, D. P. The influence of symbolically modeled instrumental aggressive and pain cues on the disinhibition of aggressive behavior. Unpublished doctoral dissertation, Stanford University, 1965.

Hartmann, H. E., Kris, E., & Loewenstein, R. M. Comments on the formation of psychic structure. In A. Freud, H. E. Hartmann, & E. Kris (Eds.), *The Psychoanalytic Study of the Child.* Vol. II. New York: International Universities Press, 1947.

Hartrup, W. W. Some correlates of parental imitation in young children. *Child Development*, 1962, **33**, 85–96.

Harvard Law Review. Anthropotelemetry: Dr. Schwitzgebel's machine. *Harvard Law Review*, 1966, **80**, 403–421.

Hastorf, A. H. The "reinforcement" of individual actions in a group situation. In L. Krasner, & L. P. Ullman (Eds.), *Research in Behavior Modification: New Developments and Implications.* New York: Holt, 1965. Pp. 268–284.

Hathaway, S. R. Some considerations relative to non-directive psychotherapy as counseling. *Journal of Clinical Psychology*, 1948, **4**, 226–231.

Hawkins, R. P., Peterson, R. F., Schweid, E., & Bijou, S. W. Behavior therapy in the home: Amelioration of a problem in parent-child relations with parent in a therapeutic role. *Journal of Experimental Child Psychology*, 1966, **4**, 99–107.

Haynes, S. N. Learning theory and the treatment of homosexuality. *Psychotherapy: Theory, Research and Practice*, 1970, **7**, 91–94.

Hebb, D. O. *A Textbook of Psychology.* Philadelphia: Saunders, 1958.

Heller, K., & Goldstein, A. P. Client dependency and therapist expectancy as relationship maintaining variables in psychotherapy. *Journal of Consulting Psychology*, 1961, **23**, 371–375.

Henderson, J. D. A community-based operant learning environment 1: Overview. In R. D. Rubin, H. Fensterheim, A. A. Lazarus, & C. M. Franks, (Eds.), *Advances in Behavior Therapy*, New York: Academic Press, 1971. Pp. 233–237.

Hendry, D. P. (Ed.) *Conditioned Reinforcement.* Homewood, Ill.: Dorsey, 1969.

Henle, M., & Hubble, M. B. "Egocentricity" in adult conversation. *Journal of Social Psychology*, 1938, **9**, 227–234.

Henson, D. E., & Rubin, H. B. Voluntary control of eroticism. *Journal of Applied Behavior Analysis*, 1971, **4**, 37–44.

Herbert, J., & Swayze, J. *Wireless Observation.* New York: Columbia University, Teachers College, 1964.

Herman, S. H., Barlow, D. H., & Agras, W. S. Exposure to heterosexual stimuli: An effective variable in treating homosexuality? Paper read at the American Psychological Association meeting, Washington, September, 1971.

Herrnstein, R. J. Superstition: A corollary of the principles of operant conditioning. In W. K. Honig (Ed.), *Operant Behavior: Areas of Research and Application.* New York: Appleton Century Crofts, 1966. Pp. 33–51.

Herzberg, A. *Active Psychotherapy.* London: Research Books, 1945.

Hesse, H. *Narcissus and Goldmund.* New York: Farrar, Straus and Giroux, 1968.

Hetherington, E. M. A developmental study of the effects of sex of the dominant parent on sex-role preference, identification, and imitation in children. *Journal of Personality and Social Psychology,* 1965, **2**, 188–194.

Heyns, R. W., & Zander, A. F. Observation of group behavior. In L. Festinger, & D. Katz (Eds.), *Research Methods in the Behavioral Sciences.* New York: Dryden, 1953. Pp. 381–417.

Hilgard, E. R. The relationship between the conditional response and conventional learning experiments. *Psychological Bulletin,* 1937, **34**, 61–102.

Hilgard, E. R. *Theories of Learning.* (2d ed.) New York: Appleton Century Crofts, 1956.

Hilgard, E. R., & Bower, G. H. *Theories of Learning.* (3d ed.). New York: Appleton Century Crofts, 1966.

Hilgard, E. R., & Marquis, D. G. *Conditioning and Learning.* New York: Appleton Century Crofts, 1940.

Hill, W. F. Sources of evaluative reinforcement. *Psychological Bulletin,* 1968, **69**, 132–146.

Hingtgen, J. N., Sanders, B. M., & De Myer, M. K. Shaping cooperative responses in early childhood schizophrenics. In L. P. Ullmann, & L. Krasner (Eds.), *Case Studies in Behavior Modification.* New York: Holt, 1956. Pp. 130–138.

Hingtgen, J. N., & Trost, F. C., Jr. Shaping cooperative responses in early childhood schizophrenics: II. Reinforcement of mutual physical contact and vocal responses. In R. Ulrich, T. Stachnik, & J. Mabry (Eds.), *Control of Human Behavior.* Glenview, Ill.: Scott, Foresman, 1966. Pp. 110–113.

Hoenig, J., & Reed, G. F. The objective assessment of desensitization. *British Journal of Psychiatry,* 1966, **112**, 1279–1283.

Hogan, R. A., & Kirchner, J. H. Preliminary report of the extinction of learned fears via short-term implosive therapy. *Journal of Abnormal Psychology,* 1967, **72**, 106–109.

Holland, J. G. Human vigilance. *Science,* 1958, **128**, 61–67.

Holland, J. G., & Skinner, B. F. *The Analysis of Behavior.* New York: McGraw-Hill, 1961.

Holmberg, A. R. The changing values and institutions of Vicos in the context of national development. *American Behavioral Scientist,* 1965, **8**, 3–8.

Holt, E. B. *Animal Drive.* London: Macmillan, 1931.

Holtzman, W. H. Statistical models for the study of change in the single case. In C. W. Harris (Ed.), *Problems in Measuring Change.* Madison, Wis.: University of Wisconsin Press, 1963. Pp. 199–211.

Homme, L. E. A demonstration of the use of self-instructional and other teaching techniques for remedial instruction of low-achieving adolescents in reading and mathematics. U. S. Office of Education, Contract No. OE-4-16-033, 1964.

Homme, L. E. Contingency management. *Newsletter,* American Psychological Association Division of Clinical Psychology, Section on Clinical Child Psychology, 1966, **5**, No. 4.

Homme, L. E., Csanyi, A. P., Gonzales, M. A., & Rechs, J. R. *How to Use*

Contingency Contracting in the Classroom. Champaign, Ill.: Research Press, 1969.

Homme, L. E., deBaca, P. C., Devine, J. V., Steinhorst, R., & Rickert, E. J. Use of the Premack principle in controlling the behavior of nursery school children. *Journal of the Experimental Analysis of Behavior,* 1963, **6**, 544.

Homme, L. E., & Tosti, D. T. Contingency management and motivation. *National Society for Programmed Instruction Journal,* 1965, **4**, 14–16.

Honig, W. K. Perspectives in psychology: XII, Behavior as an independent variable. *The Psychological Record,* 1959, **9**, 121–130.

Honig, W. K. Introductory remarks. In W. K. Honig (Ed.), *Operant Behavior: Areas of Research and Application.* New York: Appleton Century Crofts, 1966. Pp. 1–11.

Hovland, C. I., & Wonderlic, E. F. Prediction of success from a standardized interview. *Journal of Applied Psychology,* 1939, **23**, 537–546.

Howlett, S. C., & Nawas, M. M. Suggestion, relaxation, and desensitization. Paper presented at the meeting of the American Psychological Association, Washington, D. C., September 1969.

Huff, F. W. The desensitization of a homosexual. *Behaviour Research and Therapy,* 1970, **8**, 99–102.

Hull, C. L. *Principles of Behavior.* New York: Appleton Century Crofts, 1943.

Hull, C. L. *Essentials of Behavior.* New Haven: Yale, 1951.

Hull, C. L. *A Behavior System: An Introduction to Behavior Theory Concerning the Individual Organism.* New Haven: Yale, 1952.

Humphrey, G. (Ed.), Introduction, *The Wild Boy of Aveyron,* by Itard, J. M. G. (translated by George & Muriel Humphrey). New York: Appleton Century Crofts, 1962, v–xix.

Humphreys, L. *Tearoom Trade: Impersonal Sex in Public Places.* Chicago: Aldine, 1970.

Hunter, W. S., *Human Behavior.* Chicago: Univ. of Chicago Press, 1928.

Huntington, M. J. The development of a professional self-image. In R. K. Merton, G. G. Reader, & P. L. Kendall (Eds.), *The Student Physician.* Cambridge, Mass.: Harvard, 1957. Pp. 179–187.

Hurvitz, N. Psychotherapy with one spouse. *Journal of Consulting Psychology,* 1967, **31**, 38–48.

Hurvitz, N. Peer self-help psychotherapy groups and their implications for psychotherapy. *Psychotherapy: Theory, Research and Practice,* 1970, **7**, 41–49.

Huszar, R. J., & Haloburdo, J. EKG transmission from emergency vehicles. Paper presented at the IEEE National Telemetering Conference, Washington, D. C., 1969.

Hutchinson, R. R., & Azrin, N. H. Conditioning of mental-hospital patients to fixed-ratio schedules of reinforcement. *Journal of the Experimental Analysis of Behavior,* 1961, **4**, 87–95.

Huxley, A. Education on the nonverbal level. *Daedalus,* 1962, **91**, 279–293.

Hyman, H. Do they tell the truth? *Public Opinion Quarterly,* 1944, **8**, 557–559.

Hyman, H. Interviewing as scientific procedure. In D. Lerner, & H. D. Lasswell (Eds.), *The Policy Sciences.* Palo Alto: Stanford, 1951. Pp. 203–216.

Isaacs, W., Thomas, J., & Goldiamond, I. Application of operant conditioning to reinstate verbal behavior in psychotics. *Journal of Speech and Hearing Disorders*, 1960, **25**, 8–12.

Itard, J. M. G. *The Wild Boy of Aveyron.* (G. Humphrey, Ed., translated by M. Humphrey, New York: Appleton Century Crofts, 1962.

Jacobs, R. C., & Campbell, D. T. The perpetuation of an arbitrary tradition through several generations of a laboratory microculture. *Journal of Abnormal and Social Psychology*, 1961, **62**, 649–658.

Jacobson, E. *Progressive Relaxation.* Chicago: University of Chicago Press, 1938.

Jacobson, J. L., & Wirt, R. D. MMPI profiles associated with outcomes of group psychotherapy with prisoners. In J. N. Butcher (Ed.), *MMPI: Research Developments and Clinical Applications.* New York: McGraw-Hill, 1969. Pp. 191–205.

James, B. Case of homosexuality treated by aversion therapy. *British Medical Journal*, 1962, **1**, 768–770.

Jeffrey, C. R. *Proposal for the Establishment, Operation and Maintenance of a Research Center in Washington, D. C.* Vol. I. Los Angeles, Calif.: Packard Bell Electronics Corporation, 1965.

Jenkins, J. G., & Corbin, H. H. Dependability of psychological brand barometers –II: The problem of validity. *Journal of Applied Psychology*, 1938, **22**, 252–260.

Jersild, A. T., & Meigs, M. F. Direct observation as a research method. *Review of Educational Research*, 1939, **40**, 472–482.

Jessor, R., Graves, T. D., Hanson, R. C., & Jessor, S. L. *Society, Personality, and Deviant Behavior.* New York: Holt, 1968.

John, E. R., Chesler, P., Bartlett, F., & Victor, I. Observational learning in cats. *Science*, 1968, **159**, 1489–1492.

Johnson, S. M., & White, G., Self-observation as an agent of behavioral change. *Behavior Therapy*, 1971, **2**, 488–497.

Jones, M. C. A laboratory study of fear: The case of Peter. *Journal of Genetic Psychology*, 1924, **31**, 308–315.

Judicial Council, American Medical Association. Requirements for experiments on human beings: Report of the Judicial Council adopted by AMA House of Delegates, Dec. 1946. *Journal of the American Medical Association*, 1946, **132**, 1090.

Jung, C. G. *Neue bahnen der psychologie, Raschers Jahrbuch für Schweizer Art und Kunst.* Zurich: Rascher, 1912. Reprinted in J. Jacobi (Ed.), *Psychological Reflections.* New York: Harper, 1961. P. 71.

Jung, C. G. *Psychological Reflections: An Anthology of the Writings of C. G. Jung.* J. Jacobi (Ed.). New York: Harper, 1961.

Junker, B. H. *Field Work: An Introduction to the Social Sciences.* Chicago: Univ. of Chicago Press, 1960.

Justesen, D. R. Allergic and classically conditioned asthma in guinea pigs. *Science*, 1971, **173**, 82.

Kagan, J. On the need for relativism. *American Psychologist*, 1967, **22**, 131–142.

Kagan, N., Krathwohl, D. R., & Miller, R. Stimulated recall in therapy using video tape: A case study. *Journal of Counseling Psychology*, 1963, **10**, 237–243.

Kahl, J. A. *The American Class Structure*. New York: Holt, 1962.

Kahn, M. A polygraph study of the catharsis of aggression. Doctoral dissertation, Harvard University, 1960.

Kahn, R. L., & Cannell, C. F. *The Dynamics of Interviewing: Theory, Technique, and Cases*. New York: Wiley, 1957.

Kamin, L. J. The effects of termination of the CS and avoidance of the US on avoidance learning. *Journal of Comparative and Physiological Psychology*, 1956, **49**, 420–424.

Kamin, L. J. Temporal and intensity characteristics of the conditioned stimulus. In W. F. Prokasy (Ed.), *Classical Conditioning: A Symposium*. New York: Appleton Century Crofts, 1965. Pp. 118–147.

Kanareff, V. T., & Lanzetta, J. T. Effects of success-failure experiences and probability of reinforcement upon the acquisition and extinction of an imitative response. *Psychological Reports*, 1960, **7**, 151–166.

Kanfer, F. H. Vicarious human reinforcements: A glimpse into the black box. In L. Krasner, & L. P. Ullmann (Eds.), *Research in Behavior Modification: New Developments and Implications*. New York: Holt, 1965. Pp. 244–267.

Kanfer, F. H. Self-monitoring: Methodological limitations and clinical applications. *Journal of Consulting and Clinical Psychology*, 1970, **35**, 148–152.

Kanfer, F. H., & Marston, A. R. Human reinforcement: Vicarious and direct. *Journal of Experimental Psychology*, 1963, **65**, 292–296.

Kanfer, F. H., & Phillips, J. S., *Learning Foundations of Behavior Therapy*. New York: Wiley, 1970.

Kantorovich, N. An attempt at association reflex therapy in alcoholism. *Psychological Abstracts*, 1930, **4**, 493.

Kaplan, A. *The Conduct of Inquiry: Methodology for Behavioral Science*. San Francisco: Chandler, 1964.

Kaplan, M. (Ed.), *Essential Works of Pavlov*. New York: Grosset & Dunlap, 1966.

Karpman, B. *The Sexual Offender and His Offenses: Etiology, Pathology, Psychodynamics, and Treatment*. New York: Julian Press, 1962.

Katz, D. Do interviewers bias poll results? *Public Opinion Quarterly*, 1942, **6**, 248–268.

Katz, R. An investigation into the meaning of the idiographic approach to exploratory research on personality assessment. Unpublished manuscript, Harvard University, 1962.

Katz, R., & Kolb, D. Outward bound and education for personal growth. Report prepared for the Massachusetts Youth Service Board, Boston, 1967.

Kaufman, A., Baron, A., & Kopp, R. E. Some effects of instructions on human operant behavior. *Psychonomic Monograph Supplements*, 1966, **1**, 243–250.

Kay, E., French, F. R. P., & Meyer, H. *A Study of the Performance Appraisal Interview*. New York: Management Development and Employee Relations Services, General Electric, 1962.

Keating, E., Paterson, D. G., & Stone, C. H. Validity of work history obtained by interview. *Journal of Applied Psychology*, 1950, **34**, 6–11.

Kelleher, R. T. Chaining and conditioned reinforcement. In W. K. Honig (Ed.),

Operant Behavior: Areas of Research and Application. New York: Appleton Century Crofts, 1966. Pp. 160–212.

Keller, F. S. *Learning Reinforcement Theory.* New York: Random House, 1954.

Keller, F. S., & Schoenfeld, W. N. *Principles of Psychology.* New York: Appleton Century Crofts, 1950.

Kelly, G. *The Psychology of Personal Constructs.* Vols. I and II. New York: Norton, 1955.

Kelman, H. C. Processes of opinion change. *Public Opinion Quarterly,* 1961, **25**, 57–78.

Kelman, H. C. Manipulation of human behavior: An ethical dilemma for the social scientist. *Journal of Social Issues,* 1965, **11**, 31–46.

Kelman, H. C. *A Time to Speak: On Human Values and Social Research.* San Francisco: Jossey-Bass, 1968.

Kelman, H. C., & Parloff, M. B. Interrelations among three criteria for success in psychotherapy: Comfort, effectiveness, and self-awareness. *Journal of Abnormal and Social Psychology,* 1957, **54**, 281–288.

Kilpatrick, F. P., & Cantril, H. Self-anchoring scale: A measure of the individual's unique reality world. *Journal of Individual Psychology,* 1960, **16**, 158–170.

Kimble, G. A. *Hilgard and Marquis' Conditioning and Learning.* New York: Appleton Century Crofts, 1961.

Kimbrell, D., & Blake, R. R. Motivational factors in the violation of a prohibition. *Journal of Abnormal and Social Psychology,* 1958, **56**, 132–133.

Kinne, S. The clinical use of the Rep Test. Unpublished manuscript, Harvard University, 1963.

Kinsey, A. C., Pomeroy, W. B., & Martin, C. E. *Sexual Behavior in the Human Male.* Philadelphia: Saunders, 1948.

Koffka, K. *Principles of Gestalt Psychology.* New York: Harcourt, Brace, 1935.

Kolb, D. A. Achievement motivation training for underachieving high school boys. *Journal of Personality and Social Psychology,* 1965, **1**, 783–792.

Kolb, D. A., & Boyatzis, R. E. Goal-setting and self-directed behavior change. *Human Relations,* 1970, **23**, 439–457.

Kolb, D. A., Rubin, I. M., & McIntyre, J. M. *Organizational Psychology: An Experiential Approach.* Englewood Cliffs, N.J.: Prentice-Hall, 1971.

Kolb, D. A., Winter, S. K., & Berlew, D. E. Self-directed change: Two studies. *Journal of Applied Behavioral Science,* 1970, **4**, 453–471.

Kraft, T. A case of homosexuality treated by systematic desensitization. *American Journal of Psychotherapy,* 1967, **21**, 815–821.

Kraft, T. Treatment for sexual perversions. *Behaviour Research and Therapy,* 1969, **7**, 215.

Kraft, T., & Al-Issa, I. Behavior therapy and the treatment of frigidity. *American Journal of Psychotherapy,* 1967, **21**, 116–120. (a)

Kraft, T., and Al-Issa, I. Alcoholism treated by desensitization: A case report. *Behavior Research and Therapy,* 1967, **5**, 69–70. (b)

Krasner, L. Studies of the conditioning of verbal behavior. *Psychological Bulletin,* 1958, **55**, 148–170.

Krasner, L. Operant conditioning techniques with adults from the laboratory to

"real life" behavior modification. Paper read at the American Psychological
Association meeting, Chicago, 1965. (a)

Krasner, L. The behavioral scientist and social responsibility: No place to hide.
The Journal of Social Issues, 1965, **21**, 9–30. (b)

Krasner, L. Verbal conditioning and psychotherapy. In L. Krasner, & L. P.
Ullmann (Eds.), *Research in Behavior Modification: New Developments and
Implications*. New York: Holt, 1965. Pp. 211–228. (c)

Krasner, L., & Atthowe, J. Token economy bibliography. Unpublished manuscript, State University of New York at Stony Brook, 1970.

Krasner, L., & Ullmann, L. P. (Eds.), *Research in Behavior Modification*. New
York: Holt, 1965.

Krech, D., Crutchfield, R., & Ballschey, E. *Individuals in Society*. New York:
McGraw-Hill, 1962.

Lane, H., Kopp, J., Sheppard, W., Anderson, T., & Carlson, D. Acquisition,
maintenance, and retention in the differential reinforcement of vocal
duration. *Journal of Experimental Psychology Monograph Supplement*,
1967, **74**, Part 2, No. 2 (Whole No. 635).

Lang, P. J. The mechanics of desensitization and the laboratory study of human
fear. In C. M. Franks (Ed.), *Behavior Therapy: Appraisal and Status*. New
York: McGraw-Hill, 1969. Pp. 160–191.

Lang, P. L., & Lazovik, A. D. The experimental desensitization of a phobia.
Journal of Abnormal and Social Psychology, 1963, **66**, 519–525.

Lang, P. J., Lazovik, A. D., & Reynolds, D. J. Desensitization, suggestibility and
pseudotherapy. *Journal of Abnormal and Social Psychology*, 1965, **70**,
395–402.

LaPiere, R. T. Attitudes vs. actions. *Social Forces*, 1934, **13**, 230–237.

Larsen, G. Treatment of obesity. *Tedsskrift for den Norske Laegeforening*, 1949,
69, 442–446.

Lasagna, L., Laties, V. G., & Dohan, J. L. Further studies on the "pharmacology"
of placebo response. *Journal of Clinical Investigation,* 1958, **37**, 533–537.

Lavin, N. I., Thorpe, J. G., Barker, J. C., Blakemore, C. B., & Conway, C. G.
Behavior therapy in a case of transvestism. *Journal of Nervous and Mental
Disease*, 1961, **133**, 346–353.

Lazarus, A. A. New methods in psychotherapy: A case study. *South African
Medical Journal*, 1958, **33**, 660–663.

Lazarus, A. A. The treatment of chronic frigidity by systematic desensitization.
Journal of Nervous and Mental Disease, 1963, **136**, 272–278.

Lazarus, A. A. Broad-spectrum behavior therapy and the treatment of agorapho-
bia. *Behaviour Research and Therapy*, 1966, **4**, 95–97.

Lazarus, A. A. Behavior therapy and marriage counseling. *Journal of the
American Society of Psychosomatic Dentistry and Medicine*, 1968, **15**,
49–56. (a)

Lazarus, A. A. Aversion therapy and sensory modalities: Clinical impressions.
Perceptual and Motor Skills, 1968, **27**, 178. (b)

Lazarus, A. A. Behavior therapy and graded structure. In R. Porter (Ed.), *The
Role of Learning in Psychotherapy*. London: A. Churchill. 1968. Pp.
134–143. (Ciba Foundation Symposium). (c)

Lazarus, A. A. *Behavior Therapy and Beyond.* New York: McGraw-Hill, 1971.

Lazarus, R. S. *Patterns of Adjustment and Human Effectiveness.* New York: McGraw-Hill, 1969.

Lazovik, A. D., & Lang, P. J. A laboratory demonstration of systematic desensitization psychotherapy. *Journal of Psychological Studies,* 1960, **11,** 238–247.

Lederhendler, I., & Baum, M. Mechanical facilitation of the action of response prevention (flooding) in rats. *Behaviour Research and Therapy,* 1970, **8,** 43–48.

Lefkowitz, M. M., Blake, R. R., & Mouton, J. S. Status factors in pedestrian violation of traffic signals. *Journal of Abnormal and Social Psychology,* 1955, **51,** 704–706.

Leighton, A. H. The chairman's remarks. *Planning evaluations of mental health programs: Report of the second meeting of the advisory council on mental health demonstrations.* New York: Milbank Memorial Fund, 1958. Pp. 59–62.

Leitenberg, H., Agras, W. S., Barlow, P. H., & Oliveau, D. C. Contribution of selective positive reinforcement and therapeutic instructions to systematic desensitization therapy. *Journal of Abnormal Psychology,* 1969, **74,** 113–118.

Leitenberg, H., Rawson, R. A., & Bath, K. Reinforcement of competing behavior during extinction. *Science,* 1970, **169,** 301–303.

Lemere, F., & Voegtlin, W. An evaluation of aversion treatment of alcoholism. *Quarterly Journal of Studies on Alcohol,* 1950, **11,** 199–204.

Lenski, G. E., & Leggett, J. C. Caste, class and deference in the research interview. *American Journal of Sociology,* 1960, **65,** 463–467.

Lesser, G. S. Conflict analysis of fantasy aggression. *Journal of Personality,* 1958, **26,** 29–41.

Letemendia, F. J. J., & Harris, A. D. The influence of side effects on the reporting of symptoms. *Psychopharmacologia,* 1959, **1,** 39.

Leuba, C. Images as conditioned sensations. *Journal of Experimental Psychology,* 1940, **26,** 345–351.

Levin, G. R., & Simmons, J. J. Response to praise by emotionally disturbed boys. *Psychological Reports,* 1962, **11,** 10.

Levin, S. M., Hirsch, I. S., Shugar, G., & Kapche, R. Treatment of homosexuality and heterosexual anxiety with avoidance conditioning and systematic desensitization: Data and a case report. *Psychotherapy: Theory, Research and Practice,* 1968, **5,** 160–168.

Levinson, D. J. The psychotherapist's contribution to the patient's treatment career. In H. H. Strupp, & L. Luborsky (Eds.), *Research in Psychotherapy.* Vol. II. Washington, D. C.: American Psychological Association, 1962. Pp. 13–24.

Levis, D. J., & Carrera, R. Effects of ten hours of implosive therapy in the treatment of outpatients. *Journal of Abnormal Psychology,* 1967, **72,** 504–508.

Levy, D. M. Trends in therapy: III. Release therapy. *American Journal of Orthopsychiatry,* 1939, **9,** 713–737.

Lewin, K. *Principles of Topological Psychology.* New York: McGraw-Hill, 1936.
Lewin, K., Dembo, T., Festinger, L., & Sears, P. S. Level of aspiration. In J. McV.
  Hunt (Ed.), *Personality and Behavior Disorders.* New York: Ronald, 1944.
  Pp. 49–68.
Liberman, R. P. A view of behavior modification projects in California. *Behaviour
  Research and Therapy,* 1968, **6,** 331–341.
Lick, J. R., & Bootzin, R. R. Expectancy, demand characteristics, and contact
  desensitization in behavior change. *Behavior Therapy,* 1970, **1,** 176–183.
Likert, R. *The Human Organization.* New York: McGraw-Hill, 1967.
Lindeman, E. C. *Social Discovery.* New York: Republic, 1924.
Lindsley, O. R. Operant conditioning methods applied to research in chronic
  schizophrenia. *Psychiatric Research Reports,* 1956, **5,** 118–139.
Lindsley, O. R. Characteristics of the behavior of chronic psychotics as revealed
  by free-operant conditioning methods. *Diseases of the Nervous System,*
  Monograph Supplement, 1960, Vol. XXI, No. 2.
Lindsley, O. R. A behavioral measure of television viewing. *Journal of Advertis-
  ing Research,* 1962, **2,** 2–12.
Lindsley, O. R. Experimental analysis of social reinforcement: Terms and
  methods. *American Journal of Orthopsychiatry,* 1963, **33,** 624–633.
Lindsley, O. R. Experimental analysis of cooperation and competition. In: T.
  Verhave (Ed.), *The Experimental Analysis of Behavior: Selected Readings.*
  New York: Appleton Century Crofts, 1966. Pp. 470–501.
Lindsley, O. R. A reliable wrist counter for recording behavior rates. *Journal of
  Applied Behavioral Analysis,* 1968, **1,** 77–78.
Lindsley, O. R. Direct behavioral analysis of psychotherapy sessions by conju-
  gately programmed closed-circuit television. *Psychotherapy: Theory, Re-
  search and Practice,* 1969, **6,** 71–81.
Linton, R. *The Study of Man.* New York: Appleton Century Crofts, 1936.
Loew, C. A. Acquisition of a hostile attitude and its relationship to aggressive
  behavior. *Journal of Personality and Social Psychology,* 1967, **5,** 335–341.
Lomont, J. F., & Edwards, J. E. The role of relaxation in systematic desensitization. *Behaviour Research and Therapy,* 1967, **5,** 11–25.
London, P. *The Modes and Morals of Psychotherapy.* New York: Holt, 1964.
London, P. The end of ideology in behavior modification. *American Psychologist,*
  1972, **27,** 913–920.
Long, E. R., Hammack, J. T., May, F., & Campbell, B. J. Intermittent reinforce-
  ment of operant behavior in children. *Journal of the Experimental Analysis
  of Behavior,* 1958, **1,** 315–339.
LoPiccolo, J. Case study: Systematic desensitization of homosexuality. *Behavior
  Therapy,* 1971, **2,** 394–399.
Lorenz, K. *On Aggression.* New York: Harcourt, Brace & World, 1963.
Lovaas, O. I. Effect of exposure to symbolic aggression on aggressive behavior.
  Child Development, 1961, **32,** 37–44.
Lovaas, O. I., Berberich, J. P., Perloff, B. F., & Schaeffer, B. Acquisition of
  imitative speech by schizophrenic children. *Science,* 1966, **151,** 705–707.
Lovibond, S. H. Aversive control of behavior. *Behavior Therapy,* 1970, **1,** 80–91.
Lovitt, T. C., & Curtiss, K. A. Academic response rate as a function of teacher-

and self-imposed contingencies. *Journal of Applied Behavior Analysis,* 1969, **2**, 49–53.

Lowell, E. L. The effect of need for achievement on learning and speed of performance. *Journal of Psychology,* 1952, **33**, 31–40.

Lubin, B., & Eddy, W. B. The laboratory training model: Rationale, method, and some thoughts for the future. *International Journal of Group Psychotherapy,* 1970, **20**, 305–339.

Luborsky, L. The patient's personality and psychotherapeutic change. In H. H. Strupp, & L. Luborsky (Eds.), *Research in Psychotherapy.* Vol. II. Washington, D. C.: American Psychological Association, 1962. Pp. 115–133.

Luborsky, L., Chandler, M., Auerbach, A. H., Cohen, J., & Bachrach, H. M. Factors influencing the outcome of psychotherapy: A review of quantitative research. *Psychological Bulletin,* 1971, **75**, 145–185.

Luborsky, L., & Schimels, J. Psychoanalytic theories of therapeutic and developmental change: Implications for assessment. In P. Worchel, & D. Berne (Eds.), *Personality Change.* New York: Wiley, 1964.

Luchins, A. S., & Luchins, E. H. Learning a complex ritualized social role. *The Psychological Record,* 1966, **16**, 177–187.

Luria, A. R. *The Nature of Human Conflicts: An Objective Study of Disorganization and Control of Human Behavior.* (Translated and edited by H. W. Gantt). London: Liveright, 1932. (Republished: New York, Grove Press, 1960.)

Lynch, J. J., & McCarthy, J. F. The effect of petting on a classically conditioned emotional response. *Behaviour Research and Therapy,* 1967, **5**, 55–62.

Lynch, J. J., & McCarthy, J. F. Social responding in dogs: Heart rate changes to a person. *Psychophysiology,* 1969, **5**, 389–393.

Maccoby, E. E., & Maccoby, N. The interview: A tool of social science. In Lindzey (Ed.), *Handbook of Social Psychology.* Addison-Wesley, 1954. Pp. 449–487.

Maccoby, E. E., & Wilson, W. C. Identification and observational learning from films. *Journal of Abnormal and Social Psychology,* 1957, **55**, 76–87.

Maccoby, N., & Sheffield, F. D. Theory and experimental research on the teaching of complex sequential procedures by alternate demonstration and practice. Technical Memorandum ML-TM-57-31, Air Force Personnel and Training Research Center, Maintenance Laboratory, Lowry Air Force Base, Colorado, 1957.

MacCulloch, M. J., Feldman, M. P., Orford, J. F., & MacCulloch, M. L. Anticipatory avoidance learning in the treatment of alcoholism. *Behaviour Research and Therapy,* 1966, **4**, 187–196.

MacCulloch, M. J., Feldman, M. P., & Pinshoff, J. M. The application of anticipatory avoidance learning to the treatment of homosexuality: II. Avoidance response latencies and pulse rate changes. *Behaviour Research and Therapy,* 1965, **3**, 21–43.

Mackay, R. S. Biomedical telemetry: Applications to psychology. *American Psychologist,* 1969, **24**, 244–254.

Madge, J. *The Tools of Social Science.* London: Longmans, 1953.

Mahoney, M. J. Sequential treatments for severe phobia. *Journal of Behavior Therapy and Experimental Psychiatry*, 1971, **2**, 195–197.

Malleson, N. Panic and phobia. *Lancet*, 1959, **1**, 225–227.

Mallick, S. K., & McCandless, B. R. A study of catharsis of aggression. *Journal of Personality and Social Psychology*, 1966, **4**, 591–596.

Maltz, M. *Psycho-Cybernetics*. Englewood Cliffs, N.J.: Prentice-Hall, 1960.

Mandel, K. H. Preliminary report on a new aversion therapy for male homosexuals. *Behaviour Research and Therapy*, 1970, **8**, 93–95.

Mann, J., *Changing Human Behavior*, New York: Scribner, 1965.

Margolis, J. Juvenile delinquents: The latter-day knights. *The American Scholar*, 1960, **29**, 211–218.

Marks, I., & Gelder, M. Transvestism and fetishism: Clinical and psychological changes during faradic aversion. *British Journal of Psychiatry*, 1967, **119**, 711–730.

Marquis, J. M. Orgasmic reconditioning: Changing sexual object choice through controlling masturbation fantasies. *Journal of Behavior Therapy and Experimental Psychiatry*, 1970, **1**, 263–271.

Marshall, G. R. Toilet training of an autistic eight-year-old through conditioning therapy: A case report. *Behaviour Research and Therapy*, 1966, **4**, 242–245.

Marshall, W. L. A combined treatment method for certain sexual deviations. *Behaviour Research and Therapy*, 1971, **9**, 293–294.

Marston, A. R. Imitation, self-reinforcement, and reinforcement of another person. *Journal of Personality and Social Psychology*, 1965, **2**, 255–261.

Maslow, A. *Motivation and Personality*. New York: Harper, 1954.

Max, L. W. Breaking up a homosexual fixation by the conditioned reaction technique: A case study. *Psychological Bulletin*, 1935, **32**, 734.

May, R. Historical and philosophical presuppositions for understanding therapy. In O. H. Mowrer (Ed.), *Psychotherapy: Theory and Research*. Ronald, 1953. Pp. 9–43.

May, R. *Existence*. New York: Basic Books, 1958.

Mayerson, P., & Lief, H. I. Psychotherapy of homosexuals: A follow-up study of nineteen cases. In J. Marmor (Ed.), *Sexual Inversion: The Multiple Roots of Homosexuality*. New York: Basic Books, 1965. Pp. 302–344.

McClelland, D. C. *Personality*. New York: Dryden, 1955.

McClelland, D. C. Risk taking in children with high and low need for achievement. In J. W. Atkinson (Ed.), *Motivation, Fantasy, Action and Society* Princeton, N.J.: Van Nostrand, 1958. Pp. 306–321.

McClelland, D. C. *The Achieving Society*. Princeton, N.J.: Van Nostrand, 1961.

McClelland, D. C. Toward a theory of motive acquisition. *American Psychologist* 1965, **20**, 321–333.

McClelland, D. C., Atkinson, J. W., Clark, R. W. & Lowell, E. L. *The Achievement Motive*. New York: Appleton Century Crofts, 1953.

McClelland, D. C., & Winter, D. G. *Motivating Economic Achievement*. New York: Free Press, 1969.

McConaghy, N. Penile response conditioning and its relationship to aversion therapy in homosexuals. *Behavior Therapy*, 1970, **1**, 213–221.

McCord, J., & McCord, W. Cultural stereotypes and the validity of interviews for research in child development. *Child Development,* 1961, **32,** 171–185.

McCord, W., McCord, J., & Zola, I. K. *Origins of Crime: A New Evaluation of the Cambridge-Somerville Youth Study.* New York: Columbia University Press, 1959.

McFall, R. M. Effects of self-monitoring on normal smoking behavior. *Journal of Consulting and Clinical Psychology,* 1970, **35,** 135–142.

McGlynn, F. D., Reynolds, E. J., & Linder, L. H. Systematic desensitization with pre-treatment and intra-treatment therapeutic instructions. *Behaviour Research and Therapy,* 1971, **9,** 57–63.

McGraw, M., & Molloy, L. B. The pediatric anamnesis: Inaccuracies in eliciting developmental data. *Child Development,* 1941, **12,** 255–265.

McGuire, R., & Stigall, T. T. Psychotherapy by television: A research paradigm. University of Mississippi, School of Medicine, 1967 (mimeo).

McGuire, R. J., Carlisle, J. M., & Young, B. G. Sexual deviation as conditioned behavior: A hypothesis. *Behaviour Research and Therapy,* 1965, **2,** 185–190.

McGuire, R. J., & Vallance, M. Aversion therapy by electric shock: A simple technique. *British Medical Journal,* 1964, **1,** 151–152.

McNamara, J. R. Some methodological considerations in the design and implementation of behavior therapy research. *Behavior Therapy,* 1972, **3,** 361–378.

Meehl, P. E. Psychotherapy. *Annual Review of Psychology,* 1955, **6,** 357–378.

Melamed, B., & Lang, P. J. Study of the automated desensitization of fear. Paper presented at the meeting of the Midwestern Psychological Association, Chicago, Ill., May 1967.

Merton, R. K. The self-fulfilling prophecy. *Social Theory and Social Structure.* New York: Free Press, 1965. Pp. 421–436.

Merton, R. K., Reader, G., & Kendall, P. (Eds.), *The Student-Physician.* Cambridge, Mass.: Harvard, 1957.

Metcalf, M. Demonstration of a psychosomatic relationship. *British Journal of Medical Psychology,* 1956, **29,** 63–66.

Metz, J. R. Conditioning generalized imitation in autistic children. *California Mental Health Research Digest,* 1966, **4,** 71–73.

Michon, J. A., & Koutstaal, G. A. An instrumated car for the study of driver behavior. *American Psychologist,* 1969, **24,** 297–300.

Milgram, S. Behavioral study of obedience. *Journal of Abnormal and Social Psychology,* 1963, **67,** 371–378.

Milgram, S. Issues in the study of obedience: A reply to Baumrind. *American Psychologist,* 1964, **19,** 848–852.

Milgram, S. Some conditions of obedience and disobedience to authority. *Human Relations,* 1965, **18,** 57–76.

Miller, B. A., Pokorny, A. D., Valles, J., & Cleveland, S. E. Biased sampling in alcoholism treatment research. *Quarterly Journal of Studies on Alcohol,* 1970, **31,** 97–107.

Miller, N. E. Limitations of the consummatory response hypothesis of reinforcement. In D. Bindra & J. Stewart (Eds.), *Motivation.* Baltimore, Md.: Penguin, 1966. Pp. 252–254.

Miller, N. E., & Dollard, J. *Social Learning and Imitation.* New Haven: Yale, 1941.

Miller, S., & Konorski, J. Sur une forme particulière des reflexes conditionnels. *C. R. Soc. Biol.,* 1928, **99,** 1155–1157.

Moan, C. E., & Heath, R. G. Septal stimulation for the initiation of heterosexual behavior in a homosexual male. *Journal of Behavior Therapy and Experimental Psychiatry,* 1972, **3,** 23–30.

Montgomery, G. T., & Crowder, J. E. The symptom substitution hypothesis and the evidence. *Psychotherapy: Theory, Research and Practice,* 1972, **9,** 98–102.

Moore, N. Behaviour therapy in bronchial asthma: A controlled study. *Journal of Psychosomatic Research,* 1965, **9,** 257–276.

Moore, O. K., & Anderson, A. R. Autotelic folk-models. *The Sociological Quarterly,* 1960, **1,** 203–216.

Moore, R., & Goldiamond, I. Errorless establishment of visual discrimination using fading procedures. *Journal of the Experimental Analysis of Behavior,* 1964, **7,** 269–272.

Morganstern, K. P., & Ratliff, R. G. Systematic desensitization as a technique for treating smoking behavior: A preliminary report. *Behaviour Research and Therapy,* 1969, **7,** 397–398.

Morris, N. Impediments to penal reform. *University of Chicago Law Review,* 1966, **33,** 627–656.

Morse, W. H., & Skinner, B. F. Some factors involved in the stimulus control of operant behavior. *Journal of the Experimental Analysis of Behavior,* 1958, **1,** 103–107.

Moss, H. A., & Kagan, J. Stability of achievement and recognition-seeking behaviors, from early childhood through adulthood. *Journal of Abnormal and Social Psychology,* 1961, **62,** 504–513.

Mowrer, O. H. *Learning Theory and Behavior.* New York: Wiley, 1960.

Mowrer, O. H. The behavior therapies, with special reference to modeling and imitation. *American Journal of Psychotherapy,* 1966, **20,** 439–461.

Mowrer, O. H., & Lamoreaux, R. R. Avoidance conditioning and signal duration: A study of secondary motivation and reward. *Psychological Monographs,* 1942, **54,** No. 5.

Murphy, J. V., Miller, R. E., & Brown, E. Secondary reinforcement and avoidance conditioning. *Journal of General Psychology,* 1958, **59,** 201–209.

Murray, H. A. *Explorations in Personality.* New York: Oxford University Press, 1938.

Mussen, P. H., & Naylor, H. K. The relationships between overt and fantasy aggression. *Journal of Abnormal and Social Psychology,* 1954, **49,** 235–240.

Mussen, P. H., & Parker, A. L. Mother nurturance and girls' incidental imitative learning. *Journal of Personality and Social Psychology,* 1965, **2,** 94–97.

Myers, R. D. Alcohol consumption in rats: Effects of intracranial injections of ethanol. *Science,* 1963, **142,** 240–241.

Nathan, P. E., Schneller, P., & Lindsley, O. R. Direct measurement of communication during psychiatric admission interviews. *Behaviour Research and Therapy,* 1964, **2,** 49–57.

Nawas, M. M. Devising scheduled taped desensitization. Research Resume No. 1, University of Missouri, Department of Psychology, 1969 (mimeo).

Nawas, M. M., Mealiea, W. L., & Fishman, S. T. Systematic desensitization as counterconditioning: A retest with adequate controls. *Behavior Therapy*, 1971, **2**, 345–356.

Nelson, C. M. & McReynolds, W. T. Self-recording and control of behavior: A reply to Simkins *Behavior Therapy*, 1971, **2**, 594–597.

New York Times. 169 hours in the shower. June 7, 1972, 4.

Nielsen, G. *Studies in Self Confrontation: Viewing a Sound Motion Picture of Self and Another Person in a Stressful Dyadic Interaction*. Cleveland: Howard Allen, 1964.

Noelpp, B., & Noelpp-Eschenhagen, I. Das experimentelle asthma bronchiale des meerschweinschens: III. Studien zur bedeutung bedingter reflexe, bahnungsbereitschaft und heftfahigkeit unter stress. *International Archives of Allergy*, 1952, **3**, 108–135.

Oakes, W. F., Droge, A. E., & August, B. Reinforcement effects on participation in group discussion. *Psychological Reports*, 1960, **7**, 503–514.

O'Connel, E. J. The effects of probability of reinforcement, cooperative-competitive set, sex of model, and sex of subject in imitative behavior in a two-choice situation. *Dissertation Abstracts*, 1963, **23**, 4769.

O'Connor, R. D. Modification of social withdrawal through symbolic modeling. *Journal of Applied Behavioral Analysis*, 1969, **2**, 15–22.

Oliveau, D. C. Systematic desensitization in an experimental setting: A follow-up study. *Behaviour Research and Therapy*, 1971, in press.

Oliveau, D. C., Agras, W. S., Leitenberg, H., Moore, R. C., & Wright, D. E. Systematic desensitization, therapeutically oriented instructions and selective positive reinforcement. *Behaviour Research and Therapy*, 1969, **7**, 27–33.

O'Neil, D. G., & Howell, R. J. Three models of hierarchy presentation in systematic desensitization therapy. *Behaviour Research and Therapy* 1969, **7**, 289–294.

Orne, M. T. On the social psychology of the psychological experiment: With special reference to demand characteristics and their implications. *American Psychologist*, 1962, **17**, 776–783.

Orne, M. T. From the subject's point of view, when is behavior private and when is it public: Problems of inference. *Journal of Consulting and Clinical Psychology*, 1970, **35**, 143–147.

Ost, J. W. P., & Lauer, D. W. Some investigations of classical salivary conditioning in the dog. In W. F. Prokasy (Ed.), *Classical Conditioning: A Symposium*. New York: Appleton Century Crofts, 1965. Pp. 192–207.

Ottenberg, P., Stein, M., Lewis, J., & Hamilton, C. Learned asthma in the guinea pig. *Psychosomatic Medicine*, 1958, **20**, 395–400.

Ovesey, L., Gaylin, W., & Hendin, H. Psychotherapy of male homosexuality. *Archives of General Psychiatry*, 1963, **9**, 19–31.

Parloff, M. B., Kelman, H. C., & Frank, J. D. Comfort, effectiveness, and self-awareness as criteria for improvement in psychotherapy. *American Journal of Psychiatry*, 1954, **111**, 343–351.

Parry, H. J., & Crossley, H. M. Validity of responses to survey questions. *Public Opinion Quarterly*, 1950, **14**, 61–80.

Parsons, T. *The Social System.* Glencoe, Ill.: Free Press, 1951.

Parton, D. A. Imitative response to an animated puppet. Paper presented at the meeting of the Society for Research in Child Development, New York, March 1967.

Pascal, G. R. *Behavioral Change in the Clinic—A Systematic Approach.* New York: Grune & Stratton, 1959.

Pascal, G. R., & Jenkins, W. O. A study of the early environment of workhouse alcoholics and its relationship to adult behavior. *Quarterly Journal of Studies of Alcohol*, 1960, **21**, 40–50.

Pascal, G. R., & Jenkins, W. O. *Systematic Observation of Gross Human Behavior.* New York: Grune & Stratton, 1961.

Patterson, G. R. Responsiveness to social stimuli. In L. Krasner & L. P. Ullmann (Eds.), *Research in Behavior Modification: New Developments and Implications.* New York: Holt, 1965. Pp. 157–178. (a)

Patterson, G. R. An application of conditioning techniques to the control of a hyperactive child. In L. P. Ullmann & L. Krasner (Eds.), *Case Studies in Behavior Modification.* New York: Holt, 1965. Pp. 370–375. (b)

Patterson, G. R., & Anderson, D. Peers as social reinforcers. *Child Development*, 1964, **35**, 951–960.

Patterson, G. R., Shaw, D. A., & Ebner, M. J. Teachers, peers, and parents as agents of change in the classroom. In F. A. M. Benson (Ed.), *Modifying Deviant Social Behaviors in Various Classroom Settings.* Eugene, Ore.: Univ. of Oregon, College of Education, 1969. Pp. 13–47.

Paul, G. L. *Insight vs. Desensitization: An Experiment in Anxiety Reduction.* Stanford, Calif.: Stanford, 1966.

Paul, G. L. Inhibition of physiological response to stressful imagery by relaxation training and hypnotically suggested relaxation. *Behaviour Research and Therapy*, 1969, **7**, 249–256. (a)

Paul, G. L. Outcome of systematic desensitization II: Controlled investigations of individual treatment, technique variations, and current status. In C. M. Franks (Ed.), *Behavior Therapy: Appraisal and Status.* New York: Mc-Graw-Hill, 1969. Pp. 105–159. (b)

Pavlov, I. P. *Conditioned Reflexes: An Investigation of the Physiological Activity of the Cerebral Cortex.* (Translated and edited by G. V. Anrep.) London: Oxford Univ. Press, 1927. (Republished: New York, Dover, 1960.)

Pavlov, I. P. *Lectures on Conditioned Reflexes.* (Translated by W. H. Gantt.) New York: International Publishers, 1928.

Pavlov, I. P. The conditioned reflex (written in 1935). In I. P. Pavlov, *Conditioned Reflexes and Psychiatry.* (Translated and edited by W. H. Gantt.) New York: International Publishers, 1941.

Payne, S. L. Interviewer memory faults. *Public Opinion Quarterly*, 1949, **13**, 684–685.

Peak, H. Problems of objective observation. In L. Festinger & D. Katz (Eds.), *Research Methods in the Behavioral Sciences.* New York: Dryden, 1953. Pp. 243–299.

Peck, R. F., & Havighurst, R. J. *The Psychology of Character Development.* New York: Wiley, 1960.

Persons, T. *The Social System.* Glencoe, Ill.: Free Press, 1951.

Peterson, R. F. Imitation: A basic behavioral mechanism. In H. N. Sloane, Jr., & B. D. MacAulay (Eds.), *Operant Procedures in Remedial Speech and Language Training.* Boston: Houghton Mifflin, 1968. Pp. 61–74.

Pfaffman, C. Sensory processes and their relation to behavior: Studies on the sense of taste as a model S-R system. In S. Koch (Ed.), *Psychology: a Study of a Science.* Vol. IV. New York: McGraw-Hill, 1962. Pp. 380–416.

Phillips, E. L., & Wiener, D. N. *Short-Term Psychotherapy and Structured Behavior Change.* New York: McGraw-Hill, 1966.

Piaget, G. W., & Lazarus, A. A. The use of rehearsal-desensitization. *Psychotherapy: Theory, Research and Practice,* 1969, **6**, 264–266.

Pinneau, S. R., & Milton, A. The ecological veracity of the self-report. *Journal of Genetic Psychology,* 1958, **93**, 249–276.

Polansky, N., Freeman, W., Horowitz, M., Irwin, L., Paponia, N., Rapaport, D., & Whaley, F. Problems of interpersonal relations in research on groups. *Human Relations,* 1949, **2**, 281–291.

Polsky, N. *Hustlers, Beats, and Others.* New York: Doubleday, 1969.

Powell, J., & Azrin, N. The effects of shock as a punisher for cigarette smoking. *Journal of Applied Behavior Analysis,* 1968, **1**, 63–72.

Powers, R. B., Cheney, C. D., & Agostino, N. R. Errorless training of a visual discrimination in preschool children. *The Psychological Record,* 1970, **20**, 45–50.

Premack, D. Toward empirical behavioral laws: I. Positive reinforcement. *Psychological Review,* 1959, **66**, 219–233.

Premack, D. Reversibility of the reinforcement relation. *Science,* 1962, **136**, 255–257.

Premack, D. Reinforcement theory. In D. Levine (Ed.), *Nebraska Symposium on Motivation.* Lincoln, Neb.: Univ. of Nebraska Press, 1965. Pp. 123–180.

Public Health Service. Clarification of procedures on clinical research and investigations involving human subjects. December 12, 1966.

Purcell, K. The TAT and antisocial behavior. *Journal of Consulting Psychology,* 1956, **20**, 449–456.

Purcell, K., & Brady, K. Adaptation to the invasion of privacy: Monitoring behavior with a miniature radio transmitter. *Merrill-Palmer Quarterly of Behavior and Development,* 1966, **12**, 242–254.

Pyles, M. K., Stolz, H. R., & Macfarlane, J. W. The accuracy of mothers' reports on birth and developmental data. *Child Development,* 1935, **6**, 165–176.

Pytkowicz, A. R., Wagner, N. N., Sarason, I. G. An experimental study of the reduction of hostility through fantasy. *Journal of Personality and Social Psychology,* 1967, **5**, 295–303.

Rachman, S. Aversion therapy: Chemical or electrical? *Behaviour Research and Therapy,* 1965, **2**, 289–300.

Rachman, S. Studies in desensitization—II. Flooding. *Behaviour Research and Therapy,* 1966, **4**, 1–6.

Rachman, S. *Phobias: Their Nature and Control.* Springfield, Ill.: Thomas 1968.

Rachman, S. Clinical applications of observational learning, imitation and modeling. *Behavior Therapy*, **3**, 379–397.

Rachman, S., & Teasdale, J. *Aversion Therapy and Behaviour Disorders: An Analysis.* Coral Gables, Fla.: Univ. of Miami Press, 1969.

Rapp, D. W. Detection of observer bias in the written record. Unpublished manuscript, University of Georgia, 1965. Cited in Rosenthal, R. *Experimenter Effects in Behavioral Research.* New York: Appleton Century Crofts, 1966.

Raush, H. L., Dittman, A. T., & Taylor, T. J. Person, setting, and change in social interaction: II. A normal control study. *Human Relations*, 1960, **13**, 305–332.

Regester, D. C. Change in autonomic responsivity and drinking behavior of alcoholics as a function of aversion therapy. *Proceedings, 80th Annual Convention*, American Psychological Association, 1972, 409–410.

Reinhert, R. E., & Bowen, W. T. Social drinking following treatment for alcoholism. *Bulletin of the Menninger Clinic*, 1968, **32**, 280–290.

Riesman, D., & Ehrlich, J. Age and authority in the interview. *Public Opinion Quarterly*, 1961, **25**, 39–56.

Riley, M. W. Sources and types of sociological data. In R. E. L. Faris (Ed.), *Handbook of Modern Sociology.* Chicago: Rand McNally, 1964. Pp. 978–1026.

Rimm, D. C., & Mahoney, M. J. The application of reinforcement and participant modeling procedures in the treatment of snake-phobic behavior. *Behaviour Research and Therapy*, 1969, **7**, 369–376.

Rimm, D. C., & Medeiros, D. C. The role of muscle relaxation in participant modeling. *Behaviour Research and Therapy*, 1970, **8**, 127–132.

Risley, T., & Wolf, M. M. Experimental manipulation of autistic behaviours and generalization into the home. In R. Ulrich, T. Stachnik, & J. Mabry (Eds.), *Control of Human Behavior.* Glenview, Ill.: Scott, Foresman, 1966. Pp. 193–198.

Ritter, B. The Group densitization of children's snake phobias using vicarious and contact desensitization procedures. *Behaviour Research and Therapy*, 1968, **6**, 1–6.

Ritter, B. Treatment of acrophobia with contact desensitization. *Behaviour Research and Therapy*, 1969, **7**, 41–45. (a)

Ritter, B. The use of contact desensitization, demonstration-plus-participation and demonstration alone in the treatment of acrophobia. *Behaviour Research and Therapy*, 1969, **7**, 157–164. (b)

Robbins, L. C. The accuracy of parental recall of aspects of child development and of child rearing practices. *Journal of Abnormal and Social Behavior*, 1963, **66**, 261–270.

Robbins, L. L., & Wallerstein, R. S. The research strategy and tactics of the psychotherapy research project of the Menninger Foundation and the problem of controls. In E. A. Rubinstein, & M. B. Parloff (Eds.), *Research in Psychotherapy*, Vol. I. Washington, D. C.: American Psychological Association, 1959. Pp. 27–43.

Roberts, R. R., Jr., & Renzaglia, G. A. The influence of tape recording on counseling. *Journal of Counseling Psychology*, 1965, **12**, 10–15.

Robie, W. F. An unsolicited life-story, *The Art of Love*. New York: Paperback Library, 1963. Pp. 188–206.

Robinson, D., & Rohde, S. Two experiments with an anti-Semitism poll. *Journal of Abnormal and Social Psychology*, 1946, **41**, 136–144.

Roethlisberger, F. J. *Management and Morale*. Cambridge, Mass.: Harvard, 1950.

Roethlisberger, F. J., & Dickson, W. J. (1939), as cited in J. Madge, *The Tools of Social Science*. New York: Doubleday, 1965. P. 154.

Rogers, A. H. Videotape feedback in group psychotherapy. *Psychotherapy: Theory, Research and Practice*, 1968, **5**, 37–39.

Rogers, C. R. *Client-Centered Therapy*. Boston: Houghton Mifflin, 1951.

Rogers, C. R. *On Becoming A Person*. Boston: Houghton Mifflin, 1961.

Rogers, C. R., and Dymond, R. F. (Eds.), *Psychotherapy and Personality Change*. Chicago: Univ. of Chicago Press, 1954.

Rosekrans, M. A., & Hartup, W. Imitative influences of consistent and inconsistent response consequences to a model on aggressive behavior in children. *Journal of Personality and Social Psychology*, 1967, **7**, 429–434.

Rosen, I. *The Pathology and Treatment of Sexual Deviation: A Methodological Approach*. London: Oxford Univ. Press, 1964.

Rosenbaum, M. E. The effect of stimulus and background factors on the volunteering response. *Journal of Abnormal and Social Psychology*, 1956, **53**, 118–121.

Rosenbaum, M. E. Effect of direct and vicarious verbalization on retention. *Child Development*, 1962, **33**, 103–110.

Rosenbaum, M. E., Chalmers, D. K., & Horne, W. C. Effects of success and failure and the competence of the model on the acquisition and reversal of matching behavior. *Journal of Psychology*, 1962, **54**, 251–258.

Rosenblith, J. F. Learning by imitation in kindergarten children. *Child Development*, 1959, **30**, 69–80.

Rosenhan, D., & White, G. M. Observation and rehearsal as determinants of prosocial behavior. *Journal of Personality and Social Psychology*, 1967, **5**, 424–431.

Rosenthal, D. Changes in moral values following psychotherapy. *Journal of Consulting Psychology*, 1955, **19**, 431–436.

Rosenthal, D., & Frank, J. D. Psychotherapy and the placebo effect. *Psychological Bulletin*, 1956, **53**, 294–302.

Rosenthal, R. *Experimenter Effects in Behavioral Research*. New York: Appleton Century Crofts, 1966.

Rosenthal, R., & Halas, E. S. Experimenter effect in the study of invertebrate behavior. *Psychological Reports*, 1962, **11**, 251–256.

Rosenthal, R., & Jacobson, L. Teacher expectations for the disadvantaged. *Scientific American*, 1968, **218**, 19–23.

Rosenthal, T. L. Stimulus modality and aerophobia: Cautions for desensitization therapy. *American Journal of Clinical Hypnosis*, 1967, **9**, 269–274.

Roshal, S. M. Effects of Learner Presentation in Film—Mediated Perceptual-Motor Learning. Pennsylvania State College Instructional Film Research Program, 1949.

Roth, J. A. Hired hand research. *The American Sociologist*, 1966, **4**, 190–196.

Ruebhausen, O. M., & Brim, O. G. Privacy and behavioral research. *Columbia Law Review*, 1965, **65**, 1184–1211.

Ruesch, J., Block, J., & Bennet, L. The assessment of communication: I. A method for analysis of interpersonal relations. *Journal of Psychology*, 1953, **35**, 58–80.

Saenger, G., Factors in recovery of untreated controls. *Psychiatric Quarterly*, 1970, **44**, 13–25.

Safren, M. A., & Schlesinger, L. E. Driving skill and its measurement. Unpublished manuscript, The George Washington University, 1964.

Saint-Exupéry, de A. *Airman's Odyssey*. London: Reynal and Hitchcock, 1942.

Salter, A. *Conditioned Reflex Therapy: The Direct Approach to the Reconstruction of Personality*. New York: Farrar, Straus & Young, 1949. (Republished: New York, Capricorn Books, 1961.)

Salter, A. *The Case Against Psychoanalysis*. New York: Holt, 1952.

Salzinger, K., Feldman, R. S., Cowan, J. E., & Salzinger, S. Operant conditioning of verbal behavior of two young speech-deficient boys. In L. Krasner & L. P. Ullmann (Eds.), *Research in Behavior Modification: New Developments and Implications*. New York: Holt, 1965. Pp. 82–105.

Sanders, R. M., Hopkins, B. L., & Walker, M. B. An inexpensive method for making data records of complex behaviors. *Journal of Applied Behavior Analysis*, 1969, **2**, 221–222.

Sapon, S. M. Contingency management in the modification of verbal behavior in disadvantaged children. Paper presented at the meeting of the American Psychological Association, Washington, D. C., 1967.

Sarason, I. G. Verbal learning, modeling, and juvenile delinquency. *American Psychologist*, 1968, **23**, 254–266.

Sarbin, T. R., & Allen, V. L. Role theory. In G. Lindsey, *Handbook of Social Psychology*, I. Reading, Mass.: Addison Wesley, 1954. Pp. 488–567.

Sargent, H. D. Methodological problems of follow-up studies in psychotherapy research. *American Journal of Orthopsychiatry*, 1960, **30**, 495–506.

Schaefer, J. B., & Norman, M. Punishment and aggression in fantasy responses of boys with antisocial character traits. *Journal of Personality and Social Psychology*, 1967, **6**, 237–240.

Schaeffer, R. W. Contributions of the operant level of the instrumental response to the reinforcement relation. Unpublished doctoral dissertation, University of Missouri, 1962.

Schaffer, L., & Myers, J. K. Psychotherapy and social stratification: An empirical study of practice in psychiatric outpatient clinic. *Psychiatry*, 1954, **17**, 83–93.

Schanck, R. L. A study of a community and its groups and institutions conceived of as behaviors of individuals. *Psychological Monographs*, 1932, **XLIII**, No. 2.

Schein, E., & Bennis, W. *Personal and Organizational Change through Group Methods*. New York: Wiley, 1965.

Schopenhauer, A. *Collected writings*. In T. Bailey (Ed.), *Complete Essays of Schopenhauer, Book IV—Studies in Pessimism*. New York: Wiley, 1942.

Schubot, E. D. The influence of hypnotic and muscular relaxation in systematic desensitization of phobias. Unpublished doctoral dissertation, Stanford University, 1966.

Schuldt, W. J., & Truax, C. B. Variability of outcome in psychotherapeutic research. *Journal of Counseling Psychology*, 1970, **17**, 405–408.

Schulmann, J. L., & Reisman, J. M. An objective measurement of hyperactivity. *American Journal of Mental Deficiency*, 1959, **64**, 455–456.

Schwitzgebel, R. K. *Streetcorner Research: An Experimental Approach to the Juvenile Delinquent.* Cambridge, Mass.: Harvard, 1964.

Schwitzgebel, R. K. Electronic innovation in the behavioral sciences: A call to responsibility. *American Psychologist*, 1967, **22**, 364–370. (a)

Schwitzgebel, R. K. Positive concepts of privacy in research. *New England Journal of Medicine*, 1967, **276**, 282–283. (b)

Schwitzgebel, R. K. Analysis of data sources used by behavioral science disciplines. Unpublished manuscript, Harvard University, Department of Social Relations, 1967. (c)

Schwitzgebel, R. K. Electronic alternatives to imprisonment. *Lex et Scientia*, 1968, **5**, 99–104. (a)

Schwitzgebel, R. K. Ethical problems in experimentation with offenders. *American Journal of Orthopsychiatry*, 1968, **38**, 738–748. (b)

Schwitzgebel, R. K. Confidentiality of research information in public health studies. *Harvard Legal Commentary*, 1969, **6**, 187–197. (a)

Schwitzgebel, R. K. Development of an electronic rehabilitation system for parolees. *Law and Computer Technology*, 1969, **2**, 9–12. (b)

Schwitzgebel, R. K. Issues in the use of an electronic rehabilitation system with chronic recidivists. *Law and Society Review*, 1969, **3**, 597–611. (c)

Schwitzgebel, R. K. *Development and Legal Regulation of Coercive Behavior Modification Techniques with Offenders.* Washington, D. C.: National Institute of Mental Health, 1970. (a)

Schwitzgebel, R. K. Ethical and legal aspects of behavioral instrumentation. *Behavior Therapy*, 1970, **1**, 498–509. (b)

Schwitzgebel, R. K., & Baer, D. J. Intensive supervision by parole officers as a factor in recidivism reduction of male delinquents. *The Journal of Psychology*, 1967, **67**, 75–82.

Schwitzgebel, R. K., Schwitzgebel, R. L., Pahnke, W. N., & Hurd, W. S. A program of research in behavioral electronics. *Behavioral Science*, 1964, **9**, 233–238.

Schwitzgebel, R. K., & Traugott, M. Initial note on the placebo effect of machines. *Behavioral Science*, 1968, **13**, 267–273.

Schwitzgebel, R. L. A simple behavioral system for recording and implementing change in natural settings. Unpublished doctoral dissertation, Harvard University, 1964.

Schwitzgebel, R. L. Short-term operant conditioning of adolescent offenders on socially relevant variables. *Journal of Abnormal Psychology*, 1967, **72**, 134–142.

Schwitzgebel, R. L. Survey of electromechanical devices for behavior modification. *Psychological Bulletin*, 1968, **70**, 444–459.

Schwitzgebel, R. L. Preliminary socialization for psychotherapy of behavior-disordered adolescents. *Journal of Consulting and Clinical Psychology,* 1969, **33**, 71–77.

Schwitzgebel, R. L. Behavior instrumentation and social technology. *American Psychologist,* 1970, **25**, 491–499.

Schwitzgebel, R. L., & Schwitzgebel, R. K. (Eds.) *Psychotechnology: Electronic Control of Mind and Behavior.* New York: Holt, 1973.

Schwitzgebel, R., & Kolb, D. A. Inducing behaviour change in adolescent delinquents. *Behaviour Research and Therapy,* 1964, **1**, 297–304.

Scott, J. P., & Fuller, J. L. *Genetics and Social Behavior of the Dog.* Chicago: Univ. of Chicago Press, 1965.

Sears, R. R., Maccoby, E. E., & Levin, H. *Patterns of Child Rearing.* New York: Harper & Row, 1957.

Sechrest, L. Situational sampling and contrived situations in the assessment of behavior. Unpublished manuscript, Northwestern University, 1965.

Secord, P. F., & Backman, C. W. *Social Psychology.* New York: McGraw-Hill, 1964.

Seitz, P. F. D. Experiments in the substitution of symptoms by hypnosis: II. *Psychosomatic Medicine,* 1953, **15**, 405–422.

Sells, S. B. Dimensions of stimulus situations which account for behavior variance. In S. B. Sells (Ed.), *Stimulus Determinants of Behavior.* New York: Ronald, 1963. Pp. 3–15.

Selltiz, C., Jahoda, M., Deutsch, M., & Cook, G. W. *Research Methods in Social Relations.* New York: Holt, 1959.

Shah, S. A. Preparation for release and community follow-up: Conceptualization of some basic issues, specific approaches, and intervention strategies. In H. L. Cohen, I. Goldiamond, J. Filipszak, & R. Pooley (Eds.), *Training Professionals in Procedures for the Establishment of Educational Environments.* Silver Spring, Md.: Educational Facility Press, 1968. Pp. F6-1–F6-20.

Shapiro, A. K. A contribution to the history of the placebo effect. *Behavioral Science,* 1960, **5**, 109–135.

Shapiro, M. B. A method for measuring psychological changes specified to the individual psychiatric patient. *British Journal of Medical Psychology,* 1961, **34**, 151–155.

Shaw, G. B. *The Adventures of the Black Girl in Her Search for God.* London: Constable, 1932.

Sheffield, F. D. Relation between classical conditioning and instrumental learning. In W. F. Prokasy (Ed.), *Classical Conditioning: A Symposium.* New York: Appleton Century Crofts, 1965. Pp. 302–322.

Sherif, M., & Sherif, C. *Groups in Harmony and Tension.* New York: Harper, 1953.

Sherrington, C. *Man on His Nature.* New York: Doubleday, 1955.

Shils, E. A. Social inquiry and the autonomy of the individual. In D. Lerner (Ed.), *The Human Meaning of the Social Sciences.* New York: World Publishing, 1959. Pp. 114–157.

Sidman, M. *Tactics of Scientific Research: Evaluating Experimental Data in Psychology.* New York: Basic Books, 1960.

Sidman, M. Operant techniques. In A. J. Bachrach (Ed.), *Experimental Foundations of Clinical Psychology.* New York: Basic Books, 1962. Pp. 170–210.

Sidman, M., & Stoddard, L. The effectiveness of fading in programming a simultaneous form discrimination for retarded children. *Journal of the Experimental Analysis of Behavior,* 1967, **10**, 3–15.

Sidowski, J. B. (Ed.), *Experimental Methods and Instrumentation in Psychology.* New York: McGraw-Hill, 1966.

Sidowski, J. B., & Ross, S. Instrumentation in psychology. *American Psychologist,* 1969, **24**, 187–198.

Simkins, L. The reliability of self-recorded behaviors. *Behavior Therapy,* 1971, **2**, 83–87. (a)

Simkins, L. A rejoinder to Nelson and McReynolds on the self-recording of behavior. *Behavior Therapy,* 1971, **2**, 598–691. (b)

Skinner, B. F. Two types of conditioned reflex and a pseudo type. *Journal of General Psychology,* 1935, **12**, 66–77.

Skinner, B. F. *The Behavior of Organisms: An Experimental Analysis.* New York: Appleton Century Crofts, 1938.

Skinner, B. F. *Science and Human Behavior.* New York: Macmillan, 1953.

Skinner, B. F. A case history in scientific method. *American Psychologist,* 1956, **11**, 221–233.

Slack, C. W. Introducing intensive office treatment for unreachable cases. *Mental Hygiene,* 1960, **44**, 238–256.

Smith, H. L., & Hyman, H. The biasing effect of interviewer expectations on survey results. *Public Opinion Quarterly,* 1950, **14**, 491–506.

Smith, W. I., & Moore, J. W. *Conditioning and Instrumental Learning.* New York: McGraw-Hill, 1966.

Solomon, R. J. Operant conditioning techniques as applied to juvenile delinquency. Senior thesis, Harvard University, 1966.

Solomon, R. W. An extension of control group design. *Psychological Bulletin,* 1949, **46**, 137–150.

Soskin, W., & John, V. P. The study of spontaneous talk. In R. Barker (Ed.), *The Stream of Behavior.* New York: Appleton Century Crofts, 1963. Pp. 228–282.

Speer, D. C., & Zold, A., An example of self-selection bias in follow-up research. *Journal of Clinical Psychology,* 1971, **27**, 64–68.

Spence, K. W. The role of secondary reinforcement in delayed reward learning. *Psychological Review,* 1947, **54**, 1–8.

Spence, K. W. *Behavior Theory and Conditioning.* New Haven: Yale, 1956.

Spielberger, C. D., & DeNike, L. D. Descriptive behaviorism versus cognitive theory in verbal operant conditioning. *Psychological Review,* 1966, **73**, 306–326.

Staats, A. W. *Learning, Language, and Cognition.* New York: Holt, 1968.

Staats, A. W. Development, use, and social extensions of reinforcer (motivational) systems in the solution of human problems. Paper presented at the Conference on Behavior Modification, Honolulu, January 1969.

Staats, A. W., & Staats, C. K. *Complex Human Behavior.* New York: Holt, 1964.

Stafford-Clark, D. Essentials of the clinical approach. In I. Rosen (Ed.), *The Pathology and Treatment of Sexual Deviation.* London: Oxford University Press, 1964. Pp. 57–86.

Stampfl, T. G., & Levis, D. J. Phobic patients: Treatment with the learning theory approach of implosive therapy. *Voices,* 1967, **3**, 23–27.

Stampfl, T. G., & Levis, D. J. Implosive therapy—a behavioral therapy? *Behaviour Research and Therapy,* 1968, **6**, 31–36.

Stekel, W. *Sexual Aberrations.* Vol. 2. London: Liveright, 1952.

Sternberg, R. S., Chapman, J., & Shakow, D. Psychotherapy research and the problem of intrusions on privacy. *Psychiatry,* 1958, **21**, 195–203.

Stinchcombe, A. L. *Rebellion in High School.* Chicago: Quadrangle, 1964.

Stoller, F. H. Group psychotherapy on television. *American Psychologist,* 1967, **22**, 158–162.

Strauss, A. Regularized status-passage. In W. G. Bennis, E. V. Schein, D. E. Berlew, & F. I. Steele (Eds.), *Interpersonal Dynamics.* Homewood, Ill.: Dorsey, 1964. Pp. 409–416.

Strupp, H. H. *Psychotherapists in Action.* New York: Grune & Stratton, 1960.

Strupp, H. H. Psychotherapy. *Annual Review of Psychology,* 1962, **13**, 475–478.

Strupp, H. H. Discussion of "The effects of psychotherapy." *International Journal of Psychiatry,* 1965, **1**, 165–169.

Strupp, H. H. *Psychotherapy and the Modification of Abnormal Behavior: An Introduction to Theory and Research.* New York: McGraw-Hill, 1971. Chapter 8.

Stuart, R. B. Operant-interpersonal treatment for marital discord. *Journal of Consulting and Clinical Psychology,* 1969, **33**, 675–682.

Subcommittee on Evaluation of Mental Health Activities, Community Services Committee, National Advisory Mental Health Council. *Evaluation in Mental Health: A Review of the Problem of Evaluating Mental Health Activities.* Washington, D. C.: Department of Health, Education and Welfare, 1955.

Sulzer, E. S. Behavior modification in adult psychiatric patients. In L. P. Ullmann & L. Krasner (Eds.), *Case Studies in Behavior Modification.* New York: Holt, 1965. Pp. 196–200.

Sutherland, E. H., & Cressey, D. R. *Principles of Criminology.* New York: Lippincott, 1960.

Sutherland, G. F. Salivary conditional reflexes in man. In J. Wortis (Ed.), *Recent Advances in Biological Psychiatry.* Vol. IV. New York: Plenum Press, 1962. Pp. 29–37.

Tamisian, J. A., & McReynolds, W. T. Use of parents as behavioral engineers in the treatment of a school-phobic girl. *Journal of Counseling Psychology,* 1971, **18**, 225–228.

Tasto, D. L. Systematic desensitization, muscle relaxation and visual imagery in the counterconditioning of a four-year-old phobic child. *Behaviour Research and Therapy,* 1969, **7**, 409–411.

Terrace, H. S. Discrimination learning with and without errors. *Journal of the Experimental Analysis of Behavior*, 1963, **6**, 1–27.

Terrace, H. S. Stimulus control. In W. K. Honig (Ed.), *Operant Behavior: Areas of Research and Application*. New York: Appleton Century Crofts, 1966. Pp. 271–344.

Thibaut, J., & Kelley, H. *The Social Psychology of Groups*. New York: Wiley, 1959.

Thimann, J. Conditioned reflex treatment of alcoholism. II. The risks of its application, its indications, contraindications, and psychotherapeutic aspects. *New England Journal of Medicine*, 1949, **241**, 406–410.

Thomas, G., & Pattison, L. The world of the dropout. Unpublished technical report, Human Resources Development Corporation, Cambridge, Mass., 1963.

Thorne, G. L., Tharp, R. G., & Wetzel, R. J. Behavior modification techniques: New tools for probation officers. *Federal Probation*, 1967, **31**, 21–27.

Thorpe, J. G., Schmidt, E., Brown, P. T., & Castell, D. Aversion-relief therapy: A new method for general application. *Behaviour Research and Therapy*, 1964, **2**, 70–82.

Thorpe, J. G., Schmidt, E., & Castell, D. A comparison of positive and negative (aversive) conditioning in the treatment of homosexuality. *Behaviour Research and Therapy*, 1963, **1**, 357–362.

Thorpe, R. G., & Wetzel, R. J. *Behavior Modification in the Natural Environment*. New York: Academic Press, 1969.

Timmons, J. A. Black is beautiful—is it bountiful? *Harvard Business Review,* 1971, Nov–Dec, 81–94.

Tolman, E. C. *Purposive Behavior in Animals and Men*. New York: Appleton Century Crofts, 1932.

Tolman, E. C. *Collected Papers in Psychology*. Berkeley, Calif.: Univ. of California Press, 1951.

Tolman, E. C. Principles of purposive behavior. In S. Koch (Ed.), *Psychology: A Study of a Science*. Vol. II. New York: McGraw-Hill, 1959. Pp. 92–157.

Trachtman, G. M. Pupils, parents, privacy, and the school psychologist. *American Psychologist*, 1972, **27**, 37–45.

Trist, E. L., & Bramforth, K. W. Some social and psychological consequences of the Longwall Method of goal-setting. *Human Relations*, 1951, **4**, 3–38.

Truax, C. B., & Carkhuff, R. R. Significant developments in psychotherapy research. In L. E. Abt & B. F. Riess (Eds.), *Progress in Clinical Psychology*. Vol. VI. New York: Grune & Strarron, 1964. Pp. 124–155.

Tucker, H., Lewis, R. B., Martin, G. L., & Over, C. Television therapy. *A. M. A. Archives of Neurology and Psychiatry*, 1967, **77**, 57–69.

Turnbull, J. W. Asthma conceived as a learned response. *Journal of Psychosomatic Research*, 1962, **6**, 59–70.

Turner, L. H., & Solomon, R. L. Human traumatic avoidance learning: Theory and experiments on the operant-respondent distinction and failures to learn. *Psychological Monographs*, 1962, **58**, 111–116.

Tyler, V. O., Jr. Exploring the use of operant techniques in the rehabilitation of delinquent boys. Paper presented at the meeting of the American Psychological Association, Chicago, September, 1965.

Tyler, V. O., Jr. The Application of operant token reinforcement to the academic performance of an institutionalized delinquent. Paper presented at the meeting of the American Psychological Association, Chicago, September, 1965.

Tyler, V. O., Jr., & Brown, G. D. The use of swift, brief isolation as a group control device for institutionalized delinquents. *Behaviour Research and Therapy*, 1967, **5**, 1–9.

Uhlinger, C. A., & Stephens, M. W. Relation of achievement motivation to academic achievement in students of superior ability. *Journal of Educational Psychology*, 1960, **51**, 259–266.

Ullmann, L. P. On cognitions and behavior therapy. *Behavior Therapy*, 1970, **1**, 201–204.

Ullmann, L. P., & Krasner, L. (Eds.) *Case Studies in Behavior Modification*. New York: Holt, 1965.

Ullmann, L. P., & Krasner, L. *A Psychological Approach to Abnormal Behavior*. New York: Prentice-Hall, 1969.

U. S. Adjutant General's Department. *Trials of war criminals before Nuremberg Military Tribunals under Control Council law no. 10*. 1947, **2**, 181–182.

van den Berg, J. H. *The Changing Nature of Man: Introduction to a Historical Psychology*. New York: Dell, 1961.

VanderMeer, A. W. The economy of time in industrial training: An experimental study of the use of sound films in the training of engine lathe operators. *Journal of Educational Psychology*, 1945, **36**, 65–90.

van Egeren, L. F. Psychophysiological aspects of systematic desensitization: Some outstanding issues. *Behaviour Research and Therapy*, 1971, **9**, 65–77.

Vannette, W. M., & Heynen, A. J. Announcement for open house of I. T. M. Academy, Grand Rapids, Michigan, 1967.

Vaughan, W. T. *The Practice of Allergy*. London: Henry Kimpton, 1939.

Veatch, R. M. Models for ethical medicine in a revolutionary age. *The Hastings Center Report*, 1972, **2**, 5–7.

Verhave, T. An introduction to the experimental analysis of behavior. In T. Verhave (Ed.), *The Experimental Analysis of Behavior*. New York: Appleton Century Crofts, 1966. Pp. 1–47. (a)

Verhave, T. The pigeon as a quality-control inspector. In R. Ulrich, T. Stachnik, & J. Mabry (Eds.), *Control of Human Behavior*. Glenview, Ill.: Scott, Foresman, 1966. Pp. 242–246. (b)

Verplanck, W. S. The control of the content of conversation: Reinforcement of statements of opinion. *Journal of Abnormal Social Psychology*, 1955, **51**, 668–676.

Verplanck, W. S. The operant conditioning of human motor behavior. *Psychological Bulletin*, 1956, **53**, 70–83.

Wagner, M. K. Parent therapists: An operant conditioning method. *Mental Hygiene*, 1968, **52**, 452–455.

Wagner, M. K., & Cauthen, N. R. A comparison of reciprocal inhibition and operant conditioning in the systematic desensitization of a fear of snakes. *Behaviour Research and Therapy*, 1968, **6**, 225–227.

Wahler, R. G. Oppositional children: A quest for parental reinforcement control. *Journal of Applied Behavior Analysis*, 1969, **2**, 159–170.

Walker, N. *A Short History of Psychotherapy*. London: Routledge, 1957.

Walker, R. G., & Kelly, F. E. Short-term therapy with hospitalized schizophrenic patients. *Acta Psychiatrica et Neurologica Scandinavica*, 1960, **35**, 34–56.

Wallerstein, R. S. (Ed.) *Hospital Treatment of Alcoholism*. New York: Basic Books, 1957.

Walsh, W. B. Validity of self-report. *Journal of Counseling Psychology*, 1967, **14**, 18–23.

Walsh, W. B. Validity of self-report: Another look. *Journal of Counseling Psychology*, 1968, **15**, 180–186.

Walters, R. H., Bowen, N. V., & Parke, R. D. Experimentally induced disinhibition of sexual responses. Unpublished manuscript, University of Waterloo, 1963. [Cited in Bandura, A., & Walters, R. H. *Social Learning and Personality Development*. New York: Holt, 1963. Pp. 76–78.]

Walters, R. H., Leat, M., & Mezei, L. Response inhibition and disinhibition through empathetic learning. *Canadian Journal of Psychology*, 1963, **16**, 235–243.

Walters, R. H., & Parke, R. D. Influence of response consequences to a social model on resistance to deviation. *Journal of Experimental Child Psychology*, 1964, **1**, 269–280.

Walton, D., & Mather, M. D. The application of learning principles to the treatment of obsessive-compulsive states in the acute and chronic phases of illness. *Behavior Research and Therapy*, 1963, **1**, 163–174.

Warren, S. D., & Brandeis, L. D. The right to privacy. *Harvard Law Review*, 1890, **4**, 193–220.

Wasik, B. H. A postcontingency test of the effectiveness of reinforcement. *Psychonomic Science*, 1968, **13**, 87–88.

Watson, J. B. *Psychology from the Standpoint of a Behaviorist*. Philadelphia: Lippincott, 1919.

Watson, J. B., & Rayner, R. Conditioned emotional reactions. *Journal of Experimental Psychology*, 1920, **3**, 1–14.

Weber, M. *The Protestant Ethic and the Spirit of Capitalism*. (1st ed. 1904) T. Parsons (translator). New York: Scribner, 1930.

Webb, E. J., Campbell, D. T., Schwartz, R. D., & Sechrest, L. *Unobtrusive Measures: Nonreactive Research in the Social Sciences*. Chicago: Rand McNally, 1966.

Weiner, I. B. Behavior therapy in obsessive-compulsive neurosis: Treatment of an adolescent boy. *Psychotherapy: Theory, Research and Practice*, 1967, **4**, 27–29.

Weiss, D. J., & Davis, R. V. An objective validation of factual interview data. *Journal of Applied Psychology*, 1960, **44**, 381–385.

Weiss, D. J., Davis, R. V., England, G. W., & Lofquist, L. H. Validity of work histories obtained by interview. *Minnesota Studies in Vocational Rehabilitation*, 1961, **12**, 1–3.

Wells, P. T., & Feather, B. W. Effects of changing the CS-US interval on human salivary responses. *Psychophysiology*, 1968, **4**, 278–283.

Wenar, C. The reliability of mothers' histories. *Child Development*, 1961, **32**, 491–500.

Wenar, C., & Coulter, J. B. A reliability study of developmental histories. *Child Development*, 1962, **33**, 453–462.

Westin, A. *Privacy and Freedom.* New York: Atheneum, 1967.

Wetzel, R. Use of behavioral techniques in a case of compulsive stealing. *Journal of Consulting Psychology*, 1966, **30**, 367–374.

Wheeler, L., & Smith, S. Censure of the model in the contagion of aggression. *Journal of Personality and Social Psychology*, 1967, **6**, 93–98.

Wheeler, S. Delinquency and crime. In H. S. Becker (Ed.), *Social Problems: A Modern Approach.* New York: Wiley, 1966. Pp. 201–276.

White, J. G. The use of learning theory in the psychological treatment of children. In H. J. Eysenck (Ed.), *Experiments in Behaviour Therapy: Readings in Modern Methods of Treatment of Mental Disorders Derived from Learning Theory.* New York: Macmillan, 1964. Pp. 463–466.

White, R. W. Motivation reconsidered: The concept of competence. *Psychological Review*, 1959, **66**, 297–333.

White, W. *Beyond Conformity.* New York: Free Press, 1961.

Whyte, W. F. *Street Corner Society.* Chicago: Univ. of Chicago Press, 1943.

Wickens, D. D., & Wickens, C. D. Factors related to pseudo-conditioning. *Journal of Experimental Psychology*, 1942, **31**, 518–526.

Wickramasekera, I. The application of learning theory to the treatment of a case of sexual exhibitionism. *Psychotherapy: Theory, Research and Practice*, 1968, **5**, 108–112.

Willems, H. F. An ecological orientation in psychology. *The Merrill-Palmer Quarterly*, 1965, **2**, 317–343.

Williams, C. D. The elimination of tantrum behavior by extinction procedures. *Journal of Abnormal and Social Psychology*, 1959, **59**, 269.

Winter, S., Griffith, J., & Kolb, D. A. The capacity for self-direction. *Journal of Consulting Psychology*, 1968, **32**, 35–41.

Wolf, M. M., Risley, T., & Mees, H. Application of operant conditioning procedures to the behavior problems of an autistic child. *Behaviour Research and Therapy*, 1964, **1**, 305–312.

Wolfe, D. L., & Wolfe, H. M. The development of cooperative behavior in monkeys and young children. *Journal of Genetic Psychology*, 1939, **55**, 137–175.

Wolfe, J. B. Effectiveness of token-rewards for chimpanzees. *Comparative Psychology Monographs*, 1936, **12**, No. 60.

Wolfensberger, W. Ethical issues in research with human subjects. *Science*, 1967, **155**, 47–51.

Wolpe, J. Reciprocal inhibition as the main basis of psychotherapeutic effects. *A. M. A. Archives of Neurology and Psychiatry*, 1954, **72**, 205–226.

Wolpe, J. *Psychotherapy by Reciprocal Inhibition.* Stanford: Stanford Univ., 1958.

Wolpe, J. The resolution of neurotic suffering by behavioristic methods: An evaluation. *American Journal of Psychotherapy,* 1964, **18**, 23–32.

Wolpe, J. Discussion of "The Effects of Psychotherapy." *International Journal of Psychiatry,* 1965, **1**, 173–175.

Wolpe, J. *The Practice of Behavior Therapy.* Oxford: Pergamon, 1969. (a)

Wolpe, J. Basic principles and practices of behavior therapy. *American Journal of Psychiatry,* 1969, **125**, 136–141. (b)

Wolpe, J., & Flood, J. The effects of relaxation on the galvanic skin response to repeated phobic stimuli in ascending order. *Journal of Behavior Therapy and Experimental Psychiatry,* 1970, **1**, 195–200.

Wolpe, J., & Lazarus, A. A. *Behavior Therapy Techniques: A Guide to the Treatment of Neuroses.* Oxford: Pergamon, 1966.

Wolpin, M., & Raines, J. Visual imagery, expected roles, and extinction as possible factors in reducing fear and avoidance behavior. *Behaviour Research and Therapy,* 1966, **4**, 25–37.

Woodward, A. E., & Williams, A. D. Present and future applications of infra-red technology to law enforcement. In S. A. Yefsky (Ed.) *Law Enforcement Science and Technology.* London: Academic Press, 1967. Pp. 835–841.

Wooster, H. Basic research. *Science,* 1959, 130, 126.

World Medical Association. *Declaration of Helsinki.* Helsinki: WMA, 1964.

Wortis, J. Pavlovianism and clinical psychiatry. In J. Wortis (Ed.) *Recent Advances in Biological Psychiatry,* vol. IV. New York: Plenum Press, 1962. Pp. 13–23.

Yates, A. J. The application of learning theory to the treatment of tics. *Journal of Abnormal and Social Psychology,* 1958, **56**, 175–182.

Yates, A. J. Symptoms and symptom substitution. *Psychological Review,* 1958, **55**, 371–374.

Yerkes, R. M. Suggestibility in chimpanzee. *Journal of Social Psychology,* 1934, **5**, 271–282.

Zachs, G. Collaborative therapy for smokers. Unpublished manuscript, Harvard University, 1965.

Zahn, C. J., & Yarrow, M. R. Conditions influencing imitative performance. *Proceedings, 76th Annual Convention,* American Psychological Association, 1968, 339–340.

Zax, M., & Klein, A. Measurement of personality and behavior change following psychotherapy. *Psychological Bulletin,* 1960, **57**, 435–448.

Zetzel, E. R. Discussion of "The Effects of Psychotherapy." *International Journal of Psychiatry,* 1965, **1**, 144–150.

Zigler, E. Social reinforcement, environmental conditions and the child. *American Journal of Orthopsychiatry,* 1963, **33**, 614–623.

Zimmerman, E. H., & Zimmerman, J. The alteration of behavior in a special classroom situation. *Journal of the Experimental Analysis of Behavior,* 1962, **5**, 59–60.

Zwerling, I., & Rosenbaum, M. Alcoholic addiction and personality. In S. Arieti (Ed.) *American Handbook of Psychiatry.* Vol. I. New York: Basic Books, 1959. Pp. 623–644.

Name Index

Adams, J. M., 228, 237
Adamson, R., 73
Addison, R. M., 78
Afflect, D. C., 213
Agostino, N. R., 90
Agras, W. S., 23, 117, 133, 137, 247
Al-Issa, I., 16, 24
Allen, B. P., 228
Allport, G. W., 161, 220
Alschuler, A. S., 148, 153
Alumbaugh, R. V., 265
American Medical Association, 262, 264
American Psychological Association, 262
Anant, S. S., 109
Anderson, D., 135
Anderson, N., 236
Anderson, T., 42
Aronoff, J., 155
Asch, S. E., 140

Athey, K. R., 232
Atkinson, J. W., 150, 151, 157
Atthowe, L., 79
Auerbach, A. H., 212
Ayllon, T., 78, 82
Azrin, N. H., 52, 53, 78, 82, 115, 116, 230, 246

Bachrach, H. M., 212
Bach-y-Rita, G., 249
Backman, C. W., 172
Baer, D. M., 54, 92, 124
Bailey, J. B., 52, 56
Ball, J. C., 229
Ballachey, E., 220
Bamforth, K. W., 238
Ban, T. A., 96
Bancroft, G., 228

Bancroft, J. H. J., 115
Bandura, A., 55, 125, 126, 128–130, 132–
136, 138, 149, 166
Barch, A. M., 142, 257
Barclay, A. M., 115
Barker, R. G., 234, 235
Barlow, D. H., 117, 133, 247
Baron, A., 54
Barrett, B. H., 78
Barron, F., 213, 216, 218
Bass, M. J., 100
Bath, K., 68
Baum, M., 23
Baumrind, D., 266
Becker, H., 184, 186, 188, 189
Becker, H. S., 236
Becker, R., 247
Beecher, H. K., 255
Benne, K., 167
Benney, M., 232
Bennis, W. G., 167, 198, 200, 202
Bentler, P. M., 13, 27, 28
Berger, S. M., 144
Bergin, A. E., 18, 207
Berk, R. A., 228, 237
Berkowitz, L., 134, 138
Berlew, D. E., 172, 174, 192, 198
Bernal, M. E., 56, 68–70, 139
Berzon, B., 166, 167, 169, 170, 203
Bevan, W., 73, 74
Bijou, S. W., 137
Blake, R. R., 141, 142
Blakemore, C. B., 115
Blanchard, E. B., 130, 133
Blane, H., 231
Blumberg, A., 167
Bond, I. K., 16
Bookbinder, L. J., 19
Bootzin, R. R., 133
Bostow, D. F., 52, 56
Boulding, K., 201
Boulougouris, J. C., 23
Bowen, N. V., 140
Bowen, W. T., 110
Boyatzis, R. E., 172
Bradford, C. P., 167
Brady, K., 248
Braginsky, B. M., 230
Braginsky, D. D., 230
Brandeis, L. D., 249
Branel, D. A., 247

Brayfield, A., 179
Breger, L., 21, 25
Bremer, D., 108
Breuer, J., 5–7
Brill, N. Q., 223
Brim, O. G., 249
Broden, M., 243
Brown, B. M., 21
Brown, G. D., 136
Brown, P., 138
Brown, P. T., 116
Brown, R., 140, 173, 196, 197
Brunswik, E., 212, 220
Bryan, J. H., 142, 143, 257
Buber, M., 145
Buehler, R. E., 140
Buell, J., 54
Burchard, J. D., 81
Burns, B. J., 68
Burton, R. V., 229
Butler, J., 219

Callahan, E. J., 133
Campbell, B. A., 66
Campbell, D. T., 135, 208–211, 216, 217
Cannell, C. F., 228
Cantril, H., 221, 232
Carkhuff, R. R., 177
Carlisle, J. M., 113
Carlson, D., 42
Carrera, R., 10
Carter, C. W., 253
Cartwright, D. S., 215
Castell, D., 116
Cautela, J. R., 78, 109
Cauthen, N. R., 27
Cavan, S., 238
Chalmers, D. K., 140
Champaign, S. D., 10
Chandler, J. P., 141
Chandler, M., 212
Chapman, J., 247
Chassan, J. B., 245
Cheney, C. D., 90
Chittenden, G. E., 138
Church, R. M., 66, 115
Clark, D. F., 10
Clark, R. W., 150
Cleveland, S. E., 110
Cloward, R. A., 139

Cocteau, J., 103
Cohen, B. B., 16
Cohen, H. L., 79–82, 89, 91
Cohen, J., 212
Cohler, B., 219
Coleman, J. E., 232
Coleman, J. S., 189
Condon, W. S., 235
Cook, G. W., 212
Cook, S. W., 254, 262, 266, 269
Cooke, G., 22, 28
Cooper, C. L., 167
Corbin, H. H., 228
Coulter, J. B., 229
Cowles, J. T., 79
Cox, D. E., 270
Cox, G. H., 246
Crawford, M. P., 51
Cremerius, J., 215
Cressey, D. R., 139
Crisp, A. H., 20
Cronbach, L. J., 219
Crowder, J. E., 19
Crumpton, E., 223
Crutchfield, R., 220
Csanvi, A. P., 77
Cumming, W. W., 39, 40
Curtiss, K. A., 166

Daniel, W. J., 51
Darley, J., 268
Darlington, R. B., 142
Davidson, H. A., 207
Davis, D. L., 110
Davis, D. P., 167
Davis, R. V., 228, 230
Davis, V. E., 110
Davison, G. C., 16, 22, 23, 26, 51
Dawe, P. G., 247
de Baca, P. C., 77
Declaration of Helsinki, 262
Dekker, E., 96, 98
Delgado, J. M. R., 249
Dembroski, T. M., 228
DeMyer, M. K., 51
DeNike, L. D., 54
Denton, J. C., 228
Deutch, M., 237
Deutsch, M., 212
Devine, J. V., 77

Ditman, K. S., 109
Dittman, A. T., 234
Dohan, J. L., 216
Dollard, J., 124
Donner, L., 24
Dulany, D. E., 54
Dunlap, K., 10
Duryea, R., 142
Duryee, J. S., 68
Dykman, R. A., 99
Dymond, R. F., 209, 211, 212, 214, 222

Ebner, M. J., 203
Eddy, W. B., 167
Edington, E. S., 245
Edwards, A. L., 219
Edwards, J. E., 22
Efran, J. S., 25
Ehrlich, J., 232
Eiduson, S., 223
Eisenberger, R., 92
Ekman, P., 247
Elliott, R., 138
Ellison, G. D., 107
England, G. W., 228
Erikson, E. H., 185, 189
Ervin, F., 249
Evans, R. I., 228
Eysenck, H. J., 3, 4, 17, 18, 20, 206, 212–
    215, 219

Fairweather, G. W., 219, 222
Feldman, M. P., 116
Fenichel, O., 142
Fesbach, S., 136–138
Festinger, L., 180, 194
Filipczak, J., 79
Findley, J. D., 71, 72, 78
Fishman, S. T., 23
Flood, J., 22
Folkins, C. H., 25
Forsyth, P. P., 219, 222
Foshee, J. G., 246
Fowler, H., 67
Fox, R., 189
Frank, J. D., 179, 180, 210–212, 214, 216,
    217, 222, 223
Franks, C. M., 109
Freed, A., 141

Freeman, W., 237
French, E. G., 151
French, F. R. P., 178
French, N. R., 253
Freud, S., 5–8, 37, 141, 149, 223, 247
Freund, K., 113
Friedlander, B. Z., 246
Friesen, W. V., 247
Fuller, J. L., 118
Furniss, J. M., 140

Gaier, E. L., 247
Gantt, W. H., 106, 107, 118
Garfield, S. L., 207
Gaylin, W., 111
Geen, R. G., 134
Geer, B., 184, 186
Geer, J. H., 129
Gelder, M. G., 20, 115
Gewirtz, J. L., 92
Gibb, J., 167
Gibbs, D. N., 16
Glover, E., 18, 141, 207
Goffman, E., 144, 236
Gold, M., 136
Golden, R. I., 101, 102
Goldfried, M. R., 27
Goldiamond, L., 79, 90, 91, 95, 162, 164,
    165, 179, 230, 241
Goldman, J., 246
Goldstein, A. J., 22, 27
Goldstein, A. P., 179, 214, 217, 222
Golembiewski, R. T., 167
Gonzales, M. A., 77
Goodwin, D. W., 108
Gordon, J. E., 136
Gordova, T. N., 109
Graubard, P. S., 81
Graves, T. D., 139
Grayson, H. M., 223
Graziano, A. M., 16
Griffith, J., 172
Groen, J., 96, 98
Gruber, R. P., 28
Grusec, J. E., 129
Guerner, G. G., 24
Guest, L., 231
Guthrie, E. R., 21, 92

Haggard, E. A., 247
Hagiwara, R., 249

Haith, M. M., 247
Halas, E. S., 240
Haley, J., 184, 193–195
Hall, C. S., 176
Hall, D., 202, 204
Hall, R. V., 243
Haloburdo, J., 249
Hamilton, C., 98
Hanson, R. C., 139
Harby, S. F., 126
Haring, N. G., 246
Harlow, H. F., 172
Harris, A. D., 240
Harris, F. R., 54
Hartup, W., 135
Harvard Law Review, 249
Hathaway, S. R., 222
Havighurst, R. J., 142
Hawkins, R. F., 137
Haynes, S. N., 115
Heath, R. G., 117
Hebb, D. O., 92
Heller, K., 222
Hellman, L. I., 223
Henderson, J. D., 83
Hendin, H., 111
Hendry, D. P., 42
Henle, M., 253
Henson, D. E., 115
Herbert, J., 248
Herman, S. H., 117
Herzberg, A., 31, 32
Hesse, H., 103
Heymen, A. J., 81
Hicks, L. H., 254, 262, 266, 269
Hiken, J. R., 247
Hill, W. F., 42, 107
Hingtgen, J. N., 51
Hirsch, I. S., 116
Hoenig, J., 21
Hogan, R. A., 22
Hoine, H., 108
Holland, J. G., 43, 65
Holmberg, A. R., 258
Holt, E. B., 124
Holtzman, W. H., 245
Holz, W. C., 116, 230
Homme, L. E., 74, 77, 78, 177
Hopkins, B. L., 246
Horne, N. C., 140
Horowitz, M., 237
Howell, R. J., 28
Howlett, S. C., 24

Hubble, M. B., 253
Huff, F. W., 16, 36
Hughes, E., 184, 186
Hull, C. L., 92, 100, 148–150
Humphrey, G., 58
Humphreys, L., 238
Hunt, H. F., 217
Huntington, M. J., 189
Hurd, W. S., 171
Hurvitz, N., 170
Huszar, R. J., 249
Hutchinson, H. C., 16
Huxley, A., 11
Hyman, H., 229, 232

Irwin, L., 237
Isaacs, K. S., 247
Isaacs, W., 91
Itard, J., 59–61

Jacobs, R. C., 135
Jacobson, E., 15
Jacobson, J. L., 224
Jacobson, L., 179
Jahoda, M., 212
James, B., 113
Jeffrey, C. R., 81
Jenkins, J. G., 228
Jenkins, W. O., 92, 229
Jersild, A. T., 237
Jessor, R., 139
Jessor, S. L., 139
John, V. P., 248
Johnson, S. M., 245
Jones, H. G., 115
Jones, M. C., 13
Judicial Council of the American Medical
    Association, 255
Jung, C. G., 227
Junker, B. H., 237
Justesen, D. R., 98

Kagan, J., 151
Kagan, N., 247
Kahl, J. A., 185
Kahn, M., 138
Kahn, R. L., 228
Kamin, L. J., 99
Kanareff, V. T., 140
Kanfer, F. H., 245, 265

Kantorovich, N., 109
Kapche, R., 116
Kaplan, A., 239
Karpman, B., 111
Katz, D., 232
Katz, R., 198, 220
Kaufman, A., 54
Kay, E., 178
Kean, J. E., 16
Keating, E., 229
Keller, F. S., 44
Kelley, H., 260
Kelly, F. E., 218
Kelly, G., 223
Kelman, H. C., 201, 222, 223, 269, 270
Kilpatrick, F. P., 221
Kimble, G. A., 254, 262, 266, 269
Kimbrell, D., 141
Kinne, S., 221
Kinsey, A. C., 93, 113, 232, 237
Kirchner, J. H., 22
Koenig, W., 253
Kolb, D. A., 49, 157, 171, 172, 174, 185,
    192, 198
Konorski, J., 107
Kopp, J., 42
Kopp, R. E., 54
Koutstaal, G. A., 247
Kovalev, N. K., 109
Kraft, T., 16, 24, 116
Krasner, L., 3, 79, 228
Krathwohl, D. R., 247
Krech, D., 220
Kupers, C. J., 166

Lane, H., 42
Lang, P. J., 16, 23
Lanzetta, J. T., 140
Lasagna, L., 216
Lasater, T. M., 228
Latane, B., 268
Laties, V. G., 216
Lauer, D. W., 99
Lawson, K., 25
Lazarus, A. A., 3, 16, 26, 27, 35, 36, 109,
    133
Lazarus, R. S., 25
Lazovik, A. D., 16
Leary, T., 216, 218
Leat, M., 135, 140
Lederhendler, I., 23

Lefkowitz, M. M., 141
Leggett, J. C., 232
Leitenberg, H., 23, 68, 133, 247
Lemere, F., 110
Lenski, G. E., 232
Lesser, G. S., 135
Letemendia, F. J. J., 240
Levin, G. R., 140
Levin, H., 115
Levin, S. M., 116
Levinson, D. J., 214
Levis, D. J., 10
Lewin, K., 180, 198
Lewis, J., 98
Lick, J. R., 133
Likert, R., 178
Lindeman, E. C., 236
Lindsey, G., 176
Lindsley, O. R., 52, 53, 66, 78, 241, 247
Linton, R., 185
Litwin, G. H., 151, 155
Lofquist, L. H., 228
Lomont, J. F., 22
London, P., 10, 20
LoPiccolo, J., 36
Lorenz, K., 161, 162
Lovaas, O. I., 134
Lovibond, S. H., 110, 115
Lovitt, T. C., 166
Lowell, E. L., 150, 151
Lubin, B., 167
Luborsky, L., 192, 212, 213, 217
Luchins, A. S., 127
Luchins, E. H., 127
Luria, A. R., 102
Lynch, J. J., 118

McCarthy, J. F., 118
McClelland, D. C., 149–153, 155–157, 234
Maccoby, E. E., 115
Maccoby, N., 126
McConaghy, N., 37, 113
McCord, J., 136, 229
McCord, W., 136, 229
MacCulloch, M. J., 116
McFall, R. M., 245
Macfarlane, J. W., 229
McGaugh, J. L., 21, 25
McGlynn, F. D., 23, 24

McGuire, R., 113, 247
McGuire, R. J., 115
McGuire, W. J., 254, 262, 266, 269
McIntyre, J. M., 174
Mackay, R. S., 249
Macker, C. E., 142
McNamara, J. R., 9
McReynolds, W. T., 56, 245
Madge, J., 237
Mahoney, M. J., 122, 133
Maltz, M., 193
Mandel, K. H., 115
Mangham, I. L., 167
Mann, J., 259
Marcia, J. E., 25
Mark, V., 249
Marks, I. M., 20, 23, 115
Marley, E., 246
Marquis, J. M., 117
Marset, P., 23
Marshall, G. R., 51, 56, 78
Marshall, W. L., 117
Marston, A. R., 166
Martin, C. E., 93, 113
Maslow, A., 172
Mather, M. D., 16
Max, L. W., 114
May, R., 221, 228
Mealiea, W. L., 23
Medeiros, D. C., 133
Mednick, S. A., 213
Meehl, P. E., 207, 209, 210
Mees, H., 51, 56
Meigs, M. F., 237
Melamed, B., 23
Menlove, F. L., 129, 130
Merton, R., 26
Merton, R. K., 185, 186
Metcalfe, M., 98
Meyer, H., 178
Mezei, L., 135, 140
Michon, J. A., 247
Milgrim, S., 260
Miller, B. A., 110
Miller, N. E., 77, 124
Miller, R., 247
Milton, A., 229
Mitts, B., 243
Moan, C. E., 117
Montgomery, G. T., 19
Moore, N., 98

Moore, O. K., 190
Moore, R., 90
Moore, R. C., 23
Morganstern, K. P., 16
Morris, N., 264
Morse, W. H., 89
Moss, H. A., 151
Mouton, J. S., 141
Mowrer, O. H., 115, 129
Murray, H. A., 150
Mussen, P. H., 135
Myers, J. K., 214
Myers, R. D., 110

Nagle, J., 142
Nathan, P. E., 247
Nawas, M. M., 23, 24
Naylor, H. K., 135
Nelson, C. M., 245
Newton, J. E. O., 118
Nielsen, G., 247
Noelpp, B., 98
Noelpp-Eschenhagen, I., 98
Norman, M., 135

O'Connell, E. J., 140
O'Conner, R. D., 143
Ogston, W. D., 235
Ohlin, L. E., 139
Oliveau, D. C., 23, 27
O'Neil, D. G., 28
Opton, E. M., Jr., 25
Orne, M. T., 133, 217, 245, 256
Ost, J. W. P., 99
Ottenberg, P., 98
Ovesey, L., 111

Pahnke, W. N., 171
Papania, N., 237
Parke, R. D., 135, 140
Parloff, M. B., 217, 222
Parsons, T., 186, 190
Pascal, G. R., 92, 229
Paterson, D. G., 229
Patterson, G. R., 56, 135, 140, 203
Pattison, L., 192
Paul, G. L., 16, 17
Pavlov, I, P., 3, 9, 96, 99–101, 104, 105,
    118–120

Payne, S. L., 231
Peak, H., 235
Peck, R. F., 142
Pelser, H. E., 96
Peterson, R. F., 124, 137
Pfaffman, C., 74
Phillips, E. L., 177
Phillips, J. S., 265
Piaget, G. W., 133
Pinneau, S. R., 229
Pokorny, A. D., 110
Polansky, N., 237
Polsky, N., 236
Pomeroy, W. B., 93, 113
Pooley, R., 79
Powell, B., 108
Powell, J., 246
Powers, R. B., 90
Premack, D., 75–77
Pruett, H. L., 68
Pullan, B. R., 115
Purcell, K., 135, 248
Pyles, M. K., 229
Pytkowicz, A. R., 138

Rachman, S., 20, 22, 109, 110, 113, 117,
    123, 126
Raines, J., 22
Rapaport, D., 237
Rapp, D. W., 240
Ratliff, R. G., 16
Raush, H. L., 234
Rawson, R. A., 68
Rayner, R., 12, 13
Rechs, J. R., 77
Reed, G. F., 21
Regester, D. C., 109
Reinhert, R. E., 110
Reisal, J., 167
Reiser, M. F., 217
Reisman, J. M., 246
Reitman, A. P., 232
Renzaglia, G. A., 247
Reynolds, D. J., 16
Reynolds, E. J., 23, 24
Rice, L. N., 219
Richard, R. A., 223
Rickert, E. J., 77
Riesman, D., 232
Riley, M. W., 233
Rimm, D. C., 133

Risley, T., 51, 56
Ritter, B., 28, 130, 131, 133, 144
Robbins, L. C., 229
Roberts, R. R., Jr., 247
Robie, W. F., 112
Roethlisberger, F. J., 256
Rogers, C. R., 161, 172, 177, 178, 209, 211, 212, 214, 222, 247
Rosekrans, M. A., 135
Rosenbaum, M., 110
Rosenbaum, M. E., 140, 142
Rosenblith, J. F., 140
Rosenhan, D., 142
Rosenthal, D., 129, 216
Rosenthal, R., 50, 179, 240, 256
Rosenthal, T. L., 30
Roshal, S. M., 126, 144
Ross, D., 134
Ross, H. L., 209
Ross, S., 246
Ross, S. A., 134
Roth, J. A., 231
Royer, F. L., 118
Rozelle, R. M., 228
Rubin, H. B., 115
Rubin, I. M., 174
Ruebhausen, O. M., 249

Saenger, G., 214
Safren, M. A., 247
Saint-Exupery, de A., 1
Salter, A., 4, 32, 34
Sanders, R. M., 246
Sapon, S. M., 78
Sarason, I. G., 138, 143
Sarbin, T. R., 191, 194
Sargent, H. D., 210
Schaefer, J. B., 135
Schaeffer, R. W., 84
Schaffer, L., 214
Schein, E. V., 167, 198, 199, 202
Schlesinger, L. E., 247
Schmidt, E., 116
Schneller, P., 247
Schoenfeld, W. N., 44
Schoggen, P. H., 254, 262, 266, 269
Schubot, E. D., 22
Schuldt, W. J., 207
Schulmann, J. L., 246
Schwartz, R. D., 246, 253
Schweid, E., 137

Schwitzgebel, R., 49
Schwitzgebel, R. K., 26, 45, 49, 78, 136, 231, 233, 238, 241, 245, 246, 249, 251, 263, 264, 267, 269
Schwitzgebel, R. L., 78, 179, 246
Scott, J. P., 118
Sears, R. R., 115
Sechrest, L., 141, 246, 253
Secord, P. F., 172
Seitz, P. F. D., 19
Sells, S. B., 73
Selltiz, C., 212
Shah, S. A., 85
Shakow, D., 247
Shannon, G., 56, 69
Shapiro, A. K., 216
Shapiro, M. B., 221
Shaw, D. A., 203
Shaw, G. B., 104, 105, 118
Sheffield, F. D., 107, 126
Sheppard, W., 42
Sherif, C., 237
Sherif, M., 237
Sherman, J. A., 124
Sherrington, C., 228
Shils, E. A., 270
Shugar, G., 116
Sidman, M., 41, 48, 65, 90
Sidowski, J. B., 246
Simkins, L., 242
Simmons, J. J., 140
Sipprelle, C. N., 270
Skinner, B. F., 3, 39, 43, 52, 64, 66, 89, 104, 105, 165
Slack, C. W., 238
Smith, E., 136
Smith, H. L., 232
Smith, M. B., 254, 262, 266, 269
Smith, S., 136
Solomon, L. N., 166, 167, 169, 170
Solomon, R. J., 47, 48, 209–211
Soskin, W., 248
Speer, D. C., 211
Spielberger, C. D., 54
Staats, A. W., 41, 51, 79, 85
Staats, C. K., 41
Stafford-Clark, D., 111
Stampfl, T. G., 10
Star, S., 232
Steele, F. I., 198
Stein, M., 98
Steinhorst, R., 77

Stekel, W., 111
Stephens, J. H., 118
Stern, J., 108
Sternberg, R. S., 247
Stevens, M. W., 157
Stewart, R. B., 81, 82
Stigall, T. T., 247
Stinchcombe, A. L., 189, 192, 195
Stoddard, L., 90
Stoddard, P., 54
Stoller, F. H., 247
Stolz, H. R., 229
Stone, C. H., 229
Strauss, A., 184, 186, 190
Straussman, H. D., 223
Strupp, H. H., 129, 207, 219
Stuart, R. B., 78
Summers, M., 265
Sutherland, E. H., 139
Swayze, J., 248
Sweet, W., 249

Tamisian, J. A., 56
Tang, J., 232
Tasto, D. L., 28
Taylor, T. J., 235
Teasdale, J., 110, 117
Terrace, H. S., 89, 90
Test, M. A., 142, 143, 257
Tharp, R. G., 81
Thibaut, J., 260
Thimann, J., 109
Thomas, G., 192
Thomas, J., 91
Thomas, W. I., 26
Thorne, G. L., 81
Thorpe, J. G., 116
Thorpe, R. G., 144
Timmons, J. A., 156, 157
Tolman, E. C., 92, 125
Traux, C. B., 177, 207
Trist, E. L., 238
Trost, F. C., 51
Trumbo, D., 142
Turner, E. D., 73
Turteltaub, A., 129
Tyler, V. O., Jr., 81, 136

Uhlinger, C. A., 157
Ullmann, L. P., 3, 26

Unger, A. A., 223
United States Adjutant General's Department, 262, 265
United States Public Health Service, 262

Valins, S., 26
Vallance, M., 115
Valles, J., 110
van den Berg, J. H., 5
VanderMeer, A. W., 126
van Egeren, L. F., 23
Vannette, W. M., 81
Vaughan, W. T., 97
Veatch, R. M., 262
Verhave, T., 40, 106
Verplanck, W. S., 256
Voegtlin, W., 110

Wagner, M. K., 27, 56
Wagner, N. N., 138
Wagstaff, A. K., 219
Wahler, R. G., 56
Walker, M. B., 246
Walker, N., 7
Walker, R. G., 218
Wallerstein, R. S., 109, 110
Walsh, M. J., 110
Walsh, W. B., 230
Walters, R. H., 125, 126, 135, 136, 138
  140, 149
Walton, D., 16
Warren, S. D., 249
Wasik, B. H., 77, 84, 85
Watson, J. B., 12, 13, 228
Webb, E. J., 246, 253
Weiner, D. N., 177
Weiner, I. B., 34
Weiss, D. J., 228, 230
Weiss, G., 249
Wenar, C., 228, 229
Westin, A., 251
Wetzel, R., 69
Wetzel, R. J., 81, 144
Whaley, F., 237
Wheeler, L., 136
White, G., 245
White, G. M., 142
White, R. W., 51, 172
White, W., 218
Whyte, W. F., 236

Willems, H. F., 237
Williams, A. D., 247
Wincze, J. P., 133
Winter, D. G., 155, 156
Winter, S. K., 172, 174, 192
Wirt, R. D., 224
Wolf, M. M., 51, 56
Wolfe, D. L., 51
Wolfe, H. N., 51
Wolfe, J. B., 79
Wolfensberger, W., 264, 270
Wolff, H. H., 20
Wolpe, J., 3, 14–16, 18, 19, 22, 29, 30, 35–37
Wolpin, M., 22
Woodward, A. E., 247
Wooster, H., 239

Wright, D. E., 23
Wright, H. F., 234

Yarrow, M. R., 125
Yates, A. J., 10
Yerkes, R. M., 143
Young, B. G., 113
Young, S., 56, 69

Zachs, G., 172, 174, 179, 192
Zahn, C. J., 125
Zetzel, E., 18
Zola, I. K., 136
Zold, A., 211
Zwerling, I., 110

Subject Index

Achievement motivation:
  cognitive supports, 154
  goal setting, 153
  group support, 154
  historical development, 149
  measurement of, 150–152
  motive syndrome, 153–154
  relationship to academic achievement,
    157–159
  relationship to entrepreneurship, 151–
    152, 155–157
  relationship to Thematic Apperception
    Test, 150
Adaptation level, 73–74
Alcoholism, treatment of, 16, 108–111
Altruism, 142–143
Assertive responses, 29
Assessment, 206–226
  control procedures: control groups,
    211–213

Assessment:
  control procedures: control phenomena,
    211
    matched controls, 212
    random-assignment control groups,
      212
      stratified sampling controls, 212
    control subjects: own control, 214–215
      population base rates, 215–216
      waiting list, 213–214
    expectation, 216
    placebo effect, 216–218
    pretest—posttest control group, 208
    research structure: experimental mortali-
     ty, 209
    history, 208
    instrument decoy, 208
    maturation, 208
    selection, 209
    Solomon four-group design, 210

Assessment:
  research structure: spontaneous
      remission, 216
    statistical regression, 208
    testing, 208
    type I error, 213
    type II error, 213–214
Asthma, conditioning of, 96–98
Avoidance learning, 114

Behavior exchange, 260–270
  agreement as binding, 268–269
  interaction matrix, 260–262
  matrix awareness, 265–268
  respondent choice, 262–265
Behavior modification, 3
Behavior therapy, 3, 4

Catharthis, 6, 137–138
Classical conditioning (see Conditioning,
    classical)
Client-centered therapy, 161
Cognition, 25–27, 29
  (See also Systematic desensitization,
      cognitive factors)
Compulsive behavior, treatment of, 29–30,
    34–35
Conditioned emotional reaction, 13
Conditioning:
  classical: backward conditioning, 99
    compared with operant conditioning,
        106–108
    conditioned reflex, 96
    conditioned response, 96
    conditioned stimulus, 96
    delayed conditioning, 99
    effect of person, 117–119
    eliciting stimuli: compared with dis-
        criminative stimuli, 104–108
      described, 104
      relationship to sexual behavior, 113
    excitation, 99–101
    extinction, 21–22, 100
    freedom reflex, 117, 119
    higher-order conditioning, 101–104
    inhibition, 99–101
    procedures, as generally used, 96–101
    simultaneous conditioning, 99
    social reflexes, 118
    unconditioned response, 96
    unconditioned stimulus, 96
    trace conditioning, 99

Conditioning:
  classical: use in treatment: of alcoholics,
      108–111
    of homosexuals, 113–117
  operant: chaining, 43–44
    compared with classical conditioning,
        106–108
    extinction, 42
    schedules (see Reinforcement, sched-
        ules)
    (See also Discriminative stimuli)
Contact desensitization, 130–133
Contigency management, 74–78
Control groups, 211–213
Control subjects, 213–216

Delinquency, 44–50, 79–81, 128, 139–140
Differential association, 139
Discrimination learning:
  described, 89
  errorless procedure, 90
  traditional procedure, 89–90
Discriminative stimuli:
  behavior as, 134
  compared with eliciting stimuli, 104–108
  compared with time-out stimuli, 89
  meaning of, 94–95
  people as, 90–93
  relationship to sexual behavior, 93–94
  in social context, 92, 94–95
Disinhibition, 126
Drive reduction, 149

Eliciting stimuli:
  compared with discriminative stimuli,
      104–108
  described, 104
  relationship to sexual behavior, 113
Emotions, 103–104
Encouragement, 27–28
Ethics in research, 253–271
  behavior exchange, 260–270
  ethics advisory group, 269
  human distinctiveness, 257–258
  humanistic influence, 259–260
  indigenous ethic, 254
  informed consent, 262–267, 270
  medical influence, 255–256
  with mental patients, 264, 267
  with offenders, 264, 267
  pathology versus normality, 256–257

Ethics in research:
  privacy, 270
  right to informed participation, 270
Excitation, 99–101
Experimenter bias, 23
Extinction:
  in classical conditioning, 21–22, 100
  in operant conditioning, 42, 63, 89

Fears (*see* Phobias)

Generalization of responses, 83–86

Homosexuality:
  cause, 36, 111
  treatment, 16, 37, 113–117
Hypnosis, 32

Imitation (*see* Observational learning)
Inhibition:
  in classical conditioning, 99–101
  in observational learning, 126
Instrumental conditioning (*see* Conditioning, operant)
Instrumentation, 235, 246–249
Interpersonal relationships:
  affection, 198
  intimacy, 198, 200–201
  power, 198
  solidarity, 196–197
Interview data:
  reliability of, 229–231
  validity of, 228–232
Interviewer bias, 231–232
Interviewer error, 231
In vivo treatment procedures, 27–29

Kelley's Role Construct Repertory Test, 221–222

Lie detection, 101–102

Marital discord, 80–82, 92–93
Modeling:
  assertive responses, 34, 35
  compared with operant shaping, 55
  effectiveness, 35
  in self-directed change, 179

Observation:
  of behavior, 91–92
  need for, 227–228

Observation:
  privacy, 249–251
  procedures: instrumentation, 235, 246–249
    in natural settings, 234–236
    participant observation, 235, 240–246
    self-observation, 235–240
Observational learning:
  aggressive behavior, 134–139
  compared with identification, 128
  compared with operant shaping, 126–128
  compared with trial-and-error methods, 127
  courses using modeling, 144
  deviant behavior, 139–141
  disinhibitory effect, 126
  generalized imitation, 124
  imitation, 126
  inhibitory effect, 126
  learning to imitate, 124
  live modeling, 123
  participant modeling, 130–133
  prosocial behavior, 141–143
  punishment of model, 135–137
  relationship to operant conditioning, 124–125
  response-facilitation effect, 125
  symbolic modeling, 130
  treatment of phobias, 122–123, 129–134
Operant conditioning (*see* Conditioning, operant)

Parents, shaping behavior, 56
Peer group, as change agents, 201–204
Phobias:
  in childhood, 8
  encouragement, 123
  experimentally produced, 12–13
  of snakes, 122
  treatment of, 13–14, 16, 24–30, 123
Placebo effect, 25–26, 216–218
Play, 190–192
Premack principle, 75–78
Privacy, 249–251
Psychoanalysis, 3–8
Punishment:
  compared with active avoidance learning, 114
  compared with conditioned suppression, 114
  compared with passive avoidance learning, 114

Punishment:
  defined, 66
  of model, 135–137
  use in changing behavior, 67–70, 109

Rater bias, 223–224
Reciprocal inhibition:
  effectiveness, 9, 14, 16–20
  procedures, 14–17, 22–24, 31
  (See also Assertive responses;
    Sexual responses; Systematic
    desensitization)
Reciprocal-role expectations, 222–223
Recording of behavior:
  graphs, 164, 170–171
  records, 179
Reinforcement:
  of competing responses, 68
  negative, 66–70, 107
  positive, 66–70
  schedules: combined, 66
    continuous, 63
    extinction, 63
    intermittent, 63–64, 66
    interval, 64–66
  (See also Punishment; Reinforcers)
Reinforcers:
  generalized, 42–43
  negative, 68
  positive, 66
  primary, 42
  secondary, 42–43

Secondary gain, 190
Self-directed change:
  feedback, 174–176
  helping interventions, 176–180
  individual determination, 162–166
  personality factors, 173–174
  process of goal-setting, 174
  self-directed groups, 166–170
  self-reinforcement, 166
  self-research, 170–176
  social demand, 160
  theoretical developments, 160–162
Self-observation, 235, 240–246
Sexual behavior:
  exhibitionism, 16
  frigidity, 16
  homosexuality, 16, 36, 37
  impotence, 35–36
  positive reinforcement of, 37

Sexual behavior:
  stimulus control of, 93–94
Sexual responses:
  classically conditioned, 113
  inhibited by anxiety, 35–36
  positive reinforcement of, 37
  stimulus control of, 93–94
  used to reduce anxiety, 35
Shaping of behavior:
  advantages, 53–56
  attitude of experimenter, 50–51
  cooperative behavior, 51–53
  delinquent attendance, 44–50
  limitations, 53–56
  priming, 54
  procedures, 40–43
  use of "timeout," 52, 56
Smoking, 16
Stimulus control, 88–121, 163–164
Stuttering, 16
Symptom substitution, 19–20
Systematic desensitization:
  automated, 23–24
  cognitive factors, 25–27, 29
  effectiveness, 16–20, 29
  encouragement, 27–29
  essential elements, 20–28
  hierarchy construction, 14
  in vivo, 27–31
  relaxation, 14, 15, 22
  suggestion, 24

Token economies, 79–83
Transitional roles:
  acceptance of role occupant, 184–185
  autotelic folk models, 190
  goal-setting, 192–193
  identification, 199–201
  interpersonal relationships: affection, 198
    intimacy, 198, 200–201
    power, 198
    solidarity, 196–197
    status, 196–197
  involvement, 193–194
  peer group, 201–204
  scanning, 199, 201–202
  terminal status, 194–196

Vicarious conditioning, 144–145

Wild Boy of Aveyron, The, 58–62